3/99

THE LUSTRE OF OUR COUNTRY

JOHN T. NOONAN, JR.

THE LUSTRE OF OUR COUNTRY

THE AMERICAN EXPERIENCE OF RELIGIOUS FREEDOM

UNIVERSITY OF CALIFORNIA PRESS

Berkeley · *Los Angeles* · *London*

University of California Press
Berkeley and Los Angeles, California

University of California Press, Ltd.
London, England

© 1998 by
The Regents of the University of California

Library of Congress Cataloging-in-Publication Data

Noonan, John Thomas, 1926–
    The lustre of our country : the American experience
of religious freedom / John T. Noonan, Jr.
        p.   cm.
    Includes bibliographical references and index.
    ISBN 0-520-20997-4 (alk. paper)
        1. Freedom of religion—United States—History.
    2. United States—Church history. I. Title.
    BR516.N59   1998
    323.44'2'0973—DC21   97-49327
                                                   CIP

Printed in the United States of America
9 8 7 6 5 4 3 2

TO THE LAW CLERKS, STAFFS, AND JUDGES
OF THE UNITED STATES COURT OF APPEALS
FOR THE NINTH CIRCUIT

CONTENTS

ILLUSTRATIONS

ACKNOWLEDGMENTS

I am indebted to the hospitality of the National Center for the Humanities, Durham, North Carolina, where I started work on this book and to the generous support of the Institute for Advanced Study, Princeton, New Jersey, where I completed it. Harold Berman of Emory University provided helpful information on the American advisers to Russia. David Frederick furnished me with data on Judge Denman. Peter Stern provided translations and advice on the chapter on Japan; Anton Leof was a valuable consultant on French and the chapter on France; Patrick Brennan did an initial investigation of the material on Russia. Nancy Eisenhauer, Jerome Farris, Aram Jack Kevorkian, and Richard Stookey have read the manuscript critically in whole or in part. Nine externs—Samir Bukhari, Laura Gerrity, Andrew Heimert, Nina Hong, Anna Itoi, Christel Laine Kelly, Brett McDonnell, Colin Moran, Miranda McGowan—checked and critiqued the citations. Rochelle Levy was of great help in gathering the illustrations. Lisa Marie Watanabe has advised me on copyright and other questions. I am indebted to the librarians of the Bancroft, Boalt, and Doe Libraries at the University of California at Berkeley; of the Graduate Theological Union at Berkeley; of the Firestone Library, Princeton University; of the Institute for Advanced Study; of the Divinity School, Lamont, and Widener Libraries at Harvard University; of the Manuscripts Division of the Library of Congress; of the Post Office Division of the National Archives; and of the United States Court of Appeals for the Ninth Circuit.

I have been especially fortunate in the secretarial skills of Karen Thomson and Evelyn Lew.

In discussions with my wife Mary Lee on specific topics and the general theme of the book I have benefitted from her insightful comments and sustaining encouragement.

John T. Noonan, Jr.
Berkeley, California
December 8, 1997

INTRODUCTION

I cannot write about the killing of the Quakers without the surprised excitement of discovery. Kill Quakers for God's sake? Kill them in America and at the very beginning of America? Kill them in Boston in the Cradle of Liberty at the direction of the General Court of Massachusetts? Not a theme of history in the Boston suburb in which I grew up, although such Massachusetts men as Nathaniel Hawthorne, John Greenleaf Whittier, and Brooks Adams thought that this early instance of intense religious violence and religious bigotry had its place in the American devotion to the free exercise of religion; and today a statue of Mary Dyer stands before the State House on Beacon Street. Negative experience has been as powerful in shaping our minds as the abundant good fruits of our ideal, not to mention that it's instructive to see that the fiercest feelings are directed at deviants who are closest, and that the verbal champions of freedom can be the persecutors.

Of all the violences and hatreds of humankind, that based on religion has been the most injurious, not because of the intensity of feeling and ferocity of execution that it has engendered—mere political ideologies have done greater damage in these respects—but because of the harm it has done religion itself, mocking its mandates, denying its duties, perverting its purpose. None, I dare declare, is more hateful to God.

For God must enter any account of religious bigotry and religious freedom. On that point you cannot be neutral. Religion is either the worship of a being distinct from the worshipers who is God for the worshipers, or God is the projection of personal and collective need. It makes a difference. The latter alternative, the common humanistic interpretation of religious phenomena, affords no secure footing for religious freedom. For my part, I approach this most difficult and fundamental of subjects not without diffidence and doubt but with the belief that religion is a projection (for who could deny the freight of human desires that every religion has borne?), and that religion is also a response to another, an other who is not a human being, an other who must have an intelligence and a will and so be, analogously, a person. Heart speaks to heart, says

Newman with poignant lucidity. There is a heart not known, responding to our own. Such is human experience. Religion is ineradicable because of this other and greater to whom we relate and respond.

One overriding problem exists: how can religion be treated neutrally? It is a problem for me, writing about it, a problem for any executive agency or legislature dealing with it, a problem for the courts enforcing the constitutional guarantee of freedom for it. Sociologists and historians, bureaucrats and judges, seek to categorize religion. But religion is a relationship to God; God is not a category; and categorization misses the living communication between believer and God that is the heart of the matter. In the end, categories must yield to empathy and its necessary ingredient, imagination.

That religion has caused many acts of violence and perpetuated many hatreds is a datum of history. So has sex. Humankind cannot do without sex; sex cannot be eliminated in order to eliminate its attendant evils. No more so can religion. For the evils, at least for most of the evils that religion brings, a sovereign remedy exists—free exercise!

Free exercise—let us as Americans assert it—is an American invention. How foolish it would be to let a false modesty, a nervous fear of chauvinism, obscure the originality. That sayings and principles in favor of freedom may be found in other civilizations is evident. Christ tells his followers to do unto others as they would have others do unto them. From such sayings a deduction in favor of religious freedom seems obvious; but such sayings have been contained in cultural contexts that made the deduction imperfect. There have also been whole societies more tolerant than not of religious diversity. A great empire like the Roman knew how to let most sects survive and even prosper. In exceptional circumstances a small state might do likewise: so, it is reported, the rulers of eighth-century Khazaria, poised between Christian and Muslim rivals, converted to Judaism and let the people of the country remain in their old religions. Tolerance is a policy, an acceptance of religious difference because it's more trouble than it's worth to eliminate it, a prudential stance of wise statesmen. It is something else to inscribe in fundamental law an ideal of freedom for the human activity most potentially subversive of the existing order. Never before 1791 was there a tablet of the law, a legal text guaranteeing to all a freedom from religious oppression by the national legislature. Never before 1791 such a public, almost unalterable commitment to this ideal. In that year, both the French and the American constitutions committed themselves to the ideal. But the first commitment was stillborn; and the second had to shed an arguable ambiguity and develop.

"To know the law is not to know the words of the law, but their force and power." The old Roman adage, focused on law's *vim* and *potentiam*, is inscribed high on a wall of Langdell Library at Harvard Law School. It echoes now in my mind. Words alone do not do the trick. They are a starting point and a direction. To know the force and power of the First Amendment I have looked at a variety of experiences, a variety that is great because the amendment itself has encouraged a variety of religious experiences that have interacted with the law and affected its meaning.

I begin with the story of the experiences that gave free exercise life in the Boston of my youth. One might, but should not, attempt to conceal the experiences that color one's own conception of the issues. Let each one addressing this theme say where he or she comes from, and goes. I grew up in a church that formally denied free exercise and live now in the same church that has come to champion it. This whole book is a reflection on the experience. The prologue gives my perspective. Thereafter I use a variety of forms to express the variety of perspectives that bear on reading our national experience and the paradoxes it contains. That the doctrine of religious liberty should itself be adaptable to catechetical exposition is an irony, or a sign of how religion and religious freedom are entwined. That a younger sister might be more uncompromising than a more famous older brother was suggested to me by knowing Laura Nader, but the chosen form permits the sister's critique to use Tocqueville's own words against himself. Theodore Parker was a charismatic Boston preacher whom our modern media would dismiss as "a controversial figure"; how capture his disturbing power and contemporary relevance except by a clash of critic and eulogist, undergirded by a selection of his own declarations? That the purported archival history of the occupation of Japan should smack of smugness only underlines the puzzle of imposing freedom by command. The chosen forms are my invention, the views expressed real. No doubt my own opinions breathe beneath these masks.

The book is divided into three principal parts. The first, "History," looks at religious freedom as it existed, cramped and confined, before the First Amendment, and then turns to James Madison, the man primarily responsible for religious freedom becoming the first of our liberties. Of course, Madison did not act alone. Of course, he had critics and opponents. Of course, he had his own intention—documents are not drafted unintentionally. Of course, he succeeded only because he incorporated ideas already common currency, only because he accepted ambiguities understood differently by different factions, and only because he diluted the clarity of his intention with compromising phrases. But to follow Madison is to catch the quintessence of the drive, at once deeply religious and deeply political, for more than religious tolerance—for free exercise itself. It is Madison whom American experience has vindicated.

With an even greater sense of surprise than I had encountered the killing of the Quakers, I discovered Madison and his accomplishment. Modest in all things, including his Christian commitment, James Madison was, so far as I know, the first statesman who, himself a believer, and not knowing any persecution himself, had enough empathy with the victims of persecution to loathe the idea of enforced religious conformity and to work to produce law that would forever end it. It is easy to be tolerant if you don't believe. To believe and to champion freedom—that is Madison's accomplishment. Overshadowed by Jefferson, Madison was the better workman. In the phrase "free exercise" that the founder of seventeenth-century Maryland had brought to America, Madison found the perfect expression, an expression that in his mind excluded the establishment of a church as well as the enforcing of religious opinion. The First Amendment's prohibiting of laws "respecting the establishment of religion" is not a text that, at the time it was adopted, had the effect of preventing a church establishment. For Madison the whole burden of freedom was carried by the formula of free exercise. It was his belief and hope that freedom of religion "promised a lustre to our country."

What that formula meant had to be worked out. The most influential, perhaps the best interpreter in the first fifty years was a Frenchman. I levy on his treatise, designed for his compatriots, and on his journal, kept for himself, to explore the common views of free exercise in the 1830s. Yet a reality check must also be made to determine if Tocqueville's vision corresponded to the laws and politics of the America he observed. Ideal and reality are brought together here in the course of a cento composed from his own writings.

Free exercise was a negative on Congress. It was also a charter for religious organizations, which multiplied, and religious interventions in society, which intensified. Of these interventions one was traumatic, paradigmatic, and triumphant—the Christian demand for the abolition of slavery. I look at the event through the correspondence, autobiography, and above all the sermons of Theodore Parker and the poetry of Julia Ward Howe. The free exercise of religion fed the fires of internecine war. I once wrote that we had never had a war of religion in America. Strictly speaking, that is true but I see now how severely this claim must be qualified by the events leading up to the war that began in 1861. The consequences of free exercise are neither controllable nor predictable nor invariably benign.

Not predictable. The American experience of religious freedom has also included the federal prosecution of the leaders of a religion for fraud in their profession of faith. The religion itself, a kind of cousin of Christianity, was put on trial. Humbug, not heresy, the justices of the Supreme Court thought was at stake. The line may lie in the eye of the beholder. The examination of this case, *United States v. Ballard*, permits inspection of how the judges' views of religion interact with the freedom of religion that is guaranteed. To recognize a new religion requires empathy, and to empathize the judge must become a pilgrim. Judicial line drawing is not apt to produce such pilgrims.

Reflection on *Ballard* leads by a natural progression to the second part of this book, ominously entitled "Problems," where I look at questions built into the coexistence of government with the free exercise of religion. The questions run through the teachings of the United States Supreme Court on the subject. For advocates before that tribunal and for judges subject to its mandate, these teachings are identical with the Constitution. Professors of constitutional law often perpetuate the view. The Supreme Court's own rhetoric occasionally supports it. "The Constitution commands," a justice or a clerk will write, meaning that there are five votes for the proposition being announced as the law by the court. In fact, this hybrid judicial tribunal and political committee is a channel. Through its pronouncements current conventions about the Constitution take compact shape, decide cases, provide guidance to public officials, and stimulate debate, reaction, and the development of further pronouncements.

Development is key to understanding the work of this court and other courts in relation to free exercise. The concept is borrowed from theology, specifically from John Henry Newman's *Essay on the Development of Doctrine*. In the course of time Christian doctrine has undergone many shifts and turns and is noticeably expanded from its evangelical form. How account for the changes? By supposing that the process has been one in which an idea or set of ideas have had their implications worked out, with the basic or dominant idea gradually driving out ideas incompatible with that dominant idea's mastery; or to put it in less patriarchal or Hegelian terms, human beings in conflict have come to see that commitment to certain basic principles excludes accommodations and deviations once accepted as normal. So, for example, Christianity has gone from endorsing slavery to abhorring it, all as a firmer grasp of the central commandment of charity has been had.

Something similar has happened, or is happening, in the realm of free exercise. For a century and a half the development of the idea was the work of legislators and government officials, of schools and colleges, of churchmen and civic leaders, of treatise-writers and law professors. None of these has abandoned the field, but only in the last half century has development been accomplished by the activity of courts. In this era that began in 1940, particular judicial shapes have been given to free exercise. The results, inspected closely, appear chaotic. No mystery surrounds what is happening. By trial and error, by exaggeration and careful qualification, by broad declarations and hairsplitting distinctions, by retreats and reaffirmations, human beings in conflict are developing doctrine. A central idea, I argue, exists.

On the whole, the Supreme Court has moved in the direction of freedom. For that reason, especially for those acknowledging no other authority, the court is special; it seems even sacred. But no institutional guarantee has been given that the movement will continue or be uninterrupted. After all, until the 1860s this tribunal was the citadel of the Slave Power. As for religion, the court's early precedents declined to extend freedom to the Church of Jesus Christ of Latter-day Saints and ratified the confiscation of that church's property. Since 1940 the court has known major regressions such as the first Flag Salute Case and the Sacramental Peyote Case and the Religious Freedom Restoration Act Case. No certainty exists that the court will do the right thing. With the aid of the other branches of government, the criticism of the legal profession and the voices of the electorate, the direction toward freedom has been kept.

Hanging as a dark shadow over all the judicial efforts to uphold free exercise is the difficulty—no, the impossibility—of separating the courts from government. The federal courts are the third branch, coordinate with Congress and the president in authority and power and identification with the state. The judges are appointed, promoted, and paid by the executive. Their confirmation, their salary level, and their jurisdiction depend on the national legislature. Beyond these bonds that bind them tightly to the other two organs of government, the courts exist, speak, have a role only because they act governmentally. Can the judicial institution resolve a quarrel within a church, or determine what religious claim will be honored, or even decide what set of beliefs and practices constitute a religion, without committing the authority of the state to particular churches or theologies? Experience says no. The freedom of religion from the state depends upon the judgment of the state.

To be sure, the federal government does not have the unity of design and purpose that characterized the General Court when it banned the Quakers, judged them, and hanged them. Our three branches do rub against one another. Yet rarely does the judicial branch subvert the other two. Where religious freedom is at issue, the stance of the national court before the national interest as determined by the national legislature or executive has always been extra-deferential.

The courts from one perspective are part of the problem; at the very least they must be so as long as they act without self-consciousness, without acknowledging that the judicial hand on religion can be as hard as the legislator's or the bureaucrat's. But the problem—the dilemma if one likes—is larger. The problem is, Can you have a nation without a national religion? Rhetoric says, Of course. Realities are different—observe the employment of prayer and the celebration of religious holidays by all three branches; the tax exemption of religious bodies and the draft exemption of the clergy and certain conscientious objectors; the integration of religion into the armed services, whose chapels and chaplains, bibles and torahs and sacramental stock are provided at governmental expense according to congressional appropriation and appropriate service regulation. And when the nation actually goes to war, its leaders call on God to grant it victory. Judicial rhetoric is deployed to disguise the realities because they are doctrinally embarrassing; the disguise is easily penetrated. Religion is entangled with government. Yet free exercise has survived in the face of the enmeshment. Will ultimately free exercise work itself free, so to speak, and end all the entanglements, or will free exercise coexist, and even require coexistence, with them? I explore but do not answer the question.

To leave such a question unanswered will appear evasive to some and be disappointing to others. Ironically, there is as much dogmatism in defining and defending religious freedom as in defining and defending any creed. Shibboleths are dear to newspaper editors. Certainties are dear to all of us. But I am not able to answer. I point to such a question as one raised by the American experience or American experiment, as Madison described it. The experiment goes on. Final answers are premature.

Marred by occasional persecutions, halting in its progress, the experiment to date has not produced perfection; but it has succeeded. How much of the success has depended on the First Amendment, how much on the demographics of immigration and the frontier, how much on the decline of religious zealotry, how much on the growth of religious insights into what God requires will continue to be matters of examination, argument, and estimation. Beyond dispute, the free exercise of re-

ligion in America has manifested itself in the propagation and flowering
of many religions, in the vigorous growth and occasional decline of particular churches, in the unmolested cultivation of the criticism of religion and the gradual spread of a secular spirit, in the usually peaceful
coexistence and cooperation, intermarriage, and friendship of believers
and unbelievers of various kinds, in a freedom from national domination by any denomination, in religious contributions to the morals of the
community, and in the active, sometimes avid, often effective, occasionally repulsive intervention of religion into public life. In the most sustained of such interventions, here treated as crusades, religion, untram-
meled by governmental restraints, has been the foremost of our political
institutions.

Not everyone will see all these fruits as good, but none can deny that
they are abundant, and few would find all bad. Abroad, America has not
always been the model, but the pioneering American example has had
its substantial effect. Free exercise has added a lustre to American
democracy. The light has been reflected round the world.

In part three, "Influences," I examine that light as it has played on
France, Japan, Russia, and the Catholic Church. France beat the United
States by a few weeks in introducing freedom of religion into the country's constitution, and France proceeded to persecute religion and then
establish it. The formula of freedom, owed in part to American influences symbolized by Jefferson's diplomatic mission to Paris, was a frag-
ile directive in a country whose history and culture had so little prepared
the way. Only in the twentieth century has France moved toward real religious freedom. In contrast, Japan owes its present constitutional guarantee of religious liberty to its defeat in World War II, the American occupation, and MacArthur's making of its constitution. The American input
has been large. It is still being assimilated in a nation where the national
religion has been said to be Japaneseness. For Russia religious liberty came
only with the overthrow of Communism. The drafters of the new constitution and laws have looked candidly and confidently to the American experience and to American law professors for guidance; the past,
czarist and Communist, affects the absorption of their ideas; the outcome
for religious freedom is still uncertain. The Catholic Church, once a defender of the repression of heresy, became in 1965 a champion of religious liberty on the grounds of both revelation and natural law. A principal draftsman of the new stand was an American Jesuit.

An American diplomat, American officers, American law professors,
an American Jesuit—through these individuals, as well as in the count-

less ways a culture is disseminated, the American experience has been communicated. In each instance the idea of free exercise has been dependent on the conditions in which it has been received. Like religion itself free exercise is culture-bound. Yet there is a direction in which the nations have moved. The American experience has lighted up the skies.

PROLOGUE

CHAPTER 1

BOSTON, 1926-1956

WILLIAM CARDINAL O'CONNELL
Archbishop of Boston, 1936

*"The march to our duty here, not merely to ourselves, but to
our surroundings, must proceed. God wills it."*

I was born in Boston on October 24, 1926, and writing about a subject as to which personal perspective means so much, I find it incumbent to give some account of my own religion as it was exercised from that date forward. I will begin with a bit of family history.

My father's grandfather was a Protestant. He must have been Presbyterian, for he came from Scotland, but nothing was ever said in family memory of his specific denomination, because when he married my great-grandmother he became a Catholic, as was she. Over five centuries, all Protestants have had Catholic ancestors, and many Catholics have had Protestant ancestors, making the Christian community as a whole more of a family than is often acknowledged. In this case, the extra seriousness of the adult convert had a surprising result: the couple's two sons became priests of the diocese of Worcester. Three of the four daughters remained unmarried—"the girls in Springfield," as they were called even in their seventies, cheerful and intelligent maidens. Only my grandmother married and perpetuated the line.

On my mother's side there were only Catholics and, as far as I know, no ecclesiastical connections. Growing up in Concord, Massachusetts, she had a faithful friend and wise counselor in her pastor, Matthew or Mattie Flaherty; and Father Flaherty, as he was alliteratively known, remained until his death a family friend, closer geographically and empathically than the somewhat remote and reserved uncles in Worcester.

My parents were married in 1925 in St. Mary's in Brookline, where my mother had moved. Monsignor Splaine, the pastor, presided, as canon law provided. I often heard the story. "The uncles are all right," he said, i.e., the two priests from Worcester could sit on the altar, "but Mattie will have to stay to home," i.e., he was not to intrude into the monsignor's domain, a conclusion dictated by church politics and a sense of territoriality. To outsiders the Catholic Church in Boston looked like a monolith; within, the parish was the operative unit of everyday life, the religious orders provided variety, and there were intense internal battles.

To isolate my religious education from the rest of my experience is to compose an artifact, arbitrary but for its relevance to the themes of this book. Specifically religious instruction began with my mother, who taught me to pray. She herself prayed regularly and, basing herself on experience, believed in the power of prayer. Her religious views were wide in the respect she accorded other faiths—she had been educated by similarly broad-minded nuns and priests at Trinity College in Washington—and she had no use for a bigotry that denied the sincerity, the goodness, and the ultimate salvation of those not of her persuasion. She had a number of close friendships with Protestants, formed chiefly in her Concord schooldays. She had more Catholic friends, including two members of the Congregation of Notre Dame de Namur, one ex-nun of that order, and one ex-postulant; those who had left the religious life had remained extraordinarily devout without their habits, and my mother valued their prayers and their love.

My father should also be described as a religious man, although one less confident of eliciting the responses of God. His mind was critical, and he examined theological doctrines as well as priestly pronouncements from the pulpit critically. Wholly committed to Catholicism—what else was there? he thought—he meditated a good deal on its paradoxes and problems. As he and I grew older, he took delight in theological debate. I remember keenly his assaults on the teaching that then passed as orthodox, and had for over a millennium, that an ideal state would repress by force any heretical deviation from the Church; incredulity and scorn characterized his reaction to the doctrine. At a later date I recall his tormenting Richard McBrien, then teaching theology at Boston College, with the question, "What is the difference between 'begotten' and 'made' in the statement of the Creed that the Son was 'begotten not made'?" And at a later date I recall his asking me how I thought Christ could have suffered on the cross if he was conscious that he was God as well as man. At the same time as he grew older his devotion to Lourdes, where he and my mother went as volunteers, grew. He was willing to believe that miracles had occurred there; it was the concreteness of the proofs that caught his eye and mind. And he translated from the French a long biography of Bernadette Soubirous.

In this household, attendance at Sunday mass was a matter of course, never questioned, never neglected; and similarly attendance on all holy days of obligation. After my father's mother's death we usually went to mass on her anniversary; other ordinary days we did not. On Good Friday, from the age of about eleven, I would go to the Three Hours with my mother; the sermon sequence on those occasions is the only long exposure to preaching that I experienced.

There were sermons—very short by Protestant standards, too long by ours—given usually, but not always, at Sunday mass. The mass was the thing, not the preaching. The latter was rarely eloquent and sometimes incoherent; delivery ranged from mediocre to bad. I cannot recall social issues or party politics ever being discussed. Sin was a topic, sex in general was referred to, materialism was often denounced. A literal-minded paraphrasing of the gospel of the day was standard. Memory does call from its depths several Jesuits and one or two Redemptorists who spoke with fire while preaching retreats.

An event that took place as much as three or four times a year was a letter, read from the pulpit, opening with the salutation, "To the clergy and faithful of the archdiocese of Boston, health and benediction!" and concluding with the signature, "William Cardinal O'Connell, archbishop of Boston." The cardinal lived in an Italianate palazzo on Commonwealth Avenue, which was pointed out to me as a child from a distance. The letters were how he was chiefly present to the parishes. He, or his ghostwriters, had a classical rotundity of phrase that appealed to me and seemed to match the portliness of the cardinal himself. It was in observing the cardinal's relationship to civic affairs that I gained my first sense of the difference between the Church and governmental authorities and the interaction between them.

William Henry O'Connell was born in Lowell, Massachusetts, in 1859 and lived until 1944. Educated at Boston College and the North American College in Rome, of which he was later rector, he had been appointed coadjutor with right of succession in 1906 and had become the archbishop the next year; he was promoted to the cardinalate in 1911 by Pius X; and he continued as cardinal-archbishop until his death. Coming into office in 1906 at the age of forty-seven, a man of energy, ambition, and political adroitness, he personified the Catholic Church to the world in Boston. He was resisted by stubborn pastors and nuns. He was bereft of his Roman patrons with the death of Pius X and the eclipse of Pius X's secretary of state, Merry del Val. He was undermined with his fellow bishops by his cover-up (unsuccessful from them) of the secret marriage of his priest-nephew, whom he had improvidently made archdiocesan chancellor. None of these setbacks and disasters were topics for the press of the day, nor matters of gossip among the faithful he addressed by letter, nor exploited by other religious leaders outside his flock. Untroubled by defeat and unharassed by the media, he maintained the image of a strong, steady bulwark of Rome and sound morality.

Morality was his stock in trade, a stock that appealed as much to the majority of his Catholic audience as it did to many inheritors of the Puritan ethic. Distinct as they were in origin, education, imagination, methods, beliefs, and aspirations—so distinct that they make an incongruous pairing—O'Connell and Theodore Parker, Boston's moral mentor of the 1850s, were linked by their focus on the moral side of religion. In chapter five, Parker's free exercise of religion to influence the morals of the community is set out at length. "The Puritan has passed; the Catholic remains," O'Connell declared in an hour-long address at the Cathedral of the Holy Cross, marking in 1908 the centenary of Boston as a diocese of the Catholic Church. "The march to our duty here, not merely to ourselves, but to our surroundings, must proceed. God wills it." God was still marching as in the 1850s, or directing the march; moral progress and duty, the Parkerian watchwords of sixty years earlier, were still battle cries; but a different trumpeter blew the trumpet.

O'Connell chose the issues on which he would commit himself and calibrated the degree of his commitment, with some care. Honesty in public office was one theme, superficially safe but practically fraught with danger if made particular and applied to individuals. Without pronouncement from the pulpit or circular letter to the parishes, he let be known his disapproval of James Michael Curley, the most prominent of rascals in Boston politics. In 1932 the cardinal's lawyer, Frederick Mansfield, defeated Curley for mayor of Boston and promptly began a lawsuit that succeeded in establishing in a specific case the kind of corruption that Curley had been suspected of engaging in on a wide scale; Curley was forced to disgorge his bribe. Yet Curley was irrepressible, and he went on to be governor: the cardinal was far from omnipotent.

A subsequent election year the cardinal observed in public, "The walls are raised against honest men in civic life." On Tuesday, November 2, 1937, All Souls' Day and Election Day in Boston, Curley was again on the ballot for mayor, opposed by a young newcomer, Maurice J. Tobin. Above its masthead that morning the *Boston Post* quoted the cardinal's words about the walls raised against honesty and followed them with the newspaper's own advice: "You can break down those walls by voting for an honest, clean, competent young man, Maurice J. Tobin today. He will redeem the city." As was later remarked, "only the most careful reader" would have noticed where the quotation from O'Connell stopped. The cardinal took no steps to clarify the impression made. Curley's resounding defeat is attributed, at least in part, to the *Post*'s proclamation. The method was more indirect than one that Parker would have used but the effect was one he would have applauded: a dishonest officeholder was denied reelection.

I was eleven at the time of this campaign and would lie if I said I recalled the *Post* headline; but I do remember the cardinal's general hostility to the old mayor. My parents shared the former's deep antipathy to corrupt politicians, and as a rule of thumb in a state where Catholics were the largest bloc of voters, it was generally believed that a Catholic candidate for statewide office, running against a Protestant, would prevail, unless his honesty and competence fell signally below his opponent's; then, respect for governmental integrity would normally trump the fellow feeling of a once-oppressed minority that now could exercise political power.

Geographic, economic, ethnic, and political overlaps existed. The Catholics as immigrants or the children of immigrants tended to be urban and poor, but some had reached the Berkshires and were farmers, or the suburbs and were doctors, lawyers, or real estate brokers; conversely, there were poor Protestants, occasionally referred to in political jargon as "swamp Yankees." The largest body of Catholics was of Irish descent; but Italian, Portuguese, Polish, and French immigrants had also brought Catholicism with them, and there was a small number of converts. The majority were Democrats, but the Republicans had wooed the Italians and the rising Irish. There were odd pockets such as Quincy where John Quincy Adams's grandson Thomas as a Democrat had turned the local Irish into Republicans. The stereotypical Catholic was urban, poor, Irish, and Democratic, with all factors reinforcing one another. Reality was more complex. Affected by, and affecting, all these forces, religion itself came in various shades, from the quiet fervor of the daily massgoer to the disinterest of the fallen-aways.

To have combined all these disparate factors into a solid political bloc capable of action on a wide range of issues would have been a next-to-impossible task. A Catholic Party on the model of the Center Party in Germany could not have been formed, if it had been wanted. And it was not wanted—not by the politicians, not by the church leaders.

Religion, nonetheless, remained a factor to be taken into account by politicians, analysts, and ordinary voters in Massachusetts elections. For one thing, in the 1930s it was still used as an index to ethnic identity. The William James family, to give a literary example, were of Irish descent but in this country had never been Catholic; neither William nor Henry were looked on as Irish; it startled me recently to hear the critic Denis Donoghue describe Henry as "Ireland's second greatest novelist." For another, the residue of political discrimination based on religion was just disappearing. It was a century since Catholics had been barred by law from public office. In the cities the Catholics had become dominant; but it had taken a long time for any Catholic to achieve statewide office. The first Catholic governor had been David Ignatius Walsh, in 1914, and he had gone on to become the first Catholic senator in 1922. No Catholic sat on the Supreme Judicial Court until Walsh appointed James Bernard Carroll in 1915; there were none on the federal bench in Boston until George Sweeney in 1936. If voters did take religion into account, this pattern of exclusion, not a clerical conspiracy, was a cause. Once all traces of discrimination disappeared—say by the 1950s—the cohesiveness of religion declined markedly.

O'Connell himself was conspicuous and explicit in saying that the Church endorsed no party. He had a friendly relation with only one president, William Howard Taft. He did nothing to forward the election of Al Smith, the first Catholic presidential candidate, for whom Massachusetts voted overwhelmingly. His relations with Franklin Delano Roosevelt, for whom Massachusetts was equally strong, were cool. He was suspected by militant Catholic Democrats of being a Republican. But he gave no public sign.

To return to his public stand on issues he saw as moral, he spoke publicly in 1935 on a lottery to raise money for the state. The lottery bill, sponsored by Curley, was supposedly assured of passage. Opposition by newspapers and by Protestant church groups was unable to stop its inevitable success. The day before the final vote in the House, the cardinal publicly condemned the idea: lotteries were "a tremendous source of corruption and demoralization." The next day the bill was defeated 187 to 40. There is little question that the cardinal's voice was decisive.

Besides corruption and the lottery, a third battle I was aware of as a boy—even more aware of because it brought sexuality into public discussion—was over birth control. In the 1870s, at the urging of the Protestant reformer Anthony Comstock, devices for preventing conception had been federally banned from the mails. Massachusetts had followed suit by forbidding their sale in the commonwealth. In 1941 a move to repeal the law was started in the legislature. Through his lawyer, Mansfield, O'Connell indicated his opposition. The sponsors, noting what had happened to the lottery bill, changed their tactics and introduced repeal by way of referendum to be voted on by the electorate at large. In November 1942 the issue was on the ballot—a moral issue if ever there was one, in Cardinal O'Connell's eyes. Yet the subject of sex was not one he would speak on personally, nor did he care to describe contraception. Instead, the archdiocesan newspaper, *The Pilot*, thundered against "this unholy, unpatriotic, loathsome thing." Voters were told not to permit "a practice which God Almighty has forbidden." Pastors were encouraged to enroll voters and themselves to speak out in general terms against the initiative. I still have a clear memory of riding by car from Boston to Worcester in October 1942, seeing the highway at various strategic places carrying billboards with the stark and simple message: BIRTH CONTROL IS AGAINST GOD'S LAW. VOTE NO ON PROPOSITION TWO. I couldn't vote, but I could ask questions, and I did ask why. The answer—the orthodox one—was that it stopped a natural process. "Is it wrong to cut your fingernails, then?" I asked. The analogy was far from perfect but was enough to make me think that the message could be wrong.

The cardinal did not lose that time on that one. But as he could effect nothing by force, and as such old-fashioned ecclesiastical methods as interdicts were out of style, he could succeed only if his views tapped a fund of moral sentiment already present in his audience. He occasionally lost, not only in his battles with Curley. At the explicit request of Cardinal Gasparri, Pius XI's secretary of state, he wrote Governor Fuller asking clemency for Sacco and Vanzetti and was rebuffed. Following his own sense of propriety, he rebuked (by category, not name, the same method used in his treatment of Curley) the demagogic Detroit priest Charles Coughlin: "Almost hysterical addresses by ecclesiastics" were out of place in political discourse. Catholic Boston remained Coughlinist in sympathy. Even where the welfare of churchly charities was at stake he did not necessarily prevail. A Massachusetts constitutional convention in 1917 considered a ban on state aid to sectarian institutions, including schools and hospitals. The proposal went exactly contrary to the old Protestant constitution's aid to the clergy and to Harvard. The former had been ended in 1833, and Harvard had not received appropriated funds since the 1840s; but other Protestant agencies had been subsidized. Sentiment to end state aid seemed to coincide with fear that Catholic entities would benefit. So at least O'Connell thought, declaring publicly: "even before we have a chance to speak, the door is slammed in our face." Despite the cardinal's admonitions, the amendment was supported by Boston Catholic politicians such as Martin Lomasney, the boss of the West End, and John McCormack, the future congressman and

Speaker of the House; the convention adopted it; and the voters approved it overwhelmingly.

As Lomasney, McCormack, and Curley illustrated, the Catholic politicians were not all in the cardinal's camp. Even the one political figure he regarded as a friend, Senator Walsh, received no political directives from him. O'Connell's reserve was in sharp contrast to Parker's interventions with Senator Charles Sumner, and O'Connell's maneuvering against Curley bears little comparison with Parker's denunciation of Senator Daniel Webster. In general, O'Connell can be fitted into one Tocquevillian insight—religion embodied in him operated as the foremost of American political institutions because it played no party game but sought to advance what its advocate saw as common morality.

Growing up in this environment where Catholicism embodied moral energy—an energy that reinforced that of my parents—I did not take much interest in the dogmatic disputes of earlier centuries, and the implications of modern biblical criticism had not been absorbed by the Catholic mainstream. The Bible came in the regular readings of the gospels at mass, where the biblical text became part of the liturgy and enjoyed the liturgy's sense of being outside time; it was not history. My first recollection of the Bible outside this confining liturgical context is of reading at about age nine a set of "Bible stories" in my grandmother's house; Abraham's proposed sacrifice of his son I found a terrifying tale. Earlier, say when I was about seven, my mother had told me the story of Adam, Eve, and the snake, and I had asked, "In what language did the snake talk?"—a scientific rather than skeptical question. My first flash of real doubt occurred at Christmas when I was eleven or twelve: the whole story of Bethlehem struck me as improbable because of the detail. It was the same sensation I was to have later reading *Paradise Lost*: Milton's thick embroidery made the whole business fantasy. The accounts provided by Matthew and Luke, now styled "the Infancy Narratives," were to be analyzed in Raymond Brown's *The Birth of the Messiah* as largely midrashim, stories composed to convey a theological insight. But Brown's book came half a century later. Such freedom from literalism in reading the New Testament was uncontemplated in my education. In the case of Christmas I suppressed my thoughts. Religion in relation to morality was my focus.

My formal religious education was completed at the Cenacle—first by kind sisters (I did not encounter the surly nuns of legend), then by a brilliant young priest, John Wright, later a cardinal and the lost hope of the American liberals (to be specific, he did not go to bat for them on the subject of contraception and similar issues). Besides the parish in Brookline of St. Lawrence, named for a saint renowned for being grilled, there was the Jesuit church of St. Ignatius, the chapel of Boston College; the Passionist monastery of St. Gabriel in Brighton; and the Franciscan friary in Brookline. As in Chaucer's day, the Franciscans were favorites as confessors. The religious range within Catholicism was rich enough to accommodate a variety of inclinations, moods, needs, and intellectual interests.

The Protestant clergy was unknown to me, but the Protestant approach was familiar. Public school in Brookline opened class daily with a prayer —the Our Father and the Twenty-third Psalm. The Our Father was the Protestant version, with the extra line on "the power and the glory." As the Catholic form was the first prayer I knew, I was aware of the difference, and soon—I am not sure how soon—learned the reason for it and would be silent when the apocryphal addition was prayed. No teacher commented. Nor did any student or parent object to the prayers. The John D. Runkle School—later jocularly called "the Jewish Groton"— had then a mixed Protestant-Jewish-Catholic clientele.

After four years at Runkle I attended the Rivers Country Day School for eight. Here the headmaster, Clarence Allen, began each week with a school assembly, at which he prayed and Protestant hymns were sung. There was a vestigial sense about this short weekly service, less frequent than our public school prayers, a faint remainder of the robust religious rites of High Church boarding schools. It was a tincture of religion. Nonetheless, I enjoyed the hymns, and some of their stirring stanzas still echo in my brain. I had of course a number of Protestant and Jewish friends, none of them, so far as I could tell, particularly religious or interested in religion. As usual, an exception to such a generalization comes to mind: my Rivers classmate, Arthur Chute McGill, who later became a professor at Harvard Divinity School. But at Rivers I thought of Arthur as my chief academic rival, doubly formidable because his uncle, Austin Chute, was our Latin teacher. Protestants outnumbered Catholics on the faculty and in the student body, but religious discrimination was not known.

One final note on the Protestant heritage, a note moving from the explicitly religious to cultural history, but of relevance to the theme of this book: in the study of history and in general conversation the Salem witch trials were sometimes referred to, perhaps partly because witches were a topic for merriment at Halloween and partly because we would visit our Shea relatives in Salem, the site of the trials. But no one ever mentioned that in the nineteenth century Unitarians had dispossessed Congregationalists; that in the eighteenth century Congregationalists had jailed Baptists; that in the seventeenth century Congregationalists had beaten Baptists and killed Quakers. Nineteenth-century New Englanders had tried to keep alive the memory of the persecution of the Quakers. Nathaniel Hawthorne, descendant of one persecutor, memorialized the horror of it in 1832 in "The Gentle Boy," an early tale as haunting and guilt-ridden as vintage Hawthorne. John Greenleaf Whittier, himself a Quaker, put to verse the ordeal of the Southwick children. Brooks Adams, John Adams's great-grandson, in a book polemically entitled *The Emancipation of Massachusetts*, ascribed to "the Quaker martyrs" "our own perfect liberty of thought and speech." These efforts to preserve the cautionary legacy were in vain. That part of the Protestant past was swallowed up by a picture of Protestant amity and tolerance, a united Protestant front.

Because of the war, I left Rivers early, in January 1944, to follow my father's footsteps to Harvard. No alternative was considered by me or my parents; not even the hint of a Catholic college was heard from them or from me. At Harvard in the spring of 1944 I plunged into the study of the New England Transcendentalists with F. O. Matthiessen as mentor. Emerson's Divinity School Address of 1836 made an immediate impression. But how far that seemed from the moribund Divinity School of the Harvard of my day! In similar ways religious themes ran through many of the courses I then took in English, although the religious as such was not isolated from the cultural and not often emphasized. Matthiessen was an exception, and I think of him reading "Ash Wednesday" as though trying to understand and empathize with T. S. Eliot's religious preoccupation. Eliot, at all events, stood as the best of American poets and was indubitably religious.

The finest of teachers outside the English department was Joseph Schumpeter, the former finance minister of Austria. (Another ex. was Heinrich Brüning, the Center Party leader and former German chancellor whom Hitler had pushed aside; I met him in Lowell House but did not know him well enough to learn from him). Schumpeter was a master teacher, and I took the Economics of Socialism from him. He thought that as an economic system socialism could work. I asked him why anyone would want it if it was not in the interest of their class. He answered, "Some men pursue women, some religion, some hunting." In his view socialism was a species of religion and was as arbitrarily and as personally chosen. He himself was reported to prefer the pursuit of women; but we gossiped remarkably little about our professors.

My tutor was Jack Bate, then known to me as Assistant Professor W. Jackson Bate. With him I read Boswell on Dr. Johnson and was immediately captured by the great moralist. Encouraged by Bate, I embarked on a senior thesis comparing Johnson and Harvard's humanist, Irving Babbitt; my theme was the place of "absolute values" in the work of a critic, and I compared Johnson's Christian beliefs favorably with Babbitt's more tentative foundations. Harry Levin took an interest in this thesis, too, and I benefited from his sensitivity to issues of belief.

I took no Philosophy, but on my own read *The Unity of Philosophical Experience*, the William James lectures given at Harvard by Etienne Gilson, a marvel of synopsis and simplification. I read some Newman, some Maritain, and was above all affected by a philosophical novel, George Santayana's *The Last Puritan*. Set in part in Boston, with a stifling Puritan legacy contrasted with a vital Catholic current and both set off against pagan unbelief, the work exhibited Santayana's clear grasp of the alternatives; the next year I was to visit him in Rome.

With wartime acceleration, I graduated at the end of the summer of 1946, just as the war ended, and I had a sense that my college education had been too short and that I should continue it. Thanks to my parents' generosity, I did so at St. John's College, Cambridge University. In Europe I saw for the first time what a Christian culture had created, from universities like Cambridge to cathedrals like Siena's. For a believer, the cathedrals were not the museums they are for tourists, but still sacred places. I visited Lourdes, no great cathedral city, but a place where the palpable miracle was the faith of pilgrims, spiritually exalted whether they were bettered physically or not. I visited Rome and, through Cardinal Spellman and his friend Count Galeazzi, met Pius XII. Our conversation was not memorable, but my impression of the pope's intelligence remains. I visited the ancient church of San Clemente, built on a shrine to Mithras, and in its bowels encountered a Roman bust of Cardinal O'Connell, who had paid for the restoration. With Santayana I spoke at length, as also with Eliot in his office at Faber & Faber; I was struck by the photograph of Pius XII he had on his London desk.

The European experience cumulatively confirmed what I already felt in my bones, that Catholicism was the largest intellectual force in my life, yet I knew so little about it. I had never studied it as a subject. My religious education, except for occasional reading, had not gone beyond the high school level. It seemed to me absurd to place such confidence in what I had examined so little. I took the advice of the chairman of the Harvard English department, George Sherburn. After consultation with his colleagues he recommended either the Pontifical Institute of Medieval Studies at Toronto University or the Catholic University of America in Washington. Toronto looked like a cold place, Washington one that presented political vistas as well as academic ones. I chose Washington.

My plan was to obtain a doctorate in philosophy, but first it was necessary to know enough philosophy to enter the Graduate School of Philosophy. The first year I pursued a private tutorial with Vincent Smith, one of the few persons I have known who had a pure philosophical mind, that is, who had internalized philosophical concepts as though they actually contained insights into reality. It was a pleasure to read and debate Thomas Aquinas with him. At the same time I studied Church History with Alfred Rush, Scripture with Edward Arbez, Apologetics with Edmund Benard. Smith was a layman and allowed himself to be paid for his work. The other three were priests and insisted that their tutorial efforts could not be compensated. I became friends with Arbez, an exile from France after the suppression of Modernism and an excellent Scripture scholar, too cautious one would say today, but fully aware of all modern methods of investigating the ancient texts. Benard was only a dozen years my senior, an expert on Newman, a pure Gallic intelligence from the diocese of Springfield, Massachusetts. With him and his Paulist colleague Eugene Burke I became a dinner companion, golfing companion, and traveling companion. Our debates were unending.

Of these debates the most relevant here (I see I have strayed into matters not strictly germane but perhaps they are excusable as context) was over the relation of religion to governmental power. In June 1948 the Catholic Theological Society met in Chicago. The society was only three years old. It was about to elect Burke its president. "Bliss was it in that dawn to be alive." John Courtney Murray, then forty-one years old, a graduate of Boston College and professor of theology at the Jesuit seminary at Woodstock for the past eleven years, presented a seventy-page paper entitled "Governmental Repression of Heresy," a subject which he accurately identified as "the neuralgic point on a contemporary controversy." He contended that it was *not* the duty of a good Catholic state to repress heresy even when it was practicable to do so.

All the modern theological textwriters were against him—the Dominican Louis Bender; the curialist Alfredo Ottaviani; a variety of French, German, Italian, and Spanish Jesuits. In the United States the leading authority on "Catholic principles of politics," Monsignor John A. Ryan— "Right Reverend New Dealer," the liberal theological supporter of Franklin Delano Roosevelt—had studied the papal encyclical *Mirari vos* and taken specific note of its condemnation of "the doctrine of liberty of conscience and separation of Church and State." As recently as 1941 Ryan had published this pronouncement: "If there is only one true religion, and if its possession is the most important good in life for States as well as individuals, then the public profession, protection and promotion of this religion, and the legal prohibition of all direct assaults upon it, becomes one of the most obvious and fundamental duties of the State." From this principle Ryan drew the conclusion that in an ideal state the Catholic Church would be established and heresy would be repressed.

The unanimity of the theologians was no accident. They were united because they followed what Gregory XVI had taught in *Mirari vos*, what Pius IX, following Gregory XVI, had taught in *Quanta cura*, what Leo XIII in the wake of his predecessors had proclaimed in *Immortale Dei*. In *Mirari vos* Gregory XVI had responded to the efforts of Félicité de Lamennais to make the Church a champion of religious liberty. The pope assailed "indifferentism," described as the doctrine that anyone could obtain eternal salvation, whatever his beliefs, provided that he lived a decent moral life. "From this most foul font of indifferentism," Gregory XVI went on, "flows that absurd and erroneous opinion, or, rather, madness, that freedom of conscience must be affirmed and defended for everyone." In *Quanta cura* Pius IX repeated Gregory XVI's attack on "the madness that freedom of conscience and of worship is the proper right of every human being and ought to be proclaimed by law and maintained in every rightly-constituted society." These teachings were dated respectively on the Feast of the Assumption, 1832, and the Feast of the Immaculate Conception, 1864, giving a Marian cachet to what were sent as encyclical letters to all the bishops of the Catholic Church. Their teaching was endorsed again in 1885 by Leo XIII in *Immortale Dei*, an encyclical explicitly focused upon "the Christian constitution of States."

These pronouncements, as a reading of the next chapter will confirm, were consistent with Catholic teaching since St. Augustine on the coercion of heretics. They were, however, notably one-sided in ignoring Catholic teaching since Lactantius on the rights of conscience and the Catholic teaching incorporated in St. Thomas Aquinas on the duty to follow conscience. Gregory XVI, a former Camaldolese monk, and Pius IX, a disillusioned liberal, spoke with excited anxiety and anger as they contemplated the social ruin they thought freedom of conscience and freedom of opinion had brought to France and the Papal States. Read outside the broader context of Christian teaching, the encyclicals stood like boulders barring recognition of the universal freedom of conscience.

Encyclicals are known from their opening words. *Mirari vos* (You have wondered) and *Quanta cura* (With what great care) resonated in my ears. I had wondered. The Church, with great care, had apparently answered. Small wonder that the Redemptorist Francis Connell, then Catholic America's best known moral theologian, announced at Chicago after hearing Murray, "I, for one, shall continue to uphold the traditional view." The furthest that orthodox theologians would go in glossing the papal position was to advocate a theory, daring when first conceived, that there was a thesis and an hypothesis. The thesis was that a Catholic state had a duty to repress heresy. The hypothesis was that, in some circumstances, more harm than good might be done by a state doing its duty. In these hypothetical circumstances, religious toleration became the duty. In the United States, for example, it was generally agreed that the circumstances of the hypothetical held. Catholics could and should accept and extend religious freedom; but in principle, religious repression was the state's responsibility. Naturally, this view that in ideal circumstances the Catholics would repress all other beliefs caused uneasiness. The unrest was skillfully played on by Protestant polemicists like Paul Blanshard. Critics of this character were guilty of being more Catholic than the pope—of taking the authoritative texts more literally than they were taken in the Catholic Church in America or Rome; but the critics' distrust was genuine and the doctrine they exploited had once been operative.

What Murray did in defense and development of his idea was to cultivate an understanding of the difference between state and society; to critique the church-state theory of St. Robert Bellarmine; to invoke ideas on "the indirect power" of the Church first fashioned by the fourteenth-century theologian Jean Quidort (Sleeping John); and to suggest that the nineteenth-century encyclicals be read in context as polemics against a rationalism, a naturalism, and a Latin anticlericalism very different from the philosophy behind the American separation of church and state. He appealed as well to European history: "Political experience has taught us that the worst way to cope with dissidence is by legal suppression of it. Experience too has, I think, taught the Church that any attempt to establish or maintain religious unity by governmental coercion of dissenters does more harm than good to the Church."

Murray was answered not by experience but by appeal to authoritative doctrine. His scholarly articles, his tentative attempts to establish historical contexts, were replied to by firm insistence on the black letter of the papal texts. At Catholic University, Murray's fierce opponent was

Joseph Fenton, a diocesan priest from Springfield, Massachusetts, and Benard and Burke's colleague on the theological faculty. "Butch" Fenton, a bear of a man, was prepared to denounce Murray to the Holy Office in Rome and to delate Benard and Burke as well if they were in Murray's camp.

I entered debate with my two friends, taking Fenton's position, as I had with my father, and teasing them for their sole authority, Sleeping John. I did so with a double motive. On the one hand, I thought Fenton had all history on his side, so that there was intellectual integrity in sticking to his position. On the other hand, I thought that if Fenton was right, the Church must be wrong to have such a position. And remember that my general posture was that of an investigator of the foundation of faith. Could I believe in a Church so firmly attached to a doctrine my own father thought was ridiculous?

Finally tiring of my endless citation of papal pronouncements against religious freedom, Benard and Burke suggested I travel the short distance to Woodstock, Maryland and confront Murray himself. It was arranged. We spent the afternoon together. Murray stated his position. I stated my objections. He said, "The papal encyclicals must be seen in context. They spoke against the background of an anticlerical politics. They did not speak for all time." I saw what he meant; but I did not see how this background fully explained Gregory XVI's vehement denunciation in *Mirari vos* of the ideas of Félicité de Lamennais. Lamennais was not only the foremost apologist of the Church in France; he was, in contrast to the Gallican tradition, outspokenly propapal. In the early 1830s his paper *L'Avenir* had taught that the future lay with democracy and the Church. I did not understand how Murray's global explanation of the papal condemnation fitted his case. I felt the attraction of Murray's position without being persuaded of it. I put the question aside as not a practical one: after all, every Catholic accepted American democracy and liberty of religion today. But in the back of my mind I was aware that this practical comfort implicated a much larger question, the relation of history to the teaching of the Church, the question to which I have returned again and again.

Meanwhile I found in the Graduate School of Philosophy the academic context in which to pursue my examination of the claims and credentials of the Catholic Church. My master's thesis was on Alfred Loisy. Loisy, a French priest and biblical scholar, had found it impossible to reconcile the results of modern biblical scholarship with traditional presentations of the Gospel. In *L'Evangile et l'Eglise* he ventured on a theory of the development of Church teaching that explained a dogmatic change as a response to changing human needs. His views were rejected by Pius X and condemned in the encyclical *Pascendi* where his approach, stigmatized as Modernism, was characterized as "the synthesis of all the heresies." It was such a synthesis because it provided for indefinite, ecclesiastically uncontrolled development of doctrine. I could see, I could feel the attraction of Loisy's position. Was it not what John Courtney Murray was arguing in explaining the change on church and state? But I also could see the strength of the papal position. If human needs were the criteria, what content did revelation have? Was there no principle of stability?

I determined to look at the questions in terms of the philosophical postulates, explicit or implicit, in Loisy's work. My essay did not take enough account of the biblical data that had stimulated Loisy's solution, nor enough account of the theological dimensions; it did link Loisy to a chain of European subjectivism into which his speculations fitted; but my work was more an exercise than an enterprise wholly engaging me. It was different with my doctoral dissertation, into which I immediately plunged. The topic was the scholastic analysis of usury, that is, the way the Catholic theologians and canonists had presented the Church's prohibition of profit on a loan. The subject looked dusty to the outside observer. To me it had a triple appeal: its matter was moral, specifically, the demands of justice; the reasoning of the scholastic writers, while nominally philosophical, was very often legal, and already I was contemplating law school, to which I had been admitted in 1946; and finally, what I was studying was the evolution of a moral doctrine. That evolution challenged the Church's claim of constancy in its teaching.

Usury had first come to my attention at Cambridge University, where in my browsing I had encountered both William Lecky's *History of the Rise and Influence of the Spirit of Rationalism in Europe* and Bernard Dempsey, S.J.'s *Interest and Usury*. The former author chronicled the Church's abandonment of its old ban on profit on a loan as the triumph of the new rationalism over the old dogmatism. The latter, a protégé of Schumpeter, maintained that the old rule still had vitality and should be applied today in the special context of creation of credit by banks, because none of the reasons morally justifying interest existed for a banking system that created what it loaned. Both arguments interested me, and I saw that the topic had not been much explored. It was a perfect case in which to investigate the consistency of teaching by the Church, for it did not carry the emotional baggage of a moral issue affecting my own conduct (I was in no position to be a lender). And I could tuck it under the rubric of philosophy by treating the subject as a subdivision of ethics and the requirements of justice.

In two years I composed a manuscript that was twice as long as needed to qualify for the degree, and I had immersed myself in usury more than anyone in the department. At the last moment I heard of Stephan Kuttner, the erudite layman who was the soul of the School of Canon Law, and in kindly fashion he looked at my work and approved the canonical sources that I had used along with the philosophical and theological. What I had was a study of the development of Church doctrine over eight hundred years. The development was more complicated than Lecky had imagined, and the rationalism that had produced the changes was built into the scholastic method and had effected the real mutations of the doctrine by the seventeenth century. The rule was less rigid than Dempsey thought. In its mutated form, it accommodated credit creation by the banking system as it had once permitted exchange banking by the Medici and government loans by the Fuggers. The story was one of basic principles, response to changing circumstances, fine legal lines and close legal argument—the work of human beings adapting a moral rule to their experience. Plainly, the rule had not fallen from heaven. Plainly, the rule, proclaimed as ordained by God as law, had altered with the centuries. The documentation of this alteration did not directly bear on the question raised by Murray. It did prepare me to look critically at scriptural texts, conciliar canons, and papal pronouncements removed from the context of their circumstances, and to distinguish a variable rule from underlying values.

Having now spent four years examining as best I could the claims and credentials of the Catholic Church, and having pursued one case thoroughly and as a consequence having seen that one claim—that of always teaching the same morals—had to be read with major qualifications, I now turned to law school as providing a subject at once more concrete and more certain than what I had been studying. It was with surprise that I found the kind of development I had made out on usury was characteristic of the common law. No rule was fixed forever. Through changing circumstances a few fundamental insights persisted. The first-year law student's reaction was to think: Nothing is sure. Mature reflection saw both progress and stability.

In Constitutional Law, I first formally encountered the existing jurisprudence on the relation of religion to governmental power. The course was taught by Arthur Sutherland, a bland and pleasant person; it is not memorable on his account. But in the 1940s the Supreme Court had ap-

plied the First Amendment for the first time in the history of the nation
to assure the free exercise of religion and to prevent its establishment.
These cases, breaking new ground, occasionally had the ring of John Marshall announcing the existence of the power of judicial review of an act
of Congress and occasionally they found themselves caught in contradiction. Not anticipating all the problems ahead, the court sometimes
spoke boldly, sometimes delphically. At the very time I was in law school,
the court decided *Kedroff v. St. Nicholas Cathedral*, and this perplexing
and problematic case became the subject of a commentary by me in the
Harvard Law Review. With the uninhibited candor of a law student I
criticized the lone dissenter, Justice Robert Jackson, as "unrealistic" for
saying that only the property of a church, not its liberty was at stake,
and I sententiously added: "the material means are as necessary to a religion as the opportunity to have its doctrine taught and heard."

Our study was supposed to be the Constitution. In retrospect, I am
conscious of how professors of Constitutional Law identify constitutional
law with the opinions of the Supreme Court of the United States. It is
convenient for them to do so. In a single, easily accessible place they find
a body of facts assembled and analyzed and a body of doctrine announced. In an old tradition of exegesis, Jewish and Christian, the academic commentators can expand and reconcile the texts they take for
study. The world is fitted within the authoritative books.

Prior to 1940 if one looked at a textbook on Constitutional Law, or
at the casebooks in which students learned this law, there was a single
set of cases under "Religion, Freedom of." This set comprised the *Mormon Cases*. According to them, this was the understanding of the free
exercise of religion by the United States Supreme Court: conduct in accordance with one's idea of one's obligation to God could be federally
proscribed if the conduct conflicted with morality as conventionally understood by Christians. Specifically, polygamy could be proscribed even
though plural marriage was prescribed as the duty of male Mormons by
the Church of Jesus Christ of Latter-day Saints. An old device of ecclesiastical inquisition, an oath disavowing church membership, could be
employed to purge Mormons from federal juries. As a final squeeze, the
property of the offending church could be seized and used by the government. Upholding this mass of intolerant legislation, the Supreme Court
had introduced Jefferson's phrase "the wall of separation" into constitutional discourse and paid it lip service.

In this way, congressional power to affect the free exercise of religion
stood affirmed at the time of my birth in 1926. As for the states, the

Supreme Court had ruled in 1845 that the Constitution "makes no provision for protecting the citizens of the respective states in their religious liberties." It was not evident in 1866 when the Fourteenth Amendment was proposed that its laying on the states the obligation to observe due process of law would alter this result; nor had the Fourteenth Amendment altered it as late as 1926. Even if the Fourteenth Amendment had made free exercise operative against a state government, the *Mormon Cases* would have permitted the governmental interest to trump the religious claims. The *Mormon Cases* were still being cited as controlling law in 1937 when the Supreme Court dismissed for want of federal jurisdiction a plea of Jehovah's Witnesses that a municipal ordinance unconstitutionally abridged their freedom of religion. Then in 1938 things began to change, and in 1940 a constitutional right to free exercise against a state's interference was suddenly discovered and proclaimed.

What brought about the change? I do not believe the question was asked in our class in Constitutional Law. As is sometimes the case, the most fundamental question is too awkward for a new orthodoxy to ask. Now, retrospectively, I offer two hypotheses: First, that the change was the inevitable consequence of incorporating other First Amendment rights into the Fourteenth Amendment, thereby making them binding on the states. As early as 1925 the Supreme Court had observed for the purposes of the case that freedom of speech and freedom of the press were incorporated in the Fourteenth Amendment; thereafter these freedoms were used to strike down state restrictions. The Jehovah's Witnesses in 1938 had successfully invoked freedom of the press against the city ordinance to which in 1937 they had vainly objected as a prohibition of religion. It was just a matter of time before the logic of these cases made it apparent that the first of the First Amendment freedoms must also apply to the states.

Still, the inevitable occurs only with effort, and the timing of its arrival is critical. What made religion come to the fore in 1940? Here the second hypothesis kicks in. Many legal and moral positions, I believe, are formed in reaction to movements or situations perceived as terrible evils. In the course of the 1930s, the persecution of the Jews in Germany had become notorious. With the beginning of World War II the Nazis' identification with religious persecution loomed large in America. Other religious persecutions had, of course, occurred earlier in the century— of Christian Armenians by Turks, of Catholics by anticlerical Mexicans and anticlerical Spaniards, of Christians and Orthodox Jews by the Soviet Union. But that Germany, a Western nation, known for its academic and artistic accomplishments, should stage pogroms, and that that now Nazified nation should be engaged in mortal struggle with a nation whose cause the United States supported, was strong reason to assert the difference of America and to raise in particular the banner of religious freedom. In its landmark decision obliging the states to respect free exercise, *Cantwell v. Connecticut*, the Supreme Court explicitly alluded to the violence of those who acted "in the delusion of racial or religious conceit," a danger it said that had been "emphasized by events familiar to all."

Against the concept of a court interfering with local government was none of the feeling that New Dealers had built up against a court interfering with acts of Congress. True, the general liberal theory of constitutional interpretation, dating back to Holmes's 1905 dissent in *Lochner*, was that courts should not substitute their judgment for that of legislatures unless the legislation was plainly contrary to a specific liberty as that liberty was understood in American tradition. When the Supreme Court struck down a local ordinance as inconsistent with the free exercise of religion, it had no judicial precedent to show that the court's understanding was the traditional one. The court was innovating. But already a reasonably liberal justice, Harlan Stone, had drawn a distinction as to types of judicial federal intervention and had defended intervention to prevent the oppression of what he memorably catalogued as "a discrete and insular minority." The Jehovah's Witnesses were indisputably discrete, insular, and a tiny minority; they fitted Justice Stone's description beyond challenge. All the Supreme Court had to do was to announce that religious oppression by a state was something such a minority must be guaranteed against.

A final factor made change possible: a displacement was going on. The Supreme Court was no longer in the business of invalidating the government regulation of business. Courts abhor vacuums. Power unexercised is power gone. The energy spent, the power exercised in examining economic regulation, could and must be used elsewhere. The active men on the court had no desire to reduce their power. A judicial empire had been created by the Supreme Court's willingness to limit the regulatory power of Congress to activity "directly" affecting commerce. The empire reached its zenith in the cases invalidating parts of the New Deal. It was now about to disappear. A new and vaster world lay open to judicial supervision.

In response to these factors and to the vigorous argument of the Witnesses' counsel, the Supreme Court held in *Cantwell v. Connecticut* that the "fundamental concept of liberty embodied in [the Fourteenth]

Amendment embraces the liberties guaranteed by the First Amendment," among them the free exercise of religion. In other words, the states were henceforth to respect religious liberty. That liberty came in two parts—freedom to believe, which was absolute, and freedom to act, which, "in the nature of things," was not. Absolute freedom was beyond any state interference. Regulation of action by a state could not infringe religious freedom "unduly"—the adverb was deliberately broad and vague.

In *Cantwell* a general statute of Connecticut forbade solicitation of funds for a religious, charitable, or philanthropic cause without a certificate from the Connecticut secretary of state, who was to determine if the cause was religious, charitable, or philanthropic before issuing the certificate. Newton Cantwell and his two sons, Jesse and Russell, were soliciting money for the Jehovah's Witnesses without a certificate from the secretary and were convicted of the crime of so acting. The Supreme Court held that it "unduly" put "a forbidden burden" on the free exercise of religion to make solicitation for a religious purpose rest "in the exercise of a determination by state authority as to what is a religious cause."

Jesse Cantwell had also been convicted of the common law offense of breach of the peace. He had been playing a phonograph on a public street of New Haven. The record he played attacked all organized religions as systems of Satan and attacked the Catholic Church in particular. Cantwell's purpose was to persuade his hearers of the truth of the position of the Witnesses. His views were offensive to Catholics and to "all others who respect the honestly held religious faith of their fellows," but he was not personally abusive or threatening. Vilification and false statements, the Supreme Court observed, were used both in politics and religion. The court held that Cantwell's conduct was protected by the constitutional freedoms of both speech and religion.

The opinion was unanimous. It was written by Owen Roberts, an Episcopalian and a Republican, appointed to the court by Hoover. Roberts made the momentous proclamation without fanfare, without a single signal that the court had embarked on new waters. Nor was this opinion the occasion to explain the difficulties densely surrounding the new doctrine. What restrictions acted "unduly"? Could a public official never determine if a cause was "religious"? If a public official could not make this determination, how could a judge? Was false religious speech beyond the power of the state? Neither asked nor answered, these questions remained.

I was fourteen at the time of *Cantwell*, old enough to read *Life* and *Time* and take an intelligent interest in the world. Neither journal nor the *New York Times* paid attention to the case. *Cantwell* made not the slightest impression on my mental environment; but it made the Supreme Court, for the first time in American history, the active upholder of religious freedom.

Encountering *Cantwell* in the 1950s, along with the subsequent court victories of the Jehovah's Witnesses, and never having met a Witness in our lives, we law students used to joke, "The Witnesses are an invention of the Constitutional Law professors, designed by them to illustrate the First Amendment." The joke was not very sprightly or serious, but it pointed to an underlying reality: the Witnesses were an obscure group, without power in the society. To grant them rights was virtually costless for the society and for the courts. Religious freedom was vindicated in principle with almost nothing paid. Reading the cases as students, however, we resonated to the rhetoric of freedom that resounded in them. We in the fifties were in the afterglow of the American crusade in Europe, as Dwight Eisenhower had called it. Intolerance abroad had been crushed. Victory over intolerance here was celebrated.

My exposure in law school to the cases on Free Exercise was theoretical, but they reinforced a conclusion I had already reached on religious freedom: my father, Benard, Burke, and Murray were right, and the Catholic Church did not have to stay with its old position. I intend to say in the penultimate chapter of this book how the change was made. But before it happened I had a good taste of politics in Massachusetts as it was affected by religious identities and institutions and by the intervention of churchmen in their own interest and in that of social justice. I was practicing law in Boston with Herrick, Smith, Donald, Farley & Ketchum and still living in my hometown of Brookline. I was approached by a group I thought of as "the Jewish elders," who asked me to run for office in Brookline. The town by then had a Jewish majority, divided between families who had been in the town at least a generation and recent arrivals from Mattapan and Roxbury. The elders came from the former but had influence with both contingents. Catholics were the second largest bloc, divided too—the Villagers grouped around St. Mary's, some of them in an area known as the Farm that was by Brookline standards a slum; and lawyers, doctors, stockbrokers living on Fisher Hill in St. Lawrence's parish or nearer to Boston in St. Aidan's where John F. Kennedy was born. The third group, the Protestants, were identifiable as swamp Yankees near the Boston border and aristocrats living around The Country Club, Roundheads and Cavaliers as I sometimes imagined them to be. With the attention to religious affiliation so important still in such a middle-class suburb as Brookline, the elders put together a ticket composed of one Catholic, one Jew, and one Protestant to run for the Redevelopment Authority. I was the Catholic.

The authority, newly formed, had as its first task to eliminate the Farm by redeveloping it. The pastor of St. Mary's, Monsignor Joseph Robinson, bitterly opposed the project as eliminating part of his parish, and he had his own candidate for the authority, the president of the school custodians' union; like Cardinal O'Connell in the old days, the monsignor entered politics with a pawn.

Whether the monsignor's interest was strictly moral could have been debated. There was no teaching of the Church against redevelopment. It was plain that part of his displeasure was at his loss of parishioners who, if poor, were loyal. But he was also looking out for their good, material and moral. Why should they be forced out without compensation (they were largely tenants not owners and so not entitled to the proceeds of eminent domain)? Would not the destruction of their compact community be detrimental to their family life?

In the November election of 1956 there were nine candidates for four available seats (the governor was to appoint the fifth member). Sarah Wallace, president of the town's League of Women Voters, and I were victorious on our slate; it had not hurt me that a selectman of the town was named Tom Noonan. Our Protestant running mate was defeated; there were not enough Protestant voters interested in the project, and he had little charisma. Another defeated candidate was Michael Dukakis. He was young—a student at Harvard Law School—and there were not many Greek Orthodox in Brookline. The monsignor's candidate did win. The governor appointed a Democrat from the Village, who looked to the monsignor for advice. The monsignor had two votes certain and nearly a majority, for the fifth member was another of his parishioners. But this man was in his eyes a sell-out. He had spoken in favor of the redevelopment. To punish him the monsignor told his other two representatives to vote for me for chairman.

In this way I was made the leader of the project and began bargaining as to the contents of the redevelopment program to meet the monsignor's legitimate objections. It seemed unfair that the government confiscate the land and make it available in one package to a developer who would reap all the benefits, while the people most affected would be dispossessed and get nothing. The land was very valuable, not like so many redevelopment projects mired in urban decay but immediately contiguous to prosperous suburban residences. We could ask much from the developer to whom we would award the project. We made it a requirement that the successful bidder agree to subsidize in his new project the rent of any old tenant of the area who chose to return. The developer's profits would in part go to providing better housing for the dispossessed. Our requirement was an innovation, designed to do equity to the dispossessed. In this concrete way, in the 1950s, in Massachusetts, at this entirely parochial level, the Church entered into politics. To a degree, its pastor acted for the poor. To a degree, combined with other factors, religion played a part in the election. To a degree, the monsignor affected the choice of chairman. Theodore Parker would probably have understood; William Cardinal O'Connell certainly would have.

PART ONE

HISTORY

CHAPTER 2

TO KILL A QUAKER,
TO BEAT A BAPTIST

Religious Liberty before the Revolution

MARY DYER
executed June 1, 1660

*"My life not availeth me in
comparison to the liberty of the Truth."*

As befits the matter, I set it out in catechetical form.

Where are the roots of religious liberty to be found?
In Holy Writ, which makes obligations to God superior to those to any human being or any human contrivance. As the Acts of the Apostles have Peter say, summing up one strain of the precedent tradition, "We must obey God rather than man." Hence, conscience comes first.

An example before Peter?
The prophets of Israel denouncing the rulers of Israel, e.g., Nathan denouncing David.

What was the theological significance of the action of the prophets?
The sovereignty of God and His law was proclaimed.

What sociological significance?
A split of authority was created. The split provided space in which liberty of conscience appeared. Two interests were set in competition with each other. Legitimate power was no longer unitary.

By liberty of conscience in this ancient context you mean?
Liberty of certain charismatics to speak in judgment of the government, e.g., Isaiah: "Your very rulers are rebels, confederates with thieves; every man of them loves an offering and itches for a gift; they do not give the orphan his rights and the widow's cause never comes before them."

Did ancient Hebrew have a word for conscience?
It had the concept, not the word. For example, Solomon to Shimei: "You know all the evil that your heart knows that you did to my father David."

How did Christianity perpetuate this split of authority, this space for conscience?

By creating a Church that could speak such judgments.

How did Christianity enlarge the split and the space?

In two ways: by proclaiming the crucifixion of Christ at the hands of a lawful Roman governor, with the unspoken but momentous implication that lawful authority could make stupendous mistakes. By separating religion from obligation to family, obligation to tribe, obligation to nation, obligation to empire; in short, by making it personal.

What central moral notion of the pagan world converged with the Christian tradition?

Conscience.

Explain.

Conscience, as early as Cicero, is an inner judge. As Cicero first uses the word, "Bad thoughts and the consciousnesses of the mind terrify; these are the constant domestic Furies who day and night seek punishment on behalf of parents from their wickedest sons." From a state of mind, conscience becomes for Cicero a judge: "Your mind's conscience," he tells the senators judging Cluentius, "you receive from the immortal gods. It cannot be torn from you. You will live without fear and with the height of decency if this will be for you, for your whole life, the witness of your best counsels and deeds." Witness and judge, conscience has the character of the Stoic concept of divine reason in which all share. Witness, judge, reason, voice of God, conscience enters the moral consciousness of Christians.

Sum these answers.

By the first century A.D. there is in the Mediterranean world a religion, which will spread widely in the West, that carries the concepts of a God, living, distinct from and superior to any human being, society, or state; of obligations to that God, distinct from and superior to any society or state; of authorized teachers who can voice these obligations and judge any society or state; of an inner voice of reason that is one way God speaks as well as by His authorized teachers. According to these concepts as taught by this religion, each person, individually and not as part of a family, tribe, or nation, will have to account to God as Judge for every thought and deed. Collectively, these concepts are at the core of liberty of conscience and liberty of religion.

Explain why liberty of religion was not recognized at once?
The pressures of inherited convention, the lure of power, the sense that fidelity should be enforceable.

Explain further.
The Mediterranean world linked religious practice to civic security and success. To separate religion entirely from public life required a vision held by no one. Christianity moved from the status of a minority religion persecuted to a minority religion entrenched, a religion promoting the power of its ministers, enjoying discrimination in favor of its adherents, and encouraging the persecution of dissidents from its teachings.

Why was fidelity a key?
By force of analogy. In the words of Augustine, "Is it a lighter matter for a soul not to keep faith in God than for a woman not to keep it with her husband?" Adultery was punished by the law, so then should unfaithfulness in keeping the faith.

To whom were these words applied?
To those who were Christians, who departed from orthodoxy. In particular, to the Donatists whose error was to believe that for Christians the surrender of the sacred books of Christianity under pagan persecution was an unforgivable sin; so that by an irony not rare in religious history those Christians most adamant in their Christianity were themselves persecuted by other Christians for their adamancy.

What kind of force was employed?
Fines; civic disabilities and disinheritance; corporal punishment.

What was the practical benefit of such persecution?
According to Augustine, it worked.

Were other Christian heretics subject to disabilities and penalties under Christian emperors?
Yes. The Apollinarians, the Arians, the Eunomians, the Macedonians, the Montanists, the Phrygians, and the Priscillianists, to name those proscribed in Augustine's day.

Is it accurate to assert that persecution was the logical corollary of the absolute conviction of the truth of one's faith drawn by those with the power to persecute?

It is inaccurate. At no time did Christian thought embrace this proposition, which ran directly counter to two fundamental axioms: first, that faith was a gift and second, that the acceptance of that gift must be free—two convictions forged in blood when the Christians suffered savagely from persecutions by defenders of the old gods. "Religion," Lactantius had then written, "cannot be compelled. The whole thing must be done with words, not whips, so that it be voluntary." Religion, the Roman persecutors were informed, is to be defended "not by killing but by dying." "None of us," Lactantius could add, "are kept against our will. For he who lacks faithful devotion is of no use to God." In this time of their oppression, religious persecution by the empire was said by the Christians to be "against the law of humankind, against all established rightness." Only after Christianity became the established religion of the empire was breach of faith put forward as worthy of corrective punishment. Lack of belief in Christianity by a pagan or a Jew was not itself made a crime.

What was the proper approach to Jews in papal perspective?

"Those who differ from the Christian religion should be brought to the unity of the faith by mildness and kindness, by counselling and persuasion . . . not repelled by threats and terrors," declared Gregory the Great in 591, setting out for the benefit of the bishop of Terracina the way he should treat the Jewish population of his diocese.

Sociologically speaking, how is the different treatment of pagans, Jews, and heretics to be explained?

By inherited conventions, by the limits of power, by the intensity of feeling against those closest in belief who do not share the belief fully; for they are seen as those most likely to corrupt the faith, the ones most culpable in their disbelief, the ones most vulnerable to coercion.

Is it not true, nonetheless, that those who had never been Christians were at times the object of discrimination and repression that should be accounted persecution?

Undoubtedly. To give three examples, in the time of Augustine himself, the Manichaean religion was the subject of severe penal laws. In the age of the Second Crusade, Bernard of Clairvaux in a letter addressed to "all

Christians" urged that the pagan Slavic nations be converted or destroyed. Throughout the Middle Ages and up to the French Revolution, the Jews of Christian Europe were of second-class status. In the rough rhetoric of many Christian apologists, adopted by such popes as Innocent III, they were "worthy of servitude" and "bound to perpetual servitude."

The freedom of even non-Christians was then far from fully respected?

True. Even as to the performance of religious rites, Thomas Aquinas taught that Jewish ceremonies should be tolerated as foreshadowing Christian ones; but that "the rites of other infidels which bear nothing true or useful, are not to be tolerated in the same way except perhaps to avoid some evil, to wit scandal or a division that could arise from this or an obstacle to the salvation of those who would gradually be converted to the faith if they were tolerated. On this account the Church has sometimes tolerated the rites of even heretics and pagans when there was a great multitude of infidels."

Toleration when opportune, extermination of alien rites when appropriate, disadvantages at all times, but no formal compulsion of unbelievers to convert: Is that the formula?

Apparently.

As Thomas Aquinas built on Augustine to develop Christian thought, how far was it taught that the persecution of Christian heretics should go?

To death if they were warned in time and failed to correct themselves.

Could not even those heretics who had relapsed into heresy count on forgiveness inasmuch as no sin is unforgivable?

They could count on forgiveness with God, not with the Church. As Thomas Aquinas phrased it, remarkably refusing the imitation of God: God "knows who are truly returning. But the Church cannot imitate this. She presumes that they are not truly returning who, after they have been received back, have again relapsed. Therefore she does not deny them a way of salvation but she does not safeguard them from the peril of death."

What was the relation of the Church to a medieval Christian state?

The Church was established, that is, supported and used by the state. The personnel of each institution interpenetrated the other. The liberty of the Church was asserted against the power of the prince. A split in

interests, power, space remained, as the famous conflict between Henry
II and Archbishop Thomas Becket illustrates. At the same time the two
authorities often overlapped. For example, most of the bishops of England
were aligned with the king, not the archbishop. The Church was often
put to secular ends, as the condemnation of Joan of Arc on a trumped-
up charge of being a relapsed heretic illustrates. The space between Church
and state was sometimes uncomfortably small.

What happened to conscience?
It enjoyed a kind of schizophrenic recognition.

Amplify.
The supremacy of conscience was sustained, for conscience "is in a certain way the dictate of reason" and what is proposed by reason is proposed as true and therefore as "derived from God, from Whom is every
truth." Consequently although conscience could make a mistake—the
possibility of mishearing the divine voice is foreseen—one must obey one's
conscience; for "it is the same thing to flout the dictate of reason and the
commandment of God." If conscience, that is, reason, teaches one not
to believe in Christ, conscience must be obeyed.

Did not the supremacy of conscience imply the liberty of conscience?
No. The supremacy of conscience was equivalent to the obligation to conscience. The obligation to conscience implied not the liberty of conscience
but the obligation to form conscience correctly. Crass ignorance, deliberate or negligent, would lead to a deformed conscience. Although one would
act correctly in following the deformed conscience, one would have committed a moral fault by failing to form it correctly. One was consequently
open to correction not for following conscience but for forming it.

Conscience, then, had no protection against coercion?
Not if those judging the matter found fault in its formation.

Did this view of the matter change with the Reformation?
No. The Reformation created more heretics to be persecuted. The
Reformation created new churches that had their own heretics whom they
persecuted. But yes. Heretics became so numerous that they had to be tolerated for the sake of peace. The emperor Maximilian II, a Catholic, in
1568 extended legal toleration to Lutheran lords and practical toleration
to other Lutherans. The nobles of Poland in 1571 pledged themselves to

refrain from bloodshed, imprisonment, or confiscation "over differences of faith or changes of church"; the elected king of Poland swore to uphold this agreement, styled the Warsaw Confederation. The mutual toleration granted was between lords, not between lord and peasant. Still, until it ceased to exist as a kingdom, Poland was the most tolerant nation in Europe.

What else did the Reformation result in?

The Catholics of England, out of power, came, as Cardinal Allen put it in 1584, to "desire above all the liberty to exercise publicly those requirements of their worship which persecution forces them to perform secretly"; they sought "some liberty for the exercise of their consciences." When James I treated with the French for the marriage of his son Charles to a Catholic princess, Henrietta Maria, the French desired that the English should promise to the Catholics "the free exercise of their religion." But "the English would not listen to the word exercise." In the end, "free exercise" was publicly accorded by treaty only to the princess and her suite. Already by 1624, in the light of religious repression, "exercise" had a robust significance; and free exercise had a particular meaning for James's court in a way that had a consequence for America.

What more did the Reformation lead to?

It brought into existence in the sixteenth century authors who had suffered persecution and who came to write about persecution as contrary to the teaching of the Gospel, for example, Sebastian Franck; Caspar Schwenckenfeld, who gave his last name to the Schwenckenfelders; Menno Simons, who gave his first name to the Mennonites; Sébastien Castillon, a Savoyard who in 1554 urged the example of Christ and His Apostles as contrary to persecution.

What was the effect of these writings?

The creation of belief in religious freedom among small communities of Christians without the power conferred by large numbers and the possession of great material resources; the scattering of the idea of a Church not dependent on support by the state; the hardening of the hearts of the persecutors.

What happened in the following century to increase the chances of religious liberty?

The outbreak of more revolts, reversals, revolutions, and wars fed by difference of religion; the proliferation of religious sects; the founding of refuges for religious dissidents; the emergence of a learned criticism of religious persecution; the exhaustion of religious combatants; the increase of limited legal toleration of religious dissent.

Exemplify the revolts, reversals, revolutions, and wars in England.

The Revolution against Charles I; the Restoration of Charles II; Monmouth's Rebellion; the Revolution against James II.

What was the effect of the exhaustion of the religious combatants?

Widespread desire to find a basis for accommodation of theological conflict.

Exemplify the proliferating sects.

The Congregationalists; the Presbyterians, Scottish and English; the Baptists; the Quakers; the Ranters.

Name and date the refuges.

New Plymouth (1620); the Massachusetts Bay Colony (1629); Maryland (1632); Providence Plantations (1636); Pennsylvania (1680).

Name the leading learned critics of persecution.

Roger Williams; Baruch Spinoza; John Locke.

What ironies attended the refuges?

New Plymouth was founded by Separatists from the Church of England who were committed to a church composed of the born-again. It accepted the presence in the community of those not committed to the church but restricted citizenship to believers in the true worship of God. It ultimately could not survive by itself and merged with the Massachusetts Bay Colony, whose religious practices and prejudices it found congenial.

Massachusetts Bay Colony was founded by Christians seeking a purer church than the Church of England. They evolved their own distinct church, the Congregationalist, which the colony supported by local taxation. In the words of John Norton, appointed as "teacher," that is, pastor, by order of the legislature, New England was "a *Plantation religious*, not a Plantation of Trade." Consequently, "we through grace abounding abhor prejudicing the liberty of Conscience in the least measure," but "blasphemies and heresies carried on with a high hand and persisted in, are to be suppressed with weapons & punishments."

The significance of these two statements?

In one of the first American colonies, in a colony founded as a refuge from persecution, in a town sometimes self-described as "the cradle of liberty," religious freedom was prized, and religious persecution thrived.

Detail the legislation.

In 1656 the General Court—the governing body of the colony, combining legislative and judicial functions and including the executive in its membership—proscribed the presence of Quakers in the colony. One set of measures was directed to keeping "alien" or "vagabond" Quakers out; the other set was directed to such Quakers "as shall arise from amongst ourselves." Alien Quakers were to be apprehended, jailed, whipped, and deported. Ship captains bringing in Quakers were to be fined 100 pounds. The same monetary penalty, plus imprisonment, was to be inflicted as of 1657 on any inhabitant who, "directly or indirectly," caused a Quaker to be brought into the jurisdiction. Anyone harboring a Quaker was also to be fined and imprisoned. The importation of Quaker literature became criminal. By 1658 it was also criminal to propose Quaker doctrine at a church meeting or to "approve of any known Quaker" or the Quaker's tenets. The penalties were a fine and whipping. Security had to be given not to repeat the offense. If security were not given, the offender was to be banished, any return to the colony subject to the penalties provided for the return of deported "stranger" Quakers.

Was there more legislation?

Yes. Return was a particular problem. In 1657 the General Court prescribed for banished male Quakers who came back that they should lose one ear, a second time the other ear; females were to be "severely" whipped. On a third return, "he or she" should "have their tongues bored through with a hot iron." A year later, on October 19, 1658, the ultimate penalty—death by hanging—was provided for banished Quakers who returned. This punishment had hitherto been reserved for Jesuit or other Catholic priests who came back to Massachusetts after being banished.

Detail the implementation of the legislation.

Under the energetic leadership of John Endecott, repeatedly elected governor, the laws against the Quakers were enforced. The milder penalties such as flogging were inflicted on men and women alike. The General

Court ordered that Provided Southwick and her brother Daniel, two children of Quakers, be put in the stocks and then sold to Englishmen in Virginia or Barbados when their Quaker parents were unable to pay a fine. Climactically, on October 18, 1659, the General Court decreed death for returned Quakers William Robinson, Marmaluke Stephenson, and Mary Dyer. The men were hanged on Boston Common nine days later. Dyer underwent a mock execution. As the General Court then put it, through its "mercy and clemency" she had "liberty to depart within two days." She went back to her husband in Rhode Island.

Why does Dyer's statue now stand in front of the State House on Beacon Street in Boston?

She came back to Boston. She was rearrested. The General Court ruled that her sentence now be executed. On June 1, 1660, she was hanged on the Common. Her statue, erected three hundred years after the event, recalls her own view of liberty: "My life not availeth me in comparison to the liberty of the Truth."

Did any contemporary call the attention of the General Court to its inconsistency on religious liberty?

Yes. Anne Brinley Coddington, Mary Dyer's next-door neighbor in Newport, wrote the Massachusetts magistrates a month after her execution: "Would you not have thought it hard Measure, if any of you had been so used by the Bishops? Nay, did you not so think, though they did less than you yourselves have done? Is this following the Command of Christ, who said, *Whatsoever ye would that Men would do unto you, that do unto them?*"

Was Dyer the last Quaker they put to death?

No. That was William Ledra, also executed on the Common.

Was the legislation made more onerous?

Yes. In May 1661 under the double pressure of criticism in the colony and the threat implicit in the restoration in England of Charles II, a monarch open to Quaker lobbying, the General Court intensified the persecution. New legislation provided that any vagabond Quaker should by "the constable of the towne wherein he or she is taken . . . be stripped naked from the middle upwards and tied to a carts tayle and whipped thro the towne" and so in every town till reaching "the borders of our jurisdiction."

Why was the legislation so careful in its use of pronouns identifying each gender?

Because women were particularly persistent Quakers.

Was the new legislation enforced?

It was.

Why was the persecution by the colony so vigorous?

Because, in the words of the General Court, Quakers were persons "despising government and the order of God in church and commonwealth" or again, as the General Court in a theological manifesto quoting the Reverend Norton declared, the "opinion of theirs of being perfectly pure and without sin tends to overthrow the whole gospell and the very vitalls of Christianity;" or again, in the words of John Endecott to Charles II, "the Quakers died, not because of their other crimes, how capitoll soever, but had they not been restrained, so far as appeared, there was too much cause to feare that wee ourselves must quickly have died, or worse."

The real reasons?

The Quakers were "a hideous Döppelganger" dogging the Puritans' steps. They believed in the same God, the same Trinity, the same Savior, the same Bible as their persecutors. They claimed an Inner Light that guided them differently from the clergy and laity they confronted. What could be more of an affront?

The Quakers were incorrigible. They came back. Who can give a criminal more than three chances?

The Quakers might have converted Congregationalists. What else is meant by Endecott's "or worse"? "For liberty of conscience," as the General Court instructed its agents on March 17, 1681, "wee have been, as wee then conceived, necessitated to make more severe laws to prevent the violent and impetuous intrusions of the Quakers."

How long did the persecution last?

About one generation. As late as 1675 constables were instructed by the General Court to arrest persons found at any Quaker meeting and subject them to a fine and to discipline at the house of correction. Only in 1681 did the General Court actually repeal the capital punishment prescribed for Quaker returnees and suspend the other measures.

Was the persecution successful?

Yes. Quakers came to avoid Massachusetts; Quaker societies did not flourish in the commonwealth. Quakers settled on Nantucket, which fell within the jurisdiction of New York, and in Rhode Island, ruled by a refugee from Massachusetts, and ultimately in Pennsylvania, given them by Charles II. Massachusetts was spared.

What does it all show?

That neither the soil of America, nor the experience of having suffered persecution, nor explicit belief in freedom of conscience were sufficient in themselves to prevent men carrying out persecution on account of religion.

Describe the other refuges.

Maryland was founded by Lord Baltimore, a Catholic who feared for the future of his religion in England, secured the patent for his colony from the king, who was the head of the Church of England, and agreed that in his colony no Christian should be molested "for or in respect of his or her religion nor in the free exercise thereof." In this way, the exact expression "free exercise" entered the American continent, echoing the use of the phrase in England to indicate more than adherence to one's private religious belief. Before the end of the century the Anglicans controlled the government and Catholics could not hold public office or practice law within the colony.

Providence Plantations was founded by Roger Williams after he was exiled by the Congregationalists from Massachusetts. He secured a charter from Parliament, confirmed by the king who was also the head of the Church of England, that granted the widest latitude of religious practice. The colony attracted many Baptists and Quakers and a small number of Jews. By the end of the century the colony forbade Jews and Catholics to vote. Roger Williams himself as president of the colony condemned "such an infinite liberty of conscience" as would recognize the conscientious objection, held by many Baptists and Quakers, to bearing arms.

Pennsylvania was founded by a Quaker as a refuge for his coreligionists and was chartered by the king who was also the head of the Church of England. No one acknowledging "*One* Almighty God, the Creator, Upholder, and Ruler of the World" was to be molested because of his "conscientious Persuasion or Practice." Catholics, however, were not permitted to have visible churches. Only persons professing "to believe in *Jesus Christ*, the Savior of the World," were eligible for public office.

Complete religious freedom never existed in any of these refuges?
True.

How, then, did they change the situation?
Plymouth and the Bay Colony provided an ideal and a rhetoric more permanent than their descent into persecution. Rhode Island dimly (for it was poor and its reputation dingy) and Pennsylvania strikingly (for it was prosperous and well regarded) showed that organized government could exist without supporting a church. Maryland provided the phrase that is at the core of the First Amendment. All four colonies demonstrated that the Church of England could tolerate other forms of Christian worship and so prepared the ground for the English Act of Toleration.

What part was played by the proliferation of sects?
The proliferation of sects created a variety of alternatives to the established Church of England and to the old Church and thereby created political constituencies that politicians had to consider.

What was the critical contribution of Roger Williams?
Principally, *The Bloudy Tenent, of Persecution; for Cause of Conscience, Discussed, In A Conference Between Truth and Peace*, wherein he taught "that the blood of so many hundred thousand souls of Protestants and Papists spilt in the wars of present and former ages, for respective consciences, is not required nor accepted by Jesus Christ the Prince of Peace"; that civil officials are "not judges, governors, or defenders of the spiritual or Christian state of worship"; and that "it is the will and command of God" that "permission of the most paganish, Jewish, Turkish, or antichristian consciences and worships, be granted to all men in all nations and countries."

What was the critical contribution of Baruch Spinoza?
His *Tractatus theologico-politicus*, wherein he taught that "no one can transfer to another his own natural right or his faculty of reasoning freely and judging"; that hence, it is usurpation and injury when the supreme civil power attempts to prescribe "what opinions ought to move each mind with devotion to God"; that so doing, the "civil power endangers itself, creates hypocrites, causes divisions, destroys peace, and discourages those of good education, the integrity of morals and the cultivation of virtue."

And of John Locke?

His *Letter Concerning Toleration*, which answered an Arminian theologian's inquiry about the desirability of "the mutual toleration among Christians" and declares, "I esteem that toleration to be the chief distinguishing mark of a true church"; which taught that the method of "the Captain of our salvation" was to send out His soldiers "not armed with the sword, or with force, but furnished with the Gospel, the message of peace, and the exemplary holiness of their conduct"; which analyzed a civil commonwealth as limited to temporal objectives and having a jurisdiction that "neither can nor ought in any way to be extended to the salvation of souls"; which declared, "No way that I walk in against my conscience will ever bring me to the mansions of the blessed"; which argued for civil toleration to all except those who deny the being of a God (for promises and oaths, the bonds of human society, "can have no hold upon or sanctity for an atheist") and except "those who refuse to teach the duty of tolerating all men in matters of mere religion" (for they ask for toleration only until they are strong enough to end it).

The influence and effect of these teachings?

Williams's work had an especial impact on, and following among, dissenters from the Church of England, and, in the time of James Madison, upon Isaac Backus, the most forceful and effective of Baptist expositors of religious freedom in America. Spinoza's book, the work of a Jew excommunicated by his synagogue, showed the intellectuals of Europe how philosophical argument for religious freedom should be developed. Of the three, Locke's letter paid the largest dividends. Written in Latin, the language of the learned, it was within three years translated into English, the language of the politicians. Written anonymously in exile, it was ultimately known as Locke's and benefited from his prestige as the foremost English philosopher, psychologist, and theorist of government. Written by an author who was, arguably above all, a theologian, written by such a master of biblical exegesis and argumentation, Locke's *Letter* spoke with as much, or more, force to the devout Christian as it did to deists. Excepting those who did not themselves teach toleration, it excluded Catholics from benevolence, to the satisfaction of the Protestant administration that replaced James II.

How was toleration legally accepted?

By the Act of Toleration conditionally passed in 1688 after the ouster of

James II to "give some ease to scrupulous consciences in the Exercise of Religion"; confirmed by a second Act of Toleration in 1711 as a permanent settlement of full establishment for the Church of England, civil rights for Protestant dissenters willing to be regulated, legal disabilities for atheists, Catholics, Jews—an almost Lockean law for forbearance among Protestants.

What was the law, then, in 1765, as expounded by William Blackstone in the most authoritative, most influential, and most up-to-date treatise on the laws of England?

That human beings have "natural rights," which "God and nature have established" and "no human legislature has power to abridge or destroy." That "the principal aim of society is to protect individuals in the enjoyment of those absolute rights," vested in them by the "immutable laws of nature." That Christianity was once "deformed by the daemon of persecution" but the reign of Elizabeth restored "the religious liberties of the nation" while a statute of Charles II abolishing the punishments for heresy delivered "our minds from the tyranny of superstitious bigotry." That "the persecution and oppression of weak consciences, on the score of religious persuasions, are highly unjustifiable upon every principle of natural reason, civil liberty, or sound religion." That the enforcement of the penalties against papists would be "the destruction of every principle of toleration and civil liberty." That "the idea and practice" of civil liberty "flourish in the highest vigor in these kingdoms [England, Scotland, Ireland], where it falls little short of perfection."

Also, that the Church of England is established by law. That neither its canons nor its book of common prayer can be insulted; and that no other Protestant ministers may preach unless they publicly pledge themselves to hold certain Christian doctrines specified by statute. That Catholics are subject to a broad range of punishments and legal incapacities; that Catholic landowners can lose their land and Catholics educated abroad their inheritance on the claim of a Protestant relation; and that Catholic priests celebrating mass are subject to life imprisonment, and that these laws, although "seldom enforced in their utmost vigor," may be applied. That no one can hold office in the military or the national government without receiving the sacrament according to the rites of the established church and without acknowledging by oath the English king as head of the church. Nor can one be naturalized without a similar oath (a relaxation in favor of Jews in 1753 having been abandoned "with some precipitation"). Those who "falsely pretend an extraordinary commission from heaven" can be fined, flogged, or imprisoned. Those who deny the being or the providence of God or cast contumelious reproaches on Christ or expose Scripture to contempt or ridicule are subject to the same punishments; "for christianity is part of the laws of England."

After all, then, natural rights were extolled, liberty of conscience celebrated, religious bigotry deplored, religious conformity encouraged and rewarded, and religious controls retained?
Yes.

Was Blackstone less schizophrenic on the natural rights of conscience than his medieval predecessors?
Not perceptibly, but his tone was less strident.

Did Blackstone's bland representation of tolerance reflect the actual application of the law?
No. Mass had still to be celebrated covertly in London. As to Catholics of property, "several lived under great terror and some under actual contribution" in consequence of the penal statutes.

Does Mr. Thwackum of Tom Jones *accurately reflect the state of mind represented by the English law as it applied in the American colonies? That is, "When I mention Religion, I mean the Christian Religion; and not only the Christian Religion, but the Protestant Religion; and not only the Protestant Religion, but the Church of England."*
Yes as to Anglican Virginia; no as to such colonies as Congregationalist Connecticut and pluralist Pennsylvania.

Was the killing of Quakers unacceptable but the beating of unlicensed Baptist preachers acceptable in certain colonies?
As events proved, yes.

What, then, was the importance of the ideas furnished by Williams, Spinoza, Locke, and perceptible if deformed in Blackstone?
The ideas inhabited the mind of James Madison and the minds of those he addressed at the time of the American Revolution. The ideas prepared them for a more perfect expression of the ideal. The ideas pushed them toward the taking of a momentous legal step.

CHAPTER 3

JM'S ORIGINAL INSIGHT

JAMES MADISON, JR.
*age thirty-one, two years before writing
the Memorial and Remonstrance*

*"We maintain therefore that in matters of Religion, no man's right
is abridged by the institution of Civil Society and that Religion is
wholly exempt from its cognizance."*

In the south clerestory near the entrance of the Gothic chapel on the campus of the college that nurtured him JM stands enshrined, in the Window of the Law. In the same chapel, next to Charlemagne's mentor Alcuin, is JM's teacher, John Witherspoon, beneath whose feet is a legend from the Gospel according to John: "The Truth shall make you free." Through the stained glass of both windows the light enters. Setting and symbols appropriately celebrate JM; the evangelist's claim is a hope, or a program.

JM is how the modern editors of the correspondence and speeches of James Madison, Jr., briskly refer to the Founding Father whose thoughts and deeds are most relevant to this book. "Mr. Madison," a contemporary would have said. He is at once an eighteenth-century figure to be understood in the context of his day and an active prophet whose vision was so farsighted that the contraction to his initials fits the modernity of the man. JM or Mr. Madison, he cannot be confined as an icon to the stained glass of a chapel.

Let us begin with what appears at first glance to be a code and on further inspection a code whose clarity is transparent and whose theological, philosophical, political, and historical foundations are firm and deep.

JM'S NOTES, DECEMBER 23–24, 1784

Debate on Bill for Relig. Estabt proposed by Mr. Henry

1. limited
2. in particular
3. What is Xnty? Courts of law to Judge
4. What edition, Hebrew, Septuagint, or vulgate? What copy—what translation?
5. What books canonical, what apochryphal? the papists holding to be the former what protestants the latter, the Lutherans the latter what other protestants & papists the former

6. In What light are they to be viewed, as dictated every letter by inspiration, or the essential parts only? or the matter in generall not the words?

7. What sense the true one, for if some doctrines be essential to *Xnty*, those who reject these, whatever name they take are no *Xn* Society?

8. Is it Trinitarianism, arianism, Socinianism? Is it salvation by faith or works also—by free grace, or free will—&c &c &c

9. What clue is to guide Judge thro' this labyrinth? When the question comes before them whether any particular Society is a Xn Society?

10. Ends in what is orthodoxy, what heresy?

I. *Rel*: not within purview of Civil Authority.
tendency of Estabg. Xnty

1. to project of Uniformity
2. to penal laws for supportg. it

Progres[s] of Gen: Assest. proves this tendency

---

difference between estabg. & tolerating errour—

II. True question not—Is Rel: necesy.?
are Relig. Estabts. necessy. for Religion? no.

1. propensity of man to Religion.
2. Experience shews Relig: corrupted by Estabt.
3. downfal of States, mentioned by Mr. H[enry]. happened where there was Estabts.
4. Experience gives no model of Gel. Asst?
5. Case of Pa. explained—not solitary, N.J.
   See Const. of it. R.I.N.Y.D.

---

factions greater in S.C.

6. Case of primitive Xnty.
   of Reformation
   of Dissenters formerly.

III. Decl: Rig[hts]. 7. Progress of Religious Liberty

IV. Policy.
   1. promote emigrations from State
   2. prevent [immigration] into it as *asylum*

V. Necessity of Estabts. inferred from State of Conty.

---

true causes of disease
   1. War   common to other States
   2. bad laws   & produce same
      complts. in N.E.
   3. pretext from taxes
   4. State of Administration of Justice.
   5. transition from old to new plan.
   6. policy & hopes of friends to G. Asst.

---

   true remedies not Estabt. but being out war
   1. laws cherish virtue
   2. Administ: justice
   3. personal example—Association for R.
   4. By present vote cut off hope of G. Asst.
   5. Education of youth

Probable defects of Bill
dishonor Xnty

---

panegyric on it on our side

Decl: Rights

Beneath the abbreviations, JM's thought is clear. A bill establishing religion is a bill establishing Christianity. But what is this Xnty? The desperate European enterprise undertaken to impose unity by definition, by argument, by force necessarily ends in asking what is orthodoxy, what is heresy. Are the courts to judge? Civil authority is incompetent to answer. What is the true question? Not, Is religion necessary? Human beings have a propensity to religion. The true question is, Are religious establishments necessary for religion? Historical and contemporary examples answer negatively. Christianity ("panegyric on it on our side") does not need establishment. The final point: "Decl: Rights"—that is, the Declaration of Rights proclaimed by Virginia in 1776, text mainly by JM—is decisive: it determines that the free exercise of religion is the law and excludes the establishment proposed by Mr. Henry.

Mr. Madison was the son of a prosperous slaveholder and vestryman of a Church of England parish. He was baptized in the Church of England and in his last years at home tutored by Thomas Martin, one of its priests, who lived with the Madison family and was "a man of both learning and piety"; his pupil himself declared his advice would "be always gratefully remembered." Before that, Mr. Madison had studied at the school of the devout Donald Robertson, whose available library included Thomas à Kempis's *Imitatio Christi*. No sensitive fifteen-year-old, it is reasonable to guess, could have ignored this powerful presentation of the following of Jesus. The Latin he learned with Robertson would have enabled him to comprehend Thomas à Kempis's succinct and simple lines.

Mr. Madison had attended a college founded by Presbyterians in Princeton, New Jersey that was presided over by the Reverend John Witherspoon, a Presbyterian divine who had sacrificed his work in Edinburgh and had come to America, as he put it, that he "might be instrumental in furnishing the minds, and improving the talents, of those who might hereafter be the ministers of the everlasting gospel." Under these austere auspices Mr. Madison had learned to inquire, to debate, to respond to intellectual challenge, to gain, as he himself put it, his "very early and strong impressions in favor of liberty both Civil and Religious." He had been taught by the reverend preceptor-president that "the magistrate ought to defend the rights of conscience and tolerate all in their religious sentiments that are not injurious to their neighbors." He had been taught by the same authority that every man ought "to judge for himself in matters of religion"; and that maxim had been invested with explosive force by being coupled with the proposition that this "natural liberty" was one "which ought not to be alienated even in society." Neither preceptor nor students attempted to reconcile this principle, so potentially subversive of civil law, with the requirements of civil order. No doubt the main focus was on what President Witherspoon put more mildly in his lectures: "We ought to guard against persecution on religion's account." That the principles, political and religious, inculcated were kept with satisfying fidelity by the pupil is demonstrable. After the constitutional convention of 1787, Princeton gave JM an honorary degree. There was "none," his old preceptor declared, "to whom it gave more satisfaction" than himself.

Mr. Madison had stayed on in Princeton to continue the study of Hebrew with President Witherspoon: the ministry must have been on his mind. He had copied pages of commentary on the Gospels and on the Acts of the Apostles. He had turned sacred scripture over in his thought. He had become sick—with disease? with doubt? it is impertinent to speculate where evidence is inconclusive—and he had come home and read a little law and had thought about what he could do. At this time, in the fall of 1773, he was consulted by a friend and fellow Princetonian, William Bradford, then residing in Philadelphia, a man three years his junior, accounted by him "the only valuable friend I have settled in so public a place."

Mr. Bradford wrote that he was considering the choice of "callings in Life"; that he had thought of the ministry but there were "some insuperable objections"; and that he needed Mr. Madison's advice on the choice between law, medicine, and merchandising. (He ultimately became the first attorney general of the United States). Mr. Madison replied that he regretted his friend's decision about the ministry but would not press him to change his mind. He went on: "I cannot however suppress [this] much of my advice on that head that you would always keep the Ministry obliquely in View whatever your profession be. This will lead you to cultivate an acquaintance occasionally with the most sublime of all Sciences and will qualify you for a change of public character if you should hereafter desire it."

What did JM mean by the advice, to "keep the Ministry obliquely in View?" His next sentence gave his thought specific content: "I have sometimes thought there could be no stronger testimony in favor of Religion or against temporal Enjoyments even the most rational and manly than for men who occupy the most honorable and gainful departments and are rising in reputation and wealth, publicly to declare their unsatisfactoriness by becoming fervent Advocates in the cause of Christ, & I wish you may give in your Evidence in this way. Such instances have seldom occurred, therefore they would be more striking and would be instead of a 'Cloud of Witnesses.'" The closing allusion was to the Epistle to the Hebrews 12:1–2: "With a cloud of witnesses to faith around us, we must throw off every encumbrance, every sin to which we cling and run with resolution the race for which we are entered, our eyes fixed on Jesus." To follow Jesus in public life was to keep the ministry obliquely in view.

Mr. Bradford replied that he would, in accordance with Mr. Madison's advice, cultivate divinity "every vacant hour." In a place, Philadelphia, where "deistical sentiments" about religion universally prevailed, Mr. Bradford believed it "as absolutely necessary to be able to defend as well as believe the Christian religion." Mr. Madison's answering letter noted that he himself found current periodicals "loose in their principals" and encouraging "free inquiry even such as destroys the most essential Truths." The periodicals, indeed, were "enemies to serious religion and extre[me]ly partial in their Citations." Mr. Madison was not an enemy of serious religion. He implied that he already held the truths he believed essential. He commended Mr. Bradford for studying "the History and the Science of Morals," a study that settled principle and refined the judgment while "enlarging Knowledge and correcting the imagination." "I doubt not," Mr. Madison continued, "but you design to season them with a little divinity now and then, which like the Philosopher's stone in the hands of a good man will turn them and every lawful acquirement into the nature of itself and make them more precious than fine gold." And there was a final piece of spiritual counsel: "a watchful eye must be kept on ourselves lest while we are building ideal monuments of Reason and Bliss here we neglect to have our names enrolled in the Annals of Heaven." JM, surely no hypocrite, seasoned his thinking with a little divinity. JM, a builder of an ideal monument on earth, never lost desire to be enrolled in the annals of heaven.

Shortly afterwards there fell into JM's lap the issue that was to energize and animate him. Uncertain and reflective and puzzled as to his vocation, JM suddenly saw what he knew must be wrong and, in reaction, reached a resolution. From his home, in January 1774, he wrote Mr. Bradford: "If the Church of England had been the established and general Religion in all the Northern Colonies as it has been among us here and uninterrupted tranquility had prevailed throughout the Continent, It is clear to me that slavery and Subjection might and would have been gradually insinuated among us. Union of Religious Sentiments begets a surprizing confidence and Ecclesiastical Establishments tend to great ignorance and Corruption all of which facilitate the Execution of mischievous Projects."

The "slavery" reacted to was not chattel slavery. "Slavery" was a metaphor, easily derived from what JM saw about him on Virginia plantations, for the mental stagnation to which uniformity of religious opinions led. Already he was a pluralist, a believer in the salutary effects of division and competition, seeing their virtue in the realm of religion before he extolled their virtue in politics. The moral evil he perceived was the imprisonment of six Baptist preachers in Culpepper County, Virginia.

JM's mind had been prepared for the issue three years before. As a matter of principle, the Separate Baptists did not apply to the Crown for the permit to preach required of Protestant ministers not pertaining to the Church of England, the church by law established. In 1771, in Caroline County, a preaching Baptist was interrupted as he sang a hymn by a minister of the Church of England on horseback who rammed a horsewhip into his mouth and with aid of the sheriff and some others hauled him into a nearby field where he was flogged for his unlicensed activity. The Baptists interpreted the incident religiously: it was an instance of "the rage of malice of the old serpent devil," while "the Blessed Jesus was riding victorious on the White Horse of the Gospel in many parts of the world unknown to us." When, shortly thereafter, the first meeting of the General Association of the Separate Baptists of Virginia was held at Blue Run Church in Orange County, the outrage was remembered, and the preachers asserted that their license came from "King Jesus." Four to five thousand persons assembled at Blue Run Church to hear this message—the largest crowd ever assembled in Virginia. Orange County was where JM lived. Student of religion and of politics, JM could not but have known of the flogging and of the local reaction.

Mr. Madison's letter to Mr. Bradford of January 1774 linked his thoughts on religion to politics and the anti-British agitations in Boston:

"Political Contests are necessary sometimes as well as military to afford exercise and practise and to instruct in the Art of defending Liberty and property." How early "exercise" was a muscular noun for him, how early he was interested in the art by which liberty must be defended!

He continued his confidences to Mr. Bradford: "I have indeed as good an Atmosphere at home as the Climate will allow but have nothing to brag of as to the State and Liberty of my Country. Poverty and Luxury prevail among all sort: Pride ignorance and Knavery among the Priesthood and Vice and Wickedness among the Laity. This is bad enough. But it is not the worst I have to tell you. That diabolical Hell conceived principle of persecution rages among some and to their eternal Infamy the Clergy can furnish their Quota of Imps for such business. This vexes me the most of any thing whatever. There are at this [time] in the adjacent County not less than 5 or 6 well meaning men in close Gaol for publishing their religious Sentiments which in the main are very orthodox. I have neither patience to hear talk or think of any thing relative to this matter for I have squabbled and scolded, abused and ridiculed so long about it, to so little purpose that I am without common patience. So I to pity me and pray for Liberty of Conscience."

Theology, or theological metaphor, to the fore. The agents of religious repression are not comical elves but imps: in the lexicon of the day puny or subaltern devils, as in the preacher's phrase "imps of Satan." The principle on which they act comes from Hell—a dark ascription; there is no evidence that it is less than seriously asserted. Mr. Madison is as serious as the Separate Baptists in seeing the old serpent's malice. What is sacred, whose liberty must be safeguarded, is the faculty by which right is discerned from wrong, and by which God speaks to each—the conscience. What distresses Mr. Madison most is the clergy's part in persecution, a part so dramatically illustrated by the mounted priest, horsewhip in hand to stop the dissenter's mouth. Mr. Madison ends with a prayer or request for a prayer. Against the background of his piety, his words are not to be read flippantly or as an expression of futility. Prayer in these circumstances was JM's earnest response to perceived evil.

Mathematicians, it is believed, have their insights young, when their purely intellectual powers are at their height. They need no experience to see into the world of numbers. Statesmen, at least Plato thought, need experience. JM was either a mathematician or his experience, supplied vicariously by history, had come early. At twenty-two, using the Philosopher's stone of divinity, he had formed and had articulated the insight that in revolutionary America would carry the day for the free exercise of religion.

In June 1776, two years later, Virginia was in revolutionary fire. The rebels held the capital, Williamsburg, and prepared a Declaration of Rights for the new commonwealth. JM was put upon the drafting committee. Its chairman was Mr. George Mason, a man of wealth, practical experience, and Church of England principles. The Church of England was at some disadvantage, given the temper of the times. Mr. Mason's draft proposed to extend tolerance beyond what English law allowed. His declaration declared: "That Religion, or the Duty which we owe to our divine and omnipotent Creator, and the Manner of discharging it, can be governed only by Reason and Conviction, not by Force or Violence; and therefore that all Men shou'd enjoy the fullest Toleration in the Exercise of Religion, according to the Dictates of Conscience, unpunished and unrestrained by the Magistrate, unless under Colour of Religion any Man disturb the Peace, the Happiness, or Safety of Society, or of Individuals. And that it is the mutual Duty of all, to practice Christian Forbearance, Love and Charity towards Each other."

Mr. Madison, twenty-four, was the youngest member of the committee and, according to Thomas Jefferson, characterized by "extreme modesty." He had done desultory reading in the law: he was not a lawyer ("praise God!" a nonlawyer exclaims). He had read more theology: he was not a theologian ("praise God again!" murmurs a nontheologian). He was conscious, to use his own words, that he was "young and in the midst of distinguished and experienced members." He had thought about government and religious liberty. He redrafted the text.

Eliminated were the theological adjectives for the Creator. "Force" was subtly expanded to a more comprehensive noun, "compulsion." The "fullest Toleration" disappeared and the "full and free exercise of it [religion]" replaced the stricken term. Tolerance, out; free exercise, in—a decisive move. Moreover, free exercise was what "all men are equally entitled to." Mr. Mason's draft had said nothing about human equality. Equality carried, at least to some minds, the implication that any special privilege, any financial support for a particular church, was no longer acceptable. With peculiar daring, Mr. Madison added a further clause that explicitly struck the Church of England's establishment, untouched in Mr. Mason's draft: "No man or class of men ought, on account of religion to be invested with peculiar emoluments or privileges nor subjected to any penalties or disabilities unless under etc." (leaving unrevised the

Mason text with its qualifications as to injurious acts under color of religion and its injunction to Christian charity). "On account of religion," the prepositional structure of President Witherspoon's stricture in his Princeton lecture against persecution, echoed in JM's proposal.

Unexpectedly, Mr. Madison persuaded Mr. Mason that the new text said what Mr. Mason wanted to say. Surprisingly, the committee approved. Astonishingly, that bulwark of the established Church, Mr. Patrick Henry, introduced the new text to the convention. But when a delegate asked Mr. Henry if he intended to disestablish the Church of England, Mr. Henry disclaimed the intention. Mr. Madison was asked to redraft. The explicitly offending provision on privileges and penalties "on account of religion" (but not the statement on equality) was dropped. Slightly altered in the final round, the Madisonian text prevailed. The cardinal change from Mr. Mason's draft was that for "Toleration" Mr. Madison had substituted a phraseology recognizing in effect that freedom of conscience was "a *natural* and absolute right" (interpretation & emphasis JM's, as he later looked back on his accomplishment). For him, as for President Witherspoon, what was absolute and natural was beyond the civil power.

There were limitations operating to curb the full force of his insight. As he set such store on equality and on natural rights, any literally minded person would suppose that the declaration he drafted was meant to have a liberating impact on those who by law were not treated equally and were enslaved. Even if he did not intend to address their lot in general, he did intend—it could be supposed—to include them within the ambit of freedom of conscience. Nothing he did or said, however, drew this consequence; and no one suggested it.

Chattel slavery was by English law established. The Virginia statute controlling the conduct of slaves was to be subsequently written by a committee of three that included Mr. Jefferson; passage of the bill was to be managed by Mr. Madison. By its terms "the unlawful assembly" of slaves was criminal; the law became a perfect instrument for restricting the religious activity of the enslaved. "Steal away to Jesus," as the hymn puts it, is what the slaves had to do in stealth, by night, to pursue their own religious needs. Did the slaves not have human minds? Did they not stand in a relation to God that transcended human constraints upon their consciences? For Mr. Madison slaves were part of "the family," his couriers and his traveling companions and his property. He knew that they were human beings, who had human minds. Ultimately he worked for their gradual, compensated emancipation. In 1776 he put them from his sight.

As for the free exercise of religion by women, there were not the strict legal prohibitions operating on slaves. But women were severely handicapped in their educational opportunities, hence in their freedom to enlarge or liberate their minds, or to teach; no institution of higher education existed for their instruction. By law, they were restricted in their property rights if they were minors or married, and they were thus affected in their freedom to follow a religion or contribute to a church in disregard of their fathers or husbands. Barriers with these serious practical impacts on free exercise Mr. Madison left unremarked. Neither set of restrictions was absolute in its effects: slave religious practices had their own dynamism, women were not helpless in their individual spiritual development. The emancipation of conscience established by law was simply not as thorough as required by logic and the existing practical impairments of freedom.

Following the adoption of the Declaration of Rights, the new general assembly of Virginia repealed the specific acts of Parliament bearing on opinion in religion "or the exercising any mode of worship whatsoever." The English common law remained untouched. Blackstone had celebrated only the repeal of certain statutory proscriptions. Despite the Declaration, heresy—so Jefferson observed polemically—remained in theory an offense punishable by the burning of the heretic to death. Colonial Virginia statutes on religion stayed on the books. No atheist nor anyone denying the existence of the Trinity or the authority of Scripture could hold public office, receive a gift or legacy, or act as guardian of his own children, as executor of a will, or as an administrator of an estate. Mr. Jefferson as governor proposed to mop up this incongruous and unenforced residue of religious prejudice with a bill that, instead of establishing a church, proposed "establishing religious freedom." In 1779 the assembly agreed to make permanent the defunding of the Episcopalian clergy but rejected Mr. Jefferson's bill. In Mr. Jefferson's words, the people were willing to remain under "religious slavery." For him, as for Mr. Madison, slavery was the most powerful of negative metaphors.

In 1784, with the Revolution won and Mr. Jefferson in Paris, the battle in Virginia resumed. Mr. Henry, probably the most popular politician in Virginia, proposed a bill "Establishing a Provision for Teachers of the Christian Religion." The preamble began: "Whereas the general diffusion of Christian knowledge hath a natural tendency to correct the morals of men," and went on to explain that this diffusion was not possible without teachers. The bill proper equated "ministers" and "teachers of the Gospel." For the ministers' support a state property tax was to be levied.

The key term was "establishing." The establishment of religion was to return. The beauty of the scheme was that it would bring all Christian denominations aboard. Each taxpayer could choose the Christian church that would receive his tax. Quakers and Mennonites, who had no clergy, were to be exempted. Catholics were too few to matter. Across the board the Protestant clergy were to be helped. The Baptists, with their scruples about governmental support, were taken to be bribable. The main beneficiaries were to be the Episcopalians and the Presbyterians. "The *Episcopalians* have again shown their teeth and fangs," Mr. Jefferson wrote Mr. Madison from Paris. The bill demonstrated what JM had already called "the exquisite cunning of the old fox," no longer his ally. Mr. Henry proceeded to schedule the third and final reading of the bill for Christmas Eve, a kind of extraordinary present to the churches.

The same day he wrote Jefferson, JM drew up his notes in opposition. They have been set out at the start of this chapter. They speak for themselves. On December 24, 1784, he and other opponents persuaded the legislators to put off the bill. The notes ripened into a Memorial and Remonstrance, addressed in the summer of 1785—the bill still pending—to the assembly. To paraphrase or quote selectively is not to do JM justice. I single out these points, grouped topically in a way that JM did not choose to arrange them but that illustrates most graphically the nature and range of the considerations driving him.

Theological:

1. Religion is "the duty which we owe to our Creator."
2. The duty is to render the homage that each person determines in conscience "to be acceptable to him [the Creator]."
3. The right to determine this duty in conscience belongs to each person and is "unalienable" for two reasons: first, the exercise of the right must depend on evidence, and each person will determine what evidence is sufficient for conviction; and second, the duty, as it runs to the Creator, can never be relaxed by any human being.
4. The duty trumps—"is precedent, both in order of time and in degree of obligation"—the claims of "Civil Society," whether those claims are made by society at large or are made by a legislature. In religion the sole authority is "the Governour of the Universe," to whose government each person is subject. Religion is therefore "wholly exempt" from the "cognizance" of civil society or civil government. That "the Civil Magistrate is a competent

Judge of Religious Truth" is a falsehood. That the Civil Magistrate "may employ Religion as an engine of Civil policy" is wickedness.

5. If freedom of religion is abused, it is "an offense against God, not against man."

6. To rely on governmental support is "a contradiction to the Christian Religion itself for every page of it disavows a dependence on the powers of the world."

7. To use governmental coercion to support the Christian clergy is to discourage conversion and to surround Christianity "with a wall of defense" characterized by "an ignoble and unchristian timidity."

Civic:

1. Government must not act beyond the limited powers it has. This imperative, this "great Barrier," is what assures the right of liberty of conscience exempted from civil authority because it is under God's. A ruler can "overleap" the great Barrier but to do so is to become a tyrant and to submit to such a ruler is to become a slave.

2. If the government can "establish Christianity," it can establish a particular sect of Christianity. The opening step must be resisted lest worse follow.

3. To give exemption to some denominations and not to all offends the equality with which all men enter society.

4. To impose a burden on those who are Quakers and Mennonites (for they will be taxed though they have no denomination to support) offends equality.

5. Religion is not necessary for the support of the government; so (it may be inferred) its support is not a proper governmental objective.

6. Religious establishments make a government tyrannical.

7. Seeking governmental support for religion "will destroy harmony and forbearance among the denominations."

8. To enforce a law obnoxious to a great part of the citizenry will "tend to enervate the laws in general, and to slacken the bands of Society."

9. The law will drive citizens out of the commonwealth.

10. The law will keep immigrants out, acting as a "Beacon on our

Coast" warning off "the persecuted and oppressed of every Nation and Religion." In contrast, the former policy of offering them "an Asylum" was a policy that "promised a lustre to our country, and an accession to the number of its citizens."

Historical:

1. The fruits of ecclesiastical establishments, "more or less in all places," have been "pride and indolence in the Clergy, ignorance and servility in the laity, in both, superstition, bigotry and persecution."
2. "Torrents of blood have been spilt in the old world, by vain attempts of the secular arm, to extinguish Religious discord, by proscribing all differences in Religious opinion."

The Memorial and Remonstrance ended with a prayer to "the Supreme Lawgiver of the Universe." Like JM's final word to Bradford, the prayer should not be read as a polite bow to a distant deity; it is addressed to the God whose cause is that of conscience. Prophetically, the advocate of religious freedom announced its promise of universal approbation, of adding "lustre to our country."

Drafted by Mr. Madison and circulated anonymously, the Memorial and Remonstrance gained 1,552 signatures. The memorial, according to Mr. Madison, "met with the approbation of the Baptists, the Presbyterians, the Quakers, and the few Roman Catholics, universally; of the Methodists in part; and even of not a few of the Sect formerly established by law." Another anonymous petition, asserting the assessment to be against "the Spirit of the Gospel," obtained 4,899 signatories, no doubt chiefly Baptist. In all, 10,929 petitioners indicated their opposition. In a state in which legal qualifications for voters disqualified women, blacks, Indians, males under twenty-one, and males who were not landowners, the number of persons actually voting in a Virginia election did not exceed 40,000. Probably not every signer was a voter, but 10,929 signatures meant that the electorate was in arms. In the November 1785 session of the assembly, Mr. Henry's plan was "crushed."

The aftermath yielded Mr. Madison a second satisfaction. He carried Mr. Jefferson's bill for establishing religious freedom wiping out all the antique penalties and incapacities for religious opinion or religious teaching. The strongest statements were contained in the bill's preamble, "the enacting clauses" in Mr. Madison's terminology. "Almighty God hath created the mind free," was the preamble's foundational declaration. From it there followed, implicitly, that the mind was not to be influenced "by temporal punishments, burdens or incapacities" or to be bribed "by worldly honors or emoluments." To compel support of a religion from a disbeliever was "sinful and tyrannical." To compel support from a believer was to deprive a believer of "the comfortable liberty" of choosing his own pastor. In either case governmental coercion was "a departure from the plan of the holy author of our religion, who being lord both of body and mind, yet chose not to propagate it by coercions on either." An attempt to identify the "lord" as Jesus Christ was defeated in committee. At the same time the success of the bill was assured by its being "espoused by some members who were particularly distinguished by their reputed piety and Christian zeal." With that fine sensitivity to language that characterized Mr. Jefferson and Mr. Madison, the tables were turned. Conscience, not church, became by law established. Freedom to believe and to profess was classified as a natural right. With unusual optimism Mr. Madison wrote Mr. Jefferson that the enacting clauses "have in this Country extinguished for ever the ambitious hope of making laws for the human mind."

Concede what Mr. Madison's theology assumes: there is a God living and distinct from every human creature; this God is the Creator and the Lawgiver and the Governor of the world; he is a "he"; he takes an interest in, and satisfaction from, the homage humans render him and he will condignly punish humans who neglect to observe the commands that he communicates through conscience. Then on what basis can a mere human or mere association of humans intrude their regulations to prevent an individual from obeying God? As JM stated half a century later, the right is "*natural* and absolute." The "absolute," unitalicized, crowns the emphasized "natural."

For every upholder of the supremacy of the state JM's defense of free exercise is a scandal, a stumbling-block. The "great Barrier" stands against the sovereignty of the state. Each individual's religion "wholly exempt" from social control? No qualifications whatever on the right and duty to pay homage to God as one sees fit? Surely, in the heat of battle, JM exaggerates! No, his theological premises compel these radical conclusions.

REPRESENTATIVE MADISON

Two years after the establishment of religious freedom in Virginia, Mr. Madison in Philadelphia became the chief architect of a constitution that prohibited religious tests for public office but that was without a provision for religious liberty. Why? Mr. Madison's explanation to Mr. Jefferson in Paris made three points. First, to restrain the federal government in this regard was to imply that it had a power in this regard, which he denied. Second, to seek was to be disappointed. Mr. Madison was "sure that the rights of Conscience in particular, if submitted to public definition, would be narrowed much more than they are likely ever to be by an assumed power. One of the objections in New England was that the Constitution by prohibiting religious tests opened a door for Jews, Turks & infidels." New England, he implied, would balk at more freedom. The third reason was Mr. Madison's own disillusionment. "Repeated violations of these parchment barriers have been committed by overbearing majorities in every State." How quickly his confidence in enacting clauses had waned!

Absence of a written guarantee of conscience was a stick with which the anti-Federalists struck the Constitution and sought to prevent its ratification. In Virginia Mr. Henry led the attack and pointed to the absence. Mr. Madison could not help reminding him of Mr. Henry's own disregard—so Mr. Madison implied—of Virginia's Declaration of Rights in seeking in 1785 to enact the general assessment for the clergy. JM's thrust was not pure rhetoric. He knew as well as Mr. Henry that he had had to amend the Declaration of Rights to eliminate disestablishment, yet in the Memorial and Remonstrance he had argued that compulsion to support the clergy violated the rights of conscience. His notes in preparation for the great debate over Mr. Henry's bill had twice referred to the "Decl. Rig" as though it were dispositive, as if the Virginia declaration of 1776 had itself done the job and equality of religious exercise forbade establishment. He had stuck to his own reading of the declaration, however contrary he knew it was to the views of Mr. Henry, Mr. Mason, and the majority of the legislators who had enacted it. Now, debating the Constitution, Mr. Madison appeared to confess a disillusionment with paper barriers. He asked Mr. Henry, "Is a bill of rights a security for religion?" He answered his own question. In America, he said, religious freedom "arises from that multiplicity of sects, which pervades America, and which is the best and only security for liberty in any society."

Already argued by JM in number 10 of *The Federalist* was the proposition that the security against oppression by any single political faction is a multiplicity of interests each contending with the others. His first illustration of the proposition was that "zeal for different opinions concerning religion" produced a balance. In the argument and illustration he was following Mr. David Hume, eliminating, however, Mr. Hume's sneer at religious "interests," and he was thinking of Virginia where in the fight over the general assessment Baptists and Presbyterians had defeated Episcopalians. The argument was enlarged in *Federalist* no. 51, where Mr. Madison distinguished the government of men from the government of angels (a nice theological contrast) and continued, saying "the security for civil rights must be the same as for religious rights. It consists in the one case in the multiplicity of interests, and in the other, in the multiplicity of sects." Speaking now to Mr. Henry, Mr. Madison paralleled his argument in *The Federalist*: the numbers have it; only by dividing the numbers can your freedom survive. The reply also echoed Mr. Madison's early letter to Mr. Bradford: disharmony is better than harmony, intellectually; uniformity of religious opinion is slavery. Still, the starkness is startling. The best security, maybe. But the *only* security? What had Mr. Madison and Mr. Jefferson been struggling for when they set up parchment barriers in Virginia?

On further reflection—on the force of his opponents' position, on his own prospects for election to federal office—JM changed his tune, came to his senses, saw that thought articulated on paper in lapidary command has a force of its own. In the same letter he wrote to Mr. Jefferson in Paris saying why there was no bill of rights, he gave two reasons why there should be one: "1. The political truths declared in that solemn manner acquire by degrees the character of fundamental maxims of free Government, and as they become incorporated with the national sentiment, counteract the impulses of interest and passion. 2. Altho' it be generally true as above stated that the danger of oppression lies in the interested majorities of the people rather than in usurped acts of the Government, yet there may be occasions on which the evil may spring from the latter sources; and on such, a bill of rights will be a good ground for an appeal to the sense of the community." With Mr. Jefferson's encouragement Mr. Madison came to favor a federal bill of rights.

In November 1788 Mr. Madison was put up in the Virginia assembly for election to the United States Senate. He was not chosen. As JM has it, "The attempt was defeated by Mr. Henry who is omnipotent in the present legislature. . . . He has taken equal pains in forming the Counties into districts for the election of Reps. to associate with Orange such as are most devoted to his politics and most likely to be swayed by the prejudices excited agst. me." JM doubted he could even be elected to Congress when his home county, Orange, was combined with pro-Henry counties in this fashion. Nonetheless, he ran to become a representative.

At a critical juncture of his campaign he wrote the Reverend George Eve, the pastor of Blue Run Church where the great protest meeting of Baptists had been held before the Revolution. The Baptists were now even more numerous and active. Their leader, the Reverend John Leland, based in Orange County, had baptized 300 persons in 1788 alone. Even if not all 300 were voters, in an election in which about 2,200 persons voted, the Baptists had to be a major force. Mr. Madison assured Pastor Eve that he was now committed to amendments to achieve "the most satisfactory provisions for all essential rights, particularly the rights of Conscience in the fullest latitude."

A campaign advisor, Mr. George Nicholas, told the candidate he must do more—appeal to the Reverend Reuben Ford, the Baptist minister at Goochland Church, and get the Reverend Leland to "exert himself." JM, it may be inferred from the results, made the contacts. A preelection meeting was held at Blue Run Church. The participants were reminded of Mr. Madison's "many important Services" to the Baptists. JM inserted a notice of his support of a "specific provision" on "the Rights of Conscience" in the Fredericksburg, Virginia *Herald*. On February 2, 1789, Mr. James Madison was elected over Mr. James Monroe by a margin of 336 votes. The Reverend John Leland wrote at once to congratulate him and to remind him of the Baptists' interest in religious liberty. With the aid of these dedicated evangelicals, by the active intervention of the preachers in politics, Mr. Madison became the spokesman for religious freedom in the Congress that was to begin the government of the United States.

JM was more than that—recognized by his keen Massachusetts adversary, Mr. Fisher Ames, to be by common consent the "first man" of the House and so a leader in all the institutional arrangements needed to be made. He was heavily relied on by President Washington for advice and penmanship. Not until he became president himself would he, his editors note, "possess so much power and influence." In the capacity of ghostwriter he drafted Washington's first address to Congress, April 30, 1789, and took the opportunity to insert a quiet reminder that Congress had constitutional power under Article V to propose amendment of the Constitution and could judge it expedient to do so. As chairman of the House committee to reply to the presidential address on May 5, 1789, he drafted the response, picking up the president's words and underlining them: "The question arising out of the fifth article of the Constitution, will receive all the attention demanded by its importance; and will we trust, be decided, under the influence of all the considerations to which you allude." JM made sure that the House would pay attention to altering the Constitution.

Over two hundred amendments had been proposed by the ratifying states. From the mass, JM culled nineteen, which in his original plan would not have been attached separately but incorporated into the existing Constitution. He added one amendment of his own devising, to be inserted among the existing restrictions on the states in Article I, section 10. It read: "No State shall violate the equal rights of conscience, or the freedom of the press, or the trial by jury in criminal cases." Not only the federal government but the individual states were to be bound to religious freedom, phrased precisely in terms of the equality of consciences.

Mr. Madison brought the plan to the floor on June 8, 1789. For the occasion he had again prepared notes, among them:

> *Contents of Bill of Rhts . . .*
> 3. *natural rights*, retained—as Speech, Con. . . .
>   Object of Bill of Rhts . . .
>   ought to point to greatest danger which
>   in Rep: is Prerogative of majority . . .
>   Objectns. vs. Bill of Rhts. . . .
> 2. In fedl Govt. all not given retained . . .
> 5. Not effectl. vs. sts also—but Ex: also . . .
>   Time sanctify—incorporate public Sentiment
>   Bill of Rhts ergo. proper . . .

Observe the close connection of the two rights asserted to be "natural": speech and conscience, the emphasis on "natural" stressing its talismanic importance. Mr. Madison's presentation moved a reluctant House. His plan was referred to a select committee, one member from each state, JM for Virginia. His bill proposing amendments was reported back on July 28. It was debated in August.

To assure religious liberty at the national level JM proposed for insertion in Article 1, section 9, an amendment to fit between clauses 3 and 4, that is, to appear in the limitations on the powers of Congress. The amendment would have followed the words, "No Bill of Attainder or ex post facto law shall be passed." The proposed text read: "The civil rights of none shall be abridged on account of religious belief or worship, nor shall any national religion be established, nor shall the full and equal rights of conscience be in any manner, or under any pretext infringed."

In several respects the draft differed from JM's maiden effort in Virginia. Religion was not defined. The "mutual duty" to practice Christian charity went unmentioned. The qualification limiting liberty when it disturbed peace, happiness, or safety under color of religion, was dropped. Most notably, "free exercise" was not employed. The ban on infringing the rights of conscience "in any manner or under any pretext" made conscience the centerpiece. The equality of the rights of conscience was emphasized, as in Virginia. A national established religion was banned.

JM put forward as an amendment immediately after that on religion the following: "The people shall not be deprived or abridged of their right to speak, to write, or to publish their sentiments; and the freedom of the press, as one of the great bulwarks of liberty, shall be inviolable." The natural right to speech followed the natural right of religious freedom but was distinct from it. The text also made a nice distinction between a natural right absolute in itself and the liberty of press that was auxiliary and essential.

The text on religion was thinned in committee, but one Madisonian point was added. The downsized draft emerged to read: "No religion shall be established by law, nor shall the equal rights of conscience be infringed." Ban of an establishment, however, drew criticism. Suppose, said Mr. Huntington of Rhode Island, that a minister brought suit in federal court for his salary, the amendment might lead to denial of his suit, for "a support of ministers might be construed [as] a religious establishment." The critics were afraid that the amendment applied to the states. JM suggested the difficulty be met by restoring "national" to modify religion. He withdrew the suggestion when Mr. Gerry of Massachusetts pointed out that "national" was objectionable because it implied a "consolidated," rather than a "federal," government. "Congress" was introduced as a term that did not have the objectionable implication. Pointedly, the prohibition was designed to operate only against the federal legislature. Ultimately, on August 20, the amendment passed the House in a form proposed by Mr. Ames: "Congress shall make no law establishing religion, or to prevent the free exercise thereof, or to infringe the rights of conscience."

The Bill of Rights went to the Senate where the amendment JM thought "the most valuable"—his own, binding the states not to violate the rights of conscience—was killed. The Senate also meddled with the text affecting the national government and religion. The Senate version declared: "Congress shall make no law establishing articles of faith or a mode of worship or prohibiting the free exercise of religion." The precise reason for the change is unreported. Plainly a twist was given to the prohibition against establishment: the Senate draft forbade not financial support but theological fiats by Congress.

Confronted by the Senate's action, the House refused to recede and asked for a conference. Three senators and three representatives met, JM among them. From the conference emerged the final text which Congress passed and the states ratified: "Congress shall make no law respecting an establishment of religion, or prohibiting the free exercise thereof." In two prepositional phrases (not clauses) the job was done. The first phrase assumed that establishments of religion existed as they did in fact exist in several of the states; the amendment restrained the power of Congress to affect them. The second phrase was absolute in its denial of federal legislative power to inhibit religious exercise. Succinct, the amendment referred to religion twice but used the term only once: no room to argue that the term changed its meaning in the second reference. Pleonastically the practice that could not be prohibited was denominated "free."

JM would not have been troubled by this duplication for emphasis nor bothered by "free exercise" encompassing a prohibition of any establishment. As he was to write later, expounding the power conferred by the Constitution to regulate trade, "Pleonasms, tautologies + the promiscuous use of terms + phrases differing in their shades of meaning, (always to be expounded with reference to the context and under the general controul of the general character + manifest scope of the Instrument in which they are found) are to be ascribed sometimes to the purpose of greater caution; sometimes to the imperfections of language; + sometimes to the imperfection of man himself."

Imperfect, cautious, exact—peculiarly the triumph was Mr. Madison's. At twenty-two he had seen what government and religion required—seen it in the transparent clarity with which a brilliant mathematician perceives a new relationship of numbers. For over fifteen years he had worked to have his idea incorporated into fundamental law—worked not singlemindedly, not as though it was the purpose of his life, but as for an ideal he knew to be sound, of importance, and plausibly attainable. At times he had hesitated, disillusioned or doubtful. The ironies of politics had put him in the position of skeptic of any written security for freedom. Another turn of politics had made his election depend on a religious denomination and its ministers entering the political battle. Always he had counted votes. He was ready to compromise to gain his end. He was not wedded to words. He was conscious that words alone would not work, although it was by words, after all, that the doctrines of religious establishment and religious persecution had been forged. By words they might be exorcised. Patient, flexible, persevering, he prevailed. He dared to believe that time would sanctify and public sentiment would incorporate the ideal put in words.

JM had triumphed. Or had he? He had lost the restriction on state religious establishments. That ideal would have to wait a century and a half for its proclamation. He had lost any reference to equality, to his mind a significant reinforcement of religious liberty. He had lost—and here was a crux—his clear ban on a national religious establishment and had had to accept language ambiguous at best and arguably merely meaning that the federal legislature should not touch, that is, disturb or revise, the existing establishments from New Hampshire to South Carolina. What survived the Senate was the ban on legislation prohibiting, that is, denying or even restricting, free exercise.

The great ambiguity of the First Amendment opens wide. What free exercise meant to Mr. Madison it had not meant to Mr. Mason, Mr. Henry, and the assembly that adopted the Declaration of Rights, and what free exercise meant to Mr. Madison was not what it meant to the First Congress that petitioned the president to set a day of thanksgiving to God; created chaplaincies; and made grants of public property for the support of religion. It is plausibly argued that for many members of the First Congress the restrictions of the First Amendment were jurisdictional: the federal government was barred from interfering with religion because religion was within the power of the several states. In the absence of a national consensus on the proper relation of government to religion, the nation was taken out of the question; the states were left to make their own choices. JM, as his writings before and after 1791 demonstrate, had a different vision, that was to be vindicated by history.

Free exercise to Mr. Madison meant no government interference with the obligation of conscience. But he had offered as a separate amendment a proposal to exempt conscientious objectors from bearing arms. The amendment had been defeated. Congress as a whole did not share JM's view of the unlimited rights of a conscience exempted from civil authority. The gap between his views and the majority yawned. Radical believer, practical politician, JM took what he could get. As the Bill of Rights in its entirety applied to neither women nor slaves, the same practical and legal limits on their freedom of religion remained as in Virginia. JM did not denounce the limitations.

It was enough. It was enough in JM's view of what free exercise implied for the future. Free exercise in itself was incompatible with establishment. So he had thought in 1776 in Williamsburg; so he had argued in 1785 in the Memorial and Remonstrance; so he had answered Patrick Henry in 1788; so he observed nearly a half century later, responding to a minister who asked his opinion "on the relation of Xnity to Civil Govt." "The rights of Conscience," he then wrote, were "not included in the surrender implied by the social State" and were "more or less invaded by all religious Establishments." It was his consistent, coherent, bold position. If Mr. Madison had been a lawyer, it would be questioned as a lawyer's too close reading of language. Cognizant of legal argumentation, JM maintained his view on a stronger basis than legal dialectics. That basis was his religious conviction from the beginning that free exercise of religion excluded any governmental support of religion.

What that exclusion meant for him is spelled out in memoranda he wrote sometime after the end of his service as president, memoranda that he was too prudent to publish and too conscientious to destroy. The time was probably 1823 when he wrote Edward Livingston apropos Livingston's draft of laws for Louisiana, took up several of the topics treated in the memoranda, and spoke of the importance of "every new & successful example . . . of a perfect separation between ecclesiastical and civil matters." Published posthumously, the memoranda memorialize his thought.

Under the heading "Monopolies Perpetuities Corporations Ecclesiastical Endowments," JM turns from a consideration of necessary limits on the corporate powers of towns to "the danger of silent accumulations and encroachments by Ecclesiastical Bodies." His mind travels from the politico-economic concept of monopoly to the undesirability of a single dominant church. Implicitly he rejects the concept of church unity as Europe had known it in favor of an American concept of competition as healthier. The rejection carries with it neither a denial of the objectivity of truth nor skepticism about Christianity. The rejection of monopoly does imply that no church holds all of Christian truth. Therefore not only does he deplore an established church but any church with monopolistic possibilities.

In America, in Mr. Madison's view, "4 great religious Sects" coexisted; probably Methodists, Baptists, Episcopalians, Congregationalists were meant. But suppose in the competition, one religion prevailed. What, then, would happen to a freedom that depended on religious rivalry? With that question unarticulated in the background, JM writes of the danger of ecclesiastical institutions acquiring property because they were perpetual. In the United States the danger was doubled. The churches typically received land in new and growing cities. The land then experienced "exorbitant advances." In time the churches would have "more than is useful, and in time more than is safe." Implicitly this chain of reflection suggests the desirability of the English statutes against accumulations by ecclesiastical bodies, the invidiously named mortmain laws against "the dead hand" of a churchly corporation. JM does not go so far but he holds that no church should be incorporated; the same result followed— churchly ownership could not exceed the lives of human beings. The commonwealth of Virginia put this Madisonian view into practice from 1795 to 1845 to the evident disadvantage of churches in distinction to all other charities. The churches were only denied a privilege but as the privilege was the common one of all other charities, the denial was arguably discrimination against the free exercise of religion. JM has no qualms; his distrust of a monopolizing church runs deep.

Mr. Madison begins this meditation on monopolies with one of his recurrent hopes, that "the most enlightened States of the old world may be instructed" by American example. In Virginia, he continues, "religious liberty is placed on its true foundation and is defined in its full latitude." The "general principle" is "contained in her declaration of rights" and is "unfolded and defined" in the Act for Establishing Religious Liberty. Here "the separation between the authority of human laws, and the natural rights of Man excepted from the grant on which all political authority is founded, is traced as distinctly as words can admit." The general principle set out is "the great barrier ag[ain]st usurpations on the rights of conscience." The great barrier, here uncapitalized, is what the Memorial and Remonstrance had insisted upon. Natural rights are excepted from political authority.

Mr. Madison goes on to replay the theme of his "most valuable amendment," which Congress had rejected. He exhorts the states that retain in their own constitutions "any aberration from the sacred principle" to "revise and purify" their systems. Examples of ecclesiastical encroachments are then provided: a congressional bill in 1811 to incorporate the Episcopal church in Alexandria, which President Madison vetoed; a bill also in 1811 to reserve land in the Mississippi territory for a Baptist church, which he also vetoed; a bill in Kentucky "to exempt Houses of Worship from taxes"; and "the most notable," Mr. Henry's attempt in 1785 to establish a tax "for the support of all Xn sects," which Mr. Madison defeated. The sweep of what JM disapproves is striking. Separateness for him means no public support for a church; no incorporation; no tax exemption.

The existence of chaplains for Congress, selected by Congress and paid for by public funds, also draws his retrospective criticism. He had been the first man of the First Congress that had instituted them but the chaplains are "a palpable violation of equal rights, as well as of Constitutional principles." The fruits of this particular religious establishment are daily devotions "already degenerating into a scanty attendance, and a tiresome formality." In the same way the chaplaincies for the army and navy offend constitutional principle. The chaplaincies, if they cannot be ended, should not be used as precedent for further departure from principle.

Finally, Mr. Madison turns his mind to a practice in which he himself engaged as president: the issuance of "religious proclamations by the Executive recommending thanksgivings & fasts." These proclamations are open to two objections, first that, in general, a government should not offer mere advice, and second, that the government has no capacity to offer religious counsel; and there is a third, more powerful objection, that such proclamations "seem to imply and certainly nourish the erroneous idea of a *national* religion." The danger of imitating biblical Israel in being a theocracy is a danger for countries that "have embraced Xnity." Such proclamations may, moreover, be used for party purposes, a danger illustrated by Mr. Alexander Hamilton's effort to insert partisanship into a proclamation by President Washington. JM adds as to one of his own presidential proclamations that he responded to a request from Congress and used "a form & language" that were "meant to deaden as much as possible any claim of political right to enjoin religious observances."

A highly respected, highly informed biographer of Mr. Madison, looking at his whole life, states that "oddly" his political feelings as a young man had been most aroused by the persecution of the Baptists in Virginia. The same biographer concludes that JM's life was "given up to a political religion." These evaluations fit twentieth-century intellectual life, dominated as it is by secular assumptions. JM becomes an early secularist, who gave a ceremonial nod to the maker of the universe before getting on with the serious work of building a nation.

The memoranda on monopolies may be used to reinforce this assessment. Every secular civil libertarian must thrill to their warnings against ecclesiastical encroachments. But to take suspicion of the clergy for hostility to religion is a mistake. It is a mistake fostered by our age's habit of hazy reference to "the Enlightenment," a habit formed in the attempt to create a secular patrimony and pantheon. JM is swept into the pantheon.

"The Enlightenment," like its now discredited opposite, "the Dark Ages," is at best a way of dating a period of history. It does not function well as an analytic guide. A catchword and catchall, the term embraces every extoller of reason from Mr. Locke to M. Voltaire. The intellectual leaders of the age all celebrated reason—a reason that encompassed such a spectrum of religious convictions that the verbal convergence is not helpful in discerning the lines of division.

Where JM stood on the spectrum may be seen by comparing his stance with that of Mr. Hume, whom he sometimes cited, and M. Voltaire, whom he ignored. For Mr. Hume, religion embodied " a principle which disclaims all control by human law, reason and authority." If "reason" is removed from this sentence, it could be assimilated to JM's thought at its most radical. But removal makes all the difference. For Mr. Hume the corollary of a reasonless religion would not bring a freedom to be welcomed. The corollary is consequences too dreadful to be endured. The only solution in Mr. Hume's "perfect commonwealth" is for government to maintain strict control of the church. Not so for JM. As for M. Voltaire, JM's early desire to be enrolled "in the Annals of Heaven" stands in stark contrast to the views of a man who crusaded to "wipe out" Christianity. The distance is unbridgeable.

JM's own perspective may be gauged from his advice to Thomas Jefferson when the latter asked him in 1824 to supply "a Theological Catalogue" to stock the library of the University of Virginia. Mr. Madison did not have a theology such as a professional theologian might develop. He claimed that development of the subject was "beyond my depth" and that he had a distaste for entering theological controversies. He had scarcely ceased his acquaintance with what he had written Bradford was "the most sublime of all the Sciences." He has been described as "probably America's most theologically knowledgeable President." To whom else was Mr. Jefferson to turn except his friend of fifty years when Mr. Jefferson thought of an advisor for his university on books on theology? And Mr. Madison, stressing the students' need for "pretty full information," proceeded to reply with thoughtful deliberation until his friend pressed him for a quicker answer. His list for the university included a substantial number of the Fathers of the Church; the lights of the Dominican and Franciscan orders, Thomas Aquinas and Duns Scotus; Catholic and Protestant authors of the Reformation such as Erasmus, Calvin, Socinius; later controversialists, among them the Jesuit Robert Bellarmine and the Protestant champion William Chillingworth and the Jansenist Catholic Blaise Pascal; and "the celebrated work" of Samuel Clark, a theologian warmly recommended at Princeton by the Reverend Witherspoon and still reverently remembered by Mr. Madison. The choices were ponderous but discriminating. Not a single book of infidelity or skepticism, no Voltaire or Hume or Paine was listed, no works loose in their principles or "Enemies to religion." No deist appeared. The writers are all Christians; the most radical is Socinius, whose Christianity was a good deal lower than the Fathers but who reasoned entirely from the Christian Scriptures. Only an ecumenically minded Christian, knowledgeable in Christian sources, would have supplied such a list. Only a pious Christian would have eliminated all books hostile to Christianity. Mr. Madison himself left to the university his own possession: *The Necessary Duty of Family Prayer, with Prayers for Their Use.*

Pious education, maturation under a Presbyterian at Princeton, immersion in the study of Scripture—all leading to the conviction of "essential Truths" and the desirability of keeping "the Ministry obliquely in View" and the resolution to go beyond "building ideal monuments of Reason and Bliss": these characteristics of JM have already been remarked. That he continued to hold these beliefs in the period of his intense activity on behalf of religious freedom—that is, from 1774 to 1789—is evidenced by his writings addressed to his countrymen.

JM's central public testimony to his religious beliefs is the Memorial and Remonstrance. Here the only question, as his notes have it, is "are Relig. Estabts. necessy for Religion?" not "Is Rel. necessy?" The answer comes from "the Christian Religion itself." That religion is not "invented by human policy." That religion is "this precious gift." That religion is, in the most positive and pervasive metaphor of the age, "a light." The metaphor, used by a Christian, echoes the first chapter of the Gospel according to John: Christ is "the true light which lights everyone entering the world." Hence, JM speaks interchangeably of "the light of Christianity," "the light of revelation." This religion is to prevail not by force, which is repudiated by "every page" of the religion, and not by "unchristian timidity," but by evidence and example. By these means "Truth" will make its "victorious progress" to be "imparted to the whole race of mankind."

Public argument is not the same as personal conviction. But public argument that employs religious belief for its own ends, that makes "an Engine" of religion, precisely parallels the exploitation of religion by government that JM denounced in the memorial as wickedness. If he himself had made religion instrumental in this fashion it would make him the hypocrite no one believes he is. In the memorial JM addresses Christians as a fellow Christian; he speaks as a believer in Christianity's special light; his argument looks to the evangelization of the world.

The convictions he expressed as a young man are muted but perceptible in the reflections of the ex-president. In refutation of all predictions of doom, "the total separation of the Church from the State" in Virginia is marked by "an increase of religious instruction." At the same time the government of the state has remained stable without benefit of "an anointed hierarchy." In fact, "the number, the industry and the morality of the Priesthood, & the devotion of the people have been manifestly increased." In these terms JM in 1819 assessed the success of the experiment he had launched. The experiment is succeeding by his criteria because both state and religion are flourishing.

In the same vein is the unpublished memorandum of 1823 on monopolies. JM's exhortation to the states with establishments tells them that they should amend their constitutions where they err "by giving to Caesar what belongs to God, or joining together what God has put asunder." JM combines the explicit words of Jesus on rendering to Caesar what is Caesar's with a biblical-sounding phrase in which the separation of church and state is suggested to be of divine origin, their sundering being the mirror opposite of marriage where God joins two beings together. A human being's relationship with God is "excepted from the grant on which all political authority is founded." This radical separation is, JM declares, a "just and a . . . truly Xn principle." It is Mr. Madison's principle as a Xn.

Near the end of his life, in his answer to the minister asking about "the relation of Xnty to Civil Govt," he personally confessed his beliefs. (How modestly he held them! Even in the youthful letter to Mr. Bradford where zeal simmered to the surface he thought of "suppressing" his advice.) First, as to God: "There appears to be in the nature of man what insures his belief in an invisible cause of his present existence, and anticipation of his future existence." Second, as to "the Xn religion itself," it is "the best & purest religion." He could have made no stronger affirmation. What is natural is what is inalienable for JM. Hence religion must be safeguarded; and the best religion is a Christianity ecumenically left undefined. The Mr. Madison of 1832 is the Mr. Madison of 1774, 1776, 1785, 1819, and 1823.

To suppose that JM had only a political religion because he did not publicly display his piety is to miss the genius of the man: his modesty. He followed Jesus as a true follower will. From the beginning when, in his own words, he "spared no exertion" to save the Baptist preachers from imprisonment and to obtain their release, he had acted from "a mere duty prescribed by conscience." The mere duty carried JM all his way.

The duty was mere; the prescribing authority was supreme. It was supreme because it was not just an inner tickle, a subjective unease: it was for JM the actual voice of another, a communication, a command. The ultimate fact—the ultimate paradox if one likes—is that for the Father of Free Exercise the rightness of the doctrine is rooted in his own faith, a faith conventional in its day but for all that palpably alive, a faith stupendous in modern eyes, the faith that God in us speaks to us.

The radicalness of JM—should we say the madness of Madison?—was to suppose that each individual has a zone in which he or she responds to the voice of God, a zone beyond political authority. How could Mr. Madison, practical politician, constitutional architect, wise statesman, have imagined that that would work? It was not merely that A's conscience might lead him to injure B, it was that A's conscience might lead him to scandalize B (if Mr. Madison knew any history at all, he knew that Quakers had on occasion in the past walked naked into church); it was that A's conscience might lead to refusal to cooperate in the common defense of the community (Mr. Madison was well aware of his conscientious-objector constituents). JM was willing to run these risks without discussing them, confident, I suggest, that the difficult cases would be rare and de minimis—confident, after all, that the voice of God would not often be heard in distorted or eccentric ways. A modern reading of free exercise notes that the First Amendment forms part of a constitution; it cannot be isolated from the structure to which it is attached; its interpretation, like the interpretation of every right, requires a "balancing." JM could scarcely have disagreed with the structural considerations; but he does set out "the great Barrier" as an absolute, an absolute that, like a mathematician, he was willing to see asymptotically approached.

In the ultimate and absolute relation of each individual to God lies the limitation on civil society and civil government on which JM insists. Without that relation, why should the individual not be absorbed by the community, why should a society be constrained to respect conscience? With that relation to a Creator, Governor, Judge in existence for each individual, with that personal responsibility to a personal God, a government of human beings must be a government of limited powers. The theology underwrites the political theory on the competencies of government. The "great Barrier which defends the rights of the people"—that barrier central to JM's theory of government—depends upon the people having other business than the ordering of the temporal society, its goods and goals. By their consciences the people relate to God. The faith that there is a governing God is fundamental.

In this union of ideas JM was a representative in Mr. Emerson's sense of the term: one of those great "leaders and law-givers" who "teach us the qualities of primary nature—admit us to the constitution of things. . . . What they know, they know for us." JM knew for us. JM is also representative of his time. He embodied ideas current in his culture. Seizing those that were common coin, making them his own, combining them, energizing them, applying them, he participated in the creation of a government incapacitated from establishing a religion, from testing religious convictions for public office, from limiting the free exercise of religion. Of course he did not succeed single-handed. He had, on occasion, a mentor, Mr. Jefferson. He had allies in Virginia and in Congress. He had constituencies, of which the most decisive was the Baptists of Orange County. He worked in committees, in conferences, in legislatures. All his great contributions were anonymous—the Virginia Declaration of Rights, the Act Establishing Religious Freedom, the Constitution of the United States, *The Federalist*, the Bill of Rights. Mr. Madison's anonymity is the guaranty of his representative character.

The anonymous collective achievement obscures the great ambiguity. Judge Learned Hand once observed that constitutional restraints on government are "precipitates" of battles already won. From one perspective, his observation is true as to "Free Exercise." In 1791, even a state like Massachusetts with a church established by law claimed in its constitution to respect the rights of conscience. "Free Exercise," understood narrowly to permit establishments, was inoffensive to all. Moreover, as the federal government was believed to have no power to regulate religion, an amendment proscribing its use of such a power was harmless. The amendment was without any costs. It was the proclamation of a principle that impacted neither a church nor an individual.

In JM's perspective, the case was otherwise. Free exercise was not a commonplace enshrined. Its rightness had been reached by an insight. Its rightness had been confirmed by the disasters attending the repression of religion; and JM did not disdain experience as the way the rightness of what he had proposed should be examined. To the Reverend Frederick Adams, JM wrote in 1832, America was an experiment in which free exercise was put "finally to a decisive test." Rather than embodying a platitude, the phrase foreshadowed a program, a program pointing toward a remarkable burgeoning of religions in America. It marked a beginning, not an end, to the question what qualifications could limit a liberty so absolutely asserted, to the question how a government of limited powers could govern individual consciences first responsible to God.

It constituted a challenge and an appeal to overbearing majorities whose own free exercise of religion might lead to commitments excluding the conduct, if not the opinion, of those who had formed their consciences otherwise.

JM's "admitted Umpire" for his experiment was experience. The contradiction, or the paradox, of truth as one, plurally perceived, had yet to be resolved or completely accepted. With JM's work, the new order of the centuries began; America was a nonpareil; its political system "a new Creation"; Columbia became a gem; or the germ, the possibility, was implanted.

THE FOREMOST OF OUR
POLITICAL INSTITUTIONS

ALEXIS DE TOCQUEVILLE
1830

*"Religion—which with the Americans never mixes directly
in the government of the society—must be considered
as the foremost of their political institutions."*

Excerpts from the unpublished account of her observations in America in 1835 by Angélique de Tocqueville, the keen-eyed younger sister of the famous Alexis (the translation is mine):

On my arrival in America it was the religious aspect of the country that first struck me. One of my first encounters was with Mr. Adams, the former president, who told me: "There are two facts that have had a great influence on our character: In the North, the religious and political doctrines of the first founders of New England; in the South slavery." I could not suppress the suspicion that this way of expressing the situation— with such clear partiality to his own region—concealed within the analysis a prophecy of conflict within a national character so strangely divided. But I restrained myself from expressing this thought, for I was a guest in the country. I chose while in Boston to explore the religion dominant there. For that purpose, I could have had no better guide than Mr. Channing, the most famous preacher and the most remarkable author today in America (in a serious genre). He assured me that religion in America was being perfected with the advance of reason. I expressed some doubt as to whether the process of purifying Christianity—a process in which Mr. Channing had played a leading part—might not lead to eliminating its substance as well as its corruptions. But Mr. Channing showed no uneasiness on that account. The intellectual triumph of Unitarianism, of which he is a priest, was assured, he said; it was secure in Harvard College and in the leading churches of Boston. Mr. Dwight, another very zealous Protestant pastor, informed me that all education in America was "moral and religious. There would be a general outcry, a kind of popular uprising against anyone who wanted to introduce a contrary system, and everyone would say that it would be better to have no instruction than one given in a different manner. The Bible is where all our children learn to read."

This point as to the religious education of the young was one that had been made as well to my brother Alexis, but he had chosen not to em-

phasize it in his celebrated book, even though the same observation had
been made to him, if possible more emphatically, by Mr. Spencer, the distinguished New York legislator. According to the latter, the clergy in the
state of New York are in charge of public education; he knew of only
two exceptions; it appeared to him to be a state of affairs "conformable
to nature."

This disinterest of my brother, at least a disinterest in publishing a fact
of such importance to the proper understanding of the role of religion
in the United States, led me to investigate what other palpable phenomena he might have chosen to overlook or be silent about. I began with
the constitution of Massachusetts, fortified by the information, tactfully
provided by my hosts, that this document was one of the first of the constitutions of the new states and a prototype for several.

To my astonishment I found that the constitution of this new commonwealth asserted in unequivocal terms the obligation of all men in the
society to engage publicly in the worship of God; and that this dogmatic
affirmation had a prominent position in the part of the constitution denominated Declaration of the Rights of the Inhabitants. It was indeed
an obligation—not a right—that was affirmed and was made all the more
vigorously insistent by the consistent capitalization of all the letters of
the deity, viz., GOD. This obligation was linked in a way that both the
older and younger Adams must have found congruent with the religious
and political doctrines of their ancestors. The older Adams, I was told
on good authority, had been approached at the revolutionary Congress
by Mr. Backus, a minister of the Massachusetts Baptists, who objected
to the system then prevailing in the province, by which the inhabitants
were taxed to support the Congregational Church. Mr. Backus pointed
to the unfairness of being "obliged to support a ministry we cannot attend." Mr. Adams told Mr. Backus that he "might as well expect a change
in the solar system" as to expect the Congregationalists to "give up their
establishment."

That system had been unshaken by the passage from colony to commonwealth. As Mr. Quincy, the president of Harvard College, informed
my brother, the only change their revolution had made was "to put the
people's name in place of that of the king. For the rest one finds nothing changed among us." In keeping with the sentiment of Massachusetts
so succinctly expressed by Mr. Adams to Mr. Backus, its constitution
linked the existence of civil government itself to the existence of "piety,
religion, and morality," on which the constitution declared that civil government depended. As a corollary, the public worship of God and pub-

lic instruction in religion must be provided for by the civil government; for, without this public support, the draftsmen assumed, both worship and instruction must languish. Accordingly, the Declaration of the Rights of the Inhabitants directed the towns of the commonwealth of Massachusetts to provide at public expense for the public worship of GOD and for the support and maintenance of "public, protestant teachers of piety, religion, and morality in all cases where such provision shall not be made voluntarily." The exception envisaged by the final proviso was, I was told, Boston, where the churches and their ministers were supported by pew rent.

At first I could not believe my own eyes when I read the words of this constitution, now over half a century old—to the Americans, it must seem a venerable document. Had not my brother written that all his informants "principally attributed the peaceful empire that religion exercises in their country to the complete separation of the Church and the State"? Had he not added, "I am not afraid to affirm that during my stay in America I did not meet a single man, cleric or lay, who was not in agreement on this point"? Could he have been misled or mistaken on a matter of such importance? Perhaps the words of the constitution were like those of many hoary documents, verbiage without vitality in them.

To the contrary: I observed at once one point on which all, or nearly all, were in agreement, including the Baptists, otherwise reluctant to employ the force of the state to enforce religious obligations. That was the duty to maintain the solemnity of the day associated with the Resurrection of Christ, the day described by statute as "the Lord's Day." A law of Massachusetts, enacted in 1782, provided for a fine of ten shillings for any able-bodied person who absented himself or herself from Sunday services for a month and forbade any kind of selling, business, or labor on the Sabbath. In addition any musical concert, dancing, or "any public diversion, show, or entertainment" and "any sport, game, play, or recreation" were prohibited under a five shilling penalty; and to complete the prohibitions it was provided under similar sanctions that on this day reserved for the worship of God "no person shall recreate, disport, or unnecessarily walk or loiter, or assemble themselves in the streets, lanes, wharves, highways, common fields, pastures, or orchards of any towns or place within this State."

The legislature of once-Puritan Massachusetts, it might be thought, descended into extraordinary detail. I surmise that the Bostonians never go to the beach, for beaches are strangely omitted from the legislative list of locations where Sunday disporting is discouraged or, rather, made criminal. But the basic sabbatarian legislation is as characteristic of New York and Virginia as of the old Puritans' commonwealth. The belief of the dominant Protestant churches in the sanctity of the Sabbath was imposed on all inhabitants. By the time of my brother's arrival, an attempt had been made by a constitutional convention to lift the Massachusetts legislation imposing attendance, and the people had rejected the amendment, so that the obligation, now reduced to at least one Sunday attendance every three months, was in force when my brother came to Boston and Stockbridge. In 1833 the power of the legislature to require attendance was abrogated. The prohibition of most alternative activities remains. The Lord's Day it was meant to be, and the Lord's Day it has remained. Secular business is not to be transacted upon it. The law is such, I was told by a farsighted Boston lawyer, that if a man worked on the Lord's Day, thereby violating the statute, and in the course of his employment were injured owing to the negligence of his employer, he would nonetheless be barred from recovery for his injury: his own willful violation of law would be held to have contributed to his harm. In this draconian way, the sacredness of the day set aside for the deity is preserved.

Sabbath-keeping as a principle and a law is not disputed by any of the religious bodies. To further my astonishment I found that there had been a veritable war (not it is true with weapons) between the Congregationalists and the Unitarians. The war had been at law, and it was to obtain the benefits of the establishment effected by the constitution of the commonwealth. The victory had gone to the Unitarians, who succeeded in capturing the Supreme Judicial Court of the commonwealth; my brother was right on that point—all public disputes in America become judicial disputes. And the observant may add, the side that captures the judges will prevail.

At all events, a leading Unitarian jurist, then chief justice of the commonwealth, Mr. Parsons (aptly christened Theophilus or "God-loving"), expressed his entire satisfaction with the system on behalf of the generation following that of the constitution-makers. He declared in a judicial opinion that Christianity had been "found to rest on the basis of immortal truth." He used the following words to describe the relation of Christianity to the state's legal structure: "And this religion, as understood by protestants, tending by its effects to making every man submitting to its influence, a better husband, parent, child, neighbor, citizen, and magistrate, was by the people established as a fundamental and essential part of their constitution." I found it difficult to conceive of a more concise or a more authoritative assertion of the state's establishment of a religion than this pronouncement uttered in the course of an allocution by the state's highest tribunal allocating tax revenues to the support of a minister of the Gospel.

It will not have escaped the reader that the chief justice qualified the Christian religion as that religion is "understood by protestants," just as the constitution itself refers to "public, protestant teachers of piety," and so forth. The latter provision in the Declaration of Rights originally had a complement in the portion of the constitution dealing with "the Frame of Government" and determining eligibility for public office. Here an old device for assuring religious conformity had been resorted to, and a test oath required for eligibility for the principal executive offices and membership in the legislature of the commonwealth. The oath required the candidate to disavow any allegiance, temporal or spiritual, to any foreign prince or prelate. It was frankly designed to disqualify Catholics from public office, inasmuch as a scrupulous Catholic would decline to deny the spiritual jurisdiction of the pope. This provision remained in force for two generations in the new commonwealth but was ultimately excised due, I am informed, to an increase of the Catholic electorate, still a small minority, in Boston.

The law of Massachusetts's neighbor, New Hampshire, whose population has not been so noticeably affected by Catholic immigration, more forthrightly requires that its chief executive and each member of its Senate and House of Representatives shall be "of the Protestant religion." In general, I might add, the worst official discrimination is against those religions that are least numerous. The body of Jewish believers is not very large anywhere and most frequently suffers legal disabilities. In Rhode Island, for example, founded by Roger Williams as a sanctuary of religious freedom, Jews may not hold public office or vote in public elections.

You—indeed, any rational person—may be puzzled as to why the constitution of the commonwealth of Massachusetts, so distinctly partial to Protestants otherwise undefined, should have alienated the Baptists or led the Congregationalists and Unitarians to quarrel. As to the first question, I learned that a religious society used not to be eligible for tax support unless incorporated, and the Baptists believe that the state has no right to incorporate a church, that is, to make the church adopt a legal form prescribed by the state. They hark back to their old opposition to licensing by the English monarch; their license, they believe, is from God. If they would not capitulate to the English king, why should they bow to his secular successors? At length, after much controversy, they had their way.

As to the cause of the quarrel among the heirs of the Puritans, I learned to my fresh surprise that the town meetings—those instruments of local government so justly praised by my brother—were the bodies that actually determined which church and minister to support; and as Unitarians came to distinguish themselves from Trinitarian Congregationalists, each faction naturally wanted the town to pay those ministers who agreed with its theology. Capture of the town meeting, an assembly which did not itself impose theological qualifications for membership, provided providentially, as it seemed to the Unitarians, a way by which they could acquire not only new appropriations of town money for their use but actually take over the churches and parsonages already built by town taxes for the use of the Congregationalists; and this way was approved and ratified by the Unitarians upon the Supreme Judicial Court. The result was that in the more enlightened parts of the commonwealth, by which I understood my interlocutors to mean Boston and its environs, the Unitarian ministry came into possession of some of the finest churches, built by the towns and once enjoyed by the now-ousted Congregationalists.

The war, I next came to discover, did not end with an unqualified Unitarian triumph. The Congregationalists did learn from their defeats to desire a change in the solar system, to undo the establishment that had lasted two hundred years, from the Pilgrim Fathers to the 1820s. In the fall of 1831 when my brother visited Boston the change was being contemplated; and in 1833 it was effected by an election in which the embittered Congregationalists, joined by Baptists and Catholics, voted to amend the constitution and eliminate compulsory public support of a Protestant ministry.

Even that amendment, I came to understand, did not terminate the public largesse bestowed on the two principal rivals; for the Unitarians were enabled to retain as their own, no longer subject to the vote of any town meeting, those edifices and funds that they had won during the long struggle; and the Congregationalists similarly kept as their own the places from which they had not yet been rousted. These church buildings, parsonages, and appurtenant accounts were no longer church property provided by the town and subject to the town's religious preference as that preference might change. All this property was now simply the property of one of the two churches. It is hence characteristic of a Massachusetts town to have a central lawn or commons, at the head of which stands a simple white edifice, noble in its simplicity; the edifice is a Congregationalist or Unitarian church, once within the gift of the town, now securely within the control of a religious denomination alone. The churches have been disestablished; they retain their preeminence, physical as well as moral, in the communities of the commonwealth.

I was aware that my brother had amplified his personal observations by the study of Mr. Joseph Story and indeed had incorporated enough of Mr. Story's ideas into his major work that Mr. Story himself became indignant that the contribution levied on him had gone unacknowledged. I therefore turned to Mr. Story's commentaries on the federal constitution to see if these had generated a view of church and state that had overshadowed and even overwhelmed what my brother might have found to be the case in Massachusetts. I knew that Mr. Story, although himself a Massachusetts man, now sat on the highest tribunal of the federal government; and I supposed that, although a Unitarian, he might have a larger political view than that of his coreligionists in Boston.

To my initial gratification I found that Mr. Story had written with conviction in favor of Article VI of the federal constitution, which provides that no religious test shall ever be a requirement for federal office. Mr. Story wrote enthusiastically that this provision "cut off forever every pretense of any alliance between church and state in the national government." He did not notice, however, that in a state such as New Hampshire a religious test for federal office was effectively perpetuated to this day by the provision confining the electors of United States Senators to persons who must be Protestant and that in Massachusetts the same effect had been achieved for two generations by the oath required to enter on public office. He equally celebrated the rights of conscience—rights he asserted to be "beyond the just reach of any human power." These rights, he continued, "are given by God, and cannot be encroached upon by human authority without a criminal disobedience of the precepts of natural as well as of revealed religion." Such sentiments were so much in tune with those of my elder brother that I knew that he must have found comfort and confirmation in them. At the same time Mr. Story's words reminded me that in Massachusetts the Declaration of Rights of the Inhabitants of the commonwealth also contained a guarantee that no one "should be hurt, molested, or restrained, in his person, liberty, or estate, for worshipping GOD in the manner and season most agreeable to the dictates of his own conscience; or for his religious profession or sentiments; provided that he doth not disturb the public peace or obstruct others in their religious worship." But this guarantee occurring in the same article that imposed the obligation of public worship of God and public support of a minister had clearly nothing to do with the separation of church and state. Reading further in Mr. Story, I encountered the following passage—it irresistibly brought to mind the judicial opinion of Mr. Theophilus Parsons—that there were "few persons in this or any other Christian country who would deliberately contend that it was unreasonable or unjust to foster and encourage the Christian religion generally as a matter of sound policy as well as of revealed truth." So every colony of the former British North America, he observed, had done. "And this has continued to be the case in some states down to the present period, without the slightest suspicion that it was against the principles of public law or republican liberty." In fact, he wrote, Christianity—and in particular the Protestant religion—was peculiarly suited to republican liberty; and in obedience to that insight Massachusetts had authorized its legislature to require support "only for Protestantism."

Mr. Story therefore seemed to perceive no discontinuity between championing the rights of conscience and welcoming the separation of the national government from the church, on the one hand, and, on the other, delighting in the promotion of Protestantism by the legislature of his native state. The report of so well-informed a jurist as Mr. Story on existing practice in the United States could not have been ignored even if his personal views on the desirability of the practice might have been discounted. My poor brother! No doubt troubled by the apparent dichotomy, he had suppressed the side he found obnoxious. Plainly, Mr. Story, so highly situated in the federal judiciary and himself also the principal part of the faculty of law at Harvard College, was committed to a view that my brother averred not to have heard spoken; and that view, in Mr. Story's opinion, was the common one and the necessary foundation of the civil government.

Mentioning Harvard College, I cannot but comment on that institution's peculiar status. The crown of the educational enterprises of New England, the college was founded within a decade of the coming of the Puritans. Its purpose had been the production of a learned ministry, and its original governing board had been entitled "overseers," as had been the title of the ecclesiastical supervisors of the early Christian Church. The overseers were drawn from the extant ministry of the new settlement, all orthodox Congregationalists. When, in 1780, the revolutionary commonwealth was formed and its constitution adopted, Harvard College was made one of the institutions of government, and the new constitution devoted a separate article to it within the context of "The Frame of Government." This article acknowledged that the college had been instrumental in educating persons for "Church and State" (placing the church first in this foundational document, you see, without perceiving any disharmony in this conjunction of the two bodies) and reiterated that the purposes of the college "tended to the honor of GOD [and] the advantage of the Christian religion." The subvention by the state of this essentially ecclesiastical undertaking was taken to be a matter of course.

The theological direction of this enterprise was, quite naturally, of great importance to the commonwealth and was sensibly affected by the battle of the Unitarians with the Congregationalists for the control of the organs of the ecclesiastical establishment. Like the principal Boston churches, the college had eventually come under the domination of the Unitarian ministry. The Unitarians, while rejecting certain articles of the creed once thought essential to Christian belief, are devotedly religious and determinedly biblical, and they have not repudiated Harvard's ancient motto, *Christo et ecclesiae*, "For Christ and for the Church." I was assured by an eminent Boston lawyer that if the issue should be presented to the Supreme Judicial Court and it was alleged to be inconsistent with the constitution of the commonwealth for what is "to some extent and for certain purposes, a state institution" to have the active responsibility of maintaining a Unitarian seminary, the court would rebuff the claim on the authority of established practice.

Its government, its perpetuation, and its purpose assured by the commonwealth, the college is a model Christian institution patronized by the state.

I have said enough, perhaps, to suggest the close interconnections of church and state that prevailed in certain parts of the American republic prior to its birth and continue to prevail today. But I should add that these interconnections go further than the state financing of worship, ministry, religious education, and clerical training. They operate on the expression of ideas.

Americans are prone to speak frankly, and they have incorporated into the Bill of Rights of the federal constitution a guarantee of the freedom of speech. But there are recognized limits to this freedom, put there by religion. I conversed on this subject with Mr. Lemuel Shaw, the present presiding officer of the Supreme Judicial Court of Massachusetts. He noted that the law of the commonwealth makes it a criminal offense to engage in "reproaching Jesus Christ or the Holy Ghost," or in "denying God" in public. Somewhat boldly, I ventured to ask if the law could be enforced, especially by a judiciary led by Unitarians, such as himself, whose views on the Trinity are far from giving due honor to the Three Persons of the godhead. He assured me that there was no difficulty on this account, and that in the last fifty years the statute against blasphemy had been "frequently enforced." I drew his attention to a case I had heard of in New York where Chancellor Kent (another one of my brother's legal authorities) had enforced the blasphemy law of New York against a man who had disparaged the Virgin Birth of Christ by referring to his mother as a whore. Mr. Shaw told me that a similar verdict would be given by a Massachusetts court. I inquired if it would make any difference if the claim were made in a newspaper rather than spoken by a ruffian and whether the guarantee of Free Speech in the federal constitution had any bearing. On both points, Mr. Shaw answered negatively; a newspaper editor would be punished like any other blasphemer; any invocation of the federal constitution or any appeal to a federal court would be useless; if such an appeal were attempted in his court, he would not stay the sentence to await the result, for he knew that no federal tribunal would intervene.

This legal suppression of crude criticism of Christian doctrine and boorish offense to pious ears is supplemented by a more extensive informal censorship. As my brother had discovered, public opinion is among the most powerful forces in a democracy. On visiting Baltimore I called on a former acquaintance of my brother, a Dr. Stewart, who confessed to be an unbeliever. He pointed out to me, as he had earlier pointed out to my brother, how religion through public opinion exercises an effective censorship. Young men who have formed views contrary to Christianity are not encouraged to put them forward; it would injure their professional careers; it does not do one good to be perceived as a skeptic. The result is, he said, that religion "exercises an immense power outside the church." In particular, "anti-Christian books are never published here or at least it's a rare occurrence." His statement struck me as essentially true, comparing the numbers of anti-Christian books available in America and in France. As Dr. Stewart exclaimed, "Public opinion does what the Inquisition could not!" My brother had not seen fit to report such an observation in his masterpiece. I note it here because it seems to me that the legal machinery used against rough ridicule of Christian belief meshes with, and gives countenance to, the informal self-censorship that supports the Christian establishment.

I have yet to mention the enforcement of Christian morals by the law. I mean by morals in this context those precepts of conduct governing the intimate relations of the sexes. These relations are ruled with the utmost seriousness and strictness by the laws of the Americans. The first concern of any Christian society must be the securing of the sanctity of marriage, so that it was without surprise that I learned how closely Massachusetts had regulated the formation of these unions, permitting them only before ordained ministers of the established church or justices of the peace. I was equally unsurprised by the stern sanctions that attended unblessed unions—adulterers, male and female, are placed on the gallows for the space of one hour and may suffer as many as thirty-nine lashes. The law also provides a penalty of public whipping for the crime of duplicating a marriage by bigamy. A statute of the Commonwealth of Virginia, which Mr. Thomas Jefferson had prepared, appeared to me to go to the extreme, the partners in the latter kind of union being subject to the penalty of death; the sanction was modified to a penitentiary term in the generation after Mr. Jefferson. Those acts that are *contra naturam*, as well as against the Christian view of sexuality, are also harshly punished. The Commonwealth of Massachusetts, for example, began by punishing sodomy by death but in 1804 reduced the penalty to the milder sanction of no more than twenty years imprisonment. There was no question in my brother's mind that the Christian religion promoted the purity of morals that he observed especially among the women of the United States; but I fear that, despite his official mission to investigate the penitentiary system of the country, he gave insufficient weight to the criminal law and its threats in maintaining the morals of the place and the chaste Christian customs of the country.

Convinced by my investigations that, in at least a number of the states, the Protestant religion was patronized and protected by law, I determined to investigate further Mr. Story's declaration that there was a separation between the national government and *any* church, even though that separation had no effect upon the individual states. I had resort to a form of evidence for some reason neglected by my amiable brother, namely the laws enacted by the national legislature, more especially those relating to the appropriation of money or property. I was startled to discover that the First Congress, which, to Mr. Story's satisfaction, had separated church and state, had also established chaplains for the House and for the Senate and for the army. I could not rid myself of the notion that to pay for the services of priests must involve the government in the selection of the priests and therefore necessarily in the choice and approval of particular religious denominations and doctrines. I did not suppose that the choice would be left to chance or that Congress could be so catholic in its bounty as to include chaplains of every denomination; and I was not mistaken in my assumption.

I next discovered a far larger benefaction of Congress to religion, this time apparently left for its more precise definition to local option. I refer to the Northwest Ordinance, a law governing a vast extent of land west of the state of Pennsylvania. The original act was enacted by the Continental Congress before the federal constitution was adopted. That body took the same line advanced by the constitution of Massachusetts, viz., that "religion, morality, and knowledge being necessary to good government and the happiness of mankind, shall forever be encouraged." The First Congress, after it had adopted the Bill of Rights, also adopted this language and confirmed the grant that the Continental Congress had made to the Ohio Company of a substantial acreage of public lands to be used for the support of religion.

I confess that the mutability of democratic opinion and the winds of doctrine that may blow public sentiment in different directions might inspire some to attribute the actions of the First Congress to mere politics and to dismiss its solemn legislative enactments as authentic interpretations of the august document forming the framework of government. I myself was tempted toward this interpretation. But I was disabused of the temptation by a letter I was furnished written by the veritable architect of the constitution, Mr. James Madison. In this letter Mr. Madison was prompt to put to use the legislation and debate that took place in the First Congress "when among the members present were so many who had been members of the federal convention which framed the Constitution, and of the State Conventions which ratified it," and to declare that what the First Congress had done "proved" the point for which he was contending as to the federal power to regulate trade. Although not addressed to the religious question, the analogy appeared apt.

It is not uninstructive to note that the moving spirit in securing the conditions under which Congress regulated the Northwest Territory, in particular the conditions excluding slavery and promoting religion, morality, and education, was a Congregationalist clergyman from Massachusetts, Manasseh Cutler, who was the devout and enterprising agent of the Ohio Company; and it is further notable that in planning the government of this great wilderness, Congress wrote on a tabula rasa and was able to set out a scheme that must have seemed to its members to be an ideal form of civic government. Under the presidency of George Washington the state of Ohio was organized on the terms of the ordinance, to be followed by Indiana under President Adams, Michigan and Illinois under President Jefferson, and Missouri under President Madison. Although the two Virginians were known for their belief that no church should ever be established, neither, as far as I could tell, ever protested or regretted the federal largesse to religion in the great states organized during their presidencies.

It is characteristic of the mentality shared with Messrs. Parsons and Story that the Reverend Mr. Cutler, in a sermon preached in the Northwest Territory in 1788, could aver, "Religion ought never to be made a political machine," and he could add that, "while it is perfectly free from such a prostitution, . . . it affords the greatest aid to civil government, and has the most happy effect on society." Similarly, he could declare, "No one kind of religion, or sect of religion is established as the national religion, nor made, by national laws, the test of truth. Some serious Christians may possibly tremble for the Ark, and think the Christian religion in danger when divested of the patronage of civil power. . . . But we may dismiss our fears, when we consider that truth can never be in real hazard." Simultaneously, he could celebrate the happiness of the Ohio settlement that had a fund provided by Congress for religious instruction and improvement without the provision of the fund "being burdensome to individuals." Happy indeed the priest whose funding came from a benign federal government that did not establish a national religion or patronize Christianity or burden individuals with taxes except by providing him and his associates generous portions of virgin real estate!

There can be little doubt that a clergyman as circumspect as Mr. Cutler would have seen no prostitution of religion in its being used to civilize the Indians; and no doubt the evangelization of the savages must seem to Congress a civic as well as a religious enterprise. The Continental Congress led the way by endowing the Moravian Brethren with ten thousand acres so they might enlighten the Indians on the Muskingum, an action ratified by four later Congresses of the United States. The blameless descendants of that blameless martyr of pure religion, Jan Hus, thus became the first federally financed bearers of the Gospel.

The idea of such federal colporteurs, as I soon discovered, has become popular. I take one instance that comes easily to my hand because it resulted in a famous law case of 1832 (decided while my brother was still in New York). Congress under President Monroe appropriated funds to instruct the Indians in the territory bordering on Georgia. The chosen instruments were missionaries selected by the American Board of Commissioners for Foreign Missions, a Congregationalist enterprise. The missionaries carried out their federally financed assignment by "translating the sacred Scriptures" and "preaching the Gospel" to the Cherokees. Unfortunately, the federal agents transgressed a statute of the state of Georgia prohibiting the entry of white men into the Indian territory without the license of the state; one of their number, the Reverend Samuel Worcester, was convicted of the offense and sentenced to hard labor. Fortunately for him his federal commission from "the chief magistrate of the Union" was found to prevail over the state requirements, and he became not only a federally funded missionary but a federally liberated prisoner free to carry on his apostolic activity. The Supreme Court of the United States in exonerating him in 1832 made no adverse comment on the federal legislation that had launched his evangelical enterprise. The decision, in which Mr. Story joined, was unanimous and was written by the aged chief justice, Mr. John Marshall, a jurist well known for his scrupulous sensitivity to the commands of the country's constitution.

I am aware that my brother might possibly have regarded these instances of Indian-directed religion as falling outside the scope of his account of relationships within the American democracy. Nonetheless, I cannot conceal my own conviction that this continued congressional subsidization of the most fundamental of Christian endeavors, the bringing of the Gospel to the heathen, casts a light on the interaction of the national government with specific religious denominations, most especially as in order to effect the governmental end the government has to decide which denominations are most apt for the delicate task with which they are to be entrusted.

To return to the strictly domestic scene, I have been struck how all the leading colleges of the United States have been founded by religious bodies and funded, at least in good part, by the various colonies or states— Harvard, founded by Congregationalists, funded by the colony, later the commonwealth of Massachusetts (with an unsuccessful petition to the crown for support failing just before the revolution); William and Mary, founded by the Anglicans, funded by the colony, later by the commonwealth of Virginia; Yale, founded by Congregationalists, funded by the colony and then by the state of Connecticut; the College of New Jersey in Princeton, founded by the Presbyterians, funded by the colony and then by the state of New Jersey; King's (the eventual Columbia), founded by the Anglicans, funded by the colony, later by the state of New York; Dartmouth, founded by the Society for the Propagation of the Gospel, funded first by the province of New Hampshire, then by the state of New Hampshire; Queen's (later Rutgers), founded by the Dutch Reformed, funded by the colony and then by the state of New Jersey. Reading the reports of the federal constitutional convention, I observed that a proposal for a national university, in which "no preferences or distinctions should be made on account of religion" was rejected, partly perhaps because a majority preferred the denominational pattern that had educated them. Notwithstanding this reluctance to have a single national university, Congress under President Jackson has made land grants to Columbian and to Georgetown, both colleges within the District of Columbia. I am informed that the grant to Columbian was of special interest because it is a Baptist institution, and the Baptists have, in general, been scrupulous in resisting funding by the civil government. The grant to Georgetown was for me particularly striking because it is a Catholic institution owned and staffed by the Jesuits, and, as one reared in the Catholic faith in France, I have known how jealous some of my co-citizens have been against any extension of governmental support to the Society of Jesus. In all of these cases, I should add, that, while colleges are the culmination of the American educational system, they are not universities, and the young men who present themselves for instruction are in fact somewhat older schoolboys; so that their curriculums may be fairly described as indoctrination in the beliefs of the denominations who control them.

I have said enough to suggest the kind of evidence my brother chose to overlook or to leave unmentioned. From his possibly idealized view of the American situation he drew the following conclusion: "As long as a religion rests only on the sentiments which are the consolation of every misery, it can draw to itself the hearts of the human race. Mixed in the bitter passions of this world, it is compelled sometimes to defend allies given to it by interest, rather than love; and it is necessary for it to repulse as opponents men who often still love it while they fight those to whom it is united. Religion, therefore, cannot share the material power of a government without burdening itself with a portion of that hate that power generates."

I confess that on first reading this analysis I was struck by its penetration, and I am still not free from its sway, and that for two reasons especially: my brother foresaw accurately that compassion would rule the modern world, and so the most compassionate of religions would be the most winning one; and secondly, as he so frequently did, he employed a great general noun—in this case religion—without spoiling its effect by making it concrete. A great deal can be read into "religion" as Alexis uses it.

On the basis of this analysis, which, in the context of his book is apparently based upon his American experience and observations, Alexis went on to offer this advice: religion should found itself "upon the desire of immortality which lives in every human heart." It should eschew political power, not mix itself with political institutions, and avoid identification with political parties. It should, in a word, be a guide to the next world, not to this one.

Sage as this advice may be for the leaders of a church who must avoid open partisanship, seductive as it is as a formula for religious peace within a society, it is not, I fear, solidly founded upon the American experience. The phenomena I have just reviewed—the commitment in state constitutions to the public worship of God and the enforcement of this obligation by sabbatarian legislation; the use of public funds to endow churches, maintain ministries, commission missionaries, and benefit religious education; the control of public education by the clergy; the enforcement of a decent respect for the deity and the principal tenets of Christianity by the criminal law; and the submission of the entire sexual life of the Americans to commandments derived from Christian Scripture —point in another, more worldly direction. My brother wrote, just before he ventured upon his analysis of the role of religion in America, "The principal aim of this book has been to make known the laws of the United States." It is evident that the bulk of the laws bearing upon religion were omitted from his account.

In his earlier education, my brother had been exposed to the attractive apologia for Christianity offered by M. Lamennais, and it was only natural when this zealous priest launched his journal so winningly called *L'Avenir*, proclaiming that the Church and democracy, Christianity and freedom, were allies—it was only natural that the message should strike a deep, resonant chord in my brother's heart. It was not for him to get entangled in the ecclesiastical politics that brought *L'Avenir* to a halt the following year and then drove M. Lamennais himself from the Church. Like M. Lacordaire, my brother kept the hope for the future that the journal's name implied and, taking the way not of theological speculation but of sociological inquiry, sought to show that the hope was not a chimera.

The philosophers of the previous century, in our country at least, had thought Christianity was dead and its still kicking corpse a hideous obstacle to the proper progress of humankind. My brother, troubled by doubt though he sometimes is, does not share that view. Perhaps he is less a believer than a once-upon-a-time believer. It is strange how, in our country, men have diverged from women in the practice of faith. Were my old Ursuline teachers more committed or more loving than his instructors, or my temptations less? At all events, I dare hope that when his final hours draw near and the prospect of immortality opens before him, he will receive the sacraments and profess the Catholic religion, as he always declares publicly. But is he too infected by those views of the eighteenth century he imbibed in his reading in his youth, too ready to banish the priest to the sacristy and to confine the clergy to the cloister? Careful student that he is of historical forces, has he failed to calculate the dynamics of a religion that captured the governance of the greatest empire ever known to antiquity; that turned turbulent tribes and unlettered barbarians into statesmen and scholars and made a European civilization of cathedrals, colleges, coronations, and ordered rule; that never ceases to challenge corruption in the state or in the ecclesiastical body itself; whose reforming energies exploded the ecclesiastical and secular structure it created; whose children in one generation were Luther and Calvin and Knox (all Catholic priests when they started on the course of reform); and whose children in another generation were Voltaire and Danton and Robespierre (all Catholic schoolboys once upon a time). How can the attentive scholar expect the energies generated by the Gospel to be decorously channeled into ceremonies for the dead or sermons for the dying? History speaks otherwise. The Christian religion cannot be caged in the category of the unworldly. It comes, in the words of its Founder, to bring fire on the earth.

Our family had suffered, during our Revolution, the greatest of misfortunes, the loss of the life of our ancestor, not to mention the terrors inflicted on our father and poor mother and the impairment of our family estate. The Tocquevilles had been—may I say it frankly?—traumatized by these sad and violent events. Never again! was their silent motto and secret resolve. Now it is my brother's study to examine how the ancien régime had failed and how the new democracy offers a way to avoid the perils our Revolution had brought. It is with that concealed concern that my brother recently disclosed the true aim of his book in a letter to his good friend Eugène Stoeffels: "You seem to me to have well understood the general ideas on which my programme rests. What has most struck me about my country, more especially these last few years, is to see ranged on one side men who prize morality, religion, and order; and upon the other, those who love liberty and the equality of men before the law. This spectacle has struck me as the most extraordinary and the most deplorable ever offered to the eyes of man; for all the things that we separate in this way, are, I am certain, united indissolubly in the eyes of God. They are *holy* things, if I may so express myself, because the greatness and the happiness of man in this world can result only from their simultaneous union. From this I believe to have perceived that one of the finest enterprises of our time would be to demonstrate that these things are not at all incompatible; that, on the contrary, they are bound together by a necessary tie, so that each of them is weakened in being separated from the others. Such is my general idea." It was with that great ambition that he presented his partial and idealized account of American democracy and gave his seductive advice to the chiefs of religious institutions.

For my part, if I were asked what conclusions I would draw from the American experience in the half century it has been a republic, I would say first that the European expression "church and state" has little relevance in America; for there are many churches and many degrees of governmental power. Church and state, although the words occur in the constitution of Massachusetts, are not terms employed by the national constitution; by their abstraction and antinomy they obscure the overlap that exists. Rather than church and state there are persons who are, in varying degrees, believers in various forms of Christianity, and these persons are voters, legislators, and magistrates, both executive and judicial. Their religion often operates upon them to affect their action at the polls, in the legislative chamber, and in the executive and judicial branches of government. No watertight mental compartments exist by which their religious ideas are isolated from their civic responsibilities.

Second, the Americans have learned from the hideous experience of Europe and from a few experiences of their own as colonists that the persecution of Christian sects by one another is as destructive of religion as it is destructive of the charity that must distinguish the conduct of Christians. It is this experience that has been enshrined in their national and state constitutions' recognition of the liberty of conscience and the right to exercise religion freely. The Americans have had the happy grace to extend the toleration that England had offered to several Protestant bodies, to all Protestants, and to the Catholics. Judaism, although its numbers are not large, and local restrictions persist, has also been embraced within this national freedom. And atheists, if not vocal in public, are tolerated. I am not sure if Islam, if practiced with all its peculiarities, would be found to fit within the liberty allowed; and I have even greater doubt as to whether every new religion would be accorded the rights of belief and worship now so readily accorded the traditional varieties stemming from a common Judeo-Christian origin.

The last observation brings me to my third point, that studies of the population are relevant to the role of religion in a democracy. The enactment in Virginia of Mr. Jefferson's celebrated Act for the Establishing of Religious Freedom depended on the existence in Virginia of a majority of citizens not connected with the established church, as did the subsequent defeat in Virginia of an attempt to tax the citizenry for religious education. Similarly in Massachusetts the disestablishment that took place in 1833 was due in part to the influx of Baptists and Catholics into the commonwealth as well as the disaffection of the country Congregationalists. In a democracy the religion of the voters counts; and it would be the height of foolishness to suppose that the patterns of civil government in America have not been responsive to these religious currents, or to imagine that politics in a democracy had been, or could be, conducted without attention to religious preferences.

Why, then, do the Americans not go further in their religious differences than battles at the polls and in the courts? At least two reasons appear decisive. One is that there are so many religions that none has, or is likely to have, such power on the national scene as to be oppressive to the others. The essence of this reason was given by Mr. Spencer to my brother, who had asked him point-blank, "What causes the religious tolerance prevailing in the United States?" And Mr. Spencer had replied, "Principally the extreme diversity of sects (there is almost no end to it). If two religious faced each other, we would soon be cutting each other's throats. But as none has so much as a majority, all need toleration." Mr. Spencer's reason had indeed been anticipated by Mr. Madison, speaking in the Virginia assembly against a bill of rights and finding the "strong security" of religious freedom to be the religious diversity of the population. It is manifest, of course, why my brother did not incorporate Mr. Spencer's and Mr. Madison's analysis into his work; in France we have the situation of one religious body and its opponent at each other's throats.

The second reason why tolerance flourishes is that the minds of the Americans are primarily practical. They have a limited trust in theory and little patience for refined theological debate. The great trinitarian and christological controversies that apparently inflamed the mobs of Constantinople and Alexandria are inconceivable as sources of public passion in America. As Mr. Brown, a sophisticated planter and former American minister to France, informed my brother about his American compatriots, "In the depths of their souls they have a pretty decided indifference to dogma. One never talks about that in the churches. It is morality with which they are concerned."

No single unitary church or state; an acceptance of freedom of belief and worship for those religions known from Europe as Christian and for traditional Judaism, and a toleration of unbelief; a Christian commitment that animates many voters and many governmental officers; a division in numbers such that no Christian sect has the upper hand nationally; and a concern with religion as it bears on the practical questions of morality—such are the chief characteristics of the United States playing upon the place of religion in the society. It is the last characteristic that interests me most, for it coincides with an observation made by my brother that differs sharply from his comments on the unworldly character of religion; it points as well to the possibility of even armed religious conflict in the United States.

My brother's observation went as follows: "Religion—which with the Americans never mixes directly in the government of the society—must be considered as the foremost of their political institutions. For if it does not give them the taste of liberty, it singularly facilitates their use of liberty. It is from this perspective that the inhabitants of the United States themselves view religious beliefs. I do not know if all Americans have faith in their religion, for who can read the depths of the human heart? But I am sure that they believe religion necessary to the maintenance of republican institutions. This opinion is not peculiar to one class of citizen or one party but to the entire nation; one sees it in every social rank."

The reason that religion has this essential utilitarian role follows from a syllogism—the same syllogism so justly celebrated for its invocation by President Washington in his famous Farewell Address. Morality is necessary for the existence of republican government. Religion is necessary for morality. Therefore, religion is necessary for the continued existence of the republic.

This deep involvement of religion with morality can have no pernicious effects so long as there is general agreement on what morality, especially sexual morality, consists in. But suppose that a new religion should preach a different morality as to relations between the sexes. Would it enjoy the liberty the Americans now accord so readily to the Christian churches? Could not my brother see that, if division should occur on such a fundamental point, the Americans would not easily accept their differences? Could not my brother see that if some single, great, commanding moral good should evoke the allegiance of part of the population, logic would lead its advocates to try every expedient to advance its cause? He had only to think of Saint-Just and Robespierre in our parents' past or of Saint Bernard in our national history. I mention Frenchmen, but the compulsion of such a logic is not confined to France.

Suppose that slavery, which has, it is believed, its own special institutional impact on sexual morals—suppose that slavery were regarded from the perspective of that most elementary of Christian duties, the commandment to love one's neighbor as oneself. Could neighborly kindness, religiously inculcated, inflame passions and divide the regions of the nation? Already Congregationalist ministers in Boston are actually saying openly that slavery is a national sin. My brother anticipated an insurrection by the Southern blacks; he did not envisage a clash of North and South. But if Mr. Adams is correct, Southern slavery and Northern religion have made up the chief ingredients of the American character. May it be that the national character will dissolve into two parts? There has never been a war of religion in the new republic. But what should that conflict be called if religious righteousness led to a demand that the Southern states set aside their peculiar institution as offensive to the morals of a Christian people? Can religion be the foremost of their political institutions and not affect the liberty of each person in the country?

CHAPTER 5

GOD IS MARCHING ON

THEODORE PARKER
ca. 1850, about to become an American Saint Bernard

"My own conscience is to declare the law to me . . . "

An excerpt from the correspondence of George Frothingham:

The Somerset Club
Boston
May 30, 1860

Dear Beauregard:

I enclose for your information the report of my confidential agent on
the expected needs of Mr. Lowell's textile mills in the coming year.
Young George, whom you met at lunch, is entering the business as
if he means to make it his own. I have also communicated with our
mutual friend on the tariff.

The grand news here is that he is dead—"our Savonarola," dead,
appropriately, in the city of Savonarola. You ask who I mean by *he*.
I mean, of course, the man who has been the heart and soul of the religionists who have stirred up our fanatics not only in this commonwealth but as far west as Ohio and Illinois. I mean, of course, the
one who is not far from being Satan himself in his rank unbelief, his
smooth and slippery and hypocritical invocation of Scripture, and the
energy and determination he has thrown into the cause of wrecking our
peaceful land. I mean no other than the Reverend (?) Theodore Parker.

You may shrink a little when I am moved to speak so passionately
of the dead. Did Mr. Parker respect the dead? When our great Goliath,
indeed the Goliath of our entire country, Daniel Webster, reached the
end of his allotted days, and the city was cast in mourning, and his
passing lamented from a hundred pulpits, Mr. Parker took to his pulpit to review his life and destroy his reputation. Mr. Parker's personal
God, if he had one, was not a judging God. No, Mr. Parker had taken
upon himself the divine attribute of judge; and in that capacity he
did not hesitate to judge the divine Daniel as the worst of men, a man
whose shame was too big for any preacher to cover with his benediction, a man so small that his corpse could be insulted with impunity.

   This entry of Mr. Parker into politics, the politics of a funeral oration, was not, to be sure, the worst or earliest of his offenses against
the norms of civil behavior and religious correctness that confine
a minister of the Gospel to preaching the Gospel. As early as 1846,
at a meeting at our Faneuil Hall, he had addressed a mob to protest
against our just war with Mexico. I quote his exact words: "Men and
brothers, I call on you all to protest against this most infamous war,
in the name of the States, in the name of the country, in the name of
man—yes, in the name of God." Thank God his rhetoric was ineffec-
tive. But he was on to something.

   When Mr. Webster and Mr. Clay and other leading statesmen
of our nation painstakingly crafted the legislation we know as the
Compromise of 1850, legislation that was destined to bring peace
to our country and secure its unbreakable union, Mr. Parker again
ascended the podium at Faneuil Hall to harangue the multitude or, as
he chose to put it, "to talk the matter over, in our New England way."
His talk had scarcely begun before he was referring to the
distinguished senator from Mississippi as "Hangman Foote." But he
reserved his choicest epithets for our own senior senator. He told the
multitude that they must choose between the will of God and the will
of the devil, and he plainly indicated his belief that Mr. Webster had
chosen the will of the devil. Mr. Webster's compromise had not been
a wise solution to a political crisis; it had been, in Mr. Parker's twisted
theology, a compromise with sin.

   The Reverend Mr. Parker's incursion into politics was not confined
to oratory. As you may have heard, he more than dabbled in the business of stealing other people's property. As early as the administration
of President Fillmore he wrote the President an impudent letter
describing how he had led a bunch of ruffians, the Vigilantes, in
driving out of Boston two gentlemen from Georgia who had come in
search of two runaways from that state. He took the hypocritical line
that he was protecting the Georgia gentlemen from violence while
telling them "that they were not safe another night." And he completed his performance by performing a marriage ceremony for the
runaways, presenting "the bridegroom" with a Bible and a dagger,
one symbolizing one kind of necessary work, Parker said, the other
another.

   Then, after the passage of the Fugitive Slave Statute, part of that
wise Compromise of 1850, his ardor and impatience scarcely had a
limit. In February 1851 he applauded the mob that rescued a Negro,

called Shadrach from the courthouse itself and spirited him to liberty. "The noblest deed done in Boston since the destruction of the tea in 1773," cried Parker. How he liked those references to the Revolution in which his grandfather had played a truly heroic part!

Then when in April 1852 a Negro boy was ordered returned by George Curtis, our federal commissioner appointed under the terms of the Fugitive Slave Statute, Parker attended a meeting of the executive committee of the Vigilantes to devise means for his liberation. Tom Higginson wanted to rush the courthouse again. Parker was with him there. But Parker had an even better scheme—to practice piracy and attack the boat carrying the fugitive to Savannah. It all fell through because the marshal produced 200 policemen to guard the court. Parker took his revenge in the pulpit by lashing Curtis as one of the great monsters of history, by putting him, our precious demagogue Charles Sumner said, "in an immortal pillory to receive the hootings and rotten eggs of the advancing generation."

Now that I mention Sumner let me digress for a moment to note that there are few persons in public life so inimical to our Union than he, and there are few men in our Massachusetts more responsible for his being a United States Senator than Theodore Parker. "The senator with a conscience" was the halo Parker chose to put about his head, a head (I tell you confidentially) that deserved every blow that Representative Brooks was able to rain upon it. "The senator with a conscience!"—Great God, as if the pompous pronouncements of this portentous prig were the voice of God speaking to us through him.

To return to Parker and his sly property-stealing habits, at the very time the Nebraska bill was before the Congress and being denounced by a rabble of so-called Christian clergymen, another fugitive, one Burns, was apprehended in Boston—a Baptist preacher no less, who had taken leave of his master in Richmond. Two days after the arrest, Mr. Parker was again up on the bully platform of Faneuil Hall telling the crowd, "I have heard hurrahs and cheers for liberty many times. I have not seen a great many deeds *done* for liberty. I ask you are we to have *deeds* as well as words? . . . Gentlemen, there was a Boston once and you and I had fathers—brave fathers; and mothers who stirred up fathers to manly deeds. . . . They did not obey the Stamp Act. . . . You know what they did with the *tea*." In the wake of that exhortation the mob shouted: "To the Court House! To the Court House!" The hall was emptied. The mob ripped the banister off the stairway of the Museum. They battered in the Court House door. They charged the police. One Marshal's aide lay dead. A shot from an abolitionist's gun missed the Marshal himself. "Why didn't he hit him?" cried Parker.

Soldiers arrived. The mob was contained. The President ordered out more troops. The Marshal swore in a guard. For ten days Boston was in a state of siege and the business of the regular courts suspended. Finally, the federal commissioner, Edward Greeley Loring, ordered the return to Virginia of the slave. A cannon loaded with forty rounds of shot was put in front of the Court House. Troops under orders to fire without notice carried him to the ship that returned him to his owner. It cost the government over $100,000, but law and order had been maintained.

Mr. Parker did not offer to reimburse the government for what he and his co-conspirators caused. A Harvard law student, Albert Brown, Jr., the son of a member of our Governor's Council, was arrested for riotous conduct. But did the Reverend Parker suffer any adverse consequences? He was, indeed, indicted for a federal crime, for his part in the conspiracy that had launched the assault upon the court. The judge was to be Mr. Benjamin Curtis himself, the Supreme Court Justice for our circuit (the same Curtis who later proved a weak brother, or should I say sister?); at the time we thought he was committed to preservation of the law of the Union. In the end—perhaps a foreshadowing of things to come—he let Parker off on the most transparent of technicalities.

Some say there was a deliberate decision taken not to make Parker into a martyr. I say that one year in gaol and a good stiff fine would have done Parker and the commonwealth a better service. I remember how the municipal officials of Nashville gave that young slave-loving seminarian from Lane a thrashing he recalled the rest of his life. It is unfortunate that corporal punishment no longer exists as a sanction for such violence as Parker's conspiracy to subvert the federal judicial process.

Unrestrained by the criminal law, Parker chose to publish these words (he had meant them for the jury if he had gone to trial) addressed to Edward Greeley Loring, Judge of Probate for the County of Suffolk, and Commissioner of the United States, and Professor at Harvard College: Parker announced (referring to an unhappy incident of a few years ago), "I do not find that any College Professor has ever been hanged for murder in all the Anglo-Saxon family of men, till Harvard College had that solitary shame. Is not that enough? Now she is the first to have a Professor that kidnaps men. 'The Athens of America' furnished both!"

His shameless rhetoric did not stop there. On Ascension Sunday he told his congregation who he thought responsible for the death of the marshal's aide that resulted from the violence he had incited. Pretending to speak to Judge Loring, he said, "I charge you with the death of that man who was killed on last Friday night. He was your fellow-servant in kidnapping. He dies at your hand. You fired the shot which makes his wife a widow, his child an orphan. I charge you with the peril of twelve men, arrested for murder, and on trial for their lives. I charge you with filling the Court House with one hundred and eighty-four hired ruffians of the United States, and alarming not only this city for her liberties that are in peril, but stirring up the whole Commonwealth of Massachusetts with indignation, which no man knows how to stop—which no man can stop. You have done it all!"

Once he had tasted violence, once he saw his political machinations could make a senator, Parker had aspirations for which there were no obvious limits. He toured the country, fulminating. He backed the invasion of Kansas by the abolitionists who set out, rifles in hand, to make the territory unsafe for those with property in slaves. And then he began to patronize John Brown, to hobnob with him, to introduce him to his friends and associates in Boston, to raise money for him. Behind that violent and crazed man, that man of bloodshed and murder and insurrection, there is the benign shadow of our Boston minister.

The Reverend Parker was not at Potawatomi. The Reverend Parker was not at Harper's Ferry. But would there have been a Harper's Ferry, would the brave action of Colonel Robert E. Lee have been necessary, if the Reverend Parker and his friends had not fanned the flame and provided the fuel for Brown's murderous passions? Who is it that wrote: "The fire of Vengeance may be waked up even in an African's heart, especially when it is fanned by the wickedness of a white man; then it runs from man to man, from town to town. What shall put it out? *The white man's blood*." No, those words, fit for hysterical hyenas, did not come from the mouth of John Brown. They are words of our recently deceased patriot, Theodore Parker.

The Reverend Parker's political career began, according to an admirer's account, when, barely out of divinity school (and never having been out of New England), he felt "a general disgust" with slavery and voted as a Whig for the abolition of slavery in the District of Columbia. His political ax was whetted in the forties by working against the annexation of Texas and cheering on the so-called Conscience Whigs who opposed the war against Mexico. At that time he delivered a "Sermon on War" so remarkable in its imagery and so bristling with a repressed savagery that I cannot forego quotation.

Parker has fantasized a battle for Boston, in which eight thousand Bostonians and ten thousand men of Cambridge lie dead. He continues, "There writhe the wounded; men who but few hours before were poured over the battle-field, a lava flood of fiery valor—fathers, brothers, husbands, sons. There they lie, torn and mangled; black with powder; red with blood; parched with thirst; cursing the load of life they must now bear with bruised frames and mutilated limbs. . . . There is the battle-field! Here the horses charged; there the howitzers scattered their shells, pregnant with death; here the murderous canister and grape mowed down the crowded ranks; there the huge artillery, teeming with murder, was dragged o'er heaps of men—wounded friends, who just now held its ropes, men yet curling with anguish, like worms in the fire. Hostile and friendly, head and trunk are crushed beneath those dreadful wheels. Here the infantry showered their murdering shot. That ghastly face was beautiful the day before—a sabre hewed it half away."

What a vision of a combat he has never seen! What a taste for sadistic detail! How the preacher's old hellfire tricks (even the worms in the fire) have been translated into fierce and repulsive and attractive secular equivalents! He even speaks of God in the words of Isaiah, as One Who "treads nations as grapes in a wine-press, his garments are stained with their life's blood."

So spoke this conflicted man who in the same sermon announced that "aggressive war is a sin; a corruption of the public morals. It is a practical denial of Christianity; a violation of God's eternal law of love." A little later, after the Fugitive Slave Law was passed, he was telling his fellow ministers, "You know that I do not like fighting. I am no non-resistant, 'that nonsense' never went down with me. But it is no small matter which will compel me to shed human blood. But what could I do? I was born in the little town where the fight and the bloodshed of the Revolution began."

Small wonder that with these principles he did not hesitate to stir the city to madness over Burns. Hypocrisy and the subterranean thirst for violence, always they went hand in hand. A fellow abolitionist says of his performance at Faneuil Hall the night of the attack on the Court House: "This was certainly a direct appeal to the people to attempt a rescue, but Mr. Parker's idea was that a demonstration could be made so formidable, in point of numbers and cool purpose, as to overawe the armed guard and sweep the slave away." So Parker thought you could set fire to a house and not be guilty of arson if the conflagration should catch up a city!

When John Brown came to Boston in January 1857 the same discreet admirer "took him at once to Mr. Parker's Exeter Place house, where he was ever afterwards welcome." In April 1857 Brown sent Parker a plea for money for "the necessary supplies of the common soldiers" and asked Parker to read the plea to his congregation. Parker got the money for him. In September 1857 Brown wrote Parker for "some 500 or 1,000 dollars, for secret service and no questions asked." Brown read aloud to F. B. Sanborn of Concord, Parker's ally, the constitution that Brown was going to promulgate in some slave state which he would occupy to "establish a colony of freedmen." Parker and his immediate friends sent $500 more for the cause. Parker also drew from his well-stocked library General McClellan's recent book on the European armies, "which was thought likely to be of service to Brown," and sent it to him.

What was Brown's plan as understood by Parker and his acolytes? "To penetrate Virginia with a few comrades, help the fugitives, and defend them." On this basis, according to one of our idle young men seduced by this teacher "in the direction of pure thought and advanced independence of opinion," Parker was ready to back Brown.

Through a spy in Brown's ranks, much of the mischief he had in mind became known to Washington. Were they unaware of the ministerial prompting Brown had received? Nothing was done about our Boston divine. He could participate in a plot to levy war upon a state, he could send a textbook for the military, he could help raise the sinews of war, and all the time he remained immune in his minister's armor. Rebel and traitor!

When Brown had done his terrible work, Parker wrote the grandfather of a man who had been wounded at Brown's side (you may be sure the letter was well circulated here, with every bit of its emphasis in the author's own hand): "*A man held against his will as a slave has a natural right to kill everyone who seeks to prevent his enjoyment of liberty. . . . It may be natural duty for the freeman to help the slaves to the enjoyment of their liberty, and as means to that end, to aid them in killing all such as oppose their mutual freedom. . . . The performance of this duty is to be controlled by the freeman's power and opportunity to help the slaves. . . . My duty is commensurate with my power.*"

You have it in a nutshell, a catechism for a slave insurrection, to be led by as many John Browns as lily-livered Boston ministers can finance and send South.

Parker adds two thoughts: he would have rejoiced if Brown "had succeeded in running off one or two thousand slaves to Canada, even at the expense of a little violence and bloodshed. . . . A little success of that sort will serve us primarily for the popular cannon; it is already *loaded*." And, commenting on the shield of the commonwealth of Virginia with the emblem of a man standing on a tyrant and saying "*Sic semper tyrannis*" while chopping off the tyrant's head with a sword, Parker says, "Only I would paint the sword-holder black and the tyrant white, to show the immediate application of the principle."

You are, I know, of a philosophical turn of mind and must wonder how this murderous creature came to occupy one of our pulpits. On that point a little recent religious history is relevant. To begin with, the antislavery agitation began—I say it to my shame—in this city on the Fourth of July 1829, in the Park Street Church. William Lloyd Garrison, who had hitherto been crusading against Sabbath-breaking and alcoholism, announced that he had been converted to a new cause—abolition. Five years later 124 ministers of the Gospel, chiefly Congregationalists from this part of the world, issued a manifesto addressed to the public, in which they made the discovery that slavery was "a great and crying national sin" and that every man, in every part of the country, had a personal duty to secure its extinction by what they called "Immediate Emancipation." Thereafter, a network of ministers was formed which kept up the attack. They were always a small portion of the ministry. They did not have the countenance of the main church bodies, Methodist, Baptist, Presbyterian, Episcopalian, Roman Catholic. But they were insistent, persistent, and very noisy; and as you know, they insulted you and your fellow owners of human property to the point where you justifiably were angry and almost maddened.

Be assured that the respectable people of Boston abhor the abolitionist. Fifteen hundred merchants volunteered to send Sims the slave back to his owner in Georgia. The *Post* has asked how New England can live without the South. The *Courier* and the *Advertiser* have said that any lawyer should be proscribed who dared to come into court and defend a runaway against his lawful master. Our great educational institutions are with you. Harvard has led the way, *Christo et Ecclesiae* her motto and guide. President Lord of Dartmouth has thoughtfully made public his "Letter of Inquiry on Slavery." President Wayland of Brown has proved slavery to be a scriptural institution. The college presidents have always known their place in the community. With the battleground of politics inviting their participation, the Brattle Street Church and the Old South Church in our city have presented "the Southside view." Andover, not the least of our theological institutions, has publicly reconciled conscience and the Constitution. Three years ago Harvard would not let Parker speak at the Divinity School commencement. Everyone of sense, of moderation, of property knows that an attack on your property is an attack on his own. How Parker hated us! "Hunkers" was his choice epithet for the people of property of Boston. And how his sentiments were returned. "I cannot be otherwise than hated," he told a crowd at the Music Hall. "This is the necessity of my position—that I must be hated." Call me Ishmael!

You will ask why any member of the clergy has spoken in the way that Parker and his fellows fanatics ranted. I will tell you one reason: they were losing their congregations, who no longer believed those hell and damnation stories our ancestors rejoiced in. The ministers had to find other things to attract the crowds. Lyman Beecher, for example, now prominent among the abolitionists, first turned to baiting those of the Romish religion and helped burn a convent in Charlestown. But now there are a number of Irish in Boston; it is more convenient to make devils out of those who are remote from the scene of his preaching. Hence, those vociferous vociferations against the propertied class of the South.

I say that they were losing their congregations because of the loss of belief. They were also losing faith themselves. As our own Lowell has wittily put it:

I think I may call
Their belief a believing in nothing at all.

Parker called his God "A Father and Mother Person," a kind of hybrid hermaphrodite blessed with hebetude, a spectator not an actor in the world, a being of moral insensibility. He believed Christ to be no more divine than Daniel Webster and the Church to be no more sacred than a tavern. The Music Hall or Faneuil Hall were equally good auditoriums for his religious discourses. He could have been prosecuted for fraud, calling himself a minister of the Gospel and his church a Christian church. He should have been prosecuted for blasphemy as our Attorney General did in fact prosecute another country minister for proving that none of the Messianic prophecies were ever fulfilled by Christ. If his "Religion of Humanity" did not turn his auditors into atheists, it drove some of the more devout of them straight into the arms of Rome!

The old religious convictions were gone. Ordained to preach—what was a preacher to do? He had to vent his pent-up zeal, his sense of righteousness, his conviction of superiority, in some form other than the ancient ways. So ministers became reformers of all kinds. I have mentioned Garrison's earlier crusade for temperance. The preachers took up the rights of women and even asserted that women should have the suffrage. But nothing succeeded so much with them as the crusade on behalf of the absent black man against the absent white man.

A friend of mine at the Harvard Divinity School assures me that this kind of phenomenon is what the academics would call "displacement." Like a vigorous river that can no longer pursue its former course because of some boulder placed across the stream, and yet the water continues to pour down through the old channels until it reaches the boulder, and the penned-up waters must go somewhere, so the religious fervor of these men weaned on the Bible had to find an outlet. Unhappily the outlet is one that has been disastrous for our country.

Senator Douglas has spoken with eloquence on the problem to which I allude when he noted that at the time of the Nebraska Act between fifteen hundred and two thousand sermons were preached against the legislation by ministers in New England. I cannot refrain from copying his exact words:

> I submit, sir, whether it is fair as between man and man, whether it is honest on the part of ministers of the Gospel towards their congregations, to pursue such a course. They take a partisan view of the subject in these sermons. They fix the character of each public man. They indorse this man; they condemn that. They indorse this political party; they excommunicate that. They give what pretends to be a true statement of the facts of the question; when that statement is derived from the address and speeches of the Abolition confederates, and contradicted by the records of the country, and these records are not allowed to be produced. If these statements are put forth upon the stump, we can refute them. If they should be put forth anywhere else than in the pulpit, or except upon the Sabbath day, we can disprove them. What would these gentlemen think of me if I were to violate the Holy Sabbath day by going into Chicago, and on that day making a stump speech in vindication of the Nebraska bill? If they have a right to discuss it on the Sabbath day in opposition, may I not expose their slanders by vindicating the truth? Sir, this is an attempt to convert the Sabbath into the great day of the hustings, to make it a great day of electioneering, to get people of all modes, for if you wish to blacken the

character of a man, you can do it then with security and with impunity, because no man can rise up and expose the slander, although a dozen living witnesses may be present and know it to be a slander.

I say, sir, that the purity of the Christian church, the purity of our holy religion, and preservation of our free institutions, require that Church and State shall be separated; that the preacher on the Sabbath day shall find his text in the Bible; shall preach "Jesus Christ and him crucified." Shall preach from the Holy Scriptures, and not attempt to control the political organizations and political parties of the day.

A wise Frenchman, who visited our country and this city almost thirty years ago, noted at the time the religious peace that reigned and ventured the observation that if a religion were to be successful it should not meddle with partisan politics and practical reform. Would that Mr. Parker had meditated on the advice of Alexis de Tocqueville! I should not have to spend this afternoon in these melancholy reflections that fill my mind with news of his none too timely demise.

Yours very sincerely,
George Frothingham

THEODORE PARKER IN HIS OWN WORDS

Quotes or paraphrases taken from his journal and his letter to the members of the Twenty-eighth Congregational Society of Boston, April 19, 1859, and from his letter to Francis Jackson, November 24, 1859

"The earliest thing you [Father and Mother] taught me was *duty*—duty to God, duty to man; that life is not a pleasure, not a pain, but a *duty*."

As a youth I was attracted to the law, and friends told me that the ministry was a narrow place. But "I thought it a wide place."

In my youth I gave up on Eternal Damnation and the Trinity and the Supernatural Birth of Jesus and the miracles of the Bible and the inspiration of the Bible, and in my studies at the Divinity School I came to believe that the Christian church was "no more divine than the British State, a Dutchman's shop, or an Austrian's farm." Even the small Unitarian craft in which I launched my voyage sank. "They did not dare affirm the humanity of Jesus, the naturalness of religion to man, the actual or possible universality of inspiration." But I clung to three beliefs, then and throughout my life: the "intuition of the divine, the consciousness that there is a God"; the "intuition of the just and right, a consciousness that there is a moral law"; and the "intuition of the immortal, a consciousness that the essential element of man, the principle of individuality, never dies."

As a minister, I spoke against:

1. Bibliolatry, because the Bible is "the great fetish of Protestant Christiandom."
2. Covetousness, "the lust after property."
3. Intemperance, attacking among others, "the chief magistrate of the city," who was "notoriously the comrade of drunkards."
4. War, "showing its enormous cost in money and men."
5. Slavery, "more than any concrete wrong, because it is the greatest of all."

And I spoke for:

1. Religion. "According to my experience and observation, the religious element is the strongest in the spiritual constitution of man, easily controlling all the rest for his good or ill."
2. Woman. "A woman is man's equal, individually and socially entitled to the same rights. . . . I have demanded that she should have the vote and be eligible to any office."
3. Educational reform: Education of the spirit is especially neglected by our colleges. "The educated is also the selfish class. . . . No one would like to be tried by a jury of twelve scholars."
4. Prison reform. I learned "that the criminal is often the victim of society."
5. The rights of labor.
6. The rights of humankind.

I prophesied these things:

1. "An anti-slavery party, under one name or another, will before long control the Federal Government, and will exercise its constitutional rights and perform its constitutional duty, and 'guarantee a Republican form of government to every State in the Union.'"
2. The "strife between the Southern habit of despotism, and the Northern principle of democracy . . . any day may take the form of civil war, and one day must."
3. John Brown will die "like a martyr and also like a saint. . . . None of the Christian martyrs died in vain."

In memoriam: THE REVEREND THEODORE PARKER

*Taken from a memorial service for Reverend Parker held in Faneuil Hall on
the tenth anniversary of his death*

Theodore Parker once wrote of Saint Bernard that he was a man who
had "projected a crusade" and who had "shed his luster over many a
land. . . . Yet this man is forgotten in less than eight centuries from his
birth. His books, no man reads them. . . . But if he is thus quickly for-
got, who of modern great men can stand?" Theodore Parker needed not
have had such a fear for his own memory. He had indeed shed his luster over England and Germany and all of the United States. He had projected a crusade, the greatest the world has seen for human liberty. And
his memory will survive more than eight centuries from his birth.

Theodore Parker was born, the tenth child of his parents, in the cradle of our Revolution in Lexington, Massachusetts, the town in which
his own grandfather, Captain John Parker, had begun the battle for freedom against British tyranny. The elected head of the Lexington militia,
Captain Parker was the first American to engage British regulars in open
combat. The captain had said, "If they mean to have a war, let it begin
here." Those words, handed on by family tradition, were to have a special significance for Mr. Parker when he began his own war for freedom.
His pious parents named him Theodore, meaning "the gift of God"; and
God's gift he was to the people of this city, and this commonwealth, and
this country.

Theodore Parker did not come from a line of ministers or lawyers or
men learned in the ways of the academy. He came of yeomen, the son of
a farmer, the descendant of farmers, who had plowed their land and kept
their homesteads and supported themselves and their families in freedom
for almost two hundred years. Theodore was true to the instincts and
the experiences of this sturdy and independent stock. How he drank up
each drop of vital blood in his family connections!

Invited to be the pastor of the Spring Street Church in the village of
West Roxbury and there ordained to the ministry of the Gospel, he loved
the life and lot of a minister in a country town. It did not take him many
years, however, to take up the theme that in the end was to mark his entire dedicated life. It was in the Spring Street Church in Roxbury, in the
year 1841, that he preached his first "Sermon on Slavery." In that initial
sermon he told his small congregation, "I know that men urge in argument that the Constitution of the United States is the supreme law of the
land and that sanctions slavery. There is no supreme law but that made

by God; if our laws contradict that, the sooner they end or the sooner they are broken, why, the better."

His religious ideas were considered by some, even by some judicious critics, to be advanced. But he understood that the meaning of Christianity lies not in books or churches but in the conduct of the followers of Christ. When not yet thirty he wrote his famous essay, "A Lesson for the Day, or the Christianity of Christ, of the Church and of Society." He denounced those who made "Christianity a Belief, not a Life." He did not deny that the Christianity of Christ depended on the institution of the Church and that true religion was still to be found in the lives of living men. But he refused not to read "the actual signs of the times." He refused to stay timidly and stuffily and dully on the "beaten path" trodden by predecessor clergymen. He insisted upon "the rigid subordination of human authority to God's."

In his high mission of reshaping society to bring it into conformity with God's law, he was one with the great reformers of his day. He was the model of a mature Unitarian, the counterpart in the pulpit of such lay Unitarians as Dorothea Dix and Horace Mann. In his life he became the hammer beating out liberty at the forge of history.

It was not that he was one of those do-gooders who in their zeal for mankind overlook their neighbor at their door. I need only give a single example. When the daughter of his Concord friend Bronson Alcott was driven in desperate melancholy to contemplate putting an end to her earthly existence, it was thanks to the ministrations of Theodore Parker that she recovered her good spirits and faith in her purposes here and went on to celebrate him under the transparent pseudonym "Mr. Power." Without his timely intervention, a "landmark" in her life, the world would never have had her classic tale, *Little Women!*

Understanding that true Christianity requires practical action, he came to see that the greatest evil of his day, an evil that had to be eradicated, was the evil of keeping millions of men and women as the property of other more fortunate men and women. He was kindness and generosity itself to those around him, to his family and friends, to those who sought his assistance. He was unswerving and unremitting in his detestation of the great evil that lay upon the country. In the name of the highest law of all, the law of obedience to God, he challenged the slavery laws of the nation and he placed responsibility on each person in the country to obey that higher law.

Speaking expressly on the topic, "Function of Conscience in Relation to the Laws of Men," he explained, "The law of God has eminent domain everywhere, over the private passions of Oliver and Charles, the special interests of Carthage and Rome, over all official business, all precedents, all human statutes, over all the conventional affairs of one man or of mankind. My own conscience is to declare that law to me, yours to you, and is before all private persons or public interest, the decisions of a majority and a world full of precedents here. You cannot move out of the dominion of God nor escape where conscience has not eminent domain."

To say, as the defenders of slavery said, that there was "no law higher than what the state can make" was, he pointed out, "practical atheism. It is not a denial of God in His person; this is only speculative atheism. It is a denial of the functions and attributes of God; that is real atheism. If there is no God to make a law for me, then there is no God for me."

Invoking conscience, he invoked the rule of life of the Fathers of the Church, of Thomas Aquinas and the leading Roman Catholic divines, the Fathers of the Reformation, and the Pilgrim Fathers who for conscience's sake founded this commonwealth. He invoked the example of the Apostle Peter, who said, "We must obey God rather than man." He invoked the example of Jesus Christ, who was obedient to God unto his death.

In the name of conscience he told the judges that they had a higher duty than to enforce the iniquitous laws on slavery. In the name of conscience he was ready to tell jurors that it was better to obey God than to obey man, and they must follow their consciences not the statute book when they returned their verdict. In the name of conscience he apostrophized the legislators of this country and even dared to tell that politician who had dominated the politics of our state that he had a duty, in conscience, to follow the law of God and not to extend the fatal grip of the Slave Power as far as California.

To recall what he said on the historic occasion on which he denounced Mr. Webster and lamented his great fall, he observed that our senior senator claimed that slavery would not flourish in the West because the conditions of nature were against it. He continued: "But Mr. Webster would not 'reaffirm an ordinance of nature,' nor 'reenact the will of God.' I would. I would reaffirm nothing else, enact nothing else. What is justice but the 'ordinance of nature'? What is right but 'the will of God'? When you make a law, 'Thou shalt not kill,' what do you but 'reenact the will of God'? When you make laws for the security of the 'unalienable rights' of man, and protect for every man the right to life, liberty, and the pursuit of happiness, are you not reaffirming an ordinance of nature?

"Not reenact the will of God? Why, I would enact nothing else. The will of God is a theological term; it means truth and justice, in common speech. What is the theological opposite to 'the will of God?' It is 'the will of the devil.' One of the two you must enact—either the will of God, or of the devil. The two are the only theological categories for such matters. *Aut Deus aut Diabolus.* There is no other alternative, 'Choose you which you will serve.'"

Mr. Parker took up the feeble and fallacious maxim of the Slave Power, "Religion has nothing to do with politics." He exposed it for what it was—"subjective atheism, with a political application."

He knew what the issue was in 1850: should evil be allowed to expand? That was the issue that Mr. Webster had sought to avoid. He understood where Mr. Webster's evasions led. He quoted with great effect the words of our local lawyer-poet:

> We see dimly in the Present what is small and what is great,
> Slow of faith how weak an arm may turn the iron helm of fate;
> But the soul is still oracular; amid the market's din,
> List the ominous stern whisper from the Delphic cave within—
> "They enslave their children's children, who make compromise with sin."

In the magnificent speech that he had prepared to present to the jury if one had been empaneled to try him on the trumped-up charge of conspiracy to obstruct federal justice, he concluded: "When a boy my mother lifted me up, one Sunday, and held me while I read the first monumental line I ever saw: SACRED LIBERTY AND RIGHTS OF MANKIND. Gentlemen, the Spirit of Liberty, the Love of Justice, was early fanned into a flame in my boyish heart. That monument covers the bones of my own kinsfolk; it was their blood which reddened the long, green grass at Lexington. It is my own name which stands chiseled on that stone; the tall captain who marshaled his fellow farmers and mechanics into stern array was my father's father. I learned to read out of his Bible, and with a musket he that day captured from the foe, I learned also another religious lesson, that REBELLION TO TYRANTS IS OBEDIENCE TO GOD."

Theodore Parker lived in obedience to God. He died in obedience to God. He died, like Moses, on the edge of the Promised Land; he did not enter it. He could foresee it. Time and again he prophesied what would come with so much desolation. Living close to the ground, he heard the electric currents course through the grass. And now we have had a great war that has confirmed, in blood, everything he said and prophesied. And the evil has been destroyed. The Slave Power is no more!

There are those today who would gladly forget the struggle we endured, the perils we ran, the blood we poured out. Caught up in a frenzy of materialism, in speculation in stocks and in speculation in land, they devote themselves, as they say, to the future of this country as though it did not have a past marked by sacrifice, stern duty, and true devotion to the Author of our being. The name of Parker is scarcely remembered by them. Hunkerism will have triumphed, or have seemed to triumph, if this materialist horde comes to determine our nation's destiny. But if they can from time to time neglect Mr. Parker, they can never forget Mr. Lincoln.

Our own martyred president was, it turned out, Mr. Parker's secret disciple. It is no accident that his younger associate Mr. Herndon should have addressed Mr. Parker in 1854 as "my Ideal—strong, direct, energetic, + charitable." Hesitant, ambivalent even, in his years as a lawyer and a candidate for high office, Mr. Lincoln nonetheless was instructed in the designs of that High Power, to whom Mr. Parker had allegiance. When the war came and the forces of the Union were sorely tried, Mr. Lincoln even made a kind of wager with God, if it be not impious so to describe what more properly might be called a vow, as in fact he did call it. On the eve of the battle of Antietam he resolved "that if God gave us the victory in the approaching battle, he would consider it an indication of Divine Will, and that it was his duty to move forward in the cause of emancipation." And when the tide of victory at Antietam turned in favor of the forces of the United States, Mr. Lincoln acknowledged his vow and his obligation to his Cabinet. "It might be thought strange," he said, "that he had in this way submitted to disposal of matters when the way was not clear to his mind what he should do. God had decided the question in favor of the slaves. He was satisfied it was right, was confirmed and strengthened in his action by the vow and the results."

When the even greater victory came to the Army of the Potomac at Gettysburg, the President announced the results to the country on Independence Day 1863, using the words given us by our Savior and especially desiring "that on this day, He whose will, not ours, should ever be done, be everywhere remembered and reverenced with profoundest gratitude." Eleven days later the President issued this proclamation of thanksgiving: "It has pleased Almighty God to harken to the supplications and prayers of an afflicted people and to vouchsafe to the army and navy of the United States victories on land and sea so signal and so effective as to furnish reasonable grounds for augmented confidence that the Union of these States will be maintained, their constitution preserved, and their peace and prosperity permanently restored. . . . It is meet and right to recognize and confess the presence of the Almighty Father and the power of His Hand equally in these triumphs and in these sorrows." The President invited the people on August 6 to gather in praise and prayer for the wonderful things God had "done in the nation's behalf" and to invoke "the influence of His Holy Spirit" to "change the hearts of the insurgents" and "finally to lead the whole nation, through the paths of repentance and submission to the Divine Will."

On November 19, 1863, the President spoke those memorable words known as the Gettysburg Address. He adopted from Mr. Parker's Independence Day Sermon of 1858 in the Boston Music Hall the latter's definition of democracy—"Direct Self-Government over all the people, for all the people, by all the people." The President then concluded in a truly Parkerian vein: "We here highly resolve these dead shall not have died in vain and that this nation, under God, shall have a new birth of freedom."

Shortly before the close of his life, Mr. Lincoln was inaugurated for a second term of office and gave an address so permeated with prayer, so embodying the themes of scripture, that it might have come from the pen of Mr. Parker himself. He acknowledged that both sides had invoked the same God and that both sides had read the same Bible. But he did not fail to imply where justice lay in the eyes of God:

> It may seem strange that any men should dare to ask a just God's assistance in wringing their bread from the sweat of other men's faces; but let us judge not that we be not judged. The prayers of both could not be answered; that of neither has been answered fully. The Almighty has His own purposes. "Woe unto the world because of offenses! for it must needs be that offenses come; but woe to that man by whom the offense cometh!" If we shall suppose that American Slavery is one of those offenses which, in the providence of God, must needs come, but which, having continued through His appointed time, He now wills to remove, and that He gives to both North and South, this terrible war, as the woe due to those by whom the offense came, shall we discern therein any departure from those divine attributes which the believers in a Living God always ascribe to Him? Fondly do we hope—fervently do we pray—that this mighty scourge of war may speedily pass away. Yet, if God wills that it continue, until all the wealth piled by the bond-man's two hundred and fifty years of unrequited toil shall be sunk, and until every drop of blood drawn with the lash, shall be paid by another drawn with the sword, as was said three thousand years ago, so still it must be said "the judgments of the Lord, are true and righteous altogether."
>
> With malice toward none; with charity for all; with firmness in the right, as God gives us to see the right, let us strive on to finish the work we are in; to bind up the nation's wounds; to care for him who shall have borne the bat-

tle, and for his widow and his orphan—to do all which may achieve and cherish a just and lasting peace among ourselves, and with all nations.

He had prayed. He had quoted the psalms and the judgments of the Lord. He had invoked the duty to the widow and the orphan set out in Deuteronomy. He had quoted Jesus on the woe due him by whom scandal comes. He had heeded the words of Jesus on not judging lest one be judged. He had concluded by expressing the law of charity that is the deepest of biblical doctrines. Six weeks later, on Good Friday, he was put to death.

Over and over again we have seen the parallels drawn between that death and the death of our Savior in blood of atonement dying for mankind. His death sealed the religious reading of that conflict that Mr. Parker had prophesied. In conclusion of this ceremony let us all join in the words written by Mr. Parker's parishioner and dear friend and close companion in the enterprise of emancipation. They are words that echo Mr. Parker's own evocation of the God of Isaiah in his famous sermon on the Mexican War, just as that sermon was a powerfully prophetic vision of the tragic war that was to come. They have been words that have sustained our troops in the field and the spirits of those at home who waited patiently and wept valiantly. Let us rise and sing together:

Mine eyes have seen the glory of the coming of the Lord:
He is trampling out the vintage where the grapes of wrath are stored;
He hath loosed the fateful lightning of His terrible swift sword:
His truth is marching on.

I have seen Him in the watch-fires of a hundred circling camps;
They have builded Him an altar in the evening dews and damps;
I can read His righteous sentence by the dim and flaring lamps:
His day is marching on.

I have read a fiery gospel writ in burnished rows of steel:
"As ye deal with my contemners, so with you my grace shall deal;
Let the Hero, born of woman, crush the serpent with his heel,
Since God is marching on."

He has sounded forth the trumpet that shall never call retreat;
He is sifting out the hearts of men before His judgment-seat:
Oh, be swift, my soul, to answer Him! be jubilant, my feet!
Our God is marching on.

In the beauty of the lilies Christ was born across the sea,
With a glory in his bosom that transfigures you and me:
As he died to make men holy, let us die to make men free,
While God is marching on.

CHAPTER 6

THE SORCERESS
AND THE SOURCE

THE MESSENGER BIRD
Cover of pamphlet with greetings from
William and Leslie Van Ness Denman, December 1946

"[He] is the only one who can carry the message
to the heart of the unknown mysteries."

Serenely shining at the end of the valley of the Sacramento stand the twin pinnacles of a mountain visible on a clear day from further than one hundred miles' distance. Veiled at times by white clouds, at times towering above them, the mountain commands the California plain. Trees cover its lower slope, then snow, even in summer, surrounds its volcanic core, whose heat, unexhausted, waits the moment when it will burst into unchanneled energy. Glimpsed from afar or approached on foot in ascent, Mount Shasta has a presence that speaks to the imagination or the heart. "In the mountains, there you feel free."

In Boston before I was born God marched to make moral truth. In the Boston of my boyhood God was still marching. Divinity, and the religious imagination that responds, is not restricted. In California, God had manifested himself on this mountain, or so a band of believers maintained.

On July 30, 1993, I stopped in the town at Shasta's base and visited a reading room of the I Am movement. The reading room, physically immaculate, was kept much as the movement's reading rooms had been kept in its glory days in the 1930s. On the walls were pictures of the movement's patron, Saint Germain, and of its founders, Guy and Edna Ballard. These pictures could be purchased, and I bought one of Edna, resplendent in evening dress, glowing with a radiance meant to reflect inner conviction and calm. I also bought the I Am decrees, as the movement styled its collective prayers. One such decree I read at random ran,

YOUNGER GENERATION; ALL INCOMING CHILDREN; ALL OUR INVINCIBLE GOD-VICTORIOUS ATTORNEYS AND ACCOUNTANTS, OURSELVES, AND ALL UNDER THIS RADIATION!

In the Mightiest Cosmic Love, Victory, Light, Freedom, Protection, and Perfection; Overwhelming Supply of every good thing, and the Ascended Masters' Divine Plan Fulfilled—expanding and surging with such Herculean Speed, Power, Force, and Action; such Overwhelming Cosmic Onrush of the Cosmic Love and Victory of the Cosmic Christ that nothing can stop—the Mightiest in the Universe—that has ever come to Earth in any age, that is never absent and never late—MANIFEST, MANIFEST, MANIFEST RIGHT NOW, this instant and forever!

"Almighty I AM"! (3)

Also on sale were the books of the movement beginning with Guy Ballard's *Unveiled Mysteries*, all in a variety of European languages and all published by the Saint Germain Foundation. These I did not buy. I had read them in the original in the Bancroft Library of the University of California at Berkeley. I also did not contribute to the small container on the counter labeled "Love Offerings." Finally, for only one dollar because the merchandise was used, I acquired a record I bought not for the songs but for the color blue, for this record was one of the paraphernalia of the movement made famous in the trial of the movement for fraud: the Ballards claimed that the blue had a special healing quality, the government maintained that it was just a form of commercial coloring.

The sole attendant was an elderly man whose name I learned on inquiry was John. I asked him how long he had been associated with the movement. "Since 1939 in Los Angeles," he replied. "Then you were there for the trial," I observed. "Yes, but I didn't go," he replied. I guessed that he had had a job and couldn't have spared the time. "What did you think of it?" I asked. "How did Edna take it?" "It was just one of those things that happen to great leaders," he said. "It happened to Jesus. She just rose above it." He added, "The black magicians were banished from the earth in 1939. But there are still Forces of Darkness." "When did Edna die?" I inquired, hesitating for a moment before saying "die," lest I offend his beliefs. "She passed on February 21, 1971," he responded, not choosing to say "ascended" as I expected but quietly rebuking my grosser terminology. I looked at a photograph depicting a group of persons reenacting the carrying of the Cross. "It's a pageant we do annually," he observed. "Followers come from everywhere, the United States and abroad. We do everything except the Crucifixion—for an obvious reason."

My purchases by my calculation came to $11.50. I offered John this amount. He returned a dollar, saying that he had added it up to $10.50. I went through my arithmetic aloud. He was unconvinced. I abandoned my effort, pocketed the dollar, and returned to my car. Suddenly I was aware that John was beside me. "I added it again," he said. "You owe me a dollar." The doggedness that had kept him a believer for fifty-four years was manifest once more in this tiny way as he collected what he was properly owed.

I had made this detour returning from the Shakespeare Festival in Oregon in order to obtain ocular evidence of what had become of this religious movement that had once been the object of prosecution by the United States; whose leader had gone through two federal criminal trials; whose protests had twice been heard in what is now my court, the Ninth Circuit Court of Appeals; and whose invocation of Free Exercise had been examined by the Supreme Court of the United States after that court had intervened to protect the freedom of religion against the states. Not before, not since, has the federal government indicted a religious leader for propagating the beliefs of her religion. Her story—the story of a criminal prosecution—shows that federal authority can prosecute a religion and did so when the Department of Justice was headed by a man particularly sensitive to the claims of religion and religious freedom. Her story shows how the constitutional protection afforded religion is weak compared to the protection afforded the rights of women. Her story illustrates how hard it is for a judge to maintain impartiality in dealing with religion. Her story reveals how a court cannot carry out the First Amendment without adopting a theory of religion that is a proxy for a theology. Her story manifests that a religion with close connections with Christianity may be put on trial and found to be a fraud in twentieth-century America.

I propose to tell the tale of her trials and the appeals with the lessons about Free Exercise implicit in her story.

THE VIGILANT VOICES OF THE POST OFFICE, THE JUSTICE DEPARTMENT, AND THE PRESS

Edna came from Iowa, Guy came from Kansas. They met in Chicago. Edna played the harp. Guy's occupation is obscure. They were both versed in two currents of religion coursing through the United States: Spiritualism and Theosophy. One can guess what they thought when the harpist found herself attracted to a man named Ballard. In the 1920s as a couple they nurtured the ideas and insights that tumbled out in the 1930s in printed matter that attracted the attention of the Post Office.

Investigation by the Post Office led that agency in 1940 to refer the Ballards to Justice for prosecution. At the head of the criminal division in Washington was John Rogge, in the late 1940s celebrated as the defender of government employees accused of being security risks, but famous in 1940 for breaking up the Huey Long machine in Louisiana. President Roosevelt was to advise Attorney General Jackson of "a lot of complaints" about Rogge: "that he is a self-seeker and that he is overbearing." Rogge's favorite law to catch malefactors was the broad federal statute making it a crime to use the mails to defraud; it was a statute whose robust development in the courts had made it an all-purpose tool for prosecutors, especially when it could be coupled with the general conspiracy statute. Everyone uses the mails.

A criminal conspiracy is proved if two persons agree to use the mails to set up a fraud, to make a fraudulent representation, or to deposit a check obtained by fraud. In Learned Hand's famous phrase the conspiracy statute is "the darling of the prosecutor's nursery"; the mail fraud statute is a close second as a favorite. With these two statutes in his briefcase a federal prosecutor could seek an indictment from a grand jury almost assured of getting what he asked. Rogge's mastery of these tools had led him to be called the Paul Bunyan of the grand jury system. Above Rogge was the attorney general, Robert H. Jackson, a man whose keen and impatient mind scorned bureaucratic conventions and brought vigor to whatever enterprise he directed. Justice under Jackson was a formidable force. In November 1940 the United States Attorney in Los Angeles persuaded a grand jury to indict Edna Ballard and her son for mail fraud and conspiracy to commit mail fraud; Guy was dead.

Beginning in November 1940 the following news accounts appeared in the *Los Angeles Times;* they are abridged, but verbatim:

11/25/40   LEGAL BATTERIES PREPARED
            FOR "I AM" FRAUD TRIAL
            BALLARDS AND EIGHT OF INNER CIRCLE
            CHARGED WITH USING MAILS TO SWINDLE

Mrs. Edna Ballard, sometimes known as Joan of Arc of the "I Am" movement, her son, Donald, and eight others [will go on trial, charged with] defrauding thousands by inducing them to join through asserted fantastic and false representations. . . .

Government attorneys, James Ruffin, special assistant to the Attorney General, and Norman Neukom and Ralph Lazarus, Assistant United States Attorneys, maintain the issue is "just another mail fraud trial," although they admit it contains "unusual features." On the other side, however, Charles H. Carr and W. J. Gilbert, representing the defendants, contend "it is no such thing" and that the religious issue is bound to be injected.

12/13/40   "I AM" JURY
            HEARS STORY
            OF MIRACLE

Ballard Writing About
Meeting St. Germain
Read at Trial

"My brother, if you will hand me your cup I will give you a much more refreshing drink than spring water." Such was the meeting had with the Ascended Master St. Germain in 1930 by the late Guy W. Ballard in the shadow of majestic Mt. Shasta. . . . Asst. U.S. Atty Ralph Lazarus yesterday read of this meeting from the "Unveiled Mysteries" written by Ballard under his pen name Godfre Ray King.

"I obeyed and instantly the cup was filled with a creamy liquid," the prosecutor read from the book. "Handing it back to me, he said 'Drink it.'

"I did so and must have looked my astonishment, for, while the taste was delicious, the electrical vivifying effect on my mind and body made me gasp with surprise."

Continuing the reading, Lazarus related to the jury that St. Germain had then informed Ballard that the drink came from the universal supply and that it was life itself.

Gold in Palm

"'Whatever I desire,'" St. Germain told the surprised Ballard, "'manifests itself when I command in love. I held out the cup and that which I desired for you appeared.

"'See! I have but to hold out my hand and if I wish to use gold—gold is here.'

"Instantly there lay in his palm a disk about the size of a $10 gold piece."

The reading of Ballard's "meeting the master" preceded the testimony of Carl Pierce, a friend of the Ballards for many years . . . :

"[Ballard] often spoke [to me in the 1920s] of St. Germain, whom he said he met in Pershing Square, and later in the Hollywood hills. He told me he looked like any other person."

12/14/40 "I AM" BOOKS QUOTED AT TRIAL
AS "STAIRWAY TO ASCENSION"

Passage Read to Jury Depicts Jesus Crediting
Ballards with More Power Than He Possessed

. . . .

Attorney Lazarus then read to the jury a lecture delivered by Ballard from the 'Beloved Master Jesus' Discourse,' wherein Jesus spoke directly to the students of the class through Ballard.

The government maintains that all of these discourses which are attributed to St. Germain and Jesus were in reality written by Ballard. . . .

"I healed many people, but only a small number in comparison to that which their calls to Life and Light have called to action for the people of America."

This remarkable utterance, wherein Jesus credits the Ballards with greater power than He possessed, the prosecution cites as one of the representations made by the Ballards and known by them to be false.

12/18/40   SUBMARINE
           PLOT ENTERS
           "I AM" CASE

Panama Canal Saved
by Power of K-17,
Mail Fraud Jury Hears

In October, 1939, three submarines from Germany, one carrying the plans of Adolf Hitler for world domination, were headed for the Panama Canal. . . .

Instead of reaching the Canal the three submarines were dissolved by the mysterious power of K-17, an Ascended Master, who operated through the late Guy W. Ballard, leader of the "I Am" groups. . . .

Mrs. Madge King, investigator for the San Francisco Better Business Bureau, had testified under questioning of Attorney Lazarus that she had heard similar "discourses" given by Ballard at a meeting in San Francisco.

12/19/40   LATE DISCIPLE'S "ASCENSION" BECOMES ISSUE AT "I AM"
              TRIAL
           DOCTOR'S TESTIMONY REFUTES
           CULT'S SUPERNATURAL CLAIMS

"Did Frank Kelly make an ascension?"

This question became a burning issue in the court of United States District Judge Leon R. Yankwich yesterday. . . .

One of the government's former witnesses, Ernest Ricord, realty salesman, had testified Ballard had stated that Kelly, being a "100 percenter," made an immediate ascension. Ricord said he went to Kelly's funeral.

Yesterday the government produced Dr. W. Curtis Brigham, Los Angeles physician, who told of treating Kelly several years ago for hardening of the arteries and told of having been called in a few moments after Kelly died in 1939. . . . It [the body] had not ascended.

11/21/40   BALLARDS SUED OVER "I AM" BOOK

"Unveiled Mysteries" Said to Have Been
Copied From Another

Asserting that the book "Unveiled Mysteries" published under the pen name of the late Guy W. Ballard, one of the founders of the "I Am" movement, was copied in part from the book "A Dweller on Two Planets" written nearly 50 years ago, a suit charging infringement and accounting was filed yesterday in Federal court.

Plaintiffs in the suit are Leslie Robert Oliver, son of Frederick Spencer

Oliver, author of "A Dweller on Two Planets," and the Borden Publishing Co.

1/8/41   "I AM" SOLVED MYSTERIES
         OF LIFE, YOUNG MAN SAYS

About Ready To Believe Human Beings Once
Swung By Tails Before He Found Himself

"I was just about ready to believe that human beings once swung by their tails and then I found myself and joined the 'I Am' movement."

John Paul Center, 27-year-old former Detroit steel worker, told a jury in United States Judge Leon R. Yankwich's court yesterday that life was quite a mystery to him until at the age of 22 he took up the teachings of the late Guy W. Ballard and his wife, Edna Ballard. . . .

The [defense] witnesses ranged from the youthful Center to 75-year-old Frank Holmes, an osteopathic physician of Spokane.

The newspaper stories stressed what would attract the attention of an average reader and, it may be inferred, the attention of an average juror. Assistant United States Attorney Lazarus had emphasized what might appear inconsistent (the belief in pure followers' ascension and their actual deaths); megalomaniac (the destruction of German submarines, greater success than Jesus); and untrue (Ballard spoke to Pierce of talking to Saint Germain in the 1920s but wrote in *Unveiled Mysteries* that he first met Saint Germain in 1930). Above all, Lazarus read the Ballards' claims as literal. A notably large amount of the government's case consisted in statements made by Guy Ballard. Guy Ballard had declared in *Unveiled Mysteries* that his adventures on Mt. Shasta were "as *real* and *true* as mankind's experience on this earth today." On Shasta he had encountered the young man who gave him the cup of life; he had met Saint Germain, clad in "a white, jewelled robe"; he had been taken back to an earlier age where he, Guy Ballard, had been a woman singing before the queen of France and to a yet earlier existence where he was an assistant priest in a temple at Luxor at which Edna was a vestal virgin and their son, Donald, the high priest. He had had a second tryst on Shasta with Saint Germain where he had been menaced by a panther, whom he, Guy Ballard, overcame with love. These were the experiences that he characterized *as real* and *true* as any other earthly event.

At the trial Lazarus tried to show that Ballard had not even been at Shasta at the time claimed. This contention was rebutted by letters from Guy to Edna sent from under the shadow of Shasta in the fall of 1930 when Ballard claimed to be there. With this little battle won by the Ballards, Lazarus persisted in suggesting that the meetings with St. Germain, understood by the government as physical events, never took place. In the same vein the government presented its case on Kelly's ascension as though the Ballards had asserted that Kelly had never met with earthly extinction. The *Los Angeles Times* did not pause to dwell on Lazarus doubting the resurrection of the dead.

The jury heard the evidence over a two-month period, with time out to celebrate Christmas. The jury heard the arguments of counsel and retired to deliberate. The jury was puzzled, as the following headlines recount:

1/20/41   RELIGIOUS ISSUE KEEPS "I AM" JURY OUT AFTER THREE
                 DAYS
                 DEFENDANTS WAIT CALMLY

Twelve Apparently Ignore
Judge's Admonition To
Ponder Fraud Angle Only

1/21/41   "I AM" JURORS
                 ACQUIT THREE,
                 SPLIT ON SIX

Government Undecided
Whether to Give New
Trial to Mrs. Ballard

GLIB PREVARICATOR OR
SPOKESMAN FOR DIVINE JUSTICE

While Justice made up its mind, the Post Office, the initiator of the criminal proceedings, took limited action. It resorted to the administrative powers within its reach and recommended that a "fraud order" be entered barring Edna Ballard and her publishing company from using the mails. Among other details, the recommendation cited the Ballards' income as reported by them and entered as an exhibit at the trial:

	Gross	Net
1935	$57,974	$9,351
1936	68,958	20,673
1937	151,961	14,297
1938	156,583	14,253

In June 1942 there was a hearing at the Post Office, but the fraud order was not put in force until the conclusion of the second criminal trial.

Meanwhile, the Justice Department, still under Robert Jackson, had signaled the United States Attorney in Los Angeles that he could try again. The government obtained what the Los Angeles *Times* benevolently described as a "streamlined" version of the 1940 indictment for mail fraud and conspiracy to commit mail fraud, limiting the defendants to Edna Ballard; her son, Donald; and four associates. The fraud was charged to consist in eighteen representations made by the defendants that they "well knew" to be "false and untrue":

1. That Guy Ballard "had attained a supernatural state of immortality";

2. That Guy Ballard was "a divine messenger," selected as a medium for communications from Saint Germain;

3. That the three Ballards had been selected as divine messengers because of their "high spiritual attainments and righteous conduct";

4. That through the three Ballards the messages of "divine entities" were transmitted to mankind;

5. That these messages were "absolutely essential to the salvation of mankind";

6. That the Ballards could transmit to others "the ability to conquer disease, death, old age, poverty, and misery";

7. That the Ballards could heal curable and medically incurable diseases and had in fact cured "hundreds";

8. That, by obeying the doctrines of the movement, their followers would "be able to achieve perfect bodies and heal themselves of all human ailments";

9. That the Ballards had a "supernatural ability to bring forth from a supernatural state, money, riches, and other material means necessary to mankind";

10. That the Ballards' books "were the result of divine visitations and dictation";

11. That their magazines, letters, decrees and musical compositions were "divinely inspired and dictated";

12. That the welfare of the United States depended on obeying their teaching;

13. That the picture of Saint Germain circulated by the defendants was the result of a visitation of Saint Germain to the artist;

14. That purchase of certain charts and phonograph records sold by the defendants would bring the purchasers "great blessings and rewards in their aim to achieve salvation";

15. That ascended masters would actually appear "in physical form" before a meeting of the followers;

16. That the end of the world was approaching within the lifetime of persons now living;

17. That criticism or question of their teachings would be punished by the ascended masters;

18. That those following their teachings "would achieve the ability to make their actual physical ascension in their physical, tangible bodies and would in fact ascend and not die."

The organization of the I Am movement itself was alleged to be part of the scheme to defraud hatched by Edna and her associates, as was the organization of the company publishing the movement's books, the St. Germain Press in Chicago, and the organization of I Am's branch offices, meeting rooms, and reading rooms in thirteen cities from Los Angeles to Boston. On its face, the indictment put the religion itself—its works and teachings—on trial as a conspiracy to commit criminal fraud.

A federal indictment is a fearsome thing. Edna Ballard was not without resources. From the beginning of the investigation by the Post Office she had had the advice of the Chicago firm of Nash & Donnelly, the leading lawyers in the country in the defense of mail fraud. Horace Donnelly, a graduate of Georgetown, had entered the service of the Post Office as a lawyer in 1910 and as recently as 1934 had been its solicitor or head of its legal department. Edna Ballard said he had written the mail fraud statute of 1909; it was not uncharacteristic of her way of putting an important idea inexactly in a flamboyant manner. With his old-fashioned first name, his courtly style, and his great experience, Donnelly could scarcely have been bettered as defense counsel in a mail fraud prosecution.

Counsel advised the Ballards to demur, the same tack they had tried unsuccessfully with Judge Leon Yankwich. The demurrer admitted all the government's allegations and raised the issue of religious freedom, asserting that, even if all the facts were exactly as the government charged, the First Amendment gave the defendants immunity. Judge Yankwich, an immigrant from Rumania, self-described as Protestant, had not been impressed and had ordered the case to trial. Here a different judge, J. F. T. O'Connor, a native of North Dakota, self-described as Catholic, was equally unmoved. Following Yankwich's precedent, he ruled that the truth of the Ballards' beliefs would not be an issue, only their sincerity; in that way, he informed the defendants, their religion would not be on trial.

Judge O'Connor was also untroubled by an attack made by the defense from a different angle: there had been no women on the grand jury that returned the indictment and there were no women in the pool from which the petit jury would be drawn. Such had been the practice from time immemorial of the federal court in Los Angeles; it was no reason, Judge O'Connor found, not to proceed with the trial. A male jury was to try the case. And the prosecutors, the trial judge, and all the appellate judges were to be male. Appropriately enough, the crime charged was mail fraud. Only the principal defendant was female.

Trial itself was conducted during the Christmas season of 1941, beginning shortly before the bombing of Pearl Harbor in December and continuing into January. The war came into the trial at its conclusion. In his closing to the jurymen Lazarus told them that they were doing "a patriotic service" in assuring a better America to which her servicemen would return.

The prosecution produced thirty-three witnesses. A number of them, former Ballard staff, were used to prove that the Ballard books were promoted by mail and were profitable; that the Ballard broadcasts were promoted by mail and were profitable; and that the love gifts at the Ballard meetings, although an average of eight cents per person, exceeded the costs. As the Post Office had already shown, the Ballards made money. None of these receipts were connected to particular representations made by the Ballards. If the profits were criminal, it would be because I Am as a whole was a scam. This part of the case established that the defendants used the mails to obtain money and to deposit it.

The second prong of the government's case went to showing that the Ballards made untrue statements. (Judge O'Connor's ruling that the truth of the religion was not an issue was not treated as an obstacle.) Phonograph records sold by the Ballards carried a blue label; their brochures stated that the blue had a special healing quality. Louis Goldberg of Hollywood, manufacturer of the records, testified that the blue he used was ordinary coloring, devoid, as far as he knew, of medicinal value. Neither the Ballards themselves nor their followers had overcome illness or death. Guy Ballard had used ointments and laxatives; according to his personal secretary, "he used Feenamint more than anything else." A chiropractor testified to treating him. An osteopath had made out his death certificate; he was mortal. Dr. Brigham again testified to seeing Frank Kelly's dead body and Ernest Ricord to going to Kelly's funeral. Ballard and Kelly were proved to be as dead as Scrooge's partner Marley. No resurrection or ascension of their bodies had occurred.

The prosecutor's third step was to show the fraudulent state of mind of the defendants. The government proved that, before the events narrated by Guy as occurring on Mount Shasta, Edna Ballard used to read similar accounts aloud to her Theosophy class in Chicago; the books she read from were named. When *Unveiled Mysteries* was still in manuscript Edna read from it to the same group, correcting the manuscript—divine dictation or revelation seemed subject to her editorial pen. Virginia La Ferrera, an organist for the movement, testified that she had written the music of "Call to Light"; Guy Ballard had informed the class that the Goddess of Light had given him the tune to give to her; she had not seen the Goddess of Light. When Guy Ballard told a San Francisco meeting that the Great Hercules would speak, Madge King of the Better Business Bureau said, the speaker who followed was merely Ballard closing his eyes and using a deep voice. When an I Am teacher had told Edna that the teacher could not make people believe that Ascended Master Hercules was standing in the building, Edna had replied, "I can make them believe anything," and added, "Most of the people would come to me on their hands and knees if I told them to." If the last statement showed arrogance rather than intent to defraud, the government did not mind suggesting that Edna was a bully at heart.

Finally, the government sought to show that the Ballards' statements had actually deceived other persons—that others had relied on their representations. The government found fallen-away followers of the movement who had understood its teachings literally: Margaret Huntley Schall, the widow of United States Senator Thomas Schall of Minnesota, testified, "I actually believed I would be able to accomplish physical precipitation," and she had moved to Los Angeles because Mrs. Ballard had said that in the coming golden age Los Angeles would be the City of Light. George Thomas Stevens, an auditor for the California Board of Equalization, declared he would not have bought the Ballards' book if he "had felt that the incidents therein related were visionary." Katherine Rogers, a singer who also wrote words and music for the movement, had developed doubts and was warned by Guy Ballard that as a consequence her physical body might dissolve in six weeks and that she would certainly not sing again; she had stayed on awhile, coerced by the fear that these things might happen.

The government produced no smoking gun—no witness who was promised, say, a cancer cure in return for cash. What the government did show was a mass of teachings about prayer, life after death, and the curing of present temporary ills, which some persons had understood literally, had purchased literature to read about, and had offered gifts to support. The government painted an unattractive picture of the two principal defendants—the son, Donald, a PK or Preacher's Kid, a teenager in the 1930s who sometimes showed a surly skepticism about his parents' oratory; and Edna, the chief organizer, the "queen bee," as Prosecutor Lazarus described her in unflattering, unconsciously antifeminist terms.

The defense, presenting forty-three witnesses in all, relied chiefly on I Am followers (not paid staff) who were satisfied by the I Am teachings. They came from around the country. They were mature persons. The defense was that if these sensible, respectable people were believers, I Am could not be a racket.

The defense led off with Alfred J. Zimmerman, an accountant for the Philco Corporation, a married man and parent of a child. Since becoming a follower, he testified, there had been "much greater harmony and peace of mind in our entire household. . . . Our health has been much better, all three of us, the entire household, and there are untold blessings that have come to us." Zimmerman was followed by Walter A. Haldy, a Cleveland physician and member of the American Medical Association, who became a follower through reading *Unveiled Mysteries*. The movement had "produced a great feeling of peace and it has produced a great feeling of inward strength." It had not led him to give up using ordinary medical procedures in the treatment of the ill and the injured. Elsa Chamberlain, a small business proprietor from Madison, Wisconsin, told how the movement had "taken away from me the feeling of futility."

So it went, with each witness testifying, in a fashion that did not appear to be contrived or concerted, to benefits of health, harmony, purposefulness, and interior strengthening. The witnesses had not understood the I Am doctrines with lethal literalism. Precipitation, the Ballards' term for an answer to a prayer, for them occurred through "normal channels that we know of in ordinary life" (Alfred J. Zimmerman); "the normal channel of precipitation would be the pay envelope" (Dewey C. B. Hawley, assistant manager for the New York Telephone Company). They had not learned that the physical body would ascend at death but "the purified essence." They had not been told that cataclysms would overtake the country or world at any specific time. The witnesses had never heard the Ballards threaten anyone. The witnesses had never been told that they must make offerings or buy Ballard books. Of their own free will, because they believed in the movement, they had been its supporters.

Even the apostates that the government had put on the stand had testified that the Ballards would say, "Don't believe us, prove us." The defense witnesses had proved them. "I proved it by applying the law" (Agnes Regina Kelly, Bureau of Statistics, Interstate Commerce Commission, no relation to the deceased Frank Kelly). "Why shouldn't I believe they were right about other things that I had not yet attained to." For at least some, Guy Ballard's stories were not the attraction: "I would have bought the books for the law even though the narratives were not true. The law I refer to is the law of life, the law of our being. . . . I have been seeking all my life to know why I am here and where I am going, and how I am going to get there. . . . It has answered everything " (Jane Magnuson of Chicago).

As one reads the testimony of the defense witnesses, one realizes that here was a movement whose patron saint could have been Alexis de Tocqueville. Already a master ascended into the pantheon of American thought, would he have savored the irony of this middle-class spiritualism meeting his criteria? Like Tocqueville's ideal religion, the I Am movement did not seek to change the world or reform the country. It did offer counsel against using tobacco. It was ostentatiously patriotic. But its methods and goals and attractions were apolitical. What it chiefly offered was a meaning for life and the assurance of immortality. According to Tocqueville, a wise religion offered no more.

The climactic defense witness was Edna herself. On direct examination she declared, "I have never intentionally or at any time made any false or untrue statements to any person in connection with the I Am activity, nor said anything that I did not honestly and sincerely believe to be for the good of the 'I Am' students and for their temporal and eternal benefit." The defense asked no further questions.

The prosecution was not so restrained and did inquire if she had met Saint Germain and if she had shaken hands with him. She responded affirmatively. Were the adventures of her husband in *Unveiled Mysteries* true? They were "true, actual experiences" and "took place at the times stated." They were not adventures "in dreamland." They were not "in the physical body." They were in "the etheric body." The Ballards had never threatened believers who doubted but the Ballards had predicted

what doubt would do: "Doubt kills just as sure as bullets." She concluded
with a discourse on her "inner work": "I represent the call of the American people for divine justice to worship God as we please."

Lazarus then addressed the jury for four hours, assailing "this Ballard
racket, as we might call it in argument," "a flim-flam scheme that has
been unparalleled in history." Jesus, "a mild self-effacing man," as
Lazarus put it, had been made into a book salesman. As for the Ballards'
invocation of Saint Germain, it was "just as I might name somebody Sam
and hold him responsible for all my answers and say, 'You will have to
ask Sam about that.'" The followers understood the Ballards' experiences
to be "real true adventures. That is where the fraud comes in, gentlemen." Edna herself was "a glib prevaricator."

The closing argument for the defense began with Guy's letters to Edna
from Mount Shasta before the I Am books were written: was Guy trying to defraud his own wife? Did both of them practice fraud on their
child, Donald? "What man is there of you, whom if his son ask bread,
will give him a stone? Or, if a fish, will he give him a serpent?" There
was no representation by the Ballards that these experiences took place
"in the physical body." They believed in the life of the spirit. "God to
these people is an everyday proposition." Of course they needed money
for their work: it is "a Christian activity— . . . it requires money to sustain it."

Parallels with Scripture were paraded. The Ballards' teaching on precipitation was matched by the parable of the mustard seed; their teaching on the ascensions of pure followers was compared to the biblical accounts of Elihu and Elisha, of the Resurrection and the Ascension. The
jury was reminded that for years after the Gospels were written "those
things were claimed to be as blasphemous and as untrue and as unworthy of belief as are these statements here." The right of the free exercise
of religion, the jury was reminded, "is a peculiar right": "all seemingly
believe in it" until "a particular case presents itself where the religion exercised is different from one's own."

The government rebutted. Judge O'Connor then instructed the jury. He
read the religion portion of the First Amendment and stated, "This case
does not present a question of the lawfulness of the calling of a mental
healer, or of a religious healer, or whether or not mental science or prayer
healing is a fraud, but it presents the question of the good faith of the defendants. . . . And I charge you that even though a person or persons are
advocating a religious activity, that they must do so in good faith. . . . The
question of the defendants' good faith is the cardinal question in this case.

"The defendants in this case made certain representations of beliefs in a divinity and in a supernatural power. Some of the teachings or representations of the defendants might seem extremely improbable to a great many people—for instance: the appearance of Jesus to dictate some of the works which have been introduced in evidence; the incident testified to by one of the defendants, Mrs. G. W. Ballard, that she shook hands with Jesus and that frequently Saint Germain and other 'ascended masters' appeared to defendant, Mrs. Ballard, and gave certain dictations— these and other similar representations and statements might seem highly improbable to many people. Whether these incidents actually happened or not is not for your consideration. The religious beliefs of these defendants are not an issue in this court and not for your consideration. The issue is: 'did these defendants honestly and in good faith, believe that these incidents actually happened?'"

THE RELIGION ON TRIAL

The practice of prayer and faith in the power of prayer, belief in the immortality of each person, a distinction drawn between what is physically observable and the underlying reality for the believer—these are thoughts and tropes, principles and practices, common to Christianity. I Am's incorporation of them was obscured by two intermediaries between the modern movement and its biblical base in the Christianity of nineteenth-century America: Spiritualism and Theosophy. If the government had had the inclination to investigate in depth, if the defense had had the opportunity to do research into the roots, a brief history of these earlier ancestors of I Am would have illuminated the connection.

Spiritualism, the older cousin, had flourished in the wake of the Civil War, attracting, at least to some degree, the attention of as many as one million Americans in a population of twenty-five million. As intelligent and indefatigable a student of religion as William James was attracted by Spiritualism's central idea, that the dead could communicate with the living. In 1890 James sent a report, to be read in London by his brother Henry, to the Society for Psychical Research relating his observations of a medium named Leonora Pipes. In a seance, she had "showed most startling intimacy with [our] family affairs." He withheld judgment as to her sources but came to the conclusion that she had not gained her knowledge "by the ordinary waking use of her ears and eyes and wits." One source, he noted cautiously, could be in "the extra-consciousness," a faculty beyond sensation. For James, spiritualists were to be taken seriously even if their methods were not understood. How enticing their beliefs were in an America where the Calvinism that had been New England's backbone had cracked, the old biblical creeds were in doubt, and the Christianity of Theodore Parker had been followed by the war that racked the republic.

From Russia, into the American cultural strain cultivated by Spiritualism, came Helena Blavatsky, neé von Hahn. At a spiritualist seance in Chittenden, Vermont, at which various deceased persons appeared, Blavatsky encountered in the flesh a New York lawyer, Henry Street Olcott; he gave her insights a corporate form. In 1875 the Theosophical Society was formed, Olcott president, Blavatsky corresponding secretary and dominant party. Drawing on a dozen other books of a similar kind, Blavatsky in 1877 published *Isis Unveiled*, a mixture of gnosticism, Buddhism, Hinduism, Spiritualism, and the Kabbala. Critics documented her extensive plagiarisms; Olcott said that she "drew from the Astral light"; she herself declared, "Somebody who knows all dictates to me," adding that this person told her what manuscripts and what published works to copy. Blavatsky might be a plagiarist but anyone familiar with the development of other religions knew that religious writers often borrowed from predecessors without sensing themselves deprived of divine inspiration. In Scripture itself, Chronicles was based on Kings, Deuteronomy was a reflection on earlier legislation, the Synoptic Gospels incorporated a common source. Copying is not a charge that causes much discomfort among believers of a creed.

In 1885 the Society for Psychical Research in London investigated and pronounced the letters to Blavatsky from her mahatmas in Tibet to be her own forgeries. Blavatsky shrugged off the condemnation: "the Forces of Darkness" were seeking to discredit her. She survived the stain. Her Russian contemporary Vsevolod Solove'v acknowledged her "unique, fiery talent" and her "stormy, wild energy," adding that these qualities were united to a "perversity of the soul." The most recent historian of her movement, Maria Carlson, describes her as "an untraditional, creative and stimulating woman," who "lied to herself and others with equal facility"; a "charismatic, hypnotic personality," who "consciously mythologized her very existence"; "a genius and a charlatan."

In Blavatsky's writings Saint Germain took shape as "this great man, this pupil of Indian and Egyptian hierophants," "until this time a living mystery." He existed during the French Revolution, which he had predicted in detail. But he also appeared to have lived at the court of Francis I and to be three hundred years old. He had the ability to turn small diamonds into large ones and transmute metal into gold. He was called "the Prince of Imposters." But, Blavatsky added, "No great man's reputation was ever yet allowed to rest undisturbed." She asked, "Did he die?" and indirectly answered negatively, for Saint Germain is "one of the grandest characters of modern times."

Theosophy thrived after Blavatsky's death in 1891, its world leadership assumed by another woman, Annie Besant, a former Anglican. In Blavatsky's native land it appealed to Russians restive under the regime of Orthodoxy but skeptical of materialism; the symbolists Andrei Belyi and Wassily Kandinsky drew on it; at the same time its success in Russia "went hand in hand with the Women's Movement"; and like the Women's Movement it was suppressed by Communism. Its largest following was in India, a land whose own religious doctrines were reflected in Blavatsky's prose. In the skeptical, faith-starved West it also struck receptive chords. Edvard Munch, the Norwegian painter, felt his faith in conventional Christianity collapse in the 1880s with the deaths of his mother and sister; he nourished himself on Spiritualism mixed with Annie Besant's version of Theosophy; his treatment of color auras is owed to her; blue became of special significance. Piet Mondrian is another artist who went through a Theosophical phase. In 1916 C. S. Lewis took note of the movement as did Maeterlinck. A particularly responsive city was Dublin. William Butler Yeats for a period was a Theosophist and borrowed "gyres" and other concepts from Blavatsky. George Russell ("A. E."—the Theosophists liked initials for names) presided over the Dublin lodge and in that capacity was mocked in *Ulysses* by James Joyce, who himself drew ideas from Blavatsky and her follower and biographer, A. P. Sinnett. Metempsychosis (Molly Bloom's "met him what?") is arguably "a directive theme" of *Ulysses*. *The Portrait of the Artist as a Young Man* closes with Stephen Dedalus's declaration that bears a Theosophical sense: "I go to encounter for the millionth time the reality of experience. . . ." Having broken from Protestant or Catholic orthodoxy, the Irish writers were still avid for immortality; and these creative spirits were captivated, at least for a period, by Theosophy's dazzling recipe that brought poetry and purpose to their lives.

Astonishing as it is to an American who encounters Theosophy only as preached by the Ballards and summarized by their prosecutors, the propositions of Theosophy were taken seriously by persons of high intellectual abilities and great creative gifts; and Theosophy exercised an attraction although Helena Blavatsky was as open to uncomfortable criticism as Edna Ballard. In a long view of cultural history, Theosophy in Europe was a spiritual symptom; it had the life of a fad and faded among Western intellectuals. T. S. Eliot teased in 1920:

> I shall not want Pipit in Heaven:
> Madame Blavatsky will instruct me
> In the Seven Sacred Trances;
> Piccarda de Donati will conduct me.

Louis MacNeice observed the triumph of mundane considerations:

> It's no go the Yogi-man, it's no go Blavatsky,
> All we want is a bank balance and a bit of skirt in a taxi.

The infiltration of theosophical ideas into high culture had, however, given Theosophy a certain respectability and seriousness. Rudolf Steiner, a member of the Theosophical Society from 1902 until 1912, founded a variant, Anthroposophy, combining Christianity, Rosicrucian doctrine, and Theosophy. In Exodus 3:14, God gives His name to Moses as "I am." In the Gospel according to John 8:58, Jesus declares, "Before Abraham was, I am." Lecturing on John, Steiner taught: "The earth exists in order that the full self-consciousness, the 'I Am', may be given to mankind." His exposition sounded a note heard in the Ballards: each must develop the "I Am" within. Like the Ballards, Steiner's "spiritual science" distinguished the physical body from the astral or etheric body that would participate actively in the spiritual world.

Steiner, Blavatsky, and the Theosophical Society are entries in the *Encyclopedia of Religion*, published in 1987 under the editorship of a renowned scholar of religion, Mircea Eliade. The Ballards and the I Am movement are not. Yet a historian of Theosophy observes that "the greatest popularity" that Theosophy achieved in America came through the Ballards' movement, whose name and theology must be seen in terms of these roots and in terms of the Christian culture from which the movement issued.

Just as Blavatsky had come from an Orthodox upbringing, Besant from Anglicanism, and Steiner from Catholicism, so a number of I Am followers had been "Bible students." They quoted the Gospel of John in corresponding with the Ballards. Muriel Bliss, familiar as she put it with "the many discrepancies in the Bible," did not find the Ballards' teaching surprising. Arthur Buck was an ordained Campbellite minister. Grace Ade was the advertising manager of the New York Greater Federation of Christian Churches. Others, such as Agnes Regina Kelly, had Catholic baptismal names. The I Am movement spoke to the earlier vision these followers had held of the universe.

To those who were unpersuaded, the language of the system appeared to consist in unsubtle neologisms that were too raw to swallow. Compared with older, more complex systems, the new religion seemed to lack balance or to lack depth. These negative metaphors—uncooked, unbalanced, shallow—convey in physical images what is a complicated spiritual response. But I Am did appeal to Americans who came out of a culture partly shaped by Christian customs and beliefs. From a European perspective, the Americans were a generation or so late; but unlike the Europeans it was Americans without strong literary or aesthetic sensibilities who were most attracted to old insights put in a new way. Theosophy spoke to a European elite, an American middle class. In most of the world, Theosophy ran its course exposed only to genteel critiques; in the Soviet Union alone it was proscribed as a religion. In America alone was its offspring prosecuted as a fraud.

"PROBABLY THE GREATEST BLOW DELIVERED TO RELIGIOUS FREEDOM"

The jury took the case Friday, deliberated late into the evening, and on Saturday returned a verdict. Edna was convicted of seven uses of the mails in furtherance of a scheme to defraud, Donald of three; their associates were acquitted. It was not possible to tell from the verdict what representations the jury found false. In terms of the indictment "any representation" was enough to convict if it were fraudulent. Judge O'Connor sentenced Edna to a year in "an institution of County Jail type," suspended the sentence, and put her on probation for a year; he also fined her $3,000. He gave Donald a suspended sentence of thirty days and a $400 fine. The Ballards appealed to the United States Court of Appeals for the Ninth Circuit.

The panel of the Ninth Circuit that heard the appeal consisted of William Denman, seventy-one, of San Francisco, the presiding judge; Albert Lee Stephens, sixty-nine, of Los Angeles, and Clifton Mathews, sixty-three, a native Georgian now of Arizona, all appointees of Franklin Roosevelt. Physically they sat together to hear the case in a grand public building at the intersection of Seventh and Mission Streets in San Francisco in a courtroom whose murals celebrated the presence of federal power in the Pacific. Bound by oath and custom, they struggled to observe the precedents, the rules of law, the Constitution of the United

States. But no judge thinks exactly like any other judge. As Benjamin Cardozo observed of all judges while stating his own experience, "We may try to see things as objectively as we please. Nonetheless we can never see them with any eyes except our own." Quoting William James, Cardozo noted that each judge will have a particular personal sense of "the total push and pressure of the cosmos" and that sense will shape what the judge will see. Of the three judges on the *Ballard* panel, Denman had the dominant personality and the keenest interest in religion. He identified himself as a Unitarian, an identification now carrying little sympathy with dogmatic Christianity. His will was to contain a substantial bequest for scholarships in comparative religion at the University of California in Berkeley. Ultimately in *Ballard* it was Denman's sense of the components of the cosmos that was to decide the case.

On the first round of argument what captured Denman's and Mathews's votes was error in the trial judge's repeated ruling that the sincerity of the Ballards, not the truth of their beliefs, was what the jury must decide. The Ballards' experienced counsel had never objected to this way of framing the issue. They had even explicitly acknowledged that it was "the law of the case," that is, the law under which it was agreed that the trial should proceed. They had conducted their short examination of Edna on that basis. Now Edna's new counsel attacked what old counsel had accepted. It was a risky and unconventional strategy, and it worked.

The opinion was assigned by Denman to Mathews, probably because his was the swing vote. He gave a mechanical recitation of the indictment and made a perfunctory analysis of the arguments. He concluded that what the mail fraud statute criminalized was not insincerity but lying. The government had to prove "that some, at least, of the representations which they [the defendants] schemed to make were false. . . . Whether such representations were false or true was a question which should have been submitted to the jury." Mail fraud consisted in untrue, not insincere statements. The Ballards had been tried for the wrong crime. Their conviction was reversed, and the case remanded for a new trial.

Stephens dissented, and the United States petitioned the court for reconsideration. Now Denman entered the lists, making clear what troubled him with Judge O'Connor's treatment of the case: "The district court did not give its reason for its ruling and instruction. If the reason be because such facts could occur in no possible chain of natural causation, it is a denial to the religious of the right to prove one of the bases of their belief in the intervention of the supernatural in the daily lives of human beings—an obvious denial of the freedom of religion of the First Amendment of the Constitution." Denman's explanation was that of a man thoroughly aware of the degree to which the intervention of the supernatural was woven into the substance of most of the religions of the world; his explanation did not address the propriety under the First Amendment of putting the truth of a religious claim before a jury.

Mathews's opinion and Denman's concurrence had an infuriating effect upon the district judge who had tried the case. When Mathews's opinion came down, Judge O'Connor fired off two letters to Charles Fahy, Solicitor General of the United States, the officer who would decide if the government would seek reversal of the Ninth Circuit in the Supreme Court of the United States. O'Connor observed that the trial had consumed two months, generating over 5,000 pages of transcript. The circuit had found a single error—an error in a ruling that he had actually taken from a 1917 decision by the circuit itself. On three separate occasions the attorneys for both sides had agreed before him to accept this ruling that sincerity not truth was the issue being tried. It was outrageous to let the defendants attack the ground rules they had accepted.

When, on rehearing before the circuit, Denman declared that the district court had committed "an obvious denial" of religious freedom, O'Connor was beside himself. The day after he received word of Denman's comments, he wrote Wendell Berge, the current head of the Criminal Division. The next day, in a letter beginning "Dear Bill," he sent a copy of his letter to Berge to Justice William O. Douglas, addressed to Douglas at his home in Silver Spring, Maryland. The letter to Berge, along with one of the letters to the solicitor general is now filed with Douglas's papers on the case in the Library of Congress. What Douglas was presented with secretly, without the knowledge of the defendants, was a vigorous petition for certiorari, penned by the trial judge. Without authorization from the law or support in judicial ethics, the trial judge had become an advocate for the prosecution.

In the letter to Berge, O'Connor recited the agreement of the attorneys to his ruling and added citations to other precedents now flouted by the Ninth Circuit. He reported that trial defense counsel had told him that the defendants had no ground for appeal; the new lawyers had offered to secure a reversal without even having read the transcript. O'Connor's legal critique was subordinate to a more personal concern. As a Catholic, he saw ominous implications for his church in Denman's approach. He wrote, "One great organization believes in the miracles of Lourdes—under this opinion it would be necessary for that particular organization, preaching this article of faith, to prove it in a court before a jury, or be subject to conviction, imprisonment or fine, or both." In his view, not the prosecution of the I Am religion as a fraud, but the decision of the Ninth Circuit was "probably the greatest blow delivered to religious freedom" in America.

THE LAW KNOWS NO HERESY?

In due course Solicitor General Fahy (himself a Catholic) did apply for certiorari, and in due course the United States Supreme Court granted it. William O. Douglas was assigned the opinion of the Court.

Politically, the court was dominated by New Deal appointees, seven in all; partisan politics played no discernible role in the decision. The justices' understanding of religion was decisive, at least the first time the court decided the case. The religious composition of the court was as follows: Chief Justice Harlan Stone, former Congregationalist; Owen Roberts, Episcopalian; Hugo Black, former Baptist; William O. Douglas, a minister's son, a former Presbyterian and former born-again Christian, now a theist sympathetic to Christian ideals; Felix Frankfurter, ethnically but not religiously Jewish; Stanley Reed, Protestant; Frank Murphy, Catholic; Robert Jackson, Episcopalian; Wiley Rutledge, Presbyterian. All came from religious backgrounds, Christian or Jewish. Four were affiliated with a specific church. Five had dropped out altogether or had only a general association with their earlier religion. The majority were unchurched; religiously liberal; basically theistic; familiar with and sympathetic to Christian ideas, taken broadly; more interested in constitutional claims than in religious doctrine.

Only four years before, the court, with many of the same members, had in *Cantwell* applied the First Amendment for the first time in favor of Free Exercise. The year before *Ballard* was heard, Justice Jackson had written a stirring vindication of the Jehovah's Witnesses' right to refuse to salute the flag: "If there is any fixed star in our constitutional constellation, it is that no official, high or petty, can prescribe what shall be orthodox in politics, nationalism, religion or other matters of opinion or force citizens to confess by word or act their faith therein." Surely this court might be expected to lend a sympathetic ear to a minority no less unorthodox, small, and beleaguered than the Jehovah's Witnesses.

But was Jackson to sit at all? Congress had legislated as to district judges, requiring their recusal when the judge was "concerned in interest" or had been "of counsel" to either party. The statute did not bind the appellate courts. In 1945, a year after *Ballard* first came before the court, Jackson made an issue over a judge's duty to recuse himself in a case where sitting would create an appearance of impropriety: he implicitly rebuked Hugo Black for failing to disqualify himself in a case argued by Black's former law partner. Jackson's stand was no small matter; it began what he realized was "a war" with Black, and the war damaged his chance of the chief justiceship. Taking the duty of recusal this seriously, could Jackson sit in *Ballard?* He had been the head of the Justice Department when the prosecution was begun—"of counsel" in the sense of the statute governing district courts. He might have been unaware personally of the Ballards' indictment or even of their reindictment. But on occasion he had exercised his supervisory authority over United States attorneys and the indictments they secured. For example, at the prompting of liberal friends, he had intervened promptly in Detroit to secure the dismissal of an indictment involving Loyalist veterans of the Spanish Civil War. He could not say that Washington was too remote from a local prosecution to be unrelated to the prosecution in Los Angeles. He could not have avoided asking himself, would it appear fair to both sides for me to sit in judgment on the appeal? Most judges would probably answer such a question negatively; each justice had to decide for himself. Jackson did not decline to participate in the case and ended by writing a solitary dissent.

Douglas delivered the decision of the court, for a majority composed of himself, Black, Reed, Murphy, and Rutledge. His opinion zigzagged; it was strongest in its command of the rhetoric of religious freedom. To begin with, he faced two preliminary problems before reaching the main issue of whether the truth of the Ballards' beliefs should have been before the jury. First, the government claimed that Judge O'Connor had removed only the issue of the truth of the religious representations from the jury; there were other false representations, not of a religious character, on which the jury could and did convict. Douglas decided that the latter were not separated from the former, and the jury had been asked to pronounce only on the sincerity of the defendants' "belief in their representations and promises." The government's first maneuver failed. The defendants' waiver of the issue of the truthfulness of their representations was the government's second contention. To that well-grounded objection Douglas answered that the defendants had demurred to the entire indictment on the grounds of religious freedom; therefore they had never abandoned their objection; they could still ask the Supreme Court to declare the whole indictment a violation of Free Exercise.

With these preliminaries cleared away and the issue of what Free Exercise required squarely before the Court, Douglas quoted from *Watson v. Jones*, a post–Civil War statutory case: "The law knows no heresy, and is committed to the support of no dogma, the establishment of no sect." He added his own eloquent gloss:

> Heresy trials are foreign to our Constitution. Men may believe what they cannot prove. They may not be put to the proof of their religious doctrines or beliefs. Religious experiences which are as real as life to some may be incomprehensible to others. Yet the fact that they may be beyond the ken of mortals does not mean that they can be made suspect before the law. Many take their gospel from the New Testament. But it would hardly be supposed that they could be tried before a jury charged with the duty of determining whether those teachings contained false representations. The miracles of the New Testament, the Divinity of Christ, life after death, the power of prayer are deep in the religious convictions of many. If one could be sent to jail because a jury in a hostile environment found those teachings false, little indeed would be left of religious freedom.

From these stirring words one might have supposed that the conclusion would be, "The indictment is quashed; the defendants are discharged." Instead, without any reason being expressed at all and without the slightest reference to the reasoning of the Ninth Circuit or to the text of the mail fraud statute, Douglas declared, "So we conclude that the District Court ruled properly." Truth had not been the issue on which the Ballards had been tried. Sincerity had been the issue before the jury; the jury had convicted. At this point Douglas was apparently ready to reverse the Ninth Circuit and uphold the Ballards' conviction.

Curiously, however, such was not Douglas's conclusion. In the first draft of his opinion he left open for reconsideration by the Ninth Circuit the contention of the Ballards that the withdrawal from the jury of the truth of their representation was an amendment of the indictment and that therefore they had been unconstitutionally tried on charges on which they had not been indicted. Douglas then abandoned this explicit reason for remand to the circuit. In the final version of the opinion he merely noted that the Ballards had argued that the reversal of their conviction was "justified on other distinct grounds," not reached by the Ninth Circuit; on that basis he returned the case to the circuit.

Chief Justice Stone took a blunter approach than Douglas's majority or Jackson in dissent. He invoked the homely teaching of the common law: the state of one's mind is as much a matter of fact as the state of one's stomach. He interpreted Judge O'Connor's ruling to mean that the Ballards had been tried on the state of their minds. If they were not sincere in their representations they were misrepresenting their mental state. This analysis slid easily into saying that if a defendant had known a fact to be untrue and represented it as happening, there had been a fraudulent representation. If Edna said she had shaken hands with Jesus in San Francisco and knew that she had not, she was guilty of misrepresenting her mind. Truth, not sincerity, became the issue. It was the Chief Justice's conclusion that "on ample evidence" the jury had rightly convicted. Stone's opinion was joined by Roberts and Frankfurter.

Robert Jackson was of various minds about the case. He voted to grant certiorari on the strength of his law clerk's recommendation that the Ninth Circuit was in error. He then inclined to dissent but to prevent a tie was going to vote with Douglas. Finally when Douglas had secured four other votes, Jackson decided to write for himself. Two recollections of his days in Jamestown, New York, afforded the background of his thought: Harmonia, a community of spiritualists, had been founded six miles south of Jamestown, and he kept a news account of the town in a file containing clippings for his autobiography. In 1917, Jackson himself had read the *Bhagavad Gita* at the funeral in Jamestown of Eaton La Rue Moses, a Theosophist.

Writing alone, Jackson first appeared to agree with Denman: truth should have been before the jury. The best proof that one sincerely believes something took place is to prove it took place. In the guise of granting protection to the Ballards' religion the trial court had denied them this opportunity. As the Ballards were not permitted to testify to the truth of their experiences, they should not have been tried at all. This conclusion was the opposite of Denman's, and Jackson went on to state reasons absolutely precluding trial of this case.

William James's pathbreaking *The Varieties of Religious Experience* was made central. Religious experience, Jackson quoted James, consists in "conversation with the unseen, visions and voices, responses to prayer, changes of heart, deliverances from fear, inflowings of help, assurances of support." These events take place in a medium distinct from that of conversations with other persons of flesh and blood. These events take place "whenever certain persons set their own internal attitude in certain appropriate ways." These events are in this way self-generated, whatever the divine reality that lies beyond the setting of the internal attitude and the invisible responses. These events form experiences with tones and colors that an individual without religious insight cannot detect. No jury should be asked to say which experiences were feigned and which real.

"Faith," William James had observed, "means belief in something concerning which doubt is still theoretically possible." Jackson said he did not know "what degree of skepticism or disbelief in a religious representation amounts to actionable fraud." He continued:

Some who profess belief in the Bible read literally what others read as allegory or metaphor, as they read Aesop's fables. Religious symbolism is even used by some with the same mental reservations one has in teaching of Santa Claus or Uncle Sam or Easter bunnies or dispassionate judges. It is hard in matters so mystical to say how literally one is bound to believe the doctrine he teaches and even more difficult to say how far it is reliance upon a teacher's literal belief which induces followers to give him money.

Jackson's reference to judges gave this passage a peculiarly personal bite. Was believing in dispassionate judges like believing in an Easter bunny? Was this allusion—unnecessary to illustrate his point—evoked by the observation that in a case involving religious beliefs the judges could not be dispassionate? The text invites these questions without answering them.

Jackson concluded, "Prosecutions of this character easily could degenerate into religious persecutions. . . . I would dismiss the indictment and have done with this business of judicially examining other people's faiths." The indictment that the Department of Justice under his leadership had secured was in his awakened eyes a mistake from the beginning.

Douglas and Jackson each spoke slightingly of the Ballards' teachings. Douglas's comment was put impersonally yet in such a way that it appeared to incorporate his own conclusion: "The religious views espoused by respondents might seem incredible, if not preposterous, to most people." Jackson's was undisguised: "I should say that the defendants have done just that for which they are indicted. If I might agree to their conviction without creating a precedent, I cheerfully would do so. I can see in their teachings nothing but humbug, untainted by any trace of truth." If no official, high or petty, can determine what is orthodox in America, why should a justice of the Supreme Court in an official opinion of the Court, or even in a published dissent, stigmatize religious doctrine as preposterous or pure humbug?

Douglas's and Jackson's statements did more than reveal their own negative beliefs about I Am. They wrote as they did to show that they were not so naive as to suppose that I Am was a serious religious movement. A desire to make such a showing, it may be reasonably inferred, arose as much from how their colleagues spoke as from their estimation of wider public feeling. If Douglas and Jackson were impelled to denigrate the doctrines before them, the judges who thought the Ballards

should be prosecuted or were in fact guilty of fraud must have made
equally negative judgments of their religion. Prosecution of the priests
or ministers of a mainline Christian church for their teaching on the power
of prayer, personal immortality, or the reality of the sacramental transformation of bread and wine would have been politically suicidal as well
as culturally inconceivable. A new religion was looked on differently, not
only by the prosecutors, but by those who were supposed to be neutral.
And—it is only a guess but a guess supported by experience—what made
it especially necessary for Christian and ex-Christian judges to distance
themselves from a religion seen as a raw parody of Christianity was its
nearness to Christianity in its essential elements.

An additional factor was at work: cultural, American, and specifically
endorsed by the great pioneering American work on religion treated not
theologically but as a psychological phenomenon, James's *The Varieties
of Religious Experience*. Practical men are "usually the slaves," so Keynes
observed, "of some defunct economist." So judges put to use the philosophy, psychology, or theology that past masters of these fields have fashioned. No American had so delved into religion in the capacity of a philoso-
pher-psychologist (his theology concealed) as had William James at the
beginning of this century. The Jamesian influence is not only explicit in
Jackson; it permeated *Ballard*.

"The mother sea and fountain-head of all religion lie in the mystical
experiences of the individual." Such was James's "basic position" in his
Gifford Lectures of 1901 that became *The Varieties of Religious Experience*. Incorporating James's own mystical experiences (one disguised as
the report of a mythical French correspondent, one the recollection of an
occurrence in the Adirondacks in 1898), *Varieties* draws from its autobiographical sources and from its author's personal identification with religious responses a secret strength. It has the force, though not the form,
of a confession. In form James is attempting to study religion objectively
while examining subjective testimony to religious phenomena and their
effects. His book focuses, its author announces, on "the feelings, acts, and
experiences of individual men in their solitude as they apprehend themselves to stand in relation to whatever they may consider the divine." Re-
lentless in this focus, James does not get into the nature of "the divine"—
that would be overt theology—and he treats individuals "in their solitude,"
that is, as they exist in their interior, in their private imaginations and hearts.

James acknowledges that he is intentionally omitting the institutional
branch of religion. He does so not merely to limit his subject but from
hostility. He defines institutional religion "as an external art, the art of

winning the favor of the gods." He stops just short of saying, "Organized religion is the technique of bribing the gods." From Prosecutor Lazarus describing the I Am movement as "a racket" to Justice Jackson calling it "humbug, untainted by any trace of truth," the same Jamesian perspective ran through *Ballard*.

Looking for religion in the feelings of individuals in their solitude, James employed a criterion. For feelings about the divine to be religious, they had to be "serious," that is, ideational commitments that were neither casual nor cynical. With this criterion James asked of religion what Wordsworth had earlier required of true poetry and Matthew Arnold had made the poetic touchstone: "the high seriousness which comes from absolute sincerity."

The majority of judges in *Ballard* made the same move. The test of belief being religious was the sincerity with which the belief was held. No matter that insincerity was not a federal crime. The judges honored the First Amendment by not putting religious truth on trial. Silently they incorporated in their decisions the cultural, American, Jamesian preference for judging not the content of the belief but the manner in which the belief was held by an individual.

THE EXCLUDED OTHER HALF

The appeal had been decided, but the case was not over. On remand to the Ninth Circuit, Mathews, half-hearted from the start, switched sides and joined Stephens in affirming the conviction. Undefeated, counsel for the Ballards asked the circuit to reconsider, sharpening their attack on the tactics of the prosecution, especially the closing speech of Lazarus with its references to "this Ballard racket" and its sneers at the Ballards' teaching on ascension. Writing for the court, Stephens was unimpressed. The prosecution could not be confined to "a listless, vigorless summation of fact in Chesterfeldian politeness."

Dissenting, Denman found much to disagree with. The prosecution had violated the trial court's ruling that the truth of the Ballards' representations was not before the jury. Over two days and two noon recesses the prosecution in closing argument had deliberately injected into the trial the question of the truth of these representations and had done so mockingly with "degrading characterization" of the Ballards. Here had been "no single unfair act, possibly excusable in the heat of argument . . . [but] two days of deliberate and continued striking of the unfair blows." The misconduct of the prosecution required reversal.

But there was more, and now in 1945, in this fourth consideration of the case by the Ninth Circuit, Denman discovered an issue overlooked before. The reason, it may be more than guessed, had much to do with his wife. Forty years earlier William Denman, age thirty-three, had married Leslie Van Ness, age thirty-seven. She was the granddaughter of the pioneer for whom a principal street of San Francisco is named and the daughter of a wealthy lawyer. They had no children. They did have a strong marriage. Isolated in his judicial office, intense in his passions, Denman concentrated his life outside of court in Leslie. In 1959 when he was eighty-eight she died and life became unbearable for him; a month after her death he shot himself. Years earlier, when soon after the 1932 election he had sought the appointment as circuit judge, he had solicited the support of a range of persons able to speak to the new Roosevelt administration: the two California senators, Hiram Johnson and William McAdoo; Senator Thomas Walsh of Montana; William Green, president of the A. F. of L.; Edward Hanna, the Catholic archbishop of San Francisco; the Jewish elders, Louis Brandeis and Bernard Baruch, plus Felix Frankfurter; and he had written a personal appeal himself addressed "Dear Franklin" and stating, "I trust that I am to be the man." But the finest letter of all came from Leslie, who knew the president, too. After telling him of a visit to the Indians of the Southwest, in whom she took a lively interest, she wrote:

At this moment, when I feel stripped of compromises, when within me there is a passion for truth, for clarity, I am moved to do a strange thing. In so doing though, there is a curious intuitive sense that there will be a complete understanding on your part.

Mr. President, I wish you might see your way to appoint my husband as the fourth judge for the Ninth Circuit of the United States Circuit Court of Appeals. I feel and know Will is fitted for the position I speak of and will bring to it many qualities that will be valuable and which will be needed in the coming crowded years. He himself has values which are and will be constructive and creative. I do not want to see these possibly unused. I do not want to see them possibly wasted. I would like to see him fulfill himself, with the knowledge that in this fulfillment he will be a vital living part of the structure you build. This is what I passionately desire.

My friend,—for the moment The President is forgotten—I have written as I think and as I feel, and as one can only write to another in whom one believes there are great understandings. This I shall know of the friend, whatever may be the decision of the President.

As her letter to the president indicated, Leslie Van Ness Denman's contacts with the Indians of the Southwest had an invigorating and liberating impact upon her. At the Christmas season, in lieu of Christmas cards, she and her husband would send to their friends a pamphlet titled GREETINGS and containing pictures and themes from the mythology of one of the tribes. In 1947, for example, the pamphlet had a rabbit and a moon on the cover and within a "Hymn to the Mother of the Gods," which proclaimed, "Hail to the goddess who shines in the thorn bush like a bright butterfly," and quoted Elie Faure: "The modeller of gods, at bottom, is the spiritual universe hastening unceasingly in pursuit of its center of gravity." This Teilhardian thought was unaccompanied by any reference to Christmas itself. Ten years later, Leslie edited an entire small book *The Peyote Ritual*, with a foreword by the anthropologist A. L. Kroeber on the Native American Church or peyote cult. Leslie herself wrote that peyote gave the Kiowas "faith in a new power and a new road." The book celebrated the paintings of Tse Tke, a young Kiowa, who had given her an explanation of his work, which showed "the messenger gods" joining "the Earth and Spirit gods" and "the peyote man trying to pray to 'the unknown mystery he can only call Light.'" As Leslie understood her informant, the peyote man "prays to the great Light to understand the light within himself."

Now one knows why Will Denman left a bequest to the University of California for the study of comparative religion. His legal, political, judicial universe was cramped and corseted in comparison with the spacious Southwest in which his wife pursued her spiritual quest. Bold, inquisitive, energetic, Leslie not only championed her husband in his career but opened windows for him to a world beyond his stone palace at Seventh and Mission. Faith in a new power and a new road, messenger gods, a universe evolving spiritually, prayer to the great Light to know the light within— Leslie had opened her mind to a spirit or source beyond the visible.

It is with such a wife that Denman must have discussed Edna Ballard's case. It is such a woman of whom he certainly thought when he now wrote in dissent, "Well could a sensitive woman, highly spiritual in character, rationalize all the money income acquired by Mrs. Ballard as being devoted to the teachings of the same Jesus as are the profits of the trust created by Mrs. Eddy for the Christian Science Monitor."

What relevance did this personal observation have to decision of the case? Why, women had been excluded from deciding it. As the Ballards' counsel had objected at the beginning of the trial, there had been no women on the jury list from which the jury was drawn. The Sixth Amendment's specification of "an impartial jury," as recently interpreted in dicta of the Supreme Court in *Glasser v. United States*, required "a body truly representative of the community." In *Glasser* a list drawn from the membership roll of the League of Women Voters was noted as having fallen below this standard. Here in *Ballard* was something more fundamental—half of the community had been excluded. And that half had a vital connection to the issues in the case. Teaching was involved and over 95 percent of public-school teachers were women. Religion was involved, and "the one large and vital religious group created in America since Joseph Smith is that of the Christian Scientists founded by a woman, Mary Baker Eddy." Attendance of women at church services of all denominations substantially outnumbered that of men. Well could "a sensitive woman, highly spiritual in character, rationalize all the money income acquired by Mrs. Ballard."

Not only the Sixth Amendment guarantee of an impartial jury had been violated. Due process of law had also been offended by the exclusion of women. Assured in all federal trials by the Fifth Amendment, due process had been denied for the same reasons that the jury had been defective. The deliberate elimination of her peers had deprived Edna Ballard of elementary justice. Blazing a constitutional path, Denman invoked both Fifth and Sixth Amendments together as controlling and dispositive.

Denman concluded this dissent, remarkable for its preciseness, its passion, its prescience, and its personal character, with what was in effect a critique of Douglas's opinion. To illustrate, he created what could be called "The Legend of Will Denman." It ran as follows: In the ancient cathedral of Quebec, sitting in a congregation that includes a cardinal and two visiting Protestant bishops, there is a young Canadian carpenter of German descent, who is thinking arrogantly of the German destruction of Rotterdam and Lidice. Suddenly another carpenter, clad in the clothes of ancient Judea, stands in the aisle. The proud young man exclaims, "You here! I did not believe, but those scars in your hands come from swinging no adze. What would you have me do?" He is answered, "Pray you may be forgiven and if you of your own free will truly believe, a greater power will come to you to speak the truth." The two carpenters leave the cathedral side by side.

The Canadian carpenter goes out to do good works in the United States in educating the descendants of slaves, but his story of his conversion leads to his indictment for mail fraud. The executive officer of the Society of White Christians testifies against him, saying that while the carpenter was working on his home he told him that he did not believe any of these things happened. The carpenter testifies to the contrary: he believes the events took place before his eyes. There is derisive laughter in the courtroom. Under Douglas's opinion in *Ballard I*, the testimony of the cardinal and the two bishops could not be offered by the defense to confirm the basis of the carpenter's beliefs. A verdict of guilty of mail fraud follows.

An extraordinary religious intensity went into this work of imagination. Denman expressly provided that the apparition in the cathedral was "not the projection of either of the bishops' minds." He added, "Perhaps an agnostic psychiatrist would say that he [the carpenter from Judea] was a projection of the cardinal's mind, for he was praying for his visitor's presence and guidance. However, none in the congregation was under an emotional hysteria of impassioned mass psychological appeal, for the services had not been begun and the old cathedral was a homely and intimate edifice familiar to them since their infancy." The Canadian carpenter himself is deliberately made a proud man. Belief gives him a new orientation and a new power. The legend of Will Denman is the work of one not a believer who sees the value of belief, who trembles at its border. The construction of the legend required its author to entertain at least the possibility that such supernatural intervention could occur. The legend was a final effort to show the shallowness of the solution to *Ballard* that held truth to be irrelevant. Denman's dissent cast into shadow the perfunctory opinion of the majority.

By imagination, extending empathy, Denman demonstrated what it was possible for a judge to do. The study of religion, the anthropologist Clifford Geertz contends, is "the social history of the imagination." By the imagination also, a religious enterprise is entered. Religion is not the worse for that. As Geertz puts it, there has been "a confusion, endemic in the west since Plato at least, of the imagined with the imaginary, the fictional with the false, making things out with making things up. The strange idea that reality has an idiom in which it prefers to be described . . . leads on to the even stranger idea that, if literalism is lost, so is fact." To make the empathetic, imaginative entry into religious thought, the judge cannot forget that he or she is a mortal creature facing death, seeking purpose in the universe and life that goes beyond death. The legend of Will Denman incorporates this experience that is every person's.

Certiorari was again granted by the Supreme Court. Now in December 1946, five years after the first trial, four years after the second trial, the Supreme Court was willing—to a very limited degree—to speak on a question it had not been presented with in 1944 even though the court's dicta in *Glasser* had said that the jury should represent the community. Ignoring the large constitutional conclusions of Denman, the Supreme Court, through Douglas, said that it would exercise its supervisory powers over the federal courts. The court held that the exclusion of women from either the grand jury or the petit jury was contrary to the scheme of jury selection set up by Congress.

A jury or grand jury with women excluded was not representative because, men and women, Douglas wrote, were "not fungible." He, so his own biography would suggest, was one to know. The "subtle interplay of influence one on the other is among the imponderables." Douglas then quoted from Denman's dissent: "a sensitive woman, highly spiritual in character" would have understood Edna Ballard. Beyond prejudice to her, the exclusion of women was prejudicial to the jury system and "the democratic ideal reflected in the processes of our courts." Accordingly, the indictment on which the defendants had been charged and convicted was invalid. Douglas left it open to the United States to reindict them and convict them again.

The Supreme Court had changed since *Ballard I*. Fred Vinson, a Democrat from Kentucky, and Harold H. Burton, a Republican senator from Ohio, had been appointed by Harry Truman to replace Stone and Roberts. Vinson was a Methodist. Burton, a native of Boston, was a Unitarian, and not any ordinary member but in 1944–1945 the moderator of the American Unitarian Association; in this lay-dominated denomination he was a ranking religious authority. In this rearranged court, Douglas kept his bare majority.

Burton thought it contrary to the statute to require women to be on juries and saw no need for the exercise of supervisory power in this case because, since 1943, federal courts in California had used women as jurors. Moreover, the error of excluding women had not been argued to the Ninth Circuit on the first round and it had not even been mentioned in the Ballards' brief to the Supreme Court in *Ballard I*. The point had been abandoned. So thought not only Burton but Felix Frankfurter, joined by Vinson, the new chief justice; and on this issue Jackson was with Frankfurter.

Frankfurter went on to gloss Douglas's opinion in *Ballard I*. That opinion, he said, had left undecided the question whether the First Amendment protected the Ballards from retrial; the court should decide that issue now, not wait for the Ballards to be reindicted and reconvicted and years later be before the court attacking the validity of the indictment. The Frankfurtian gloss alleged an extraordinary gap in Douglas's opinion meant to decide a case where Free Exercise was the main issue; yet it was true that, just at the point where logically Douglas should have concluded that the Ballards were properly tried for insincerity, Douglas had veered off to say there could be other grounds for reversal. Frankfurter had wanted to affirm the Ballards' conviction in 1944 and inferentially wanted to do so now. Only Jackson reiterated his earlier view that the First Amendment required dismissal. With the votes of Black, Murphy, Reed, and Rutledge (the old majority), Douglas prevailed. The way to reindictment was left open. No justice cared to comment on the legend of Will Denman and its challenge to Douglas's view that religious truth could not be tried.

At this point a new look was taken by the Department of Justice. The attorney general was Tom Clark, a pragmatic Texan, who had signed the government brief on the first appeal to the Supreme Court and so may have had some inclination to try again. The head of the criminal division was T. Lamar Caudle, due in time to be himself convicted of conspiracy to defraud the United States. Possibly the advice of Justice Jackson to have done with the business of examining other people's faiths had penetrated the department. In any event, Frankfurter's expectation that the Ballards would be reindicted was disappointed. No reindictment was obtained.

One penalty within the power of the Post Office to inflict remained in effect. The Ballards' books and magazines continued to be banned from the mails. Only on June 7, 1954, was the fraud order revoked, the Post Office accepting an affidavit from Edna that her use of the mails would be "for religious activities and non-profit organizations" and that she would not violate the relevant statutes. It was difficult to see how the affidavit had changed the Post Office's mind; like the unjust judge of the Gospel, it had been merely worn down. The Ballards had been worn down even more. Two trials and the series of appellate arguments had cost them thousands of dollars for which they would never be compensated. The psychic costs had been large. The damage to the reputation of the movement was irreparable. With the first indictment the I Am movement began a slide into the obscurity in which it now survives in the shadow of Mount Shasta.

The belief that divine interventions in human life have occurred has been foundational for the religions that have taken form on American soil, such as Mormonism, Christian Science, Seventh-day Adventism, Pentecostalism, Theosophy, not to mention all the varieties of Christianity and Judaism and Islam that have come from abroad and flourished here. Only in Denman's tale did one judge enter briefly on an empathetic pilgrimage of the imagination. Such an endeavor might appear to be a necessary condition for judging a religious claim, even for determining the existence of a religion when its free exercise is asserted. But can a judge be a pilgrim?

PART TWO

PROBLEMS

CHAPTER 7

THE PILGRIM'S PROCESS

WILLIAM BLAKE

"Hope lifts the Pilgrim from the Slough of Despair"
Illustration for John Bunyan, The Pilgrim's Progress.

I saw, as in a dream, the pilgrimage of Samuel Simple towards that hill of which John Winthrop once spoke and to which again John Kennedy alluded, that eminence from which the freedom of America illuminates the world. When he began his pilgrimage Simple had just been made a member of a court of the United States. He was determined to defend the free exercise of religion of every individual to whom it was guaranteed by the Constitution. He did not believe he would have far to travel. "All I need to do," he declared, "is keep government out of religion, and religion out of government. Like oil and water, they can't mix. It's too obvious for words."

"Words are what we have to work with," remarked his colleague Light.

"In that case," said Simple, "I need go no further than the words of the Constitution. I assume they mean what they say. It's like reading the Bible. The plain sense is clear to anyone of goodwill. I have nothing to do but to 'lay the article of the Constitution which is invoked beside the statute which is challenged and to decide whether the latter squares with the former.'"

"That won't quite work, Simple," said his colleague Heavy. "You see the Constitution speaks of what *Congress* may not do about religion. Fifty years or so ago it was decided that 'Congress' meant 'state' and 'state licensing agency' and 'city council' and 'school board.' The Constitution, as interpreted by the cases, applies almost exclusively to these local institutions. You can't depend on the literal exactness of the words the Constitution employs."

"I see," said Simple. "It's more complex than I thought. I guess I'd better study the cases to learn what the Constitution really means." And he asked his law clerks to brief him.

"There are over two hundred cases, federal and state, that could be considered relevant," Harvardman reported. "They essentially begin with the period when judicial enforcement of the restrictions on the government in regard to religion began, in 1940. Because there were no precedents—or rather only moth-eaten and unpersuasive precedents," the law clerk added —"the innovating justices had a free hand. They drew the lines with a breadth and a freedom that recall Chief Justice Marshall in the early days of the Republic interpreting the Contracts Clause. To understand the constitutional guarantees regarding religion we should start with the great age of the forties."

"Fine," said Simple. "Pick one of the great cases."

"All right, I'll take *Everson v. Board of Education of the Township of Ewing*. It gives the grand lines of what Justice Black inventively calls 'the establishment of religion clause.' True," Harvardman added almost apologetically, "Justice Black found clauses where another might find prepositional phrases; and he did ignore the fact that the text speaks of law 'respecting establishment,' not of law 'establishing'; and he was a bit confused about Jefferson's part in the First Amendment. But his words resonate: listen to these:

The "establishment of religion" clause of the First Amendment means at least this: Neither a state nor the Federal Government can set up a church. Neither can pass laws which aid one religion, aid all religions, or prefer one religion over another. Neither can force nor influence a person to go to or to remain away from church against his will or force him to profess a belief or disbelief in any religion. No person can be punished for entertaining or professing religious beliefs or disbeliefs, for church attendance or non-attendance. No tax in any amount, large or small, can be levied to support any religious activities or institutions, whatever they may be called, or whatever form they may adopt to teach or practice religion. Neither a state nor the Federal Government can, openly or secretly, participate in the affairs of any religious organizations or groups and *vice versa*. In the words of Jefferson, the clause against establishment of religion by law was intended to erect "a wall of separation between Church and State."

"The words do have the simplicity of the Ten Commandments," Simple observed. "I suppose you could even parse the sentences to create ten commandments. But," he paused, "I would have thought 'respecting an establishment' meant 'taking into account an establishment'—in other words, the phrase in the Bill of Rights assumed that religious establishments existed and instructed Congress not to take any establishment into account, either by endowing a state-established church or by penalizing one. Am I being too simple?"

"You're being pretty perceptive," said Boaltman, a second law clerk, "but you're a bit out of date. Everyone's agreed that 'respecting an establishment' now means 'establishing.' They call it 'the Establishment

Clause.' It'd be sheer pedantry to stick to the original language. In any case, the original language didn't seem to refer to anything at all once the states disestablished their churches. So to give the Establishment Clause a function, you had to read it in a kind of revised way."

"I thought I once heard that at least Justice Black was a great stickler for reading the Constitution literally," Simple observed. "When it said 'No law,' for example, he said it meant 'no law.'"

"He was a stickler when it suited his purposes," Harvardman rejoined, "which wasn't all the time."

"The clearest words Justice Black uses are those from Jefferson," said Simple. "A *wall*—what could be simpler? I suppose Jefferson told Madison to put in the wall when Madison consulted him about the Bill of Rights."

"Not exactly," the third law clerk broke in. "He wrote those words when he was president in 1802 responding to some of his constituents in Connecticut—these were Baptists," Yalewoman added, to clear up the point, "who were being put down by the Congregationalist establishment there. Anyway, what's important is the idea of No Aid, No Tax Money to 'any religious activities or institutions.' That's a wonderfully broad principle."

"Has it ever been observed?" asked Simple.

"Well, as a matter of fact, it's been extraordinarily hard to work out," interjected Boaltman. "In *Everson* itself, for example, Justice Black thought providing transportation to parochial-school pupils was not aiding a religious institution. To cut off the busing of children to the religious schools, he suggested, would be like cutting the schools off from police protection or the fire department. It wouldn't be neutral; it would be hostile."

"That's obvious," said Simple. "So where was the difficulty?"

"After awhile," said Boaltman, "the question came up of letting a state pay for transporting parochial-school children on school field trips. That was busing too. It helped the children. It was what the state did for children in public schools. So why shouldn't it be done for parochial-school children? The court said it was unconstitutional. It broke down the wall."

"I had no idea," Simple remarked, "that the Constitution was so precise. I do find it a little troubling that justices so often personify themselves as 'the Constitution.' Why, it may not even be the justice but the justice's law clerk who is putting his or her ideas forward as the command of that majestic document! But I suppose we must accept the habits of speech of our craft. I think I see the difference between the busing that was permissible and the busing that was unconstitutional. The field trips were more part of the school curriculum than getting to school. I suppose, too, they must have been sort of religious activity—trips to churches, for example."

"No," said Boaltman, "they were to art museums and science exhibitions. But of course busing took a burden off the religious school or maybe just off the parents. I don't entirely get the difference myself. In any event it's a fairly trivial matter. Let's look at something a little harder—instructional material, whether the state can pay for that in a church school."

"I suppose not," said Simple. "That would be aid to a religious institution."

"But," Harvardman replied, "long before *Everson*, the court had held that the state could buy textbooks—secular textbooks—for all schoolchildren, wherever they went to school. After *Everson* that decision was reaffirmed. So textbooks can be provided even if they represent tax money that helps the parochial schools. After all, it's the children who are benefited."

"I think I see," said Simple. "I guess if the state aid doesn't go to the school but just takes a financial burden off the children or their parents, the aid is okay. It doesn't make any difference that by helping the parents the state encourages the parochial school and even seems to acknowledge it as a good institution. I suppose in a modern school that means the state can supply maps and globes and tape recorders, too."

"Not so fast, judge," said Yalewoman. "All that sort of stuff is a little extra. The Constitution says it can't be paid for—or so, at any rate, the court has said. You see the school would be getting this kind of material, not the students."

"How about the kind of educational extra that's directly-bestowed on the children—things like remedial help, therapy, and counseling?" Simple asked. "I suppose they're all right since they go immediately to the kids."

"It's not that easy," Boaltman answered. "For over a dozen years they were unconstitutional on the school premises, constitutional off premises with an odd exception: the state could provide 'speech and hearing diagnostic services' on the parochial-school's premises; it was assumed that the speech and hearing specialists wouldn't provide any religious instruction. But, in general, the wall shut out the counselor, the reading teacher, and the psychological therapist. The court explained that 'the pressures of the environment' in a parochial school might alter the therapist's behavior from its normal course. That was guff, of course. In 1997 the court recognized this simple truth, without saying so so bluntly. Now it's okay for the state to subsidize strictly supplemental help at a parochial school. It's still a no-no to pay for the teaching of the regular curriculum in secular subjects."

"The line is very visible," Simple agreed. "I don't entirely understand how the Constitution drew it. It reminds me of the lines that legislatures draw when they're gerrymandering. And I know that the court has found some sorts of gerrymandering intolerable."

"It's mainly symbolic," Harvardman commented. "On premises, those things get identified with the mission of the school. Off, they're neutral."

"You mean helping a child to read has a religious flavor if you do it in a classroom of the child's school and it's different if done down the block or in a trailer?" Simple asked. "I hadn't realized line-drawing could be so simple."

"That's the way it is with the Constitution," Boaltman shot back. "What do you think of this—the Constitution says the state can't pay for the cost of administering examinations in a parochial school if the costs include both state exams and school exams but if it's just state exams the state can pay."

"I can grasp that distinction," said Simple, "though I suppose it would be easy when you're giving one test to give another, and I don't see how they can keep them separate without a lot of policing. Can the state pay the teachers for teaching ordinary secular subjects like math and physics?"

"Not at all," Boaltman replied. "Those subjects in a religious school might get a religious imprint. I never heard of them getting one. But it's surely possible. The court has been adamant—No Aid carries the day there. In a way," he added reflectively, "I suppose it's all a matter of symbols here. If the state pays part of the salary of a parochial-school teacher, it looks like the state's putting some kind of seal of approval on the school."

"The schools are accredited, aren't they?" said Simple. "I mean, going to a parochial school satisfies the state's education requirement. I'd think that was the real seal of approval."

"Maybe," said Boaltman.

"What about religious colleges?" asked Simple. "I imagine they're out of luck, too."

"No." Yalewoman spoke immediately. "They've received very generous funding for their buildings. No chapels, of course. But everything else—

libraries, science classrooms, art centers, theaters—there's been a cornucopia of state aid for them. And it's all according to the Constitution."

"Why, that's astonishing," remarked Simple. "If symbols are important, some of the most visible religious enterprises nationally are the colleges. If the government pumps money into Notre Dame, doesn't everyone get the idea that the government thinks Catholic education is a good idea?"

"Maybe," Boaltman acknowledged. "I guess symbolic action by the state can't be what the Constitution is driving at after all. I guess it's more substantive than that. I mean, I mean . . . " He paused.

"You mean the Constitution forbids aid to grammar schools and high schools because they shape their students' minds while colleges just pass them on, unaffected, going out as they came in. Is that it?" said Yalewoman, whose excited voice mingled sarcasm and skepticism.

"Must be," said Boaltman. "The Constitution thinks colleges deal with persons impervious to religious education. Before then, kids are malleable. I don't know if there's any empirical support for this constitutional premise. But let's hang on to it—it's another bright line."

"How about church schools and taxes?" asked Simple. "Taxes are a very tangible subject. We should have some good lines there, especially since *Everson* said, "No Tax Aid.""

"It's a little more complicated than that, I'm afraid," Harvardman answered in measured tones. "First of all, it depends on whether you think of a tax break as aid. Some people do—you get a break, you get something another citizen does not have. Some people don't think that way— a tax is something the government takes: when it doesn't take, it isn't giving, it's just not getting.

"Second of all, in a world where tax breaks are a major way for the government to encourage nonprofit enterprise, some people would say that to deny them to church schools would be hostile—like denying them police protection, to use Justice Black's analogy. Others would say that to give them the break is to give explicit governmental approval to their activity. Does it really make any difference whether the government gives a grant of $1 million or a tax exemption worth $1 million? We have to answer these questions before we can go further."

"I see," said Simple. "That kind of philosophical speculation I find confusing. For simplicity's sake, let's assume that a dollar of exemption is as substantively and symbolically significant as a dollar of aid, and that the government has to make the same kind of inquiry in each case: 'Is this a bona fide educational institution?' Let's also assume that an exemption is a benefit that the government bestows. After all it's totally in the power of the government to grant or to withhold. Now, on these premises, that a tax exemption is a governmental gift constituting aid, what does the Constitution say?"

"It says exemption of the school's property is all right," said Boaltman shortly. "It doesn't even present a substantial federal question."

"How about a tax deduction for tuition?" Simple asked.

"It depends," said Boaltman. "A deduction of $40 per child given poor parents in New York is unconstitutional. A deduction of $700 per child in Minnesota is constitutional."

"That couldn't be because Justices Burger and Blackmun came from Minnesota, could it?" Simple asked naively. "Or was it because $40 is too little, or maybe the court doesn't like discrimination in favor of the poor?"

"None of the above," Yalewoman said pertly. "The distinction—the court said it made the Minnesota situation 'vitally different' from that in New York—is that parents of *all* schoolchildren in Minnesota could take the $700 deduction; in New York the deduction was only for poor parents of children in nonpublic schools."

"But if parents of *public-school* children weren't paying tuition," asked Simple, "how could they use a $700 deduction?"

"I really don't know," said Yalewoman a bit vaguely. "Maybe books and uniforms could add up to a couple of hundred dollars, and they could deduct those."

"You mean even though the Minnesota public-school parents would only be able to use a $200 deduction and the Minnesota parochial-school parents could get a $700 deduction, it was all okay? The parochial-school parents could get $500 more than the others—ten times more than the nonpublic advantage in New York—and it was still all right?" asked Simple, really bewildered. "Wasn't there any other difference between the cases?"

"Ten years time," said Boaltman laconically. "The school aid cases have puzzled the commentators. My old teacher Jesse Choper has said that they are 'ad hoc judgments incapable of being reconciled on any principled basis.' When a law school dean says a case is without principles, he's making a pretty severe criticism."

"Our best authority," added Harvardman, "notes that in the religious establishment cases the court often engages in 'the incantation of verbal formulae devoid of explanatory value.'"

"But the wall!" cried Simple. "The wall was such a clear image."

"Something does not love a wall," Yalewoman paraphrased Frost. "Twenty-four years after *Everson*, the court said this: 'the line of separation, far from being "a wall," is a blurred, indistinct, and variable barrier depending on all the circumstances of a particular relationship.'"

"A blurred, indistinct, and variable barrier," murmured Simple. "That reminds me of something. I wonder what."

"I know!" exclaimed Yalewoman. "It's a sponge. A sponge is certainly blurry and indistinct, and you can make it smaller or larger depending on your purposes, and it soaks things up. I guess what the court has is a sponge to soak up any aid to schools the court thinks needs to be soaked up. We can rewrite Jefferson: 'There is a sponge of separation between church and state.'"

"I am afraid I haven't been helped a bit," Simple said. "You three have tried, but you've left me with my intuitions and prejudices and no principles. I have a sponge, I probably need a mop."

"We made a mistake right there at the start," observed Yalewoman. "We went backward instead of forward. If you're going to act like a judge, you must begin with the latest authority. And you certainly can't poke too far in the rubbish bin of history."

"I'm a pilgrim and a judge," said Simple "and it's funny to begin where I should end. But you're probably right. Let's look at the last first."

"Some of the latest cases," reported Harvardman, "say the Constitution says that a clergyman can't pray at a public high-school graduation; that a city can't adopt an ordinance whose purpose is specially designed to outlaw the ritual slaughter of animals by a Caribbean cult; that a state can adopt a statute that has the effect, but not the purpose, of outlawing the sacramental use of drugs by the Native American Church."

"They get a lot out of a few words," observed Simple. "I'm still confused."

"They've had help from an unexpected quarter," said Yalewoman mysteriously.

"What do you mean?" asked Simple.

"You see, judge," she replied, "judges are used to complaining about legislative oversights and gaps in the drafting of laws and conundrums created by legislation, so judges weren't prepared to believe that a legislature had repaired what the courts have botched."

"Has the legislature repaired something?" Simple inquired.

"Yes," she answered definitively. "In the Religious Freedom Restoration Act of 1993, Congress repaired a serious error the Supreme Court made in 1990 when it held that to enforce a law burdening the free exercise of religion (in this case the sacramental use of peyote in the Native American religion) a state didn't have to prove a 'compelling' interest but merely that the law was 'neutral' as to religion so that the impact on free exercise was incidental to enforcement. For example, sacramental confession could be turned into an aid to police investigation. It would work this way: federal wiretap law permits prisons to routinely tap and tape their prisoners' phone conversations; it's a neutral practice. A prisoner seeks to receive sacramental absolution by confession to a priest through the prison intercom. Let's say the prisoner's a murder suspect. The D.A. has the prison tape the confession to get the goods on him.

"It actually happened in Eugene, Oregon," she added authoritatively.

"Another example, less dramatic but more common, judge," Harvardman interjected, "is a state's law on the preservation of historic architecture that would override a church's desire to rearrange its altar to accord with liturgical development. That's no small effect: you see, 'landmarking has burdened churches at rates many times higher than any other class of property.' Conversely, state law on redevelopment could result in the condemnation of a church of great symbolic value to its congregation, as in fact it did in a case in Yonkers, New York. Congress made it likely that none of these restrictions of free exercise would be legal."

"What did Congress say?" Simple asked.

"It said in so many words," reported Boaltman, "'Government shall not substantially burden a person's exercise of religion even if the burden results from a rule of general applicability. . . . 'There was an exception if the government could demonstrate that the application of the burden to the person was in furtherance of a 'compelling' governmental interest and was 'the least restrictive means' of furthering that interest.'"

"It wasn't as radical as Madison," Yalewoman observed, "but it was in the right direction. Several times Congress had exercised its power to protect First Amendment rights by statutory exemptions. The possibility that courts might shrink the meaning of religion had been perceptively pointed out."

"I suppose the Supreme Court was duly grateful for this correction and the consequent expansion of the guarantee of religious freedom," said Simple.

"Not a bit of it, judge," replied Yalewoman. "You must get in tune with the psychology of judges, or at least the psychology of justices."

"What happened?" Simple asked bluntly.

Harvardman hastened to explain. "The Supreme Court declared the legislation unconstitutional. The court held that the First Amendment prohibited governmental burdens on a religion only if the burdens were inflicted with hostility to the religion. The court treated the constitutional guarantee of liberty as no more than a shield against a persecutory purpose. Madison's experiment in freedom was made into a kind of an antidiscrimination proviso. With that understanding of the amendment guiding it, the court found the Religious Freedom Restoration Act to be an overreaction by Congress; there weren't many persecutory purposes around; the law lacked 'congruence' and 'proportionality' to the harm Congress could legitimately address. Of course," Harvardman added at the end of this exposition, "the court's requirement that Congress act with congruence and proportionality was a criterion dreamed up for the occasion. I can't recall any other case where the courts gave themselves the power to measure the proportionality of a legislative response. There is the Eighth Amendment prohibition of cruel and unusual punishment but that criterion applies only to criminal cases and criminal punishments."

Simple stared at Harvardman for a moment, "You mean," he said, staggered, "you mean that the Supreme Court, and presumably therefore any court addressing federal legislation, has the ability to say what Congress had in mind and then measure the means Congress used to achieve their goal?"

"I wouldn't take it out of the context of this law, judge," Boaltman observed. "The Supreme Court was protecting its turf. It didn't like being told it was wrong. The idea of a lot of people asserting their right of free exercise under the new statute—the justices found that idea troubling, maybe even appalling. Their mindset, you must know, runs in favor of law and order. Bureaucratic regulation that impacts church activities or spooks an individual soul does not disturb the justices."

"One member of the court," Yalewoman sharply observed, "even thought that creating an exemption from general law in favor of free exercise was an unconstitutional establishment of religion!"

"Aberrations will occur, even in temperate judicial minds, I suppose," Simple remarked. "But that, from what I had read, is truly amazing. This man must have it just about backward: the free exercise of religion must be subject to every general law of the society. No doubt he would have held the Volstead Act unconstitutional for exempting sacramental wine from the Nineteenth Amendment."

"That's not like you, judge, to speculate satirically about the past," Yalewoman remarked. "We've got plenty of problems in the present. One, whether in holding the Religious Freedom Restoration Act void the Supreme Court meant to say the act couldn't apply to federal law—that is, to say Congress didn't have power to restrict its own legislation—curiously, the court dodged this central question. Two, even before it invalidated the Religious Freedom Restoration Act, the Supreme Court seemed to think *itself* exempt from that law's provisions."

"Tell me about it," said Simple.

"The Satmar Hasidim," began Boaltman, "are practitioners of a strict form of Judaism; they took advantage of a New York law to establish the Village of Kiryas Joel, an incorporated municipality embracing 320 acres inhabited only by them. Their boys were educated at the United Talmudic Academy and their girls at Bais Rachel. These private schools did not have any distinctive services for handicapped children; these services were provided by the state in an annex to Bais Rachel. When, in 1984, the Supreme Court held such state aid to parochial-school students to be unconstitutional, the state stopped helping, and the handicapped children were forced to attend a nearby public school. The children suffered 'panic, fear, and trauma' in leaving their own close community. Their parents then persuaded the New York legislature to constitute the Village of Kiryas Joel as a state school district. In this capacity the village ran a public school for forty handicapped Hasidic children, including some Hasidic children from outside the district. But then two taxpayers and the New York State School Boards Association challenged this arrangement as unconstitutional.

"In 1994 the Supreme Court agreed. The New York legislature was found to have effected an establishment of religion by the 'fusion of governmental and religious functions.' The majority made no reference to the Religious Freedom Restoration Act. Apparently when the general rule burdening the exercise of religion was of the court's own making, the court didn't see itself included. Somehow the court *isn't* 'government.'"

"Didn't the court add that 'the Constitution allows the state to accommodate religious needs by alleviating special burdens'?" Yalewoman chimed in.

"Indeed." Boaltman replied. "But the special burdens of forty handicapped Hasidim were not to be alleviated by bending the *court's* rigid rules one iota."

"I hadn't realized that the court had any general rules in this area of the law," Yalewoman responded. "One who knows most says that the court makes them up from case to case. Let's look at the court's criteria."

"For example?" asked Simple.

"For example, *Yoder*," said Yalewoman, plunging into exposition. "*Yoder* in 1972 held that a general state statute requiring students through the age of 16 to attend high school and requiring parents to see to their attendance could not be enforced against the Old Order Amish because formal high-school education was 'contrary to Amish beliefs.' The Amish take to heart the admonition of Saint Paul, 'Be not conformed to this world.' A modern high school, in the Amish view, teaches its pupils to conform, alienating them from God. Amish parents cannot conscientiously allow their children to attend high school. And the Amish don't believe alternative Amish schools are the answer. On purely religious grounds they're against any high-school education. When the state attempted to enforce its school attendance law, the Supreme Court agreed that public education is 'the very apex of the function of a State.' But the state's interest was outweighed by 'fundamental rights and interests, such as those specifically protected by the Free Exercise Clause of the First Amendment, and the traditional interest of parents with respect to the religious upbringing of their children.' In *Yoder* the religious claim trumped the law of the state even as the state was exercising its highest prerogative, the education of its citizens."

"Are *Yoder* and the sacramental drug case inconsistent?" asked Simple simply.

"Superficially, they may be distinguished because *Yoder* involved parental rights in addition to religious rights," answered Yalewoman. "And if you think cases depend mostly on facts, of course doing drugs is different from skipping school. But in terms of principle the cases are indistinguishable. The parents' 'traditional rights,' which the Constitution doesn't mention, were dependent on the parents' rights under Free Exercise to supervise the religious education of their children. *Yoder* was fought and decided on the meaning of Free Exercise. A religious practice, central to the religion, was allowed to displace the general law of the state. The sacramental drug case held that couldn't be done and added another point: a court couldn't even *tell* what a central religious belief was."

"Oh, dear," said Simple. "I see that the Supreme Court is an inconstant guide on my pilgrimage. How often does it change its mind?"

"On what the Constitution in general means, it's changed its mind over one hundred times in two hundred years, or about once every biennium," Yalewoman replied. "But as to religion it has not been in the business of interpreting that long, and the rate of change, or instability, is higher. Maybe more cases will be more helpful than statistics."

"Go ahead," said Simple limply.

"Take another fairly recent case, decided in 1989: *Texas Monthly*," suggested Boaltman. "The plaintiff was a secular magazine that observed that religious periodicals in the state of Texas were absolved from paying the sales tax imposed on other periodicals. The Texas statute in fact exempted periodicals 'published or distributed by a religious faith and that consist wholly of writings promulgating the teaching of the faith,' and it also excepted 'books that consist wholly of writings sacred to a religious faith.' The Texans had the Bible in view. According to Justice Brennan, the Constitution invalidated the exemption as 'state sponsorship of religious belief,' thereby constituting a forbidden establishment of religion. At least two other justices agreed with Justice Brennan's characterization of the problem and three others agreed with the result.

"Well, is there anything wrong with that analysis?" asked Simple.

"Only that it flatly contradicts one of the classic cases of the forties, *Murdock v. Pennsylvania*," said Harvardman. "*Murdock* said a tax on publications of the Jehovah's Witnesses which their colporteurs carried door-to-door, was like a tax on preaching. You couldn't put a tax on a minister's sermons, the court said, without hindering Free Exercise. Similarly, you could not tax the magazines. The tax exemption that was required by the Constitution in *Murdock* was held prohibited by *Texas Monthly*—unless you think only Jehovah's Witnesses spread their religion's message by writings. As Justice Brennan politely put it, the two cases are 'in tension.'"

"That does seem to be an about-face," Simple said mildly. "But as you say, the court often changes its mind. Its *Murdock* mind had a run of over forty years. I guess that's a long life in this area of law. Was there anything else wrong about *Texas Monthly?*"

Yalewoman answered: "A very big decision on a state tax exemption for 'houses of worship,' that is, churches and synagogues, was *Walz* in 1972. The National Council of Churches, the United States Catholic Conference, the Episcopal Diocese of New York, the Synagogue Council of America, the Baptist Joint Committee on Public Affairs, and even Protestants and Other Americans United for Separation of Church and State defended the exemption, and its validity was sustained. The court took note that lots of other nonprofits also got the exemption—hospitals, libraries, even playgrounds. Playgrounds—here was an especially nice touch by the court to show that religion was not being given anything so very special. The court's main idea was that all these recipients of the exemption had been found by the state of New York to be 'beneficial and stabilizing influences in community life.' The Constitution did not object to a tax break for beneficial and stabilizing influences in the community."

"What is the thrust of what you are reporting . . . ?" Simple ventured.

"Simply this," said Yalewoman, "that some might think it strange that the state could decide that houses of worship benefit the community but the state could not make a similar judgment about religious publications."

"I suppose," Simple observed, "that the good works that some churches perform for parishioners and others—family counseling, assistance to the elderly, comfort to the sick, care for children, food for the unemployed, aid to the alien, and even shelter for the homeless—I suppose that kind of activity led to the court's conclusion on the property tax exemption, even though, of course, not every church is a source of social services."

"The contrary is true," Yalewoman replied. "There's an echo of Lutheran theology in the court," she added thoughtfully. "The justification of the exemption does not come from good works but from faith. The churches, the court explicitly said, were not to be justified by 'a social welfare yardstick.'"

"Then, I don't see . . . ," Simple began.

"You don't see why it's okay to benefit religion if you benefit playgrounds at the same time, but not okay to benefit religion alone," Yalewoman said, anticipating her employer.

"The court must think worship is therapeutic if it thinks the state can judge worship to be 'beneficial and stabilizing.' But if a Bible service and a sermon are therapeutic, why isn't a magazine containing excerpts from the Bible?" Simple pondered.

"You're missing the real distinction the court made," chimed in Boaltman.

"It all depends on entanglement," added Yalewoman.

"Entanglement, what's that?" inquired Simple. "That's one term I hadn't read in the Constitution. I'm already tangled enough without dealing with a fresh complication. Every time a judge prevents an establishment of religion the judge is entangled in defining what religion is."

"Deal with entanglement, you'll have to," Boaltman continued levelly, "because the court reads the Constitution to forbid 'excessive government entanglement' with the church. The state would get entangled with the churches if it had to value church property, impose tax liens on churches, or foreclose on a church."

"Are you saying that, since the Constitution forbids that kind of interaction," asked Simple, "a tax exemption of church property is constitutionally mandated?"

"Only if the tax results in excessive government entanglement," Boaltman replied.

"What kind of entanglement is that?" Simple asked. "Entanglement by an excessive government?"

"Entanglement that the court finds excessive," Boaltman answered shortly. "But we're getting away from the enigma of *Texas Monthly* and its denial of a tax exemption. As Yalewoman said, *Walz* allowed the state to judge that religion corporately practiced and promoted was in the public interest. The court went out of its way to cite earlier dicta in favor of overt state support of religion, for example: 'When the state encourages religious instruction . . . it follows the best of our traditions.' If the state may encourage religious instruction and, if the state may judge that religion is beneficial to the community, it would have appeared that the sales tax exemption was as secure as the property tax exemption. But it was as bad as the other was good, according to the Constitution."

"*Was* the sales tax exemption as universal as the property tax exemption?" Simple asked, seeking a discernible distinction.

"At least fifteen states besides Texas had the sales tax exemption for religious literature," Boaltman answered. "Other states made food served by religious organizations or vehicles used for the transportation of persons for religious purposes exempt from sales tax. Some states exempted any wine used for sacramental purposes from liquor tax or liquor licensing. Some states exempted the residences of clergymen from property tax too. The Internal Revenue Code itself exempts from gross income the rental value of the residences provided to ministers, priests, rabbis, and cantors. *Texas Monthly*, it seems to me, went in the face of the settled understanding of Free Exercise as practiced by the states and by the federal government."

"How did the dissent put it?" chimed in Yalewoman. "It said that the majority brought 'a new strain of irrationality' into the court's exposition of the religious guarantees. That's about as tough language as Dean Choper's, especially when coming from a member of the court. What's irrational is crazy, and the holding is said to not be just an aberration but a new, or additional, strain of irrationality. There must be strain all around."

Simple at this point was genuinely bewildered. Could it be that the Constitution in this area of life, which was so dear to him, was as changeable as the political complexion of the justices? How could they commit themselves to such grand theories as Justice Black had articulated and then fail to apply them? How could they be so insensitive to, if not actually ignorant of, the historical experience of Americans? How could they find in the Constitution itself the quibbling, inconsistent lines they drew? Simple had a sudden intuition that his law clerks were too well trained in legal doctrine and legal reasoning to appreciate how a great political institution like the Supreme Court had to set its sails with the wind and not be very careful about what Emerson, after all, had called "the hobgoblin of little minds."

"Rationality in the sense of consistency doesn't seem to be the court's strong suit in this area of law," Simple observed. "Maybe I'm wrong talking to you law clerks and expecting you to make legal sense out of what's been done. You think too much of citing precedents and following rules and catching fallacies. I ought to talk about these matters to my old partners, who deal with hard facts and legal realities."

Simple accordingly left his chambers and took himself in the late afternoon to the St. Wenceslas Club where he could expect to encounter Fred Frye and Aeneas Ketchum of his old firm of Fish, Frye & Ketchum. "None of us are entirely logical," Simple reflected. "If the firm were logical, we'd have called it 'Fish, Ketchum & Frye,' but seniority was more important than logic."

Fish had been dead for many years, but Frye numbered among his clients an old Presbyterian church, while Ketchum represented the Protestant Episcopal Diocese. Simple joined them in a comfortable nook at the club and explained his problem: "I'd like some insights from your experience on this church-state thing."

"You've come at a good time," Ketchum replied. "We're still trying to work with the *Wolf* case. Some call it facetiously 'the Wolf at the door.'"

"Give me a little background first," Simple said.

"Once upon a time," Frye replied, "it *was* very simple. In a hierarchical church, the church rule controlled. As a matter of fact, the law was laid down in the case of a schism in the Presbyterian Church back in the 1860s. Some folks in Louisville didn't like the General Assembly telling them they couldn't believe the Scriptures anymore, where Saint Paul told slaves to obey their masters. The General Assembly, of course, was run by Union men and worked up about the war, and they didn't mind pushing the Southern crowd around, but the folks in Louisville thought they were hearing heresy. So they just quit and wanted to take the Walnut Street Presbyterian Church with them. The Assembly said they could quit, and good riddance, *but* the church property belonged to those who obeyed the Assembly. The Supreme Court took a hard look at it and said that if you join a church you have to obey the government of the church, and a civil court should enforce what the church government decides. So the General Assembly won. Of course it didn't make the Yankee court sorry that the proslavery crowd lost, but the rule seemed to make sense on any account."

"That rule would have stopped the Reformation dead in its tracks," Simple murmured. "But if that case goes back to Civil War times something must have happened since."

"You're right, Sam, as usual," Ketchum came in. "That early decision was federal law but not constitutional law. The constitutional law didn't come in until 1952 after the Supreme Court had discovered what it began to call the Religion Clauses. The case involved a lot of Russian history, which I had better lay out for you. The Russian Orthodox Church has always had a very close relation to the state. You might say the situation there has always been the reverse of what it's been here. In 1721 the Orthodox Church in Russia was put under government control by the Ecclesiastical Regulation of Peter the Great. Its former mode of government by a patriarch and sobors or church councils was replaced by a bureaucratic institution called the Holy Governing Synod, which took an oath to the czar as 'Supreme Judge.' The synod was supervised by a lay administrator, the chief procurator. With the abdication of Nicholas II, the church lost its temporal head. In November 1917 a sobor elected Tikhon Belavin as patriarch, giving him unrestricted administrative powers in case the new Soviet government made it impossible to convoke another sobor. In 1923 a schismatic group, the Renovationists, favored by the Soviet government, deposed Tikhon, who was already in prison, and set up a new administration.

"Tikhon had appointed Platon Rozhdestvensky to be archbishop of North America, with St. Nicholas Cathedral in New York as his seat. The Renovationists named John Kedrovsky to the same position (although he was married and so canonically ineligible to be a bishop), and in 1923, he entered the cathedral, announcing that as appointee of 'the Soviet All-Living Church' he had come 'to take control of all Russian Church property.' He dismissed Platon for counterrevolutionary acts 'directed against the Soviet.'

"Well, Platon responded by calling a sobor of the North American clergy and faithful in Detroit in 1924. This council concluded that the patriarchate in Russia was under the coercion of the Communists. The sobor then relied on a decree issued by Tikhon in 1920 authorizing archdioceses to organize on a local basis if the activity of the patriarchate should stop: 'Until the restitution of the Supreme Church government,' the local sobor could 'decide definitively all affairs.' The Detroit sobor recognized Platon as archbishop. However, the courts of New York treated the Renovationists as the church and gave Kedrovsky possession of St. Nicholas Cathedral. Most Orthodox churches in America were transferred to boards of trustees headed by Platon and so escaped Kedrovsky.

"I hope it's all clear so far," Ketchum paused.

"You're halfway there," Frye murmured, adding to Simple, "you'd better let Aeneas finish. You know he's a thorough person."

"Litigation started up again in 1945," Ketchum resumed. "By this time, Kedrovsky was dead, his son John Kedroff had taken over the cathedral, and the Renovationist Church had lost the support of the Soviet government and disappeared. Meanwhile, New York had amended its Religious Corporation Law to confirm title in the Russian Orthodox Church in North America (that's the Church governed by Platon and his successors since the Detroit sobor) as the lawful owner of all property held by the Orthodox Church before the Russian Revolution. Backed by the New York law, the American group sued for possession of the cathedral.

"Kedroff himself, having no defense, looked for a new claimant. This turned out to be Venyamin Fedchenkov, whose claim was through Sergii Stragorodsky. Sergii, since his release from prison in 1927 and his comprehensive declaration of loyalty to the Soviet government, had acted— but without canonical authority—as the de facto ecclesiastical head of the Orthodox Church in Russia; his critics saw him as a puppet of the secret police. Soviet support shifted from the Renovationists to the church headed by Sergii. Sergii removed Platon and appointed Fedchenkov archbishop of North America in 1933. In 1945, at the end of World War II a sobor was held for three days in Moscow. This sobor recognized Aleksii Simansky, Sergii's successor, as patriarch and enacted a new administrative statute to govern the church. The effect of this church rule was to make the patriarch supreme. Aleksii supported Fedchenkov, and Fedchenkov supported Kedroff. In 1952 the case reached the Supreme Court."

"That's a long story," Simple commented as his old partner finally subsided. "Where does it lead?"

"The Supreme Court applied the same law it had adopted for the Presbyterians: the church rule controlled. Only now that was said to be the requirement of the Constitution, of Free Exercise to be precise."

"But I don't see how that helped," Simple objected. "Each side said they were acting in accordance with the church rule. How did the court know which was right?"

"It went to the top," said Ketchum. "It said the patriarch was right because he *was* the top."

"But," said Simple again, "weren't there all kinds of irregularities the other side was pointing to that made the patriarch's claim of authority bogus? Whose free exercise of religion was being protected anyway?"

"The patriarch's or his appointee's and their followers, for there were a few," Ketchum answered.

"Indeed," Frye chimed in. "The case appeared to recognize that a church, as well as an individual, had the right of free exercise. 'Freedom to select the clergy,' the court said, 'must now be said to have federal constitutional protection.' What a development that was! I don't believe even Madison had thought of churches themselves having free exercise rights. And to assert the new right on behalf of a church that was united to a state! If you believe Robert Jackson's dissent, the right was even asserted on behalf of 'a foreign and unfriendly state masquerading as a spiritual institution.'"

"I suppose," said Simple, "the intrusion of the New York legislature seemed a bit rough and ready. But suppose a court had made a finding that the patriarchate really was the tool of the Soviet government and had been unfaithful to its fiduciary duties. Can't a court remove a trustee who is in breach of trust, even if the trust happens to be one for religious purposes?"

"That's what we learned in law school," Ketchum agreed. "After its first opinion, the case was reconsidered on remand by the New York Court of Appeals, which ultimately reached exactly the conclusion you suggest: that to let the patriarchate exercise jurisdiction over St. Nicholas Cathedral would be 'a perversion of the implied trust to which the property is subject.'"

"And that was the end of the matter?" asked Simple.

"No!" Ketchum laughed. "The Supreme Court seemed to think that was an end run around its previous opinion. It treated the judicial intrusion as if it were as bad as the legislative and once again gave St. Nicholas to the Muscovites."

"Constitutional law and trust law diverge, I see," said Simple.

"That's what we thought for a while," said Frye, "until the Supreme Court announced that 'there are neutral principles of law, developed for use in all property disputes, which can be applied without "establishing" churches to which property is awarded.' It's that approach that led to *Wolf*."

"What was *Wolf* about?" Simple inquired.

"It was a case of much interest to us Presbyterians," said Frye, "and came from the tensions caused by the national church becoming a good deal more liberal than the locals. The case began in 1973 when the congregation of the Vineville Church in Macon, Georgia voted, 165 to 94, to withdraw from the Presbyterian Church in the United States, the PCUS, with which the Vineville Church had been affiliated since 1904. The Presbytery of Augusta-Macon, the church court of the PCUS that had jurisdiction over the Vineville Church, investigated and ruled that the majority had 'forfeited all ecclesiastical privileges of the PCUS and all rights to the property.' The majority didn't appeal but, with the minister, remained in possession of the church. The minority then sued in federal court. What they argued is this: the Georgia statute stating that the majority 'of those who adhere to its organization and doctrines represent the church' violated the First Amendment. The majority said they wouldn't rely on the statute and that there was no constitutional issue. The district court dismissed the case for lack of federal jurisdiction. The Fifth Circuit affirmed. The Supreme Court denied certiorari."

"Well, that was easy," said Simple. "But I don't see the significance."

"The case came back to the Georgia state courts," Frye continued. "The trial court looked at the deeds of the church and the Book of Church Order of the Presbyterian Church of the United States and decided that the local majority owned the property. The Supreme Court of Georgia agreed. It said it could not find an 'implied trust' in favor of the national church. The Supreme Court of the United States then took the case."

"What happened next?" asked Simple, who was curious to learn why the Supreme Court had taken an interest.

"The Supreme Court divided 5 to 4," reported Frye. "It said there were two right ways to decide the case and called both ways the application of 'neutral principles.' One way was to examine the deeds to the property and also 'certain religious documents such as a church constitution.' The other way was for state law to create a presumption that the majority ruled, 'so long as the use of that method does not impair free-exercise rights or entangle the civil courts in matters of religious controversy.'"

"Why," exclaimed Simple, "the second method just seems to be the opposite of what was laid down in that old Civil War case and followed in *St. Nicholas Cathedral*. Unless, of course, that final caveat means *St. Nicholas* applies."

"You are so right" said Frye. "Under what we thought was the law, the highest tribunal of the Presbyterian Church would decide the case. But here the decision of the church court was apparently to be ignored even though ignoring it seemed to interfere with the free exercise of religion by the national church. That is, unless the final caveat helped us out. There was another wrinkle the court subjoined. When it said that the church constitution could be examined, it added, 'In undertaking such an examination, a civil court must take special care to scrutinize the document in purely secular terms, and not to rely on religious precepts in determining whether the document indicates that the parties have intended to create a trust.'"

"You mean," said Simple, "that the courts are supposed to read a religious document but not pay any attention to its religious content and context? That sounds counter-intuitive, if not counter common sense. I can't quite believe anyone would have written that."

"That's what *we* thought," said Frye, "but that's what the court wrote. The court did give some gratuitous advice to hierarchical churches like ours. It said we could fix up the deeds so there will always be a right of reversion in favor of the national church if the local church votes to leave. Of course, it was a little late to do that in *Wolf*."

"What happened when the case went back to Georgia?" Simple asked.

"The Georgia Supreme Court reached the same result it had before. It dutifully repeated the words of the Supreme Court and then said it had already applied neutral principles to rule in favor of the majority of the local church. It didn't bother to mention the caveat we thought might save us. The Supreme Court denied certiorari. Seven years after the dispute began, the case was over. The local majority had won. At least the process was three years shorter than in *St. Nicholas Cathedral*."

"Apart from the time taken and the expense caused, anything wrong with the result?" asked Simple.

"Just that under the previous approach the national church would have won," Frye remarked. "The upshot, according to an eminent scholar at your old school, is 'startling.' Each state gets almost carte blanche to divert the property of a religious trust depending on whether the state prefers large organizations and distant authorities or prefers small organizations and local people."

"Besides which," Ketchum added, "in giving state courts an option either to go by local property law, including majority rule, or to apply the constitution of the national church, the court caused great uncertainty. No lawyer can tell a church which approach the courts of his state will take."

"Not to mention," said Frye, "the difficulty you have already mentioned, of reading a church constitution as though it were a secular document."

"What's happened since?" asked Simple, who was always willing to learn where a rule led.

"I can tell you about California," said Ketchum. "As you may have heard, there are those of us Episcopalians who share the present Roman Catholic position on the ordination of women to the Christian priesthood and are ready to leave a bishop who accepts women priests. In Los Angeles, the churches of Holy Apostles, Our Savior, St. Mary's, and St. Matthew's seceded from the diocese. The congregations thought they could take the churches with them. But the churches belonged to the diocese, which sued for their recovery. Fortunately for the bishop, Holy Apostles was recently enough incorporated to have articles of incorporation saying that on its dissolution the property would revert to the diocese. That was good enough to get the church back. The other three had a provision in their corporate papers that the constitution, canons, and discipline of the diocese would always form part of their articles of incorporation. But the seceding churches had scrapped this provision. The California court said such provisions were 'no more restrictive of future amendments to the articles of incorporation than would be similar statements in an automobile dealer's articles that it would always distribute General Motors products and always be bound by General Motors rules and policies.' Another analogy that occurred to the court was this: 'If a Kentucky Fried Chicken franchisee secedes from its national affiliation to join a Tennessee Fried Chicken operation, neutral principles of law do not recognize any claim by the ex-franchisor.'"

"I see that you find the comparison with the Colonel's product offensive," Simple remarked perceptively. "After all, the Church isn't in the fast-food business."

"It's the kind of analogy that reading canon law without taking its purpose into account is likely to suggest," Ketchum growled.

"The diocese was lucky to get Holy Apostles," Frye interjected. "After all, even there, in order to apply the reverter, the court had to find that the church had dissolved. Well, it hadn't dissolved, it had just quit the diocese. But the court, wanting to give something to the plaintiff, said there had been 'a constructive dissolution.' That's legalese for saying 'We're going to reach the result we want to reach.'"

"My God!" Simple exclaimed more or less prayerfully. "An explicit commitment to abide by the rules of a hierarchical church can be changed to make schism successful! And a church that sticks to a prior rule of discipline can be found to have dissolved itself! It looks as though courts have a fairly free hand once a church has internal divisions."

"That's the *Wolf* at the door!" Ketchum and Frye said simultaneously, smiling at their wilted witticism.

By this point Simple had finished two drinks and had exhausted his curiosity in this arcane constitutional law of intrachurch conflict. He reflected that such cases were not common. He hoped that he would never have to decide one. "It is quite like being a Roman emperor," he thought to himself. "The judge with a little management gets to decide who the true church is, at least who the true church is for purposes of owning the church." With this not totally unwelcome conclusion in his mind, he thanked his old partners and departed.

Later that evening, still troubled by all the precedents poured into his brain, Simple stopped by his favorite coffee bar, La Strada, where he stood a good chance of encountering three of his favorite graduate students. (Before his appointment to the bench Simple had done part-time teaching at the university.) Soon the students dropped by his table. One, whose head was held high and whose blue eyes sparked challengingly, was Lucinda Logic, familiarly known as Lucy. The second, with lustrous dark hair and a warm and lively smile, was Cleopatra Sens, popularly known as Cleo. The third, a shaggy student of theology, was John Henry, sometimes called "Newman."

To these three, Simple explained the nature of his quest and his frustrations. "I want to give to each person the full measure of free exercise the Constitution has allotted. But I have tripped over contradictory precedents, been entangled in brambles of judges' making, and been showered with the thousands of words judicial decisions have added to a sixteen-word constitutional commandment. Law clerks and lawyers haven't helped me. I need fresh insights and perspectives."

"Let's start with what is clearly a complex subject," suggested Cleo: "the celebration of a day commemorating the birth of the founder of Christianity and combining his name with the word for a Catholic liturgy. For the government solemnly to mark this day in the same way it marks the birth of the nation is for the government to promote Christianity. This day, drenched in religious significance, is thereby accorded the added prestige of governmental acknowledgment and respect. In miniature— for it *is* only a day—the government behaves like only a Christian government would. For a day, the government establishes Christianity.

"One can say, as James Madison would have said, 'The law does not care about trifles,' and one day's celebration of a religious occasion is not worth bothering about. But as long as the government celebrates Christmas, its connection with Christianity will be evident. And the birth can scarcely be forgotten as long as the government uses a calendar that makes reference to it: the French revolutionaries realized that so they abolished the Christian time frames. Moreover, there are 52 Sundays a year where, less forcefully, the same association is recalled, although with Sunday it is the founder's rebirth that is recalled.

"More to the point, one can say that Christmas is 'a cultural phenomenon,' that is, it's part of our common American culture, enjoyed by everyone. Not too many, I imagine, would want to see its elimination as a holiday. The Grinch who stole Christmas would not be as unpopular as the court that decreed Christmas to be an impermissible establishment.

"But this second response ignores what makes Christmas 'a cultural phenomenon.' A good part, still, of the reasons for celebrating are religious. It wasn't the winter solstice but the Christian interpretation of what Christian theology sees as the gift of God that made Christmas the season of gift-giving. We still don't call the day 'Santagift.' What's more, our view of free exercise is that freedom of religion is constitutionally guaranteed so that no minority will be discriminated against by government. If any fraction of the population feels the government's celebration of Christmas makes them second-class citizens, there is an offense to the Constitution.

"A third response might be to say, 'It's only a symbol.' But symbols are what men and women have died for. For the government symbolically to set a Christian feast apart is an important act of government. Similarly, too, with Thanksgiving. It's not blatantly Christian, but in name and origin—and still in deed for some—it's a religious recognition of God's goodness. Neither Thanksgiving nor Christmas have been totally secularized."

"Where does your history lead?" asked Simple.

"It leads—I think inexorably—to the conclusion," said Cleo, "that one must give up the governmental celebration of Christmas and Thanksgiving or give up the idea that the government can never favor and advance religion."

"What do you say?" Simple turned to Lucy.

"I say that Cleo's logic is good, but we can still tap the resources of moral philosophy to escape her dilemma. I assume it would not betray the Constitution to use an idea put forward by an Italian preaching-friar. He was trying to avoid another difficult dilemma, how to defend oneself against a homicidal attack without violating the precept against taking human life. He argued that one act could have two effects, and the morality of the act depended on the intention with which the act was performed. In the case of self-defense, the intent was good if the intent was to defend oneself even though the act was a blow that caused the attacker's death. This so-called principle of double effect has been often applied in the analysis of moral matters. It supposes one action, one good intention, and two simultaneous effects, one good and one bad; and to be moral, the bad effect must be unintended and not be greater than the good effect. In other words, a judgment is required that the bad is not disproportionate to the good."

"How does that help here?" Simple inquired.

"Mutatis mutandis," Lucy answered. "Apply the idea analogically. If the government performs an action, and its intention is to perform a governmental not religious function and the effect of the action is double, to foster a governmental purpose and to foster religion, the action is constitutionally permissible if the religious effect is not disproportionately greater than the governmental effect.

"Let me give you an example, one well established in the law. Suppose a preacher wants to preach on Sunday in a public park. May he? For the government to provide him space promotes religion, but provision of space also performs the important governmental function of maintaining a public forum for speech. The single act of giving space has two effects. The effect of promoting religion is not disproportionately greater than the effect of permitting free speech. The government's intention is to permit free speech. The government's action is constitutional."

"That requires close consideration of what effects are proportional to each other," observed Simple. "I wonder if the test is workable."

"Of course it is," said Lucy. "It explains not only the use of the parks but Sundays, Christmas, and Thanksgiving. You can't get away from some promotion of religion by making religious days state holidays. But there *is* a double effect, and the effect of providing regular occasions of rest as with Sunday, or the effect of encouraging family gatherings as with Thanksgiving or the effect of stimulating shopping as with Christmas, is not disproportionately outweighed by the religious effect.

"The same principle is at work in the cases that have given the courts the most trouble—symbolic displays, a crèche, a Christmas tree, a menorah. Is the display constitutionally good or bad? The question calls for judgment as to the intent of the governmental body arranging for, or permitting, the display. It calls for another judgment as to whether the religious effect outweighs the civic. As the cases show, these are not easy judgments to make, but they are made. They are all instances of double effect analysis."

"You do seem to have a useful tool," Simple admitted. "It does occur to me that the judgment of proportionality can get pretty subjective."

"No doubt," Lucy agreed. "You have to keep refining such judgments, using the usual methods of history and empirical research to measure what the effects are."

"I suppose the tax exemption of churches and synagogues is susceptible to the same approach," said Simple.

"Yes," Lucy answered, "even though the judgment of governmental purpose gets trickier when it's a house of worship that is being exempted. But subtle perceptions of secular effects are not always wrong."

"Could you even say that military chaplaincies and prayers by a legislature could be justified in that way?" Simple asked daringly.

"It's been tried," Cleo reported. "I suppose it seems plausible for the military. But a praying legislature? One justice has said that legislative prayers are constitutional because prayers have the purpose 'of solemnizing public occasions, expressing confidence in the future, and encouraging the appreciation of what is worthy of appreciation in society.'"

"It's a good try," Simple agreed. "But hasn't something been omitted —namely, the intention of the persons praying, who are supposedly addressing God, not mumbling soothing incantations. Also doesn't a court have to engage in theology to find that the secular effect outweighs the spiritual?"

"You seem to be right," Lucy acknowledged. "Double effect can take you only so far. But it is a useful framework."

"Useful for you and Cleo," Simple responded, "but I doubt that many practicing lawyers or judges would care to use it. It's too ponderous. They'll probably go right ahead with their ad hoc judgments."

"I thought I was being helpful," Lucy replied, slightly nettled by this dismissal. "I imagine John Henry has something to say."

"I do," John Henry intoned. "But there is a preliminary question to resolve," he continued, sounding very much like Harvardman, "and that is whether 'religion' should or should not be subsumed within the category of speech—for constitutional purposes, I mean. A very large part of most religions consists in the use of words—in reading sacred scriptures, in repeating prescribed formulas of ritual, in preaching, and even in praying. Where there are physical actions, they are usually given significance by the speech that accompanies them. Even when the action is taken silently, it is normally intended to be a communication and could easily be accommodated to the judicial category of symbolic gesture qualifying as speech.

"If religion is speech, it is of course protected by the First Amendment, too, but without the invidious difficulties that arise from approaching it as religion. For example, an evangelical group called Cornerstone sought to use the facilities of the University of Missouri at Kansas City for prayer and religious discussion. The university made its buildings open to over one hundred student groups but explicitly barred those meeting 'for purposes of religious worship or religious teaching.' A federal district court found no violation of Free Exercise and added that if the university had acted otherwise it would have unlawfully established a religion. But the court of appeals reversed, and the Supreme Court agreed with the reversal. The university had established a public forum, open to all student organizations; it could not discriminate on the basis of the content of the speech an organization would use. To bar a religious group from what was a common good, otherwise available to all, would be like denying fire protection to a church. The dissent, marveling, asked, If verbal acts of worship could not be distinguished from all other verbal acts, why could a state university not offer a class called 'Sunday Mass'? The principle established in this case was extended to use of public-school property by another evangelical group, in *Lamb's Chapel*.

"Even *Wide Awake: A Christian Perspective*—an evangelical newspaper printed by students at the University of Virginia—was acknowledged to have the right to share in $14 collected by Mr. Jefferson's university from each student, because for the university to deny it funding on account of its Christian message would have been censorship. *Lamb's Chapel* was the operative precedent. The university by providing for funding of all kinds of student periodicals had created a public forum into which a censor of religion could not intrude. There was fine historical precedent, too. Mr. Jefferson had wanted his university well stocked with theology. Neither he nor Mr. Madison thought that the university could not pay for explicit theological messages in the library."

"I like the name of the case *Lamb's Chapel*," Simple broke out irrelevantly. "*Lamb's Chapel* is as good for the religious as *Wolf* is bad for them. *Nomen, omen* as my old Latin teacher used to say."

"Don't forget the name of the mother of all the religious cases," Cleo cut in. "*Cantwell*, as in 'cant,' 'to sing in church' or 'to speak solemnly to gain a reputation for goodness that is unfounded in fact.'"

Ignoring this interruption, John Henry went on: "The approach is marvelously seductive in a secular age where there is much more sympathy in liberal and judicial circles (they overlap but do not coincide) for robust speech than there is for robust religion. If I were an advocate advising a religious group today, I would always say, 'Try Free Speech first.' Moreover, if religion could be just treated as speech we would not need to go through that painful double effect analysis that Lucy suggests, but legislative prayer would become protected speech, the crèche and the menorah would be symbolic speech, and houses of worship could be exempted like public lecture halls.

"Another advantage would be achieved by collapsing freedom of religion into freedom of speech: from a humanistic viewpoint, what is crucial is respect for each person and for each person's fundamental values. Such values are always articulated in actual or symbolic speech. To champion the free exercise of speech is the most comprehensive way of recognizing the worth of every person.

"I have, however," John Henry continued, making a portentous pause, "to take a deeper and more principled view of what is required by religion and the Constitution. Talk is what intellectuals like and value highly. For many people, perhaps most, talk is cheap and cheaply prized. What they want is a guide to action—a religion, not a lecture; a call to duty and a response to that call; an approved and abundant way of life, leading to another life. It is that, not mere speech, that Free Exercise embraces and the First Amendment surrounds with safeguards. Religion is speech sui generis. It is attempted communication with God and the report of what God requires. It has been singled out by the Constitution for special protection. That special status reflects the belief of Madison and other makers of the Constitution that the human obligation to God is different from all other human obligations. To allow that acknowledgment of the claims of conscience to lapse into desuetude would be to abandon a precious portion of the Bill of Rights. I would look the Free Speech gift-horse in the mouth and reject it with mixed feelings of regret and pride.

"Now to get to the meat of the matter. From what you've told me, Judge Simple, the lawyers and judges have pretty well messed up. They haven't been able to articulate any clear, consistent, comprehensive doctrines to carry further the fundamental principle of Free Exercise. They have, in truth, floundered. The best that can be said for them is that they've settled a number of disputes peacefully. Given the past history of theological warfare conducted by force, that's an accomplishment, although I suppose it is an accomplishment that must be heavily discounted because theological passions have much abated in the Western world and rarely lead to bloodshed anywhere within it. Let's agree that the courts have helped us muddle through. My first point is that the judges are not markedly worse than the theologians at wrestling with religion, I guess because wrestling with religion can become wrestling with God—I mean taking into account the existence, alleged commands, and even the authority of a Being so radically distinct from our own."

"That might be the reason," Simple murmured.

"Secondly," John Henry went on, "what seems to be going on is the development of doctrine. The development of doctrine is a slow, laborious gestation. It's been compared to the way an idea in a child's mind eventually takes on its full contours in the adult mind of the same person, or to the way what a poet writes contains more than he consciously knew so that it takes readers to discover all that his words imply, or to the way a bud gradually matures into full flower. It's like all of those images with those sixteen precious words in the Constitution."

"I don't care for your analogy with the life of a flower," remarked Simple. "The analogy is a little too biological, and biological development leads to maturity and then to death. What's at issue is an idea, and ideas just don't unfold naturally, without human interaction."

"I take your point," John Henry said. "What would you think of this description of what's been going on? 'The development then of an idea is not like an investigation worked out on paper, in which each successive advance is a pure evolution from a foregoing, but it is carried on and through and by means of communities of men and their leaders and guides; and it employs their minds as its instruments and depends upon them while it uses them. . . . It is the warfare of ideas under their varying aspects striving for the mastery.'"

"I like that," Cleo broke in. "'Mastery' is rather a patriarchal metaphor but your description makes provision for the input of experience and the insights of those trying to work out the idea. In our case these are leaders like Madison and Lincoln and guides like Tocqueville and Robert Jackson."

"I *do* get a glimpse of the process with the aid of that analogy," Simple said. "But do I know how it will turn out or where I am in it? I wonder," he added, "if you are not being a bit too intellectual. Aren't you dealing with something like faith?"

"Madison's reading of the religious provisions has a religious base," John Henry observed. "There is no reading of these provisions as substantive that does not have a theological base; so no reading is utterly neutral."

"Remember," Cleo said, "what Madison said, that Free Exercise was 'an experiment.' You're part of the experiment. You do have two hundred years of experience and some notable examples to guide you. If you are a believer, you will believe that God can bring the process to a successful conclusion. Already it has replaced religious war with litigation. You can be confident that your voice and example will advance the experiment. The very incoherencies you and your advisors have encountered are opportunities for creative improvement.

"I have just one bit of advice from my reading: don't let yourself and the other judges be convinced that constitutional litigation is a way to settle old scores. Various groups have been oppressed in the past because of their religion. Their historical memory recalls the oppression and makes them dislike reminders of the oppressors. But this is America, on the brink of the twenty-first century. No religion seeks to oppress, offend, or exclude any other group. Our spirit is ecumenical. Let us not rehearse or redress ancient grudges."

"I have one thought to add, too," chorused Lucy, who had regained her spirits. "What you need is a better metaphor to describe the constitutional provision on religion. The wall has been shot full of holes. 'Sponge' is too undignified. What you want is a contemporary metaphor that is positive and dignified. I have it: *semiconductor*."

"The Constitution is a semiconductor between religion and government," said Simple stupefied.

"Yes," said Lucy triumphant. "A conductor, like gold or copper, transmits electricity without resistance; you get more electricity than you want. A nonconductor, like plastic, won't transmit at all; you have no electricity. A semiconductor, like silicon, passes on a small, controlled amount of electricity which enables you to have exactly as much power as you need.

"You don't want the full blast of religion on government, that's too much light or too much heat. But a government without religion is like a computer without electricity. A government needs the charge, in small amounts. The constitutional provision can work admirably as a semiconductor."

"Free Exercise the silicon of our society," Simple said. "If I have not found the fabled philosopher's stone, I have found an element I can put to use on my journey up the hill, which I see is about to begin."

But had Simple seen how sharp the incline might be?

CHAPTER 8

DURKHEIM'S DILEMMA

LEVIATHAN

Frontispiece to Thomas Hobbes, Leviathan, *1641.*

On June 6, 1944, President Franklin Delano Roosevelt broadcast this radio message to the nation:

> *My fellow Americans*: Last night when I spoke with you about the fall of Rome, I knew at that moment that troops of the United States and our Allies were crossing the Channel in another and greater operation. It has come to pass to success thus far.
>
> And so in this poignant hour, I ask you to join with me in prayer:
>
> Almighty God: Our sons, pride of our nation, this day have set upon a mighty endeavor, a struggle to preserve our Republic, our religion, and our civilization and to set free a suffering humanity.

What is "our religion," to which the president directs the deity's attention? Surely, in this public prayer, it is not the intensely private encounter with the beyond that William James described in such autobiographical terms. The president speaks of what is being defended against great political evil, what is common, what is American. But does America have a religion? What of "the Establishment Clause"?

Our guide to what is meant may be the sociologist whose approach to religion at the start of the century paralleled James's and opposed it. Reflecting a comparable interest in treating scientifically what had been the domain of theologians, philosophers, and lawyers, Emile Durkheim did not stop at the subjective. Individual minds, in his view, attain scientific truth such as his own analysis, but religion lies in the realm of the mythological and therefore in the realm of the collective. Instead of looking at individual intentions, he asked, what does religion do? Ruthlessly objective in its focus on function, Durkheim's work leads to a dilemma for modern interpreters of our Constitution.

A religion in Durkheim's definition "is a unified system of beliefs and practices relating to sacred things, that is to say, things set apart and forbidden, beliefs and practices which unite into a single moral community, called a Church, all those who adhere to them." Durkheim's definition appears to be as ecclesiastical as James's is individualistic, until it is ob-

served that the functional components of the definition carry it beyond
the ordinary church community and make the definition applicable to
any social body that has sacred beliefs and practices regarding things set
apart and forbidden. The nation as much as any ecclesiastical body has
such beliefs and practices. A nation's beliefs and practices perform the
function of Durkheimian religion, which is "an eminently collective
thing." That function consists in the manifestation of "the collective sentiments and the collective ideas." In manifesting them, religion unites the
collectivity and gives the society its "unity and personality." So defined,
religion becomes essential to every society, for every society seeks to manifest its ideas and to unify itself. Every society must have its sacred things
and the rites to celebrate them. Society creates the sacred. The relation
of religion and society is reciprocal: the collectivity creates religion, religion creates the collectivity. Society itself is a religious phenomenon.

Ancient Israel could serve as the paradigm for Durkheim, religion creating the community, the community creating the religion. Israel could
serve if a subtraction were made—if the acknowledgment by Israel of a
transcendent God were eliminated, if every text were reinterpreted, if the
heart of the matter were made the nation not the God that the nation
professed to worship. The national states of the nineteenth century are
more amenable than Israel to Durkheim's analysis and may be supposed
to have nourished his hypothesis. Twentieth-century totalitarian regimes
make his definition appear as prophecy. Stridently in the cases of Communism, Fascism, and Nazism, subtly but nearly as comprehensively in
the case of a national democracy, the community establishes public rites,
recognizes and celebrates public memories, and above all determines the
sacred—that is, what it is forbidden to attack. In every case the community takes steps to assure that the citizens will be educated in the beliefs necessary to maintain the structure of the society. The nation depends on these beliefs and practices, on what it stamps as sacred, for its
existence. Without these beliefs and practices, it ceases to be a nation.
Society therefore worships itself and must worship itself to survive as an
organic society. Hence, the dilemma, either no society or a society that
exists by establishing a religion. For believers in the First Amendment as
currently construed neither choice is acceptable.

Durkheim's dilemma can be denied by denying Durkheim. Why, after all, should his analysis be preferred to that of James? Each has its
problems. James's is hopelessly atomistic, proceeding as though individuals floated into connection with ultimate reality without instruction
by parents, by teachers, by books, without imprisonment in language and

linguistic conventions. Durkheim's is remarkably reductionist, eliminating the transcendent. The elimination is its strength among atheists, who cannot concede that religion is a transcendental traffic and who yet must account for what is a virtually universal phenomenon. The atheistic attraction is reinforced by the neutrality achieved; all religions are alike as community creations serving a community function. In the American intellectual milieu these two attractions have assured that Durkheim's brilliant hypothesis will have status and attention.

The dilemma is not for Durkheim, but for us. If religion is defined as an expression of the national community, and if that community must create its own religion in order to exist, must the community not establish that religion; and if the community establishes its religion, how can the exercise of religion be free? Must not every other religion in the community live in subordination and check to the communal religion? How can any other religion be permitted to intrude upon what society has sanctified as sacred? Must we not either give up our national society that depends on its own religion or give up our national constitution's guarantee of the free exercise of religion?

One possible escape from the dilemma is to deny that the national community that creates the national religion is identical with the governmental organs that are forbidden to interfere with free exercise. We can, for example, still be free from specific acts of Congress restraining our religious practice even if we cannot be free of the coercion exerted by tacit conventions, unchallenged assumptions, and implicit beliefs that go into our social fabric. Let us concede that the special telling of our national story and our national mythology are restraints upon any absolute religious freedom. Let us admit that the symbols and the rites of communal belief have a sacredness not readily challengeable by any more particular religion. Let us grant that affecting all we say and do is our language, which in its concepts, phrases, and structure already determines communally what any individual may experience, express, or even conceive. In union with others in any ecclesiastical communion, or separately in our own private imaginations and hearts, we have only the tools to think with that the culture provides. With these tremendous concessions to the community shaping and controlling our consciousness, can we not maintain that within the nation we may be free from control by the apparatus of the state?

This fundamental and familiar distinction between state and society permits escape—to a point. What the distinction does not disclose is the extent to which the organs of the state—the legislatures, the executive agencies, the courts, the schools—will be the product and the voice of the religion of society. How could they not be in a democracy? What organ of government would deny a tenet of the communal religion or attack a practice recommended by communal belief? Long ago, anticipating Durkheim, Tocqueville observed that in America public opinion would become "a sort of religion of which the majority will be the prophets." Even in the 1830s he could see that there was "an immense pressure of the spirit of all on the mind of each." That immense pressure is multiplied today by a far more powerful governmental apparatus and by far more powerful media that enjoy an effectively governmental role. In a democracy you can change the governmental organs by changing the community's beliefs and practices. You cannot prevent the governmental organs conveying democracy's religion. Without self-consciousness or guilt, the government will embody the communal beliefs and exemplify the communal religion.

Religion as it actually exists in America can never be free from the pressures generated by the communal beliefs. Making this large concession to the inescapability of Durkheim's dilemma, one could still contend that the actual organs of the national government do not perform the functions of a national religion. Does the evidence support such a contention? Or is there evidence that at least certain interests of government are placed above everything else so that they are in effect sacred, that certain organs of government are in effect supreme, so that these organs protecting those interests do create what can be sociologically described as a national religion?

At the outset of this inquiry an equivocation must be avoided. Obviously many of the activities of the government are robustly secular, not formally religious. There is nothing transcendent about the tax code. But our inquiry focuses on function, not on the explicit language and not on the intention accompanying the function. I seek to determine what is sacred by determining what is beyond touching; and in three areas, at least, those of taxation and military manpower and the judiciary, the inquiry points to secular activities that are functionally sacred.

SACRED REVENUES

What is sacred as to federal taxation may be illustrated by a story related to me by a judge in Boston:

> I sat in the case of a young man, an electrician with a wife and two children, who had read the United States Constitution in the Quincy, Massachusetts

public library and had come to the conclusion that the prohibition of unreasonable searches in the Fourth Amendment and the privilege against self-
incrimination in the Fifth Amendment prevented the United States from requiring him to file an income tax return. He was perfectly willing to pay his
taxes if he were sent a bill, and most of his income was subject to withhold-
ing anyway, but he refused to file. Encountering him was like encountering a
figure from the seventeenth century who had received a special illumination
as to God's will. With equal fervor and obstinacy this man asserted he had a
constitutional right not to file a return.

A jury convicted him of the federal misdemeanor he had committed by not
filing. Following the advice of the probation officer, I sentenced him to probation doing community service as an electrician, adding only, as the educational part of the sentence, that he learn to understand American government
by doing a book report on Tocqueville's *Democracy in America*. He performed
the service and wrote an intelligent report. But a standard condition of every
sentence of probation is that the probationer not violate another law during
the period of probation. During this period the time arrived to file the income
tax return for the past year. Reverting to his principles, he refused to file. A
revocation-of-probation hearing became necessary.

At this hearing I gave the electrician the choice of filing or going to prison.
I told him that he would not find prison a pleasant experience and that his
wife and children would miss him greatly. I told him that millions of his fellow citizens, hundreds of thousands of lawyers, thousands of judges filed income tax returns and did not read the Constitution as he did. In short, I acted
as an inquisitor might have acted in medieval Europe with one who clung to
heresy—on the one hand pointing out the terrors of the penalties that could
be imposed, on the other pointing out that all of Christendom, so to speak,
was on my side. Who was he, lone heretic, to have a different position?

In the end, he capitulated. He filed the return. I was filled with relief. My
federal role had dictated my conduct. I did not and do not regret what I did.
I do ask, If the penalty had been the stake instead of Leavenworth, would I
have imposed the sentence if he had remained obdurate?

Why did this judge coerce the young electrician to give up acting on
his beliefs? Why did the judge not regret the imposition of his beliefs on
the conscience of the other? Why did the judge even contemplate how
he would have acted if the stake had been the penalty prescribed and
perhaps see that he still would have been adamant in his demands? Because
taxes must be paid to the nation. In the unconditional words of the
Supreme Court, "Taxes are the life-blood of government." Without them
the nation must die. The necessity for regularity and order in the collec-
tion of national taxes is absolutely paramount. The judge's conduct, it
may be guessed, would not have been different if the electrician had
claimed to have based his behavior on Holy Writ or on special divine
illumination. The tax law would have prevailed whatever the authority

the individual opposed to it, whatever the penalty prescribed for defiance, however injured the electrician's conscience.

The reaction of the United States Supreme Court has been similar to
the judge's in Boston. The Old Order Amish, for whose religious way
that court showed extraordinary solicitude in 1972 when education was
the issue, in 1980 challenged the Social Security Tax as a restraint of their
religious freedom. Their religion told them to bear one another's burdens, as Paul taught in the Letter to the Galatians, and to relieve the wants
of the enfeebled, as prescribed in 1 Timothy 5:8. The intervention of the
government in these matters of personal charity they saw as wrong. Cooperation with the government by paying the tax or even by receiving
social security benefits they labeled as sin. Unanimously the Supreme
Court rejected their religious challenge to the tax. If religious denominations were "allowed to challenge the tax system," then "the tax system could not function." The Supreme Court thought it self-evident that
this result could not be permitted in the name of religious freedom.

Stark as the supremacy of the nation is where taxation is at issue, the
starkness has been softened by accommodation graciously extended by
the nation. By statute, the churches have not been subjected to federal
taxation. Glebe lands of the Protestant Episcopal Church in the vicinity
of the national capital were, in 1802, the first to experience federal exemption; eventually it became law that no church property in the District of Columbia would be taxed. By statute, federal import duties paid
on plates for printing the Bible were refunded; so were duties paid on
vestments, paintings, and furnishings for churches. Bells for churches
equally became the object of a congressional refund of the tariff collected.

When the Sixteenth Amendment was adopted, Congress was given ple-
nary power to tax income as it saw fit; Congress at once exempted the income of any corporation or association organized and operated exclusively for religious purposes and, going still further, granted a deduction
from taxable income for gifts made to such organizations. As sometimes
happens with a dominant religion, concessions to competitors willing to
acknowledge their lesser stature are easy to make and prudent to grant;
so the national religion bestowed favors upon the denominations.

Only in very recent times has the government showed the steel beneath its glove. Bob Jones University, a nonprofit corporation located in
Greenville, South Carolina, was incorporated "to conduct an institution
of learning . . . , giving special emphasis to the Christian religion and the
ethics revealed in the Holy Scriptures." Both as "religious and educational institution," it required that all its teachers be "devout Christians"

and that all courses be "taught according to the Bible." Among the convictions of those operating Bob Jones was the belief that the Bible forbade marriage between members of different races. As a corollary of this belief, the university forbade dating by students "outside of their own race." Given the many and varied moral messages that have been derived from Holy Writ or stray passages therein, this exegesis was scarcely outside the pale of theological speculation. Had not the Bible for almost two thousand years been treated as a bastion of slavery? But the university's interpretation was deeply offensive in modern America.

The Internal Revenue Service denied Bob Jones's tax-exempt status as of 1970. The university paid a Federal Unemployment Tax of $21 and sued for a refund. The national court in 1983 upheld the tax. Chief Justice Warren Burger wrote: "Charitable exemptions are justified on the basis that the exempt entity confers a public benefit. . . . [An exempt institution] must demonstrably serve and be in harmony with the public interest. The institution's purpose must not be so at odds with the common community conscience as to undermine any public benefit that might otherwise be conferred." As Bob Jones's policy was construed to foster racial discrimination, the institution was judged to subvert the public benefit it might otherwise have bestowed. Its exemption was forfeit.

Forthrightly making the criterion the common community conscience, the national court set a limit to concessions. The most powerful and the most pervasive of national laws, those imposing taxes, must prevail if the peculiar religious tenets of a church conflicted with the community consensus. And the community consensus was elevated to a religious status. It was not merely a policy or a dominant public opinion that Bob Jones University had defied, it was what the national court called "the community conscience." In terms of traditional usage the chief justice implied that God had directed the reason of the community in reaching its conclusion.

Two propositions emerge as hard facts in today's America. Federal taxation yields to no religious imperative. Any religious imperative must conform to what is perceived by the designated representatives of the nation—congressmen, judges, the Internal Revenue Service—as the ultimate concern of the nation.

SACRED MILITARY

Military manpower is similar, meeting a need not as constant but in times of emergency as pressing as the nation's need of revenue. Congress, despite the First Amendment, has had a free hand in deciding the degree to which religion shall be patronized for military purpose. True, the Constitution confides power over the military to Congress and the commander-in-chief; traditionally, the judiciary has hesitated to intrude. But one supposes that if the armed forces today refused to promote any African-American officers, a court would find such blatant discrimination to be unlawful. The Constitution does not come to a complete stop at the borders of a military encampment. Establishment-Clause jurisprudence does.

Military chaplaincies are as old as the First Congress. When, about two hundred years later, the United States Army was challenged by two students at Harvard Law School, it was found to be paying the ministers of eighty-six different religious denominations to conduct religious services. Over fourteen hundred persons were commissioned as chaplains, after having been approved by "an ecclesiastical endorsing agency recognized by the Armed Forces Chaplains Board." The army provided over five hundred chapels and had built over one hundred Religious Educational Facilities for classes in religion for soldiers and members of their families. The army paid for and distributed chaplain kits; communion material; liturgical vestments; and the Bible in Catholic, Jewish, and Protestant versions. The army had developed a Cooperative Curriculum for Religious Education of the Armed Forces. Congress appropriated approximately $85 million to pay for these religious services, supplies, and education. According to the army's affidavits, without the chaplains, military morale "would suffer immeasurable harm and our national defense would be weakened accordingly." The plaintiffs' proposed alternative of a civilian chaplaincy was characterized by Judge Walter R. Mansfield, whose opinion decided the case, as "so inherently impractical as to border on the frivolous."

Congress had the power to provide for the common defense; the War Power did not prevent judicial review but gave it a special context. Conclusively, the court declared that Free Exercise obligated Congress "to make religion available to soldiers who have been moved by the Army to areas of the world where religion of their own denominations is not available to them"; that rationale covered all chaplaincies, save those located in major American cities and used by retirees; the court was willing to permit investigation of the necessity of such services. Together, the War Power of Congress and Free Exercise shielded a program designed to supply religion "to military personnel and their families." As in the case of federal taxation, the congressional subsidy of religion was legitimated by finding that the particular religions subsidized were enlisted in serving the supreme good of the nation.

That that good remained paramount was evident in the case of an Orthodox Jew who objected to the military dress code. Serving in the United States Air Force as a major and performing his professional work for the air force as a psychologist, Simcha Goldman observed a religious precept that he cover his head with a yarmulke in token of submission to God. The air force ordered him to uncover. He sought an injunction against enforcement of the air force rule. The nation was not at war. Goldman argued that uniformity of dress was not necessary to preserve military discipline. The case reached the Supreme Court which, without elaboration, held that the military had no constitutional obligation to accommodate Goldman's religion. The "considered professional judgment" of the air force as to what good military practice required was superior to Goldman's free exercise of his faith.

The larger context of Goldman's unsuccessful appeal to religious freedom was the American position, as old as Roger Williams, on conscientious objection. Addressing the town of Providence in 1656 when its Baptists objected, in the name of religious liberty, to bearing arms, Williams wrote:

> There goes many a ship to sea, with many hundred souls in one ship, whose weal and woe is common, and is a true picture of a commonwealth, or a human combination or society. It hath fallen out sometimes that both papists and protestants, Jews and Turks, may be embarked in one ship; upon which supposal I affirm, that all the liberty of conscience, that ever I pleaded for, turns upon these two hinges—that none of the papists, protestants, Jews, or Turks be forced to come to the ship's prayers or worship, nor compelled from their own particular prayers or worship, if they practice any. I further add, that I never denied that notwithstanding this liberty, the commander of this ship ought to command the ship's course, yea, and also command that justice, peace, and sobriety, be kept and practiced, both among the seamen and all the passengers. If any of the seamen refuse to perform their services, or passengers to pay their freight; if any refuse to help, in person or purse, towards the common charges or defence; if any refuse to obey the common laws and orders of the ship, concerning their common peace or preservation; if any shall mutiny and rise up against their common peace or preservation; if any shall mutiny and rise up against their commanders and officers; if any should preach or write that there ought to be no commanders or officers, because all are equal in Christ, therefore no masters nor officers, no laws nor orders, nor corrections nor punishments;—I say, I never denied, but in such cases, whatever is pretended, the commander or commanders may judge, resist, compel and punish such transgressors, according to their deserts and merits.

Even for this great champion of religious freedom, this prophet a century ahead of his time, the common defense of the community prevailed over conscience. Functionally, the community was what was ultimately sacred.

When the Bill of Rights was debated by the First Congress Madison, as we have seen, proposed in the amendment safeguarding the people's right to carry guns to add the following: "no person religiously scrupulous shall be compelled to bear arms." Quakers, Mennonites, Schwekenfelders, and Amish, all active religiously in Pennsylvania and Virginia, wanted this kind of constitutional protection of their pacifism. Opponents observed, "No man can claim this indulgence of right. It may be a religious persuasion, but it is no natural right, and therefore ought to be left to the discretion of the Government." Madison's amendment was eliminated. The recognition of conscientious objection to war became a matter of congressional grace.

As with taxes, the nation was accommodating to a point. In the Selective Draft Law of 1917 "duly ordained ministers of religion," theological students meeting certain conditions, and members of the historic Peace Churches such as the Quakers and Mennonites were exempt. Others were not. This rank discrimination in favor of certain churches and in favor of ordained clergy survived the slight constitutional challenge offered in the courts. Writing for a unanimous Supreme Court, Chief Justice Edward D. White declared: "And we pass without anything but statement the proposition that an establishment of religion or an interference with the free exercise thereof repugnant to the First Amendment resulted from the exemption clauses to which we at the outset referred, because we think its unsoundness is too apparent to require us to do more." And could the court, which included such defenders of civil liberties as Holmes and Brandeis, have done more? The sacred is what is beyond criticism. The graced groups were not made to fight. Members of newer sects such as the Jehovah's Witnesses were prosecuted, convicted, and sentenced to prison because they were not exempted and had failed to comply with the statute establishing the national norm.

The Selective Draft Act of 1940 exempted students "preparing for the ministry in theological or divinity schools recognized as such" and "regular or duly ordained ministers of religion," and it exempted from service as a combatant any person "who, by reason of religious training and belief, is conscientiously opposed to war in any form." Application of the law required the national Selective Service Administration, local draft boards, and, in a number of instances, the courts to inquire closely into the religious beliefs and ecclesiastical status of those claiming an exemption. Use of such religious factors was not considered to operate as an establishment of the graced religions or to impede the religious freedom of individuals whose religion or ecclesiastical status was not favored by the law or to entangle government with religion. The national will, embodied in the federal statute, swept aside whatever constitutional scruples might have been raised.

In the course of applying the law, the courts distinguished between objection to a particular war and objection to war under any circumstances. The first was characterized as "usually a political objection," the latter as "a response of the individual to an inward mentor, call it conscience or God, that is for many persons at the present time the equivalent of what has always been thought a religious impulse." That a moral objection to particular wars as unjust had historically been the tradition of Western Christianity was forgotten or ignored. Under the statute, so construed, over five thousand Jehovah's Witnesses and some Catholics (most prominently the poet Robert Lowell) were convicted and imprisoned for the federal felony of refusing to be conscripted.

In the course of applying the law, the director of Selective Service issued opinion no. 14, according to which a full-time minister or the functional equivalent of a full-time minister was exempt from conscription. The Jehovah's Witnesses drew no such distinction among their followers; all were ministers of the Gospel. The director of Selective Service decided which Jehovah's Witnesses should be regarded as ministers, "regular or ordained," thereby imposing on this body of believers a set of classifications that they themselves had not used. With the usual judicial deference to administrative rule-making, opinion no. 14 prevailed in the criminal prosecution of non-exempted Witnesses for failure to serve as noncombatants. Only a minority of the Supreme Court objected to denial of the exemption to Witnesses who were colporteurs, carrying the Gospel message from house to house as some ministers preached once a week in church.

Applying the statute, the director of Selective Service for New York City established theological panels designed "to give the selective service personnel the benefit of the advice of those familiar with the educational practices of various religious groups." One such Advisory Panel on Theological Classifications consisted of persons described by a draft board member as "the most prominent" Jewish rabbis and laymen in New York City. Unfortunately, their names were not made public to the students they classified. From their advice it could be inferred that, while "Jewry is divided into three separate and distinct classes, Orthodox, Conservative and Reformed," the panel lacked understanding of, or sympathy for, the Orthodox. According to Irwin Levy, a student at Mesifta Talmudical Seminary in Brooklyn, out of fifty students applying for an exemption from the school only one was recognized by the panel as a bona fide theological student. Drafted, Levy protested the secrecy and bias of the panel and brought habeas corpus to secure his release from the army. The Second Circuit, acting through Learned Hand, the most respected judge in the country, held that the draft board had improperly delegated its authority to the panel. The decision was followed by the Third Circuit in the case of two other Mesifta students, Jacob S. Samuels and Henry Horowitz, who sought release from service. At the request of the government the Supreme Court unanimously reversed and left Samuels and Horowitz as conscripts.

Writing for the court, William O. Douglas expressed no uneasiness at a religious panel of non-Orthodox Jews judging unfavorably the Orthodox seminarians' sincerity; indeed he overlooked the difference, saying there was no showing that the students' faith had not been represented on the panel. Felix Frankfurter, who in another case had publicly asserted his Jewish identity, offered no dissent. The "variety of religious faiths," Justice Douglas observed blandly, "may create difficult questions for the boards. . . . [A]dvice from well-informed members of the faith in question may '[b]oth help and speed just classification.'" What was "the faith in question?" Neither Douglas nor Frankfurter cared to comment that, historically, the bitterest division and keenest theological hatred have been between those who are close in their religious heritage and divided as to its interpretation. In the delicate business of determining to whom the congressional grace would go it was not contrary to the statute, and apparently not contrary to the Constitution, to let the judgment of good faith be made by those of a faith like but different from those they could exempt.

The judicial business of exempting religious dissenters from the national commandment of military service led the judiciary, perhaps inevitably, into theological thickets. What was being applied was a federal law so the courts found it easy to concentrate on the statute's terms not on the scope of the First Amendment. Caught up in the familiar task of statutory interpretation, the judges insensibly slipped into theological interpretation. In peacetime, with the great national pressures of World War II abated, the national tribunal declared that the Jehovah's Witnesses were total pacifists and therefore qualified for exemption. The Witnesses professed themselves ready to fight a war commanded by God. Their theological reservation was treated by the justices as a harmless quirk, a judicial nullity. Thousands of Witnesses had been classed and punished as criminals in the two world wars because they were not opposed to all war. The Witnesses now became judicially entitled to the statutory exemption for those opposed to war "in any form."

During the Vietnam War, a conflict unpopular in many influential circles and not a war at all in the sense of having been declared by Congress, exemption was governed by the Selective Service Act of 1951. To qualify, opposition to war in any form had to be based on "religious training and belief in a Supreme Being." Daniel Andrew Seeger, Arno Sascha Jakobson, and Forest Britt Peter all claimed to be conscientious objectors, were all denied exemption, and were all convicted of refusing to serve. Seeger had a "belief in and devotion to goodness and virtue for their own sakes," derived from "a religious faith in a purely ethical creed." He left open whether or not he believed in a Supreme Being. Jakobson defined religion as the "sum and essence of one's basic attitudes to the fundamental problems of human existence"; his "most important religious law" was that "no man ought ever to wilfully sacrifice another man's life as a means to any other end." Peter declined to use the words "Supreme Being" or "God" but did consider that he was religious if religion was taken to mean "man thinking his highest, feeling his deepest, and living his best." Reversing their convictions, the Supreme Court held: "A sincere and meaningful belief which occupies in the life of its possessor a place parallel to that filled by the God of those admittedly qualifying for the exemption comes within the statutory definition." Seeger, Jakobson, and Peter all were declared to fall within the exemption accorded by the statute to those who opposed war because of "religious training and belief in a Supreme Being."

To achieve this result the Supreme Court moved to a functional definition of religion. What subjectively worked like religion was to be treated as religion. The effect of this judicial move was to deprive religion of its sui generis character and to make it a portion of a larger category embracing religion and what operated, in a court's eyes, in the same way. In *Welsh v. United States*, this line of thought was pushed further. The defendant, Elliott Ashton Welsh II, had explicitly denied to the Selective Service board that his opposition to war was based on religious belief; he had formed his ideas "by reading in the fields of history and sociology"; he objected to the war in Vietnam as a failure of the United States to live up to its responsibility as a country; he also thought that he had an absolute duty not to kill or to injure any human being. The Supreme Court noted that Welsh held these beliefs "with the strength of more traditional religious convictions." Observing that Welsh was among those "whose consciences . . . would give them no rest or peace" if they fought, the national court determined that Welsh was exempted. Conscience was thereby treated not as the voice of God to one who affirmed a belief in God but as the ultimate secular guide for one who professed no belief in God. Recognizing the secular conscience and weighing the depth of Welsh's feelings, the Supreme Court brought him within the exempted religious.

Upholding the checkered pattern of exemptions, the Supreme Court emphasized "the care that Congress realized was necessary in the fashioning of an exemption which would be in keeping with its long-established policy of not picking and choosing among religious beliefs." In fact, the "long-established policy" had been for Congress to pick and choose and to establish certain favored churches and beliefs. The policy of unequal treatment was magnified by the court's glosses on the draft law, with the result that the statute discriminated in favor of three groups: religiously motivated total pacifists; religious believers who would fight only at God's command; and nonreligious humanists who held strong convictions about killing other human beings. The Supreme Court could not bring itself to acknowledge the inequalities even in the course of denying exemption to a Catholic conscientious objector who did not fall within the favored classes because as a result of his religious training and belief he did not object to all war, only to unjust war. The court could not bring itself to admit any inequalities because that would have been to intrude upon the area that had to be untouchable. Where not a small religious denomination or a handful of educated individuals were claiming exemption, but members of the most numerous religious body in the country were asking that their faith's teaching be given respect, the Supreme Court knew that the needs of the armed services must prevail. As the opinion of the court put it: "And more broadly, of course, there is the Government's interest in procuring the manpower necessary for military purposes, pursuant to the constitutional grant of power of Congress to raise and support armies. Art. 1, § 8." What was truly sacred was not the claim of conscience but the security of the nation.

SACRED JUDICIARY

In the maintenance of these sacred institutions, a third has been indispensable—indispensable at least in a system in which judicial review of legislative action exists as a constitutional mechanism. If the courts did not protect the power to tax and the power to conscript, these powers would be in jeopardy. The courts do protect them and not only permit these institutions to be beyond effective challenge but add a benediction and a confirmation; for the courts themselves are sacred.

That the courts are sacred is suggested by their physical segregation from other law offices and from all business; by the physical isolation of the judges set apart upon a bench and their special costuming; by the solemnity of their sittings sometimes begun with a prayer; and by the often oracular character of their pronouncements. Functionally, they perform three sacred actions.

The first is so obvious that it is easy to overlook. The courts have the last word in determining what support a church may receive from the state, what exemptions a church, its clergy, and its adherents may enjoy, what religious feasts may be celebrated by public authority, what occasions may be distinguished by public prayer, what religious scruples must be respected by public officials, what religious ceremonies may not be prohibited by public law, and what constitutes a religion. Performing these tasks that they have determined to be allotted them by the First Amendment, the courts unselfconsciously place themselves above any church or creed.

Their decisions may, it is evident, be influenced by legislation. As the swift invalidation in 1997 of the Religious Freedom Restoration Act of 1993 demonstrated, the influence is at the option of the courts. In so many words, the Supreme Court declared: "The power to interpret the Constitution in a case or controversy remains in the Judiciary." The power to interpret is the power to make the Constitution what the courts want regardless of the expressed will of the people through their elected representatives. Individual decisions of the courts may on occasion be regretted, criticized, even disobeyed. Theoretically, the Constitution may be amended to alter a judicial doctrine; the theoretical possibility is of small practical significance. Only five amendments have been enacted to overrule court decisions. Actual power to change a decision, 99 percent of the time, rests only with the courts. That power is normally of the greatest practical importance, because practice usually tends to conform to what the courts decree. That there should be tribunals ultimate in their authority to resolve all the constitutional questions that religion may occasion appears as an inevitable and proper corollary of the constitutional status of religion and the institution, long established, of judicial review of legislation for constitutional infirmities.

The second function is comparably ultimate: a court must decide what is the true church—decide not always nor for every purpose, but decide when a church divides and the question is who gets the property that belonged to the undivided body. Unless there is an amicable settlement or a mutual agreement to submit to arbitration, a court must choose the winner if dogmatic divisions are not to lead to fisticuffs, bloodshed, or stalemate over property. Deciding, a court will—in effect, if not in words—determine which fragment of the broken body is the true heir. The courts will decide the kind of question that religious believers in the Christian world have quarreled over for centuries. In America a court will perform the function once assumed by church councils or theocrats.

A court will not of course determine which segment is doctrinally correct at an abstract level of correctness. Awarding one side the actual church building, a court cannot help giving the impression that the state says the winning faction is the faithful repository of the church's doctrine and discipline. If the winner were subversive of these ecclesiastical fundamentals, would the court give it the sanction of the state? Symbolically, the action of the court conveys approbation.

Such a result appears to resemble—let it be stated no more strongly than that—an establishment of religion as an establishment is now understood and condemned by constitutional law. But there is more than symbolic approval, significant though that is. There is an actual endowment. The court, an agency of the state, orders that property be possessed by a religious body that, but for the court's order, would go propertyless.

It will be objected that the court awards the property only in accordance with "neutral principles." The criteria have been discussed in the preceding chapter. Either the court will follow the state's real estate and trust law in interpreting the deeds to the church property or the state may create a presumption that the majority of a church congregation controls. In either case, however, the constitution of the church enters in. The constitution of the church can be made germane to the determination of the existence of a trust. Alternatively, if state law gives the majority control, the church constitution can make majority rule "defeasible." A court, in short, will have difficulty avoiding entirely the ecclesiastical structures affecting the property; and, experience suggests, a court will rarely be uninfluenced by the judges' own views of doctrinal matters. In the early nineteenth century the Unitarian Supreme Judicial Court of Massachusetts knew how Unitarian-Congregationalist disputes over property should be decided. In the 1860s the Lincoln appointees on the Supreme Court knew whether the pro-slavery or the pro-abolitionist Presbyterians were right. An observer who knows enough about the controversy and the judges can usually guess correctly how a contest over church property will come out. But even if a court ruled with the strictest impartiality, the court would still be the state giving property to a religious organization. It would be the state establishing a church.

The ground of this analysis was laid in 1948 in *Shelley v. Kraemer*. There the Supreme Court held unanimously that, when a state court enforces a covenant restricting the ownership of property on a racial basis, the decree of the court is action by the state. Even though the court's enforcement of a purely private agreement is in accordance with state property law, the fact that state action is involved makes enforcement subject to the Fourteenth Amendment. As the state action in *Shelley* was racially discriminatory, the Supreme Court held enforcement to be contrary to the Constitution.

Shelley v. Kraemer excited much commentary and much speculation as to how far beyond the orbit of racially discriminatory court decrees the doctrine of the case would be extended. Did it apply to court decrees in intrachurch disputes? In the second round of *St. Nicholas Cathedral* the Supreme Court applied *Shelley*. The second round question, it will be recalled, was whether a decision of a New York court holding the Moscow patriarch to be in breach of trust was state action unconstitutionally interfering with Free Exercise. Citing *Shelley* for the proposition that the court's decree was state action, the Supreme Court upheld the claim that the New York court had violated the Constitution.

Whether a judicial decree is state action for purposes of the Fourteenth Amendment cannot depend on whether that decree produces a good or bad result. First, it must be asked if the decree is state action. In *St. Nicholas Cathedral II*, the Supreme Court unequivocally decided that a court decree determining the ownership of church property is state action. The follow-up question is whether the state action passes constitutional muster. The Supreme Court has held that state aid to religion is the establishment of a religion. Therefore, it would seem, any judicial decree awarding disputed property to a church must be state action condemned as an establishment. Intrachurch disputes must be judicially resolved. Intrachurch disputes cannot be judicially resolved without violating the Constitution.

This minor dilemma is peripheral to the main Durkheimian one and may appear jejune because it can be so easily resolved. The courts merely have to hold that Free Exercise trumps the Establishment Clause. If a court does not award the disputed property in accordance with the requirements of Free Exercise, the court will be an agency of the state acting to impair religious freedom. That is worse than establishing a church, we might conclude: and such at least is the implication of the *St. Nicholas Cathedral* cases. Or we might conclude that the conventional reading of the Establishment Clause is skewed if it means that judicial action by the state may never give property to a church.

Abstract argument about establishment yields to the necessity of a court intervening. That necessity, in the end, is the capital consideration. In the disposition of the property of any church that is divided or dissolved, the word of a court will be supreme. A higher court may correct a lower court. But the court that makes the final decision will be wonderfully unselfconscious that its action is state action. At the point of performing its necessary and sacred function, a court sees itself not as a state actor in an ecclesiastical dispute, but as the guardian of the First Amendment, rising above the squabbling clerics as it performs its higher mission.

The third sacred function performed by the courts is providing theological commentary on practices with religious roots or meaning. The commentary began, harmlessly enough, with the national court's observation that Sunday was a state holiday because a uniform day of rest was a secular desideratum; that Sunday coincided with a day special for Christians was irrelevant to the constitutional status of the day. The commentary became more tendentious when the Supreme Court suggested that the civic celebration of Christmas (mysteriously called "the Holiday") had a secular purpose. The commentary became dogmatic when a justice made the remarkable statement, quoted in the preceding chapter by Lucinda, that prayers solemnize public occasions, express confidence in the future, and encourage appreciation of the appreciable. That was a recasting of the purposes of prayer, in effect a theological recasting that appeared to take scant account of the purposes of those praying and to superpose upon the prayers a meaning distinct from the declared intentions with which the prayers were said.

In the 1960s the Supreme Court recognized a new religion for constitutional purposes. In a famous footnote setting out a list of nontheistic religions Hugo Black added to the list "Ethical Culture" and "Secular Humanism." This identification was in the long run to be an embarrassment both to the judiciary and to those who could be argued to fall within the category. If Secular Humanism was a religion, it was appropriate to search out where it might be established by the state and root it out. A religious non-religion was a problem.

More recently, in an easy step from the treatment of prayer as communal therapy, the Supreme Court invented a counterpart to Secular Humanism, a nonreligious religion. The court called it "ceremonial deism," uncapitalized. Ceremonial deism was the court's description of prayers by a legislature, prayer at the opening of a court, and of "In God We Trust" imprinted on the coinage. Its contours could be expanded. In the court's usage it included prayers offered in the Nebraska legislature to the Trinity in the name of Jesus—"deism" was stretched to include this Christian act of worship. The adjective "ceremonial" apparently was intended to draw the sting out of the practices described because they were governmental and a government should not be guilty of practicing religion; in other words, the national court did not care to proscribe these practices. Just as Secular Humanism was nonreligious practice that was called a religion, ceremonial deism was religious practice that was not to be called a religion. The court created a kind of American Shinto, a state religion that for establishment purposes was a non-religion because its purposes were secular.

All three judicial functions—the channeling and restraining of support for religion; the resolution of intrachurch disputes over church endowments and church buildings; the theological commentary designed to turn nonreligious convictions into religious belief and defang religious practices—derive from the place of religion in the Constitution and especially from the Supreme Court's construction of the Establishment Clause. Interpreting the Constitution, the courts ruled on religious exemptions, restrained the claims of particular churches, defined religion, and determined what was ultimate and untouchable. With inescapable irony the very provisions of the Constitution intended to protect freedom of religion have assured the courts of control, subordinating every particular religion to the supreme interests of the nation.

THE SACRED NATION

Three sacred institutions are enough evidence to indicate that Durkheim may be right. But there is more. Other national interests identified by the national executive or national legislature trump the free exercise of individual religion. In *United States v. Ballard* the decision of a federal prosecutor to single out a branch of Theosophy as a fraud was not effectually challenged at any level of government. The federal mail fraud statute, as applied to religion, was bent but treated as decisive. The government was judicially approved in its investigation of religious sincerity.

Ballard was the first case since the *Mormon Cases* in which the Supreme Court of the United States considered a federal statute challenged by a believer's claim of Free Exercise. The statute at stake was not aimed at a specific religion, or indeed at any religion, but universal in its proscription of fraud effected by mail. It was not the statute itself but only the application of the statute that was argued to be an unconstitutional interference with religion. The case came to the Supreme Court only four years after the court in *Cantwell* had discovered Free Exercise. It came to the court only two years after Robert Jackson had written for a majority that "no official, high or petty" may prescribe what is orthodox in the United States.

The Supreme Court, nonetheless, refused to limit the breadth of the federal statute and shield a religion from its application. An act of Congress, in the eyes of the justices, was different from the local ordinances and state statutes limited or invalidated in the name of Free Exercise. A deference to the national legislature, not made explicit, guided the national court. The Constitution, of course, embodies the long-run interest of the nation. But the Constitution does not provide the same palpable presence as Congress. In the conflict of the constitutional rights of religion with federal legislation, federal legislation wins.

Similarly, in the classic *Mormon Cases*, the national preference for monogamy was judicially found not only to prevail over Free Exercise but to justify substantial restrictions on the right to vote, the right to be a juror, and the right to hold property—restrictions all intended to destroy the religious community that defied the national will. Equally in point is the more recent case of the Yurok, Karok, and Tolowa tribes whose religion treated their burial grounds as sacred. The United States Forest Service scheduled a logging road through the grounds with results judicially characterized as "devastating" for the Indians' religion. Reversing the Ninth Circuit, the Supreme Court declared: "Even if we assume that we should accept the Ninth Circuit's prediction, according to which the G-O road will 'virtually destroy the . . . Indians' ability to practice their religion', 795 F.2d at 693 (opinion below), the Constitution simply does not provide a principle that could justify upholding respondents' legal claims." Government "could not operate" if one of its programs could be frustrated by such a religious claim. Remarkably, Free Exercise was not a principle to the contrary. Whether the national interest was large, moral, and of a religious character, as in the case of monogamy, or small, economic, and utilitarian, as in the case of a logging road sponsored by an agency of the executive, no interruption of the exercise of government was judicially tolerable in the name of free exercise of religion.

No case is known to exist where the national court has weighed the national interest less than the religious interest. "Congress shall make no law respecting an establishment of religion, or prohibiting the free exercise thereof." In two hundred years Congress has never been found by the Supreme Court to have done so. A legal realist could conclude that the national legislature enjoys immunity in this regard. Empirically, the evidence suggests that Durkheim is right: for a nation the nation's interests are sacred and supreme.

Just as the national religion could be read as coopting lesser religions into its service by tax exemptions and draft exemptions, so a variety of other religious practices that are governmentally endorsed may be read as lesser religions put to use by the comprehensive national creed. The military chaplains are there to serve the armed forces in subordination to the armed forces' mission. The congressional chaplains are there to add decorum and dignity to congressional sessions, just as ceremonial deism demands. The prayer of the president in closing presidential speeches or making solemn proclamations is to enhance the speech or proclamation's solemnity and to introduce into a political occasion a tone beyond political criticism. Did not Madison himself acknowledge that religious proclamations by the president imply "a *national* religion" (JM's own emphasis)? In the same way, "God Bless America" is sung by officials on public occasions to add solemnity, dignity, a note beyond partisanship. The national religion does not merely tolerate, it incorporates the clergy and the prayers and hymns and some of the symbols of the coopted faiths so gracefully put to its own national use.

THE NATIONAL SYMBOL

The nation has its own sacred symbol: the flag. We salute it, parade it, decorate courts, schools, and even churches with it, fight for it, and honor it in our national anthem. In a statute entitled "Respect for the flag," Congress has declared: "The flag represents a living country and is itself considered a living thing." In this enactment, Congress has come close to claiming sacerdotal powers. The cloth is given life in the eyes of the beholder. If there is a national religion, it follows that the sanctity of the flag should be part of the cult. Legislation, litigation, and finally an attempted constitutional amendment, have set the American flag in the domain of what cannot be touched.

At the time of World War I the states began enacting laws against flag desecration. "To desecrate"—the very word compounds *de-* with *secrate* as in *consecrate*. To desecrate is to violate the sanctity of a sacred object by contaminating or defiling it. By 1972, there were flag desecration laws in forty-eight states. The first serious challenge to them arose out of the civil rights turmoil of the 1960s. An African-American in New York, angered by a sniper's shooting of James Meredith in Mississippi, took his own flag from his home and burned it on a street corner, saying, "If they let that happen to Meredith, we don't need an American flag." He was charged by the state with casting contempt upon the flag and burning it. The Supreme Court reversed his conviction because it was based, at least in part, upon his speech. The decision was 5 to 4, and Justice Hugo Black, dissenting, said, "It passes my belief that anything in the Federal Constitution bars a State from making the deliberate burning of the American flag an offense."

In the early 1970s, amid the unrest caused by the war in Vietnam and the incursion into Cambodia, two other flag-desecration cases came to the Supreme Court. A majority of justices voted to overturn convictions. Flag burning again became an issue in 1989 when Gregory Lee Johnson participated in a protest in Dallas during the Republican National Convention. Johnson accepted a full-size flag taken from a flagpole by a demonstrator, unfurled it in front of City Hall, doused it with kerosene and set it on fire. While the flag burned, the protesters chanted:

America, the red, white and blue,
We spit on you.

The Texas Penal Code had a section entitled Desecration of Venerated Object, making it criminal to desecrate a public monument, a place of worship or burial, or a state or national flag. "Desecrate" was defined by the statute as physically mistreating the object "in a way that the actor knows will seriously offend one or more persons likely to observe or discover his action." The Supreme Court, 5–4, held that Johnson's conduct was a communication and therefore speech entitled to protection unless the governmental interest was overriding. The conduct, indeed, was especially expressive because it involved the flag, which "as readily signifies this Nation as does the combination of letters found in 'America'." The Supreme Court denied that "the Government may ensure that a symbol be used to express only one view of that symbol or its referents."

Chief Justice William Rehnquist, dissenting, observed that the flag had served to unite the thirteen colonies; had flown proudly during the bom-

bardment of Fort McHenry, leading to its celebration by Francis Scott
Key in the words that by federal statute were the national anthem; had
been lowered at Fort Sumter, starting the Civil War; and had been held
aloft in Fredericksburg by Barbara Frietchie in the famous poem of John
Greenleaf Whittier:

> All day long that free flag tost
> Over the heads of the rebel host.

The design of the flag was ruled by federal statute. The time and occasion of its display was ruled by federal statute. The position and manner of its display was ruled by federal statute. Federal law also prescribed
"conduct during hoisting, lowering, and passing of the flag." The flag
was placed on the casket of deceased servicemen and, by law, was later
given to their families. According to statute, the flag was lowered on the
death of the president or vice president or other government officials "as
a mark of respect to their memory." In recent times the Iwo Jima Memorial
in Arlington National Cemetery had commemorated American sacrifice
and victory in World War II by celebrating the heroic Marines who had
raised the flag on Mount Suribachi.

If ever a physical secular object was treated with the reverence normally reserved for a religious object of devotion, it was the flag as its prescribed treatment was set out by the chief justice, who urged that the flag
"symbolizes the Nation in peace as well as in war." The flag was indeed
"the visible symbol embodying our Nation." It was, he might have written, our tainted nation's solitary boast.

In instant response to *Texas v. Johnson*, Congress enacted the Flag Protection Act of 1989. The law prescribed one year's imprisonment for anyone who "mutilates, defaces, physically defiles, burns, maintains on the
floor or ground, or tramples upon any flag of the United States." Flag
was defined to mean any size flag: even a miniature flag was included.
Nakedly, the national interest in the national symbol was asserted by the
national legislature.

Rarely has the Supreme Court been so quickly challenged by Congress
on the court's reading of the Constitution. The Flag Protection Act went
in the teeth of *Texas v. Johnson*. But Congress did not use its power under section five of the Fourteenth Amendment to guard a First Amendment right, thereby abstaining from the maximal legislative way of asserting its position. The court's majority held firm. The federal law, it
said, "suppresses expression out of concern for its likely communicative
impact." The alleged "national consensus" supporting the new law was

not reason to exempt it from the First Amendment. The government might "create national symbols, promote them, and encourage their respectful treatment." The government was powerless to stop a communication treating the symbol with contempt. The four dissenters emphasized "the symbolic value" of the flag: in crises it motivated citizens to sacrifice, at all times it served as reminder of the society's ideology, it embodied "the spirit of our national commitment to those ideals." The government could and should protect the symbolic value without regard to the communication intended by the flag burner.

By narrow margins, over passionate dissents, the national court had now repeatedly refused to elevate the flag into a sacred icon. The court had done so without reference to the free exercise of religion. The great liberal value of free speech, closely linked as it is to the freedom of thought, had been the dominant consideration.

In June 1995 the House of Representatives elected in the fall of 1994 took the step that Congress had not taken in 1989. It passed, by a vote of 321 to 120, a proposed amendment to the Constitution of the United States. The amendment read: "The Congress and the States shall have power to prohibit the physical desecration of the flag of the United States." The specific terms of the amendment would trump the broad inhibitions of the First Amendment. At one stroke the opinions of the Supreme Court, from 1969 to 1990, were to be overridden. At one stroke the states and the Congress were to be empowered to make the national symbol sacral. It was easy to predict that the Senate would pass the amendment by the requisite vote of two-thirds, and it was likely that ratification would then follow by the required three-quarters of the States. If forty-eight states had flag desecration in laws in 1972 and forty-nine states had called for an amendment, it was improbable that more than one-quarter would now refuse to ratify. Durkheim's analysis appeared to be vindicated.

To sum up: the interests of the nation regularly trump religious claims in the nation's courts. The untouchable domain is defined by the national interest. Congress and the nation's courts determine what particular churches may be favored in the matters of conscientious objection and what particular church factions are entitled to church property in dispute. The Supreme Court defines religion, discovers new species of religion, brings religions into existence, and disavows the religious meaning of religious practices and celebrations, sterilizing them and making them harmless. Subordinating particular religions to the national will, carefully calibrating their contributions so that they constitute assistance to the functioning of a government that the particular religions are never suffered to frustrate, the major organs of the national interest give shape and sustenance to the churches. Religious organizations are patronized by federal, state, and local tax law when they benefit the community and conform to its conscience. Clergy and theological students enjoy special exemptions from military service. The clergy of approved denominations are paid to pray for the government. A variety of religious exercises accompany official occasions, giving them a solemnity and setting them apart from quotidian politics. Presidents invoke the blessing of God upon the nation at the end of their national addresses, associating themselves with the divinity. On occasions of great urgency—the loss of Washington in 1813, the victory at Gettysburg in 1863, the invasion of Normandy in 1944—prayer is put to use to unify the country. At the same time the nation retains its own necessary institutions, necessarily superior to the claims of conscience—its system of taxation, its supply of military manpower, its courts; the nation even rates as superior to Free Exercise its Forest Service's plan for a logging road. Governmental operations cannot be interrupted. Finally, the nation has its own supreme and sacred symbol, "a living thing," to be placed beyond all desecration. The national religion functions. The dilemma is plain: we must abandon our national practices or abandon our pretense that Free Exercise is our principle, unless there is other evidence to be considered and a different analysis that can displace Durkheim.

CHAPTER 9

MARTYRS AND CRUSADERS

MARTIN LUTHER KING, JR.
crusader and martyr and evangelist of freedom,
spring 1963

"Just as the apostle Paul left his village of Tarsus . . .
so am I compelled to carry the gospel of
freedom beyond my home town."

Martyrs and crusaders—two clichéd images of Christians so old that their power to invigorate any movement might be doubted, yet so evocative of the relation of believers to the state that they are indispensable in measuring Durkheim's hypothesis that each nation has an established religion, which is the worship of itself. Worship itself and produce martyrs who defy it? Worship itself and generate crusaders who change it? I begin here with the martyrs and end with the crusaders. In between I look at those who, neither martyrs nor crusaders, accommodate themselves to the state but remain believers.

MARTYRS

The Jehovah's Witnesses held a doctrine that impelled them to challenge directly and explicitly the notion of the nation as supreme. They understood the prohibition of Exodus 20:3–5 against worship "of a graven image" to apply to the salute to the flag. Like early Christians refusing to sacrifice incense to the emperor because it was idolatry, the Witnesses refused to perform what was for many citizens a patriotic ceremony and was for others an empty ritual. In Germany in the 1930s the Witnesses for their pains were persecuted by Hitler, and in 1935 their American leader, Judge Joseph Franklin Rutherford, compared the compulsory salute of the American flag to the idolatrous Nazi salute, "Heil Hitler." All around the country Witnesses began to risk the expulsion of their children from school and their own prosecution as contributors to truancy by instructing their children not to give a salute required by law in at least thirty states. By 1939 some two hundred of their children had been expelled. The Witnesses claimed to be exercising their religious freedom. They lost everywhere. Chief Justice Arthur Rugg of the Supreme Judicial Court of Massachusetts voiced the prevailing judicial view: "The pledge of allegiance to the flag ... has nothing to do with religion." The

Supreme Court of the United States was not interested in reviewing the expulsions or convictions. The national consensus was clear.

In 1940, as part of the same impulse that led the national court to decide *Cantwell*, the court agreed to hear the case of the two Gobitis children expelled by the school board of Minersville, Pennsylvania for failure to give the obligatory salute. Two weeks after the Supreme Court in *Cantwell* had enforced Free Exercise for the first time, the court in *Gobitis* rejected the challenge to the national symbol. Writing for the court, Felix Frankfurter declared that the case involved "an interest inferior to none in the hierarchy of legal values." That interest superior to other values he identified as the interest of "national unity"—exactly what Durkheim would have predicted. Frankfurter elaborated: national unity was "the basis for national security." The corollary was also Durkheimian: the symbol must be preserved in order to preserve the substance. The nation's flag was to be saluted when law required it. There was a single dissent.

The Jehovah's Witnesses were already unpopular. Before the decision came down on June 3, 1940, they had been victims of several incidents of mob violence in Texas. After the decision, individual Witnesses were attacked in Maine (beatings, burning of the Kingdom Hall in Kennebunk), West Virginia (forced drinking of castor oil), Wyoming (tarring and feathering), Nebraska (castration), Arkansas (shooting), Illinois, Indiana, Maryland, Mississippi, Oregon (mob attacks). Two states, Oklahoma and Texas, accounted for 40 percent of the incidents. Small towns, not tolerant of outsiders, were the usual sites.

Legal measures against the Witnesses added to their woes. Many communities now adopted new flag salute requirements. In Indiana two women Witnesses were sentenced to two-to-ten years in prison for "flag desecration" because they had distributed literature opposing the salute; their convictions were ultimately overturned. The Mississippi legislature, stating that "the very life and existence of these United States and the state of Mississippi are threatened" by Germany, Italy, and Japan, made it a felony, punishable by imprisonment until the end of the war, to teach or distribute literature "which reasonably tends to create an attitude of stubborn refusal to salute, honor, or respect the flag." One Witness, R. E. Taylor, was sentenced under the statute. Affirming his conviction, 3–3, the Supreme Court of Mississippi rejected Taylor's claim of free exercise of religion and declared that religion's "primary object is a haven of rest after 'life's fitful fever is over.' It is a fallacy of the rankest kind to assume that loyalty to one's country and its flag is attributing to them any aspect of divinity or omnipotent power." In at least thirty-one states legal steps were taken to expel nonsaluting Witness children from the public schools. Planned by no central authority, unintended by the Supreme Court, overshadowed by World War II, the legal and illegal persecution of Witnesses from 1941 to 1943 was the greatest outbreak of religious intolerance in twentieth-century America. Popular religion, the national religion one would be tempted to say, appeared triumphant.

Not all subscribed. A split appeared. The *New Republic*, which Frankfurter had helped to found, said that the court had come "dangerously close" to being the victim of war hysteria. The *Harvard Educational Review* said the decision subordinated the civil liberties of minorities to "the will of the majority." *Christian Century*, the liberal Protestant magazine, said, "Courts that will not protect even Jehovah's Witnesses will not long protect anybody." *America*, the Jesuits' journal, said that the court had permitted destruction of "one of the most precious rights under the Federal and our State Constitutions." Thirty-nine law reviews discussed the decision, thirty-one of them negatively. Few decisions of the Supreme Court in modern times have met with such across-the-board rejection by journals of religion joined by the journals of the nation's law schools.

A new case, from a West Virginia town, found its way to the national court. The Witnesses, making use of the earlier briefs in *Gobitis*, drew on the heroic figures of Jewish history who had observed their duty to God and had refused to worship idols. Daniel and Esther were set before the court. Frankfurter's opinion was boldly attacked: it was the *Dred Scott* of modern constitutional law. Influenced by the intellectual revulsion against *Gobitis*, the court shifted; 6–3, in *West Virginia State Board of Education v. Barnette*, it affirmed the injunction of a federal district court forbidding state officials to require the flag salute in a West Virginia school.

Remarkably, however, the rationale that commanded a majority was not specifically Free Exercise but a global invocation of the First Amendment. The most eloquent writer on the modern court, Robert Jackson, writing the most eloquent opinion of his life, concluded: "the action of the local authorities in compelling the flag salute and pledge transcends constitutional limitations on their power and invades the sphere of intellect and spirit which it is the purpose of the First Amendment to our Constitution to reserve from all official control." The Virginia Statute on Religious Freedom had affirmed that God had made the mind free. Omitting the reference to the Creator, Jackson breathed the confidence of Madison and Jefferson that the government could not compel belief. Paradoxically, he applied the religious verb *transcend* to the secular intrusion. Climactically, he affirmed "the right to differ as to things that touch the heart of the existing order." Sweepingly, he asserted: "If there is any fixed star in our constitutional constellation, it is that no official, high or petty, can prescribe what shall be orthodox in politics, nationalism, religion, or other matters of opinion or force citizens to confess by word or act their faith therein."

Announced on Flag Day, in the middle of a great war, Jackson's opinion in *Barnette* was a manifesto for freedom, a rejection of the totalitarian philosophy of the enemy, a ringing refutation of the proposition that the highest in the hierarchy of the values of the law was national unity. Rejecting that proposition, the center of Frankfurter's opinion in *Gobitis*, Jackson effectively rejected the Durkheimian analysis. If the national symbol of unity was subordinate to other values, could the nation really be said to worship itself? Confronted by the martyrdom of the Witnesses, the Supreme Court answered No.

IN-BETWEEN BELIEVERS

Durkheim, uncompromisingly atheistic, reified the sacred as things untouchable. For Christians as for Jews religion is a relation not to a thing but to a person. The relation requires a personal response. Suppose Durkheim's thesis were made less absolute and adapted to the facts of American practice, even altered to admit the existence of God. The compelling clarity of the original concept would be lost, but a more useful explanation of the United States might be had. Such an approach was undertaken by Robert Bellah, a sociologist whose understanding of America and of religion gives his work particular distinction. In a pathbreaking essay he suggested that the United States has a "civil religion."

By "civil religion" Bellah meant more than that consensus on values that George Santayana critically described as "the genteel tradition"— the residuum of Protestantism that retains a belief in personal responsibility and civic decency under the auspices of a superintending deity concerned with the destiny of the United States; a residual content dwindled in its latter days into a vision of the good life as making a lot of money by fair means, spending it generously, moving fast, and being friendly to the neighbors. That tradition, as it once existed and as it survives in tatters, is more accurately classified as an ethos than as a religion, and although it undoubtedly has impacted government, its influence has been indirect, implicit, and barely religious.

The American civil religion as conceived by Bellah is the religion practiced by the government. It is a religion in which certain documents—the Declaration of Independence, the Constitution and the Bill of Rights, the Gettysburg Address—have had a defining force; a religion in which these documents have the sacredness of scripture. It is a religion in which certain events—the Revolution, the Founding of the Nation, the Civil War—have taken on the archetypal significance of such biblical events as the Exodus. As Bellah quoted Robert Lowell, the Civil War becomes "a symbolic and a sacramental act," confirmed by the martyrdom of President Lincoln, likened to "the Christian sacrificial act." The religion is manifested in such public holidays as Memorial Day and Thanksgiving and in the proclamations and inaugural speeches of the presidents. This religion is not specifically Christian, for it does not focus on Christ; nor is it a substitute for Christianity. Although the phrase "civil religion" is derived from Rousseau, Bellah did not reflect Rousseau's belief that a republic and Christianity are incompatible. This civil religion is not Secular Humanism nor is it ceremonial deism nor the deism that recognizes only a clockmaker creator unconcerned with his creation. Its most salient features are these: it asks that America seek justice; it recognizes that America is guided by divine providence; it acknowledges that America stands under the judgment of God. In the Declaration of Independence the Founders appealed to "the Supreme Judge of the world." The civil religion of America still makes this appeal.

Civil religion performs a Durkheimian function, but it seeks the approbation of God. Durkheim's atheism is absent. Civil religion synthesizes American history and heroes with biblical notions of divine destiny, supervision, reward, and retaliation. It is not the nation worshiping itself. It is the creed, symbols, and ceremonies uniting, directing, inspiring the nation.

For Bellah, the civil religion was not an unconstitutional establishment of religion. For him the liberalism that saw the state as "a purely neutral legal mechanism without purposes or values" was "a *reductio ad absurdum* and a sociological impossibility." Historically a neutral state had never existed. The American republic was formed and maintained by the religion that animated it. Bellah's powerful representation, drawing on Durkheim without succumbing to the monstrous implication that Leviathan must worship itself, is seductive in offering a vision for be-

lievers and troublesome and even outrageous to champions of absolute
separation of the state from religion.

I prefer a different approach, an approach not focused on the institutional but on the individual. The individual fulfilling a public office is
"an in-between"—that is, he or she is both an officeholder with particular responsibilities and a human person with all that that implies; therefore in between the state and the religion chosen by the individual's conscience. The governmental phenomena in which religion is manifested
are effected by persons enrolled in existing religions distinct from any
civil religion. The military chaplains, for example, are recruited from particular denominations; they do not enter on their service as representatives of an ecumenical creed; they say mass or preach sermons or expound
the Torah as Christian clergymen or Jewish rabbis. In the same way the
tax exemptions and the draft exemptions are accorded members of particular religious organizations or persons believing in specific theologies;
more is required to qualify for the exemptions than belief in a superintending deity. Bellah's case for civil religion, powerful as it is in what it
accounts for, leaves a good deal unaccounted for.

Civil religion is a construct, a synthesis that plausibly explains some
American practices but obscures the place of persons in creating the practices. Nations do not worship, persons do. Persons have their own religions not identified with any hypothetical religion of the nation. To say
person is to say intellection, intention, interiority. Persons make up col-
lectivities, represent them, perform parts in them, and are not identical
with them. To understand the person is to understand not only the part
played in the collectivity but to understand the personal intention as well.

No human action is performed without a human intention inseparable from description of the action. Description of the practice of persons
in terms of function must ultimately be incomplete and, if incomplete,
distorted. Attention needs to be focused on the intentions of those fulfilling the roles assigned to them in what is described as civil religion. As
individuals, they might, as an eminent church historian claimed, experience only "bemusement and puzzlement" hearing their practices por-
trayed as rites of civil religion. When the intentions of public officials are
taken into account, the acts described as civil religion may become acts
of individual believers expressing beliefs that do not depend upon their
roles but transcend them.

The general case of liturgical prayer is instructive. For Jews, for Christians, religion is a relation to a Being conceived of as having intelligence
and volition. Intelligent, willing human beings respond to an intelligent,

willing God. The relation requires a response to a Person. At the same time Jewish and Christian liturgies have standard prayers that the worshiper is invited to employ to speak to God. Prayer is an unusual form of personal communication because it consists in phrases formed centuries before the person reciting it existed. The worshiper may make the prayer personal as, say, the Our Father is for many Christians. Prayer in liturgical usage, therefore, can be at once collective and individual. Presidential piety has the same characteristic. Presidential proclamation and speeches addressing God are formulaic. They have an archaic ring. They can be personal. No one would mistake Abraham Lincoln's voice addressing the deity for the voice of Franklin Roosevelt.

Consider the example of the presidential prayer on D-Day and its invocation of "our religion" so apparently apposite to Bellah's case. After the three paragraphs already quoted at the start of the previous chapter, President Roosevelt's prayer continued, stating his request to God that "by Thy grace, and by the righteousness of our cause, our sons will triumph"; asking God as "Father" to receive the fallen into His kingdom; asking God's help "to rededicate ourselves to Thee in this hour of great sacrifice"; calling on "our people" to "devote themselves to a continuance of prayer" each morning and evening; and concluding, "Thy will be done, Almighty God."

Roosevelt's prayer may be read as a prime exhibit of civil religion or, I would contend, as a shining instance of personal convictions placed in a public context. Uttered with the urgency of a supreme occasion, it is laced with specific Christian concepts: grace; a kingdom after death in which the resurrected will live; the fatherhood of God; the efficacy of prayer; the duty of submission to the divine will. Careful not to offend Jewish listeners by explicit reference to Christ, the prayer concludes with words familiar from Jesus's improvisation of a Jewish prayer and the common Christian recitation of it. No impersonal supervisor is addressed but the God of the Our Father taught by Jesus. The prayer is that of an Episcopalian ecumenically phrasing his petitions. The strength of the prayer—its sincerity dare one say—is that it so compactly unites Christian theological themes germane to the crisis at hand. The distinctive personal cadence of the presidential prayer testifies to the vigor with which the highest officeholders have on occasion exercised their own religion.

The fusion of personal piety and public activity may trouble and outrage not only strict secular segregationists but Christians who see the fusion as the state subordinating religion to its grosser ends. The spectacle of prayer supporting the military enterprises of the state may be odious

to religious pacifists. More generally, Christians committed to social justice are appalled by the ease with which Christian officeholders have
served unjust purposes of the state. The martyrs are few, the Christians
in office, many. The critics point to the past—the long acceptance by the
mainline churches of the legal system's support of slavery, the churches'
failure to condemn the governmental spoliation of the Indian, the
churches' support of wars of conquest against the Indians, Mexico, and
Spain. The critics ask, Has religious freedom been good for religion? Their
answer is No.

The debate in the House of Representatives in 1995 on the flag desecration amendment would appear to confirm these critics' fears. In the
debate in the House there was occasional quotation from Frankfurter's
references in *Gobitis* to the national symbol. The flag was credited with
talismanic force as "what makes us all Americans" and what "makes
this America." Freedom of speech has been the value most cherished by
the courts. This amendment had the effect of removing one kind of communication from the protection of the Bill of Rights. Speech was subordinated to protection of the flag. *Barnette* appeared to be forgotten in
the desire to make the national symbol sacred.

Undoubtedly for these elected American representatives there was not
a chasm between their religion and their commitments to the government of the United States. Most of the members of Congress (all but 16)
identified themselves publicly as members of religious denominations. The
four great sects of Madison's day were still visible, supplemented by the
Catholics and the Jews. In all 143 were self-identified as Catholic, 63 as
Baptist, 61 as Methodist, 54 as Presbyterian, 50 as Episcopalian, 86 as
other Christian, and 33 as Jewish. These religious commitments coexisted comfortably with the patriotic purpose of protecting the flag. Honor
to the flag was not prayer for the members of Congress. God, who was
invited to "bless our great country," was not identified with the country. Worshiping a personal deity, the advocates of the amendment did
not suppose that the flag was God's symbol or substitute.

A critic who would see in these convictions either unjustified and blind
complacency or conscious hypocrisy would fail to do justice to the ide-
alism and the integrity of many persons in public service. Such a critic
would have to assume that only his or her judgment on America was
correct. Above all, such a critic would not give due weight to the individual intentions with which a believer might fulfill the role of representative without denying personal belief. Like pure functionalists, such
critics would deny the primacy of the personal. The critics merit the con-

demnation that colonialist anthropology has received. Their moral superiority is achieved by imposing their categories upon the persons observed. The imposition is neither humane nor Christian. As Czeslaw Milosz wrote Thomas Merton after the Trappist monk denounced the war leaders of America: "I wonder whether you, Tom, being on the side of the young America sub-society, should not think sometimes that they [the leaders] are human beings too, in spite of their benighted minds." Once humanity is recognized, religious intentions distinct from role must be acknowledged. In-betweens—a Robert Jackson, a Franklin Roosevelt —are not to be turned into robots of the state. Their religious commitments, often transcending the state, disprove the Durkheimian hypothesis. They do not, however, refute it with the irresistible force of the crusaders.

CRUSADERS

Crusades evoke the European examples. The evocation is not happy for Americans of Jewish ancestry. The etymology of the term tucks in the Christian *crux*. On more than one occasion there was an anti-Semitic spillover from the carrying out of a crusade. Nor are the examples attractive to rationalists who abhor religious fanaticism; nor do the original instances embody for most Christians an exemplary following of Christ. They were marauding military expeditions. Nonetheless, Woodrow Wilson did not hesitate to describe America's war against the Kaiser as a crusade; and President Roosevelt asking for divine blessing on D-Day prayed: "O Lord, give us Faith. Give us Faith in Thee; Faith in our sons; Faith in each other; Faith in our united crusade."

The president's chosen description was repeated after victory by the victorious commander, Dwight D. Eisenhower, whose account of it was entitled *Crusade in Europe*. Certainly the invasion had several characteristics of a crusade: the introduction of armed force into foreign land, a proclaimed belief in the righteousness of the cause and the evil of the adversary, the blessing of the clergy, and the invocation of God as guarantor of the righteousness and the victory. The general's use of the term *crusade* showed that, whatever unpleasant historical associations the word might have, for many Americans it had a positive resonance. To fight for the good in God's name appealed. Crusades are attractive to many Americans. They are the most distinctive characteristic of free exercise in this country. I shall define them now more metaphorically, and more precisely, than either Roosevelt or Eisenhower.

By *crusades* in the present context I mean campaigns to change the laws of the country and thereby to change the conduct of the people of the country; campaigns waged with intense and explicit religious conviction, with the use of religious categories and symbols, citing sacred scripture; campaigns led by churchmen and organized by churches, employing prayer in their support and contending that the crusaders seek to enact the will of God.

No guarantee exists that all crusades will be for good objects. But that crusades will occur has been made likely by the nature of Christianity conjoined with the First Amendment. From one perspective, crusades are splendid instances of the free exercise of religion. What action could be more free than the religious endeavor to change the laws that the existing government embraces and enforces? What exercise could be more vigorous than organization to effect political results? Crusades make nonsense of Tocqueville's counsel to religion to stick to preachments about eternity. Crusades make sense of Tocqueville's dictum that religion is America's foremost political institution. From another perspective, crusades challenge the assumption underlying free exercise: that no religion will win. Of the four completed crusades three have left indelible marks on the United States.

The paradigmatic crusade was for the abolition of slavery. Its chief features have been concretely illustrated in the chapter entitled "God is Marching On": a heavily clerical leadership and organized church support, especially among Congregationalists and Unitarians; an intense religious conviction that slavery was a national sin and an unrestrained use of this theological category to describe and denounce the practice of slaveholding; appeal to the Bible, especially to the Old Testament commandment against adultery (slaves were often sexually abused) and the New Testament injunction to love one's neighbor as oneself (slaves were by definition never treated as oneself); frequent assertions that it was God's will that slavery be ended, as in Theodore Parker's speech on Webster stating that one must choose between God or the devil; frequent prayers to end the evil, culminating in Julia Ward Howe's hymn to the God who was marching on.

Howe was not alone among women entering the campaign through religion. The most potent of antislavery novels, Harriet Beecher Stowe's *Uncle Tom's Cabin*, was thick with religious themes. Lydia Maria Child put out, as early as 1831, the *Anti-Slavery Catechism*. Maria Weston Chapman in 1836 published *Songs of the Free and Hymns of Christian Freedom*, addressed to those "who labor for the freedom of the American slave," urging them on in their "spiritual warfare," and reminding them that they needed "imagination and affection" in order to follow "the dictates of reason and revelation."

The crusade became the work of freed blacks as well. William and Ellen Crafts, the Georgia couple married by Theodore Parker, went on a speaking tour of New England, narrating their experience of slavery and escape. The Reverend Leonard Grimes, a free Virginian, moved to the New Bedford area of Massachusetts and then to Boston where his Twelfth Baptist Church became a key station in the underground railroad. In 1854 Grimes attempted to ransom Anthony Burns, the Baptist minister, in whose attempted rescue from the Boston Court House Parker joined. It was no accident that Burns, held there by the authorities, should address his prayers "To all the Christian Ministers of Christ in Boston."

The federal response to Southern secession resists cataloging as a crusade when for Lincoln the motive of preserving the Union avowedly predominated. Yet, once the war began, the slack spirits who had scorned Theodore Parker now acknowledged that he had started "the crusade" in which they were now joined. In this vein a young Bostonian wrote to Charles Eliot Norton, the essence of the genteel tradition at Harvard, apropos of Norton's review of Joinville's memoirs of the crusade in Palestine led by Saint Louis: "The story seems to come up most opportunely now when we need all the examples of chivalry to help us bind our rebellious desires to steadfastness in the Christian Crusade of the 19th century. If we didn't believe that this war was such a crusade, in the cause of the whole civilized world, it would be hard indeed to keep the hand to the sword; and one who is rather compelled unwillingly to the work by abstract conviction than borne along on the flood of some passionate enthusiasm, must feel his ardor rekindled by stories like this. . . . No— it will not do to leave Palestine yet." The writer is Captain Oliver Wendell Holmes, Jr., thrice wounded and much worn by over three years of war, already something of a skeptic, but with ardor rekindled willing to think of his service at the front as part of the crusade of the century. If the future justice could see the war itself as a crusade, a fortiori less critical minds must have been stirred by the analogy with Western Christendom's military reclamation of the Holy Land. Julia Ward Howe's hymn for the republic is a crusader's song.

The Civil War was brought about by the antislavery crusade, the absoluteness of whose religious-moral claims angered and alienated and frightened the slaveholding South into rebellion. And the religious dimensions of the antislavery crusade continued into the war, gave it a moral as well as political cast, and played a part in the Emancipation Proclamation, in the Thirteenth Amendment, and in Lincoln's Second Inaugural Address where the awful slaughter was given meaning as divine retribution for the sin of slavery, "the woe due to those by whom the offense came."

It did not detract from the character of crusade that the antislavery movement became associated with the Republican Party. It was characteristic of a crusade that the religious zeal of its adherents to impose their morality upon the country should make a political connection necessary. The intrusion of the religionists was resented by politicians such as Senator Stephen Douglas, who accused the preachers of converting the Sabbath "into the great day of the hustings." The preachers continued to preach against the Compromise of 1850, the Kansas-Nebraska Bill, the *Dred Scott* decision. And when the crusade issued in victory, it was the crusaders' religious judgment on slavery that was enforced in action. The competing religious view that slavery was biblically approved, fully moral, disappeared.

The crusade against polygamy was less divisive because the proponents of polygamy were few, and it was far less noble because it did not take the lives of the crusaders; no chivalry was needed. The form of campaign, however, was similar, the crusade as early as 1856 finding its alliance with the Republicans, whose party platform in that year announced "the imperative duty of Congress to prohibit in the territories those twin relics of barbarism, polygamy and slavery." The next year President Buchanan, a Democrat, was advised to try "the almost universal excitements of an anti-Mormon crusade." When he ordered federal troops into the Utah territory it was generally seen as a federal effort to "root out polygamy as an affront to Christian morality."

The Church of Jesus Christ of Latter-day Saints taught that it was the duty of an adult male Mormon to practice multiple marriages, "circumstances permitting," and that failure to perform the duty "would be damnation in the life to come." Multiple marriage was no mere option or indulgence. It was a commandment, founded on the Church's exegesis of the Bible and a direct revelation by God to Joseph Smith. The Church became the target of the crusaders, who were chiefly Methodists, Presbyterians, Congregationalists, all committed to a monogamy they perceived as a requirement of Christianity.

In 1862, with the Republicans in control of Congress, "An Act to punish and prevent the Practice of Polygamy in the Territories of the United

States" was passed. Bigamy was criminalized. The territorial legislature's incorporation of the Church was annulled. Madison's old wish for mortmain legislation was granted: in the territories no church could acquire real estate worth in excess of $50,000. Abraham Lincoln signed the bill into law. From the Mormon perspective, the majority was enforcing its morality. As one of this minority expressed it: religion in America was for every man "'a matter between himself and God alone'—providing God don't shock our moral ideas by introducing something we don't believe in. If He does, let Him look out."

When finally, in 1879, the legislation of 1862 was challenged in the Supreme Court as a breach of Free Exercise, the challenge was unanimously rejected. To accept it "would be to make the professed doctrines of religious belief superior to the law of the land and in effect to permit every citizen to become a law unto himself." Madisonian madness was out. The author of the opinion, Chief Justice Morrison R. Waite, an Episcopalian, described it as "my sermon on the religion of polygamy."

Emboldened by this success, the crusaders pressed for more stringent enforcement and harsher laws. Polygamists were disqualified from voting and from being jurors in the territories. To prove polygamy, the government was dispensed from proving sexual intercourse with two women held out by one man as his wives; his maintenance of two households was sufficient proof. Legislation for the federal territory of Idaho prescribed an oath to be taken by anyone registering to vote. The applicant had to swear that "I am not a member of any order, organization, or association which teaches, advises, counsels or encourage its members, devotees or any other person to commit the crime of bigamy or polygamy, or any other crime defined by law, as a duty arising or resulting from membership in such order, organization or association . . . ; that I do not and will not, publicly or privately, or in any manner whatever teach, advise, counsel or encourage any person to commit the crime of bigamy or polygamy . . . either as a religious duty or otherwise." The government found the oath—one of the oldest heresy-hunting techniques—to be useful and combined it in an indictment with the statute against conspiracy, the prosecutor's most useful weapon. The government charged Samuel D. Davis and others with conspiracy to register to vote, when in truth each defendant was a member of the Mormon Church, which they knew taught, advised, counseled and encouraged its members and devotees to commit bigamy and polygamy as duties arising from membership. Davis was convicted and fined $500. He appealed, invoking Free Exercise and also Article VI of the Constitution ("No religious test shall ever be re-

quired as a qualification to any office or public trust under the United
States"). Upholding his conviction, the Supreme Court stated that
polygamy was subject to punishment "by the general consent of the Christian world in modern times." Christendom's unanimity validated the crusade's objective and the law enacted to accomplish it. As Justice Stephen
Field put it for the court: "However free the exercise of religion may be,
it must be subordinate to the criminal laws of the country. . . . Crime is
not the less odious because sanctioned by what any particular sect may
designate as 'religion.'"

The Church itself in 1887 became the immediate object of legislation
directing the forfeiture of its assets apart from buildings of worship (in
this way Free Exercise was honored). The sponsor of the legislation, Representative John R. Tucker, gave the closing speech in the House on behalf of the Committee on the Judiciary. He quoted the words of Jesus
from the Gospel of Mark on marriage making two into one flesh. He declared: "Ever since Christ interpreted the Judaic law and gave it to us in
His own express words, it [polygamy] has been not only a sin against
God but has been made a crime by every Christian society." The forfeiture was enacted. It was upheld in 1890 in a case ominously entitled *The
Late Corporation of the Church of Jesus Christ of Latter Day Saints v.
United States*. Joseph Bradley wrote for a unanimous Supreme Court.
Bradley himself believed that Christ "taught no dogmas but one—that
God is our Father and that we are all brethren." Speaking for the court,
he expressed more extensive ideas about the implication of Christian belief: "The organization of a community for the spread and practice of
polygamy is, in a measure, a return to barbarism. It is contrary to the
spirit of Christianity, and of the civilization which Christianity has produced in the Western world." The crusade was complete. The Church,
its opponent, was struck. Within months of the decision, now almost
propertyless, the Church agreed to abide by the laws against bigamy. In
1894 Congress returned its property. One version of Christianity, politically advocated, federally enforced as the national will, had made another version of Christianity impracticable, morally suspect, criminal, and
bankrupt.

The third crusade made the use of alcohol its target. Ministers such
as William Lloyd Garrison and Theodore Parker were early reformers
for temperance; the movement gained momentum after the Civil War.
Drawing delegates from churches and Sunday schools, the Prohibition
Party held its first national convention in 1872. The party was sustained
by Baptists, Scandinavian Lutherans, Presbyterians, and, above all, by

Methodists. A powerful ally was an organization candidly announcing its religious roots: the Women's Christian Temperance Union. In 1887 H. H. Rutherford, a minister using "individual Protestant churches as his basic organizational unit," led the way in designing legislation authorizing local governments to abolish the saloon. The newly founded Anti-Saloon League was self-identified as "the Protestant church in action." The leader of the league's educational work, Ernest Cherrington, wrote of its success: "The church voters' lists . . . constituted the real key."

In addition to the evil effect of alcoholism on the individual the reformers stressed the damage done to such Christian institutions as marriage and the family. Alcohol was associated with sexual sin in lowering inhibitions; the saloons were seen as centers for prostitution. Just as in the crusade against slavery, the danger to chastity—a high value in Western Christianity—gave added flair to sermons against the scourge.

The religious reformers were largely effective in influencing the Republican Party. There was also a religious split, with the adherents of the more liturgical, wine-using religions—Catholics, Episcopalians, Jews—showing little appetite for the abolitionism urged by zealous preachers. The Eighteenth Amendment, when it finally passed, made all wine-using liturgies difficult if not impossible by imposing a ban on sale or transportation of "intoxicating liquors" used "for beverage purposes." No one, for example, could say that the wine used for mass was not an intoxicating liquor. No one could say that a ritual consisting in the drinking of such wine was not using the wine as a beverage. A beverage is a drink. The consumption of the wine by the priest was not imaginary. The words of the mass were "Drink of this." Whatever Catholic theology's understanding of transubstantiation as effecting the change of what looked like wine into the blood of Christ, the transportation of the wine prior to consecration violated the rule established as part of our fundamental law. How could the Catholic faith be freely exercised if its central rite had to be truncated? The criminal law, the Volstead Act, which actually enforced the constitutional prohibition, avoided the problem by diluting the constitutional command, explicitly excepting wine used "for sacramental purposes, or like religious rites." The mass, communion services, Jewish seders were saved, at the small expense of ignoring the text of the Eighteenth Amendment. The crusaders, although they captured the nation, had had to accommodate those who did not share their absolute abhorrence of alcohol. The accommodation was a token that their victory would not be lasting. They had not achieved the crushing national consensus essential for the permanent enthronement of a religious-moral doctrine.

If the third crusade was spearheaded by the Protestant church in action, the fourth crusade has been aptly described by one of its leaders, the Reverend Joseph Lowery, as "the black church coming alive." Its opening moments occurred in 1955 in Montgomery, Alabama when Rosa Parks refused to move to the back of the bus and was arrested for violating a municipal ordinance segregating bus seating by race. Martin Luther King, Jr., a local pastor, emerged as the leader of a boycott of the buses by blacks. At each critical stage King spoke in the language of religion. At the first mass meeting he quoted the words of Jesus as reported in the Gospels, told the crowd that their protest should be "with Christian love," and gave as advice, "Let your conscience be your guide." The crowd sang "Onward Christian Soldiers." When his house was bombed, King cooled the crowd saying, "What we are doing is just. God is with us." When he and the other black ministers backing the boycott went on trial for maliciously interfering with a business, their black followers filled the courtroom wearing cloth crosses bearing Jesus's words on the cross, "Father, forgive them." When the Supreme Court held the Montgomery ordinance unconstitutional, an anonymous black's exclamation was recorded: "God Almighty has spoken from Washington, D.C." The transformation of the young minister who emerged as the leader was to be not as overtly miraculous as that of the young carpenter in the Legend of Will Denman, but the fruits were to be as palpable. And for King, conscience was a trumpet.

The decisive phase of the modern movement for civil rights began at the call of one layman and four ministers for a meeting of black churchmen and other black leaders in January 1957 at the Ebenezer Baptist Church in Atlanta. From that meeting emerged the Southern Christian Leadership Conference, whose name incorporated its inspiration and purpose. The guide to what must be done was the Christian churchmen's recognition that civil rights could be won only by political means and *"that direct action is our most potent political weapon."* Who would engage in this action? The leadership answered: *"The campaign is based on the most stable social institution in Negro culture—the church."*

The Southern Christian Leadership Conference was the force that developed the infrastructure of the civil rights movement. It provided moral, material, and organizational support to local protesters, otherwise isolated and at a disadvantage before the white power structure. Acting upon local communities it cultivated the mental attitudes conducive to protest. It led to large numbers of people wanting freedom from oppressive discrimination. Its "most magnificent accomplishment" was "the creation of a disciplined mass movement of Southern blacks."

Twenty-one of the twenty-five original officers of the Southern Christian Leadership Conference were ordained ministers. Its president was the Reverend Martin Luther King, Jr. Its members (it had no individual members) were chiefly Christian churches or organizations. Its characteristic form of meeting was a rally modeled on a church revival, featuring a charismatic minister, often the Reverend King himself. Its imagery was biblical—for example, the present state of subservience was seen as "Egypt"; Moses was put forward as the exemplar of a deliverer. Financing came largely from the churches, chiefly from "black church-oriented meetings outside the South." Preaching in black churches once had focused on acceptance of one's lot in this world. The crusaders insisted that religion made a difference in society. Changing the focus and the emphasis of the sermon, the crusaders used the traditional power of religious teachers to affect cultural consciousness. The charismatic preaching of King himself "translated the message of the folk gospel" and embodied "a system of knowledge and persuasion created by generations of black folk preachers." The notion of a crusade was congenial to the religious consciousness of blacks: so Ida B. Wells, a leader against lynch law in an earlier time, called her autobiography *Crusade For Justice*. King himself was the subject of a biography entitled *Crusader Without Violence*. The Southern Christian Leadership Conference employed the term "crusade" in its 1958 drive to register blacks to vote, which was christened "The Crusade for Citizenship."

The religious intrusion into Southern politics was bitterly resented by beneficiaries of the existing order. As a letter received by the Reverend George Lee in Mississippi put it: "Preacher, instead of preaching the Gospel, what you say you are called to do, you are preaching to Negroes here in Humphreys County to register and vote. You had better do what you claim you were called to do, preach the Gospel." The crusade continued, the Reverend Lee, murdered shortly after receiving this request, one of its martyrs.

A climactic moment was the confrontation planned by the Southern Christian Leadership Conference in Birmingham in 1963—"a systematic, wholehearted battle against segregation which would set the pace for the nation." The 16th Street Baptist Church in Birmingham was chosen as headquarters. This church and three other Baptist churches provided the leadership with a starting constituency of close to five thousand. The Reverend King was in charge but avoided arrest until, choosing Good Friday as the day, he disobeyed a court injunction and was put in Birmingham City Jail. From there he penned the famous epistle addressed to "fellow clergymen": "Just as the apostle Paul left his village of Tarsus and carried the gospel of Jesus Christ to the far corners of the Greco-Roman world, so I am compelled to carry the gospel of freedom beyond my home town. . . . I hope the church as a whole will meet the challenge of this decisive hour." Nearly one million copies of the Letter From Birmingham Jail were distributed.

And Martin himself was to know a real Good Friday, killed in a way that made him a martyr as well as a crusader. By his death he accomplished what Theodore Parker, a crusading preacher, fell short of doing. His fusion of the crucified with the crusader assured the perpetuation of his memory and his dream.

His movement succeeded because of the cohesion produced by "music, religious oratory, prayers, and shared symbols." Following the confrontations in Birmingham, 758 demonstrations occurred in 186 cities across the South; 14,733 persons were arrested. One year later Congress passed the Civil Rights Act of 1964. As effectively as the northern ministers who had advocated abolition, the black ministers of the Southern Christian Leadership Conference had intervened in the political system, provoked confrontation and conflict, and carried their crusade to victory.

Probably not enough crusades have occurred to warrant the generalizations that sociologists seek to draw from, or impose on, history. Certain salient features may be noted. It has been argued that only when the religious community is united has it been successful; but the prohibitionists achieved temporary, and the abolitionists achieved permanent, success in the face of religious opposition. What has counted has been determination, organization, intensity. These outpourings of moral energy do not arise from the friendly and insipid tolerance of the genteel tradition. They horrify that tradition by their harshness, zeal, and intolerance of the evil to be crushed. Their objectives are humane; their methods and their spirit are religious in their rigor, their purity, their faith, and their fire.

That cool eighteenth-century rationalist, David Hume, had warned that religious zeal must be checked by governmental measures if disaster was to be avoided. Madison had read Hume and not followed him: the cure was worse than the disease. Madison himself had never seen a crusade. The eruption of religion into politics that he had observed had carried him to Congress, but when he proposed the First Amendment the experience of crusades was not in the forefront of his thought. When the First Amendment was adopted, it was without cost to government. Crusades have demonstrated that Free Exercise is, in fact, expensive.

Crusades make citizens uncomfortable, obviously those who disagree with their objective and some who deplore their methods. They appear to be extreme. They are typically described as abandoning preaching for politics, as making the pulpit the hustings. Invoking God, the crusaders put their opponents at a moral disadvantage; the opponents naturally resent the criticism and resist the claim. The cost in social tension is high; in the case of abolition, it was a cost measured in lives.

Religiously speaking, crusades appear to be a Christian phenomenon, with roots in the prophetic tradition of Judaism. Whether the methods of any crusade are always compatible with Christ's commandment of love may be doubted or disputed; but the Christ of the Gospel according to Luke declares: "I come to send fire upon the earth, and what do I wish but that it be kindled. . . . Think you that I am to give peace upon the earth? No, I tell you, discord." Warrant for a crusader's cast of mind can be found in such Scripture. Crusades do not come from the government (the anti-Mormon movement is arguably a partial exception) but tell the government that there is an evil that must be extirpated. They soak up the energy of churchmen who, an unbeliever might speculate, need outlets for their energy. They give purpose and prestige to the religion that backs them.

Religion has flourished in America. Once there were sixteen denominations, four of them major; now over fourteen hundred denominations exist. Between 1791 and 1991, it is estimated with some probability, the percentage of the population belonging to a church has nearly doubled from 34 percent to 62 percent. Growth and variety of this kind must be due in part to competition, as Madison predicted. Part, too, must be ascribed to the energy developed by crusades, as he did not predict.

The crusades have not, however, bestowed permanent benefits on the churches that have sponsored them. Free Exercise authorizes full mobilization on behalf of a moral imperative religiously conceived. Free Exercise stands against any takeover of the government by a church. Crusades, in fact, have sought the enforcement of a moral claim, not the setting up of an ecclesiastical regime.

Crusades do, when successful, establish as the law of the land what begins as the religious perception of a moral requirement. Employing religion as a political institution, they mold the morals of the country. They lead to the enactment into law of religious-moral doctrine. At the same time they flourish because of the First Amendment. The government is not empowered to restrain them. They respond to imperatives that transcend the secular state. They are expressions of the demands of conscience. They have played a major part in the American experiment of Free Exercise.

Before these bursts of religious belief, infiltrating the society, capturing the organs of government, the Durkheimian theory withers. These eruptions are not the worship of society but its reformation. They do confirm Bellah's insight that America wants to be under judgment. They are a call to judgment in the name of an authority above the state, and the state responds, subject to a sovereignty not its own.

Enshrined in the First Amendment, free exercise has become a cultural ideal. Imperfectly honored in practice, it is beyond verbal challenge in America: Manasseh Cutler, Joseph Story, Alexis de Tocqueville testify to this truth. Internalized by many Americans, the ideal has borne fruit in religiously mixed marriages, in religiously mixed schools, in ecumenical cooperation in charitable enterprise. These civic benefits have not been destroyed by the disruption of civic harmony that crusades have brought about. The crusade completed, no church established, Americans have come again together without those dark and bitter hatreds and ancient grudges still carrying a religious label in many parts of the world. Race has been an American problem. Religion has been the source of turmoil and of civic strength. The United States has become the active monitor and advocate of religious freedom everywhere.

It was the prophecy of James Madison that the lustre of the American light would illumine the world. That light has penetrated into many corners. Without making an encyclopedia of all the places it has reached, I propose in what follows to examine three countries and one church in their response to the American ideal.

PART THREE

INFLUENCES

CHAPTER 10

THE FLICKER FROM THE FOREST

Présentation par J.T.N.

JACQUES-LOUIS DAVID
Nude study of Pope Pius VII in Paris, 1805

*Preliminary study for David's painting of the coronation of
Napoleon with the pope's blessing; or, for our purposes, The
Free Exercise of Religion in France, fourteen years after the
declaration of the Rights of Man: the Church has been
stripped—it is about to be made the instrument of the empire.*

AN AMERICAN IN PARIS

On July 20, 1789, six days after the fall of the Bastille, with revolution crackling in the streets, the following letter was sent by Jérôme Marie Champion de Cicé, archbishop of Bordeaux, to Thomas Jefferson, the minister of the United States of America accredited to the Most Christian King of France:

Le Comité chargé par l'assemblée nationale de rediger un projet de Constitution et ne voulant rien negliger pour la perfection d'un ouvrage aussi important, desire de vous entretenir et de faire tourner au profit de la France les lumieres de Votre raison et de Votre experience. Nous esperons de vous, Monsieur, cette Complaisance. Il n'y a plus d'etrangers pour vous lorsqu'il s'agit du bonheur des hommes. Dans cette juste Confiance nous avons l'honneur de vous prier de nous accorder une Conference Mercredy prochain dans un des bureaux attenant la Salle de l'assemblée nationale à 5 heures après midy pour Six.

Si j'osois, Monsieur, je vous prierois de me faire l'honneur de diner ce même jour chez moy place dauphine No. 8. Aggréez la Consideration respectueuse avec laquelle j'ay l'honneur d'etre, Monsieur, Votre très humble et très obeissant Serviteur,

† J.M. Arch. de Bordeaux

Jefferson replied the day after he received this letter:

à Paris ce 22me juillet 1789

Je sens toute ma malheur, Monseigneur, de recevoir les ordres du Comité nommé pour la redaction de la Constitution au moment que des depeches pour l'Amerique m'occupent tout entier, et que le bâtiment qui doit les porter est pret à mettre à la voile. Je vous supplie de leur en être l'organe de mes regrets. A moi la perte est des plus affligeantes de manquer à des discusssions les plus interessantes possibles, et traitées, comme elles le seront, par des membres distingués de l'assemblée la plus eclairée qui existe. Mes foibles lumieres ne leur auroient rien valu. Elles leur auroient eté d'un trop leger dedommagement pour la mefiance et peut-etre les calomnies qu'auroient pu etre inspirées contre leurs demarches, quand on aurai publié qu'un republicain zelé y avoit assisté, qu'un etranger addressé nommement au Chef de la nation avoit eté permis de se meler à des discussions où il etoit question d'abreger les pouvoirs de ce Chef, et de changer essentiellement la forme du gouvernement. L'occupation donc qui m'empeche de profiter de l'invitation que l'honorable comité me fait l'honneur de me proposer, mettra leurs deliberations à l'abri de cette reproche, la seule à laquelle il auroit pu etre lieu, et ne me laisse que des voeux tres sinceres et tres passiones pour le parfait succès de vos travaux. Assurez les en, je vous en supplie, Monseigneur, et daignez d'agreer vous meme les assurances.

So Jefferson missed a dinner with a liberal bishop and the most interesting of all possible discussions with members of the most enlightened assembly in existence. Jefferson had just experienced a slight contretemps when the great orator Mirabeau, speaking before the National Assembly, had momentarily misunderstood a letter of Jefferson's relating to the grain shortage. The cagey American was not to be caught again. But his lights, so undervalued by him and so esteemed by the archbishop's committee, had already been at the service of substantial change in France. On June 3, 1789, Jefferson had sent to Lafayette and Rabaut Saint-Etienne the draft of "A Charter of Rights solemnly established by the King and Nation"—a sketch of what the king might come forward with. The draft said something on freedom of the press. Lafayette was a Mason, Rabaut Saint-Etienne a Protestant—each presumably interested in establishing religious liberty. But Jefferson's draft offered nothing on the subject. Then on June 30, 1789, Jefferson received from Lafayette the draft of a declaration of rights, beginning, "Nature has made man free and equal," and declaring, "No man can be troubled for his religion nor for his opinions." Six days later Jefferson had annotated Lafayette's draft, and on July 9 Lafayette returned it, writing, "Be pleased to Consider it Again and Make Your observations." On July 11, Lafayette presented his proposal to the National Assembly. His text expressed "eternal truths." It embodied "what everyone knows, what everyone feels."

We are informed only that Jefferson advised Lafayette, not his precise advice, but for this old comrade in arms of the Americans he was willing to go further than with the archbishop of Bordeaux. Lafayette, like many cultivated Frenchmen, not only had dreamed of an ideal America; he had been there; he was the friend and worshiper of Washington; and at thirty-two he was in a key role. To be in close contact with Lafayette was to be dealing with the man then in military command of Paris. On August 26, 1789, on one day's notice, Jefferson opened his house to Lafayette and seven other members of the National Assembly whom Lafayette wanted "to Coalize," that is, to turn into a small coalition, on the king's power of veto; they had dinner and six hours of discussion while Jefferson, according to his account to the king's government, remained "a neutral and passive spectator." It is not easy to imagine Jefferson silent for six hours in his own home after the plates were removed "and wine set on the table, after the American manner."

Obviously au courant with the deliberations of the National Assembly, Jefferson on August 28, 1789, informed Madison: "It is impossible to desire better dispositions toward us, than prevail in this assembly. Our proceedings have been viewed as a model for them on every occasion; and tho in the heat of debate men are disposed to contradict every authority urged by their opponents, ours has been treated like that of the bible, open to explanation but not to question." By "proceedings" Jefferson evidently meant the basic American documents, not procedural precedents. The twelve-hundred-man National Assembly (far too large in Jefferson's eyes) had not modeled itself procedurally on Congress. What was being cited in debate like the Bible was most likely what had been put in writing in America.

With "the king, the mass of the substantial people of the whole country, the army, and the influential part of the clergy," forming "a firm phalanx," the patriotic party, he concluded, "must prevail." There was no more the American minister in Paris could do, and Jefferson departed for home. However inaccurate a prophet, he had assisted, in some small degree, at the birth of a new order.

DECLARATION OF THE RIGHTS OF MAN AND OF CITIZEN

August 23, 1789, "in the presence and under the auspices of the Supreme Being," the National Assembly declared "the natural, inalienable and sacred rights of man," among them Article 10:

> No one ought to be disturbed for his opinions, even religious ones, provided their expression does not disturb the public order established by law (*Nul ne doit être inquiété pour ses opinions, même religieuses, pourvu que leur manifestation ne trouble pas l'ordre public établi par la Loi*).

The text was a slightly condensed version of Lafayette's proposal, qualified by the same kind of caution that Virginia had used in 1776, except that Christian charity went unmentioned. But what was enacted was religious tolerance, not religious liberty—a great shortfall, as Mirabeau observed. The hope of believers in the positive place of liberty was Article 1: "Men are born and remain free and equal in rights" (*Les hommes naissent et demeurent libres et égaux en droits*). Article 2 added that these rights are "natural and indefeasible" and consist in "freedom, property, security, and resistance to oppression." Article 4 said that freedom "consists in being able to do all that does not harm another."

For a country that had known centuries of religious persecution from the repression of the Albigensians in the thirteenth century to the public execution in 1766 of Jean François Lefebvre, chevalier de la Barre, for disfiguring a crucifix—a country that had plunged deeply into the religious wars of the seventeenth century; that had known the massacre of the Huguenot leaders arranged by the Catholic court on St. Bartholomew's Eve and the revocation of the tolerance granted the Calvinists by the Edict of Nantes; that had seen the royal harassment of Jansenists, whose difference from loyal Catholics was difficult to discern, and the royal destruction of Port-Royal where Pascal had once thrived and the legal supervision of adherence to the papal bull *Unigenitus* by tickets of communion; that had seen 1,200 Jesuits banished in the 1760s by the Parlement of Paris and subjected to a humiliating oath as a condition of public employment—for such a country that had ingeniously, persistently, and righteously disturbed all kinds of persons for their religious opinions, Article 10 was a milestone, a new day, an impossible dream.

THE CIVIL CONSTITUTION OF THE CLERGY

In September 1789 Talleyrand, bishop of Autun, proposed the nationalization of the property of the Catholic Church. On November 2, 1789, the National Assembly decreed that "all ecclesiastical goods are at the disposition of the nation, with the charge of providing, in a suitable manner, for the expenses of worship, the support of its ministers and for the alleviation of the poor, under the supervision and according to the instruction of the provinces." In a single stroke the Church lost all its material possessions. Now it was the job of the state to finance the religion.

February 13, 1790, the National Assembly decided that the state would not support monks or nuns. The orders in which solemn vows were taken were suppressed. Those who left could expect "a suitable pension." But the main objects of concern were the bishops and the parish clergy. A committee studied the matter. In the summer of 1790 its recommendations were decreed as "constitutional articles" in what the National Assembly labeled "the Civil Constitution of the Clergy."

The Civil Constitution began by reconstituting the dioceses of the Catholic Church in France so that they coincided with the civil departments. It went on to provide for the election of the bishops in the same way as election of the members of the National Assembly. Only one who had served as a priest for fifteen years was eligible for election. Papal confirmation of the election was not to be obtained. The parish priests or curés were to be elected in the same way as recently prescribed for members of the administrative assembly of each district; five years service as a vicar was a prerequisite for being a curé, and the bishop could examine the one elected and reject him if unfit in doctrine or morals. The salary of the clergy was fixed by law in proportion to the population of the relevant diocese, city, or village, and pensions were provided those who retired.

For Mirabeau, the establishment of the dioceses that laid the groundwork of the Civil Constitution of the Clergy was a mere piece of "ecclesiastical police"—*police* in the sense of the regulation of affairs affecting the general welfare. In the words of a perceptive modern historian the Civil Constitution was "the beginning of a holy war."

The drafters of this monumental miscalculation—*l'erreur capitale de la Révolution*—were priests and lay experts in canon law, all Catholics of some sort; the majority was Gallican, a minority was sensitive to papal prerogatives, but none of them was apparently apprehensive of creating a schism, inviting excommunication, or starting a war. The Jansenists in the Assembly saw the proposal as final revenge on *Unigenitus;* they were one faction of Christians rejoicing in the putdown of old adversaries within the Church. Their thought was to reform the institution, not destroy it. The National Assembly contained a substantial number of curés who were devoted to both the Revolution and the Church. The National Assembly received the draft on May 29, 1790, and adopted it en bloc on July 12. On July 14, 1790, the anniversary of the taking of the Bastille was celebrated as a great new feast, the Fête de la Fédération, Lafayette center stage and Talleyrand saying the mass. The old religion was still the religion of the powers that were.

The great majority of the French bishops saw it differently. In October 1790 they condemned the principles of the Civil Constitution and invited disobedience to it. But new bishops had been elected—"constitutional bishops." The Assembly provided for their installation and quickly moved to that familiar weapon of religious persecution—an oath. The oath was prescribed for every ecclesiastic to swear fidelity to the Constitution of the Clergy. Henceforth the priests of France were to be divided into swearers and non-swearers. The latter were no longer to say a public mass; they were soon to become criminals.

Escalation occurred. On March 10, 1791, Pius VI condemned the Civil Constitution, denounced Talleyrand by name, and called on loyal Catholics to prevent schism. The pope put himself in opposition to the Revolution. The Assembly decreed that Voltaire (*le plus mortel ennemi de l'Eglise et de la papauté*, a modern writer notes) be buried in the Panthéon, the unfinished church of Ste-Geneviève, now commandeered by the Assembly as a national hall of fame for heroes of the Revolution. The symbolic transfer acknowledged the tie of cause and effect in public opinion between Voltaire's championing of dechristianization and the Revolution.

The last act of the Assembly before it went out of existence was to establish on September 3, 1791, "the French Constitution," the first and far from the last written constitution France was to enjoy. The Revolution was treated as a specific event, a fait accompli. The constitution provided: *Il sera établi des fêtes nationales pour conserver le souvenir de la Révolution française, entretenir la fraternité entre les citoyens, et les attacher à la Constitution, à la Patrie, et aux lois.*" While seeking to attach the citizens to the laws by new national festivals, the Assembly incorporated the Declaration of Rights and went beyond it to state that a fundamental natural right, guaranteed by the Constitution, was "the freedom of every man to speak, to write, to print, and to publish his thoughts . . . and *d'exercer le culte religieux auquel il est attaché*—"to exercise the religion to which he subscribes." The similarity to the First Amendment was striking. The Assembly saw no incongruity between this guarantee and the Assembly's earlier remaking of the ecclesiastical organization. The Assembly was sublimely indifferent to the old bishops' point of view.

The Salon in the summer of 1791 exhibited David's famous drawing, "The Tennis Court Oath," depicting the scene in 1789 in which the three estates of France became one body, the National Assembly. At the center of the scene were Dom Gerle, a Carthusian in his monk's robe; Rabaut Saint-Etienne, a Calvinist; and between them the abbé Henri Grégoire, a Catholic priest, already noted for advocating elimination of the old civil restrictions on the Jews. The drawing can be read as a celebration of religious freedom. But by the summer of '91 religious freedom was no longer the focus of the Revolution.

In October 1791 the Legislative Assembly—elected by no more than 10 percent of the male minority eligible to vote—succeeded the National Assembly as the governing body of France and continued on the course its predecessor had taken. The majority was openly Voltairean and regretted that the Civil Constitution gave as much as it did give to the Church; the minority included priests and the constitutional bishops who had taken the required oath. Most of the bishops who had not had left France. The battle within France was carried on by the curés who had not sworn. Against them, on November 29, 1791, the Assembly decreed that persistence in not swearing would make them *suspects de révolte contre la loi*. The *réfractaires*, as they were regarded, were little short of public enemies. In March 1792, Pius VI excommunicated the priests who had taken the oath and did not now disavow it. The *réfractaires* were condemned by the law, the swearers by the Church. In April 1792 the Assembly forbade the wearing of religious garb in public. In May the Assembly decreed the exile of these stubborn *réfractaires*. Pro-Catholic revolts broke out in the provinces. September 2, 1792, nineteen priests were hacked to death at the Abbaye, now a Paris prison, and 115 more persons, mostly priests, were shot, stabbed, or bludgeoned to death at a Carmelite convent converted into a jail and now become an abattoir; among the victims were three bishops.

In the same month a new legislative body, the National Convention, took office and proclaimed France to be a republic. An even smaller number of voters—about 6 percent of those eligible—had participated in the Convention's election. The majority of its members were deists, some were atheists; they agreed that Christianity was finished in France. A minority of Catholics, including constitutional bishops led by Henri Grégoire, opposed them. A motion to stop the salary of the sworn clergy was rejected, but marriage, already by the Constitution of 1791 a civil contract, was taken entirely out of clerical hands: the priests could not deny the nuptial blessing to anyone married by the mayor. Thousands of the non-swearing priests had been expelled. Measures against those who remained or returned were intensified. The oath was required of all priests and brothers, not only bishops and curés. The penalty for defiance was "the dry guillotine": transportation to Guiana. Any six citizens could denounce a priest for *incivisme* or lack of civic commitment, a comprehensive crime.

Religion and revolt against the Revolution had gone hand in hand since the Civil Constitution. In the spring of 1793 open rebellion succeeded in the west of France in the Vendée. The rebels' manifesto, issued in May 1793, invoked "the holiest and most just of causes," the preservation of the Catholic faith. Addressing "the French," they declared: "You reproach us with religious fanaticism, you whose pretensions to liberty have led to the most extreme penalties." It was only two years from the promulgation of the constitutional protection of free exercise.

DECHRISTIANIZATION

The Convention, torn by internal fights, moved steadily left. Celibacy had been the peculiar mark of the Catholic clergy: it should be destroyed. Priests like other citizens could be married by the mayor. Bishops who put any obstacles—*soit directement, soit indirectement*—to the married priest's reception of the nuptial blessing were to be deported: the constitutional bishops were now being told exactly what their religious duties were; and their salaries were uniformly reduced.

In October 1793 the Convention discarded that most potent of Christian reminders, the celebration of the Lord's Day as a holiday, and the very dating of our era from the birth of Jesus Christ. A holiday every ten days instead of seven, a rational division of the year instead of Pope Gregory's, the Year One to begin with the founding of the republic: a new order was decreed. In the schools, civic festivals were to replace holy days and the lives of republican heroes those of saints. In the provincial cities, the commissioners sent by the Convention as its representatives confiscated the bells and the silver of churches; pressed priests to marry and, if possible, to resign; and sought to organize within the churches civic celebrations unmarred by Christianity. The prayers of the Eucharist were parodied: "this is the blood of kings, the true substance of republican communion, take and drink this precious substance." Even the Christian belief in eternal life was challenged. According to a famous *arrêté* published by Fouché at Nevers on October 10, 1793, the cemeteries should have a single statue, Sleep, and on their gates a single inscription: Death Is Eternal Sleep.

In Paris, on November 7, 1793, the constitutional archbishop and thirteen of his vicars publicly renounced their office and priesthood. On November 10 the cathedral of Notre-Dame, proclaimed as the Temple of Reason by the Paris Commune, celebrated a new feast: Liberty, played by a singer from the Opéra, bowed to the light of Reason. Similar ceremonies took place in parish churches throughout Paris. The churches were then *désaffectées*, that is, devoted to municipal use. Twenty-seven more constitutional bishops abjured their religious role; thousands of priests followed them. Many got married—according to Grégoire at least two thousand before the revolutionary period ended. Throughout the country altars were profaned, relics scattered. Reliquaries, chalices, ciboriums, crucifixes were stolen or destroyed. Statues of the saints lost their heads. Churches and chapels were sold and converted to business use or exploited for their contents. Some were razed—seventy-three in the Vendée, for example. The Gothic cathedrals, too substantial to erase, were vandalized. Chartres, for instance, was endangered as lead was stripped from its roof. The emptied monasteries were fair game. Cluny was despoiled and its library pillaged. Clairvaux was sold into private hands and allowed to become dilapidated. The assault on the religious art, architecture, and sculpture accumulated in nearly one thousand years was "one of the great cataclysms of Western culture." The religion of Reason was celebrated in Catholic churches by concerts, patriotic songfests, banquets, and dancing. Parodies of the old religious processions took place. Pigs or donkeys were dressed in sacerdotal splendor. The spirit in which these proceedings took place was that of an "angry, aggressive deism, less intent on asserting itself than on disowning Catholicism and focusing less on respect for itself as the religion of the future than on outrage against the religion of the past." In this effort it succeeded: Catholicism was denied. The religion of the past was outraged. Eighteen centuries of error have entered nothingness, declared the president of the Convention.

Deeds of death followed manifestations of hatred. How many priests were killed, how many deported? Over one thousand executed after trial, another thousand killed without trial or dead as a consequence of prison conditions, over thirty thousand forced to leave the country. At Nantes, the representative of the Convention subjected priests not to "the dry guillotine" but to "vertical deportation" or "republican baptism" by dropping them, bound, from boats into the fast and fatal current of the Loire.

How many sisters were put to death? Not as many as the priests, but women were not exempted. The story of the Carmelites is well known because of Poulenc's opera. Benedictines, Cistercians, Sacramentines, Ursulines, and Sisters of Charity, in addition to the Carmelites, were guillotined. The Vendée, the scene of actual warfare in which the republic eventually prevailed, was where the most hideous massacres took place. The defeated "grand Catholic army" was not innocent of innocent blood. The republic repressed the whole region—men, women, children, cattle, and crops. It is estimated that one-third of the population died. It was a French Rwanda.

What produced this horrible holy war in the first nation in the world to commit itself by constitution to the free exercise of religion? It was scarcely that France knew only one monolithic Church, against which was set the Revolution. By 1790, when the Civil Constitution of the Clergy was adopted, there were at least seven religious groups active in the National Assembly: the ultramontane Catholics, the Gallican Catholics, the constitutional Catholics, the Jansenists, the Calvinists, the deists, and the atheists. If religious liberty could be fostered by religious diversity, there was enough diversity here, even with some overlap of groups, to sustain it.

Undoubtedly the past history of France played a part. "The French are not a people who have just emerged from the depths of the forest," one deputy scoffed at the idea of learning from America; but six centuries of bitter religious conflict had not been a school of tolerance. The promotion of religion by force was familiar. Crown and altar had been very nearly one. For the republicans the cause of religion still appeared to be tied to that of the old regime. If they were to defend the Revolution, they had to take on all its enemies. The mounting use of terror was justified as the French response to foreign invasion and domestic insurrection.

None of these real factors explains the ferocity and the thoroughness of the campaign to dechristianize the country. While examples of cruel intolerance had occurred in the 1760s, actual religious war was not an experience of eighteenth-century France. If the higher clergy were vehemently opposed to the Revolution, the curés were part of the patriotic party in 1789. If the enemies of France, domestic and foreign, were a threat in 1793, some of the worst work was done in 1794 after the threat had been met, as in the Vendée.

The most fundamental reason is that the champions who carried the Revolution forward from 1789 sought to create a new order, a new man, a new religion. To do so the old religion had to be extirpated. Some of the men of '89 had seen that from the beginning. They had absorbed the message to which Voltaire, turning from his garden to "launch a crusade," had devoted the last decade of his life: *écraser l'infâme* was his slogan in an apostolate parodying a religious mission. The "infamous thing," never defined by Voltaire but self-evidently a complex of superstition and fanaticism eminently dangerous to society, was primarily the Catholic Church; but, detesting Calvinism as well, Voltaire included all Christianity in what should be crushed and mocked the Jews of the Old Testament as "a horde of Arabs" and "a horde of thieves." Some men of '89 believed Rousseau: Christianity and a republic are incompatible. For the intellectual fathers of the Revolution, Christianity was a fraud, imposed by force. It was easy to show the fraud, it was necessary to destroy the force. Prepared by these ideas, what the men of '89 saw happen confirmed them in a belief in force. As the composition of the legislature changed, more men in power saw it their way. The peculiar mixture of cynicism and sadism—the dry guillotine, the blood-wet guillotine, the republican baptisms—with which the old religion was pursued owed something to the psychology of those brought up in one faith who now, disillusioned and angry, repudiated it. Was not Hitler an ex-Catholic and Stalin an ex-seminarian? Nor should there be discounted the mixture of malice and self-assertion with which pupils may find it necessary to reject their teachers; the Chinese Cultural Revolution is witness.

There is, it may be observed from one theological perspective, a further reason for the violence: what Voltaire could not stand in Christianity was the idea that God had become flesh; it was the Incarnation that repelled him. The Church, presenting itself as the Body of Christ, repeated this affront to Voltaire and his disciples.

For these reasons, the Declaration of Rights and the Constitution of 1791 had to remain empty words, dead letters as far as free exercise was concerned. At the end of 1793, as the official terror swung into high gear, Robespierre prepared for the Convention a manifesto addressed to the peoples of Europe: "The French people and its representatives respect the freedom of all religions and proscribe none. They abhor intolerance and persecution whatever pretexts cover them." The American formula could be aped. It could not be made to work.

CONCORDAT AND CATECHISM

In the years following the Revolution's execution of Robespierre on 9 Thermidor in the Year II the persecution of the Catholic Church in France fluctuated, with moments of hope and moments of renewed terror. The Directory that succeeded the Convention continued to be anti-Christian and in favor of *une religion purement civile, qui n'avait pas de prêtres, pas de rites, qui ne comportait ni mystères, ni révélations, ni miracles*. A purely civil religion was desired without priests, rites, or any taint of the supernatural. The government continued intermittently to guillotine priests or to deport them to Guiana. It fostered the religious society of *Théophilanthropes* or Godlovingmen and let them carry out their rites in Notre-Dame where the reader or orator, dressed in a white robe with a rose belt, addressed the congregation before an altar piled with the fruits and flowers of the season. The Godlovingmen were distinguished by their tolerance; even atheists were welcome. Meanwhile in Italy, the forces of the Directory liberated papal territory and eventually took Pius VI prisoner; in 1799 he died their captive.

The situation changed with the election of Napoleon Bonaparte as first consul and his victory at Marengo. On June 5, 1800, he told the clergy of Milan that modern philosophers had tried to persuade France that the Catholic religion was the implacable enemy of every republican government. "France, educated by her misfortunes, has finally opened her eyes; she has recognized the Catholic religion as the one anchor that alone can hold her among disturbances and save her among storms." Now in France *la religion catholique reprend son ancien éclat*. The Catholic church was back! Bonaparte looked forward to meeting the new pope, Pius VII, and effecting an "entire reconciliation." His speech, printed and distributed, was a stroke, bold and measured, in the process by which Napoleon made himself complete master of France.

The situation at the time is well described by Mme de Staël: *les partisans les plus sincères de catholicisme, après avoir été aussi longtemps victimes de l'inquisition politique, n'aspiraient qu'à une parfaite liberté religieuse*. All the persecuted wanted was free exercise. *Ainsi donc le gouvernement consulaire eût contenté l'opinion en maintenant en France la tolérance telle qu'elle existe en Amérique*. All the government would have had to do to satisfy public opinion was to follow the American model.

It was not to be. Napoleon, not himself a religious man, wanted something more: a clergy that was a *gendarmerie sacrée*, a sacred police force, and, as a bonus, the confirmation of his role by the pope. Pius VII, in possession of Rome but deprived of much papal territory, looked for the return of the territory. Napoleon saw how a religious settlement in France could satisfy the pope and himself. He took as adviser on the details the old constitutional bishop, Henri Grégoire. Negotiations were slow. Napoleon demanded action. In 1801 Cardinal Consalvi, the papal secretary of state, was sent to Paris. Napoleon gave him five days to agree to the French draft of an agreement. Consalvi capitulated, securing one significant addition as preamble: *Le gouvernment de la République française reconnaît que la religion catholique, apostolique et romaine est la religion de la grande majorité des Français.* After all the propaganda and persecution "the great majority" could be claimed by the Church. Per the agreement this majority religion could "be freely exercised in France . . . conforming itself to the police regulations that the government will judge necessary for the public peace."

The qualification on free exercise was insisted on by the first consul. The meat of the contract followed. All diocesan bishops, whether constitutionals or loyal to the pope, were to resign. Napoleon would choose the new bishops who would swear fidelity to the republic. They would also inform the government if they learned of anything going on "to the prejudice of the State." The curés were to be appointed by the bishops from persons approved by the government. The pope's role was reduced to conferring canonical installation of Napoleon's nominees for the episcopate. In place of the elected hierarchy created by the Civil Constitution, Pius VII settled for a hierarchy named by Napoleon.

In 1806 Cardinal Caprara as papal legate instructed the bishops to celebrate each August 15 the birth of Napoleon. Had the Vendée died for this? Down the road for Pius VII lay the blessing of Napoleon's marriage and the blessing of Napoleon's imperial coronation and his own kidnapping by Napoleon and life as a prisoner of the French, his cardinals turned into *les cardinaux noirs*—the black cardinals, deprived of status—when they refused to bless Napoleon's canonically bigamous second marriage. Peace with Napoleon was always to be on his terms.

The concordat was supplemented unilaterally by Napoleon by what he labeled "Organic Articles," which provided comprehensively for the regulation of the Church in France. Every detail was thought of, beginning with the prohibition of the publication of any papal bull, brief, rescript, decree, mandate, provision to office, or any other missive from Rome without authorization by the government. The same held as to decrees of foreign synods or councils, even general councils. No papal envoys could be sent without the government's approval. No fêtes except Sunday were to be celebrated without the government's permission. Priests were to give the nuptial blessing only to those civilly married. When the government ordered public prayers they were to be said. Any cleric complaining of a superior might appeal to the *conseil d'état*. Ten archdioceses and fifty dioceses were created for France. The salaries of the archbishops, bishops, and two classes of curés were fixed. This doc-

ument, following on the papal capitulation on the concordat, surprised
the pope. He sent Cardinal Caprara to Paris to remonstrate. Napoleon
bribed the ambassador with the archdiocese of Milan. The organic articles became the law of France.

Among their many provisions was a single sentence, Article 39:
"There will be but a single liturgy and a single catechism for all the
Catholic churches of France." Napoleon's foresight in providing for a
single catechism was indicated when he became emperor and this became
the catechism's elaboration of the Fourth Commandment, the commandment to honor one's parents:

*Q. What are the duties of Christians toward the princes who govern them,
and what are our duties in particular toward Napoleon I, our Emperor?*

A. Christians owe to the princes who govern them, and we owe in particular to Napoleon I our Emperor, love, respect, obedience, fidelity, military service, the taxes that are imposed for the preservation and defense
of the empire and his throne. . . . To honor and serve the Emperor is therefore to honor and serve God himself.

*Q. Are there not particular motives that ought to attach us more strongly
to Napoleon I our Emperor?*

A. Yes; for it is he whom God hath raised up in difficult times to reestab-
lish the public worship of the holy religion of our ancestors, and to be
its protector. He has restored and preserved public order by his profound
and active wisdom; he defends the state by his powerful arm; he has
become the anointed of the Lord by the consecration that he has received
from the sovereign Pontiff, the head of the Catholic Church.

*Q. What ought we to think of those who should fail in their duty toward
our Emperor?*

A. According to the Apostle Paul, they would resist the established order
of God himself, and would render themselves worthy of everlasting
damnation.

THE AMERICAN GHOST

"To the dogmatic union of Church and State," a French historian writes,
"there followed a union that was administrative, financial, and of general supervision [by the state]." With minor vicissitudes and through multiple shifts in government, the union held good for a century. It held

because it was congenial to the government, which exercised *la police des cultes*—"the supervision of the legal forms of worship," *cultes* in this usage being reserved for the regulated religions, Catholicism, Calvinism, Lutheranism, and Judaism, which were "attached to the public service." As late as 1901 the very secular director-general of *cultes*, the government official in charge, viewed the idea of separating the churches from the state as "a madness like that of a government that had on this square [*la place de la Concorde*] some ferocious animals in a cage and opened all the bars to let the beasts throw themselves on the public." Far better keep the religions in cages, this experienced bureaucrat thought.

The government also had the benefit of missionaries abroad—French Catholics supplying more men and money to the missions than any other country, and this extension of French culture functioning in support of French foreign policy from Algeria to Indochina. Since the election manifesto of Léon Gambetta in 1869, separation of the churches and the state had been a legislative project of the Left. It was regularly repulsed by the minister of foreign affairs explaining the requirements of the concordat and the effect on French interests in the East. On the Catholic side, there was no institutional discontent. After the imperial despot had been deposed in 1815, his successors had been tractable. The parish clergy was decently salaried by the state. The bishops nominated by the government were sometimes learned and usually devout and docile. Napoleon III even posed as protector of the pope against the revolutionaries who wanted to take the pope's temporal kingdom; and French troops gave substance to the pro-papal pose.

Religious voices, it is true, were raised in favor of religious freedom. Of these, the most eloquent and prophetic, that of Félicité de Lamennais, was rejected by Rome: Gregory XVI held liberty of conscience to be a kind of *deliramentum* or madness. Liberal Catholics did not disappear. Jean-Baptiste Lacordaire—significantly not one of the salaried clergy but a Dominican—discreetly rephrased Lamennais's message and succeeded to his seat in the French Academy. Charles de Montalembert, a Catholic layman, maintained Lamennais's position in politics. French bishops like Félix Dupanloup even defended as a hypothesis that under certain conditions religious freedom was preferable to religious intolerance and contended that in modern circumstances the hypothesis was realized. Nothing altered the effective union designed by the concordat.

Tocqueville, in the wake of Lamennais, made his powerful propagandistic presentation of religious liberty in America. *De la démocratie en Amérique* was a literary sensation. It had no chance of changing the government and when, fifteen years after he had written it, Tocqueville became foreign minister for Napoleon III, he had no chance of persuading his master to adopt an American approach. What Tocqueville achieved was to make part of French intellectual life a vision of religious freedom that would always appeal to some thoughtful minds as an attractive ideal.

An example is the Swiss Calvinist, Alexandre Vinet, whose *Essai sur la manifestation des convictions religieuses et sur la séparation de l'Eglise et de l'Etat, envisagée comme conséquence nécessaire et comme garantie du principe* appeared in 1842 and had an audience not only in Switzerland but among his increasingly influential coreligionists in France. Vinet's thesis was indicated in his title: the separation of church and state was a "necessary consequence" of the principle of freedom of religious expression; and it was the guarantee of that freedom. "I want my principle to be believed for itself," Vinet wrote with Cartesian zeal, "and independent of the facts. If America did not exist, I would believe in the dogma of separation, and indeed I embraced it with all the force of conviction before having glanced at the ecclesiastical constitution of the United States." Despite this proclaimed indifference to facts, Vinet had read Tocqueville and quoted him at length, supplementing him on America with Julius's *Nord-Amerikas sittliche Zustande* and the work of Andrew Reed and James Matheson, *A Narrative of the Visit to the American Churches by the Deputation for the Congregational Union of England and Scotland*. The two Congregationalists had concluded with a paean on the essential role of religion in the United States. In words sometimes today mistakenly ascribed to Tocqueville they declared: AMERICA WILL BE GREAT, IF AMERICA IS GOOD. Vinet quoted them with relish in support of his "dogma" that needed no facts but benefited by examples. Vinet's voice, like Tocqueville's, was not lost but was not heard by those in power.

The institutional partners were content, each adjusting to the other. In the familiar pattern of bureaucratic regulation, the regulators were the captives of the regulated. The office of the director of *cultes*, its last occupant writes, bore the stamp of "the bishops, priests, nuns," who had conferred upon it "a character—an atmosphere—that was religious and even sacerdotal. The Freemasons who had also come there had not been able to dominate it with the exciting but ephemeral perfume of laicity." The partners were content, but all France was divided. Some could never forget Voltaire's message:

> Our priests are not what a foolish people think.
> Our credulity makes all their knowledge.

Others thought what William Blake had written:

Mock on, Mock on, Voltaire, Rousseau:
Mock on, Mock on: 'tis all in vain!
You throw the sand against the wind,
And the wind blows it back again.

The same person could have both thoughts; holding one firmly enough
to act upon it at one stage in his life and later acting on the other, as
Roger Martin du Gard's *Jean Barois* (1921) finely illustrates. The religious question gnawed at French citizens' vitals. It needed a great public miscarriage of justice to turn the question into a political issue.

A conservative military-clerical coalition placed the blame for es-
pionage for Germany on Captain Alfred Dreyfus, a French Jew. Anti-
Semitism, inflamed in particular by Catholic clergy such as the congregation of the Assumptionists, was instrumental in supporting his conviction,
disgrace, and punishment. The hard-line clerical press was adamant as
to his guilt, and the bishops were accomplices by silence. When popular opinion swung in favor of Dreyfus's innocence the reaction was
sharp: the religionists must be curbed. The Left and the anticlerical bour-
geoisie agreed. In 1902 under the presidency of Emile Combes, an ex-
seminarian now a Spiritualist, the government brought under its supervision all the congregations—that is, all men and women under religious
vows—and decreed that only those specially authorized by law could continue to exist. *La loi Combes* passed easily; the congregations were not
formally protected by the concordat. The Society of Jesus, with over 3,800
members, unjustly seen as the heart of a conspiracy against Dreyfus, was
dissolved. Unilateral renunciation of the concordat itself was the next step.
The state would no longer salary the clergy and select the bishops. The
legislative report was prepared by Aristide Briand.

Fierce anticlericalism animated many politicians. The old Voltairi-
anism was fed by disapproval of specific practices of the Church. "Child-
stealers," the young Alfred Loisy heard the Church called, as he set off
at age fifteen for study at a minor seminary. The radical Left would have
been glad to see the Church destroyed. The moderate Left wanted the
state free of it. The idea that the state should inspire its own devotion
was far from dead: Emile Durkheim made his analysis of religion in these
terms in this era. Henri Brisson, president of the republic in 1905 and a
high Masonic official, looked at a Gothic church in a village and told a
young assistant, "The time must come when lay buildings are the noblest and most beautiful," and spoke of the need of organizing lay cer-

emonies with songs and music and creating *la mystique civile religieuse.*
The dream of the goddess Reason was still alive.

Only in the most nominal way was France "a Catholic country." There
were wide variations in practice—95 percent received communion at
Easter 1899 in the diocese of Rennes, 12 percent in the diocese of
Chartres. There was also a huge gender gap. Believers tended to be
women; but only men had the right to vote in a French election.

The Catholic opposition, as in 1789, was far from monolithic. It
ranged from royalists and members of l'Action française, who despised
the republic, to the liberal heirs of Lacordaire and Montalembert. For
the latter opponents of the proposed law of separation of the churches
and the state, it made sense to critique the bill in terms of the religious
freedom it did not furnish. Title One, Article One of the draft legislation
declared: "The Republic assures freedom of conscience. It guarantees the
free exercise of *les cultes* under the following restrictions decreed only
in the interest of public order." It was "the following restrictions" that
cut into the free exercise that was promised. The text reminded Charles
Benoist, a Catholic deputy, of the text of 1791: "The English by their
traditions, the Americans by their precautions, have rights; we have declarations of rights. They have a substance, we the wind." The French,
he added, needed a Supreme Court functioning as "a guardian of the Constitution, a depository of its rights."

The bishops were divided, a majority anxious to work out a new accommodation with the state. The "green cardinals"—the Catholics who
were members of the French Academy—urged moderation on the bishops. Their chief spokesman, the great literary critic Ferdinand Brunetière,
wrote an article, "Quand la séparatisme sera votée," accepting the inevitable and putting forward as a model for choosing bishops the system employed in the United States. It was the canonical not the constitutional structure that Brunetière urged for imitation. The suggestion was
floated in the curia. The bishops looked to Rome for guidance.

France was "the eldest daughter of the Church," the well-worn phrase
incorporating the Roman sense of the country's loyalty and ability to be
difficult. Soon to come before the curia was another idea from France,
this one launched by Alfred Loisy, that all the Gospel could be interpreted
symbolically, adjusting the symbols as human needs required. That there
was a large admixture of symbol with fact was almost incontestable. That
all the Gospel was symbolic without more than vestiges of physical fact
was destructive of the Catholic claim of truth. Close discrimination was
called for. When confronted by this challenge, Pius X responded by stig-

matizing Loisy's views as "Modernism," a heresy, or rather, "the synthesis of all the heresies." The pope was equally intransigent facing the law of separation. The union of Church and state was, for him, like the union of soul and body, part of the divine plan. It was sacrilege to separate them. In *Vehementer nos* he invoked Leo XIII's encyclical *Immortale Dei* to describe the separation of Church and state as "a great and pernicious error."

Briand, the author of the law of separation, came from the old revolutionary tradition. In 1884 he had attacked the "odious slavery" in which religion had "systematically enchained the entire world for so many centuries." Twenty years later he was a better politician. He knew he could not destroy the Church and, according to stereotype, Briand as a Breton had a naturally religious temperament. His bill provided for "cultural associations" that would be formed locally to hold the property of the Church: the bill assumed that the Church would collaborate in their formation.

Led by the pope, the bishops declined to play. The very term "cultural associations" for religious organizations was "an inadmissible neologism," obnoxious to them, and they saw the associations as divesting the hierarchy of all control. As they would not cooperate, the patrimony of the Church in France—nearly 400 million francs' worth of foundations for masses or other pious purposes—was disposed of by the state. The state also held the church buildings and now proceeded to take an inventory of its property, down to the candlesticks on the altars. Around the country, with variations depending on the devoutness of the denizens of the region, parishioners physically prevented the inventory. Skirmishes with the gendarmerie, occasional riots, a few deaths followed. From the Catholic perspective, even as expressed half a century after the events, "the Dreyfusard revolution" was taking place. From the viewpoint of their opponents, the lay state was established, the clerical enemy smashed; the parties that had allied in order to achieve the victory broke up and formed new camps.

The French situation had an echo in the United States. Led by Cardinal James Gibbons, the American bishops expressed their solidarity with the pope and the dispossessed French church, pointed out the differences between "separation" in France and the United States, and organized protests against the French government comparable to other American protests against Russian persecution of Jews. The American response drew the attention of the French government without seriously affecting its actions.

The threat of Germany and then the war with Germany came to over-shadow the French religious division. National unity became essential; patriotism's reinforcement by religion, desirable; consolation for death, the contribution the Church could always give. After the war, with France victorious, each side made conciliatory gestures. Benedict XV canonized Jeanne d'Arc, the embodiment of religious patriotism or patriotic religion. The French government permitted the concordat it had earlier repudiated to govern the eastern provinces recovered from Germany. Pius XI approved local cultural associations, organized by diocese with bishops at their head. The state contributed to the repair of churches. The confiscated funds were, in part, restored.

In the entire development from 1789 to the present, the American example and experience had played a peripheral role, the main events being determined by French history, geography, and character. A distant, flickering, ghostly light was cast by the First Amendment. And yet . . . and yet at various points that light had helped a little. I close these reflections with one man who strove to make the separation of the churches from the state workable, fair, and beneficial to the churches: Louis Méjan, Briand's counselor on the law of separation and the official charged with its execution. A Calvinist, son of a Calvinist minister, whose family memories recalled the revocation of the Edict of Nantes, Méjan was convinced that separation would rejuvenate the churches and that in time it could be made acceptable to the Catholics. He read Vinet; he quoted Tocqueville; the American constitutional guarantees seemed to him what the French should emulate in a reform of the law of separation. For him, as for the Catholic moderates like Brunetière and the bishops who sought to accommodate the opposition, the cause of religion and religious freedom were one; and the American experience assured him that he was not wrong. Méjan and moderates like him devoted to the cause of liberty and religion brought France through its long division. In passing out of the nightmares of history the glow from America was never absent.

CHAPTER 11

IN BEHALF OF THE SUPREME COMMANDER

GENERAL DOUGLAS MACARTHUR AND STAFF
on his arrival in Japan, October 1945

"Freedom of worship shall be proclaimed promptly on occupation. At the same time it should be made plain to the Japanese that ultra-nationalistic and militaristic organizations and movements will not be permitted to hide behind the cloak of religion"(State-War-Navy Coordinating Committee, September 6, 1945).

PROLOGUE

In 1549 Francis Xavier brought the Gospel to Japan. Half a century later there were over 100 Catholic churches, one Jesuit seminary, and two colleges; a Catholic bishop, 143 missionaries, 250 catechists, and close to 300,000 Catholics. In no other civilized country had Christianity, introduced by foreigners, so quickly gained so many adherents and made a mark "not merely in numbers but in influence." By 1639, thirty years after the high point, a visible Christianity in Japan had disappeared.

The Christian faith had been rooted out or driven underground by intense persecution—by the official infliction of fire or water or earth upon the believers: by imprisonment in filthy prisons; by immurement naked in bags of straw; by placement head-down in buckets of water; by suspension in sulfuric pits; by burning at the stake; by crucifixion in imitation of the fate of the Christians' master; and by crucifixion upside down at the beach so that the tide would finish off the victims. The severity of the trials is captured in modern Japanese literature by Shûsaku Endô's *Silence*. Subjected to these methods, five to six thousand—women, men, children—died. The rest renounced their beliefs or persevered and practiced them only in secret.

Like all persecutions conducted by governments, political motives played a part in this one, and no doubt economic reasons could be found with the political. But the object was to destroy a religion and the measures taken for that purpose focused on the religion. The missionaries were expelled, the entry of others was forbidden, and death was decreed for those who remained or returned. The Christians who were accused were expected to apostasize, signaling their renunciation by trampling on a *fumie* or image of Christ or the Virgin Mary. The apostates were required to enroll as members of a Buddhist temple. In 1614 the Bakafu or "curtain government," the military dictatorship that ruled Japan, decreed that every Japanese be a member of one or another of the principal Buddhist sects; a register was established to enforce the decree. As early as 1587, Hideoyoshi had ordained: "Japan is the Land of the kami. Diffusion here from the Kirishitan Country of a pernicious doctrine is most undesirable." The 1614 decree of the Bakafu repeated that Japan was "the country of the kami and of Buddha." Buddhism and the kami could coexist, but not Christianity with them. The God of the Christians was as subversive of the state as the Christians themselves. A triumph of the anti-Christian propaganda of the time was entitled *Deus Destroyed*: the Christian God's deceit and malignity were exposed. Worship of him was a false worship. The *shûmon-aratame yaku* or Office of the Inquisitor was established to assure that he did not return.

Q. & A.: AN ORAL HISTORY PROJECT

INTERVIEW WITH COLONEL J. P. MCCAUGHAN, U.S. ARMY (RET.), HITHERTO UNRECORDED AND UNTRANSCRIBED

Q. Colonel McCaughan, as you know, I'm here to get to understand the American contribution to the constitution of Japan on religious freedom. I understand you were present, so to speak, at the creation.

A. Yes.

Q. For the record, would you please state your full name and rank, rank and function in 1945, and educational background?

A. Colonel James Paddington McCaughan, United States Army, retired. In 1945, captain, U.S. Army Reserves, assigned to the Government Section, SCAP or Supreme Commander Allied Powers, Tokyo. B.A. in History, University of Pennsylvania 1934, LL.B., Rutgers University Law School 1937. I also received training in 1943 at the language school in Monterey, California.

Q. What was the position of the Allied powers on religion?

A. On July 26, 1945, at Potsdam, Germany, they had declared that freedom of religion "shall be established" in Japan.

Q. What was the American position?

A. On September 6, 1945, the State-War-Navy Coordinating Committee [SWNCC] had declared: "Freedom of worship shall be proclaimed promptly on occupation. At the same time it should be made plain to the Japanese that ultra-nationalistic and militaristic organizations and movements will not be permitted to hide behind the cloak of religion."

Q. Who was the supreme commander of the Allied powers in Japan?

A. General Douglas MacArthur.

Q. What was Douglas MacArthur's position on Japanese religion?

A. His position was that "for centuries" the Japanese had been "students and idolators of the art of war and the warrior caste." They believed they were invincible. When they were defeated by the Allies, "it was the collapse of a faith—it was the disintegration of everything they had believed in and lived by." There was now a vacuum, waiting to be filled by faith. The General was "a practicing Christian." He did not believe in conversion by force but by example and by encouragement. At his request the Pocket Testament League distributed ten million copies of the Bible in Japanese translation.

Q. Would you indicate the information that personnel in SCAP's government section had about Japanese religion?

A. Gladly. We knew almost nothing about it. We did have a Religions Division, which we talked to.

Q. Say a word about the Religions Division.

A. I'd better outline the structure. At the top was the General—that is, MacArthur—he was the Supreme Commander representing all the Allies. Beneath him was the chief of staff. Beneath the chief was our section that Court Whitney [Brigadier General Courtney Whitney] headed. We were lawyers. There was also the Civil Information and Education section. Within that section was the Religions Division.

Q. How did the Religions Division relate to MacArthur?

A. He himself "set the tone of crusade and reform only thirty-two days after the surrender." In his Civil Liberties Directive he suspended all Japanese laws restricting political, civil, and religious liberty. The mission of the Religions Division, given it by the General, was "to expedite the establishment and preservation of religious freedom."

Q. I see you're referring to documents. Who were the key personnel in the Religions Division?

A. It was headed by Bill Bunce. He knew something about Japanese religions because he'd taught high school in Tokyo before the war. He'd also been a teacher at New Mexico Teachers College. He talked to several Japanese experts on religion including a well-known scholar, Hideo

Kishimoto. I got my knowledge about Japanese religion from Bunce and the others.

Q. Japan was a modern nation. Didn't it already have freedom of religion in the constitution?

A. Sure. The Meiji constitution of 1880 said: "Japanese subjects are, within limits not prejudicial to peace and order, and not antagonistic to their duties as subjects, to enjoy freedom of religious belief." Freedom of belief did not mean freedom of exercise. As late as the 1930s there was actual repression of new religions—Omotokyo, Honmichi, Hitonomichi. There were also occasional run-ins with fringe Christian groups like the Holiness Church of Japan. Moreover, duties of the subject could involve duties that were religious, for example participation in ceremonial rites as a government official. With the enactment of the Religious Organizations Law of 1940 only religions granted recognition by the government could operate legally. Christians were constrained toward compromising their beliefs. During the war several Catholic priests were shot and more than a hundred ministers of the United Church of Christ were tried for disturbing the peace. The ministers were put to the test: "Who do you think is greater, the Emperor or Christ?" To answer "Christ" meant imprisonment.

And there was always Shintô.

Q. What did you understand by Shintô?

A. I found it vaguely maddening. You can read a modern scholar's account of Shintô, and she finds it "maddeningly vague." But what I did know was it has to do with the worship of kami. You see, kami are the same as gods. Everybody in America in 1945 knew about kamikaze—a kamikaze or Divine Wind was what the Japanese called the hurricane that routed the Mongol Fleet in 1281. They hoped that suicide planes would do the same to our fleet. Also, the planes' pilots were about to become kami.

Q. How does Shintô relate to freedom of religion in Japan?

A. To begin with, as I understand it, kami were spirits of nature or figures out of mythology or deceased feudal chiefs or members of the imperial dynasty. The practice of honoring them at village shrines had been going on for centuries. The people would ask for their help in the harvest and for their protection against disaster. In return, the people gave them loyalty and thanks for blessings received. It was all pretty local and unorganized. There wasn't any pope or bishops or governing board. There wasn't any Bible or special sacred text or charismatic founder. It was just the way things were done in Japan. Shintô just means "the way of the kami."

Q. I still don't see how Shintô gets involved with religious freedom.

A. The Meiji restoration made a kind of integration of the nation with the local practices. Since about 1600 the emperors had performed Shintô rites on accession to the throne and presided at harvest and other Shintô rituals and followed a Shintô liturgical calendar. In 1868 the new Meiji regime emphasized the distinction between Shintô and Buddhism, which was seen as a foreign import. The regime called for the complete separation of Shintô from Buddhist temples. The status of the Shintô priest was enhanced. Shintô shrines were classified and ranked in a hierarchy with the Grand Ise Shrine, a great pilgrimage center, at the top. All Japanese subjects were enrolled in some shrine. All subjects were to install a talisman of the Ise Shrine in their homes, making each household a branch shrine of the Ise Shrine. When Emperor Meiji performed the harvest rite, the populace was ordered to worship too. A new liturgical calendar was established. The days of liturgical celebration became national holidays. The national government supported the Ise Shrine, the imperial shrines, and the national shrines financially. A Department of Divinity was made part of the national administration. By 1880 the government presented Shintô "as the nation's rites and creed."

Q. I see. The government adopted Shintô and made it a kind of national religion. How did the Emperor fit in?

A. The Emperor was the keystone. The Meiji constitution declared: "The Emperor is sacred and inviolate." The official commentary stated: "The Emperor is Heaven-descended, divine and sacred." The Emperor was a kami, a god-man, a divine incarnation.

In 1890 the Emperor issued his Rescript on Education, which taught that the "fundamental character of our empire" is "loyalty and filial piety" to the Emperor. Copies of the rescript were sent to every public school and kept in special repositories in the schools along with a photograph of the Emperor. Offerings were set before the repositories. Their contents were guarded night and day. The text of the rescript was regularly read aloud by school principals performing a priestly role. The rite was part of Shintô. It unified the educational system of the nation with the Emperor.

Q. *You said that the kamikaze pilots might have been on the way to becoming kami. What did you mean?*

A. Every Japanese who died in battle was enrolled as a kami either at a local Defense-of-the-Nation shrine or at the national shrine, Yasukuni, that the Meiji regime created. As early as 1893 a board game was popular in schools in which death on a particular square led to enshrinement at Yasukuni and winning the game.

Q. *Where is Yasukuni?*

A. In downtown Tokyo. It's an oasis under a canopy of cherry trees.

Q. *How many are enshrined at Yasukuni?*

A. Over 88,000 as a result of the Russo-Japanese War and annexation of Korea. Over two million as a result of World War II.

Q. *It sounds as though the religion of the way of the kami was part of Japanese life. How did you expect to grant freedom of religion to Japan without destroying the religion of the Japanese?*

A. We decided to distinguish between Shintô as the religion of individual Japanese and Shintô as directed and financed by the government. We got the message from Washington in October '45, about a month after the surrender. "Shintôism as a state religion—National Shintô, that is—will go."

Q. *Did you have any inhibition based on the American Constitution's guarantee of religious freedom in interfering in the religion of another country?*

A. No. Not at all. It was the other way around. We brought the American Constitution's ideal to Japan.

Q. *What was the starting point for putting religious freedom into the Japanese constitution?*

A. No doubt about it. It was the Potsdam Declaration. After they'd won the war in Germany, the United States and the other Allies announced the terms on which Japan could surrender. As I've told you, they said freedom of religion "shall be established."

Q. *How did you go about it?*

A. Bunce and the boys prepared a directive—the Shintô Directive. It wiped out the Japanese government's support of Shintô. It just prohibited any government "sponsorship, support, perpetuation, control, and dissemination of Shintô." It prohibited public officials from representing the government in any shrine ceremony. It said public officials could not do things like report their taking of office to a shrine. It even eliminated the *kamidama*, the god-shelves kept in the public offices. As the directive said, SCAP had decided "to separate religion from the state." We held our breath for the reaction.

Q. What happened?

A. The Japanese obeyed.

Q. What happened next?

A. New Year's Day 1946 the Emperor told the nation that his relation to his people did not depend on "the false conception that the Emperor was divine."

Q. Did he do that as a result of an order from SCAP?

A. No, just a hint.

Q. Was the whole religious structure ended with the Emperor's declaration and the Shintô Directive?

A. For the time being. There was, of course, a shock effect. But we needed to work on the constitution too. The General had told the Japanese government back in October that they had better prepare a new constitution.

Q. What did the government do?

A. They dragged their feet, then came up with an inadequate draft that we learned about on February 1, 1946. As far as religion was concerned, they did nothing. I guess it wasn't seen by them to be a big deal and it wasn't much of a big deal for us, just a few points to be made in the course of making a whole constitution.

Q. How long did it take you to come up with your version of the constitution?

A. Eight days.

Q. That was very fast. What was the urgency?

A. The Far Eastern Commission—that was a new Allied set-up that the General could see was going to monkey with his work in Japan. It was going to have its first meeting February 26, 1946. So General Whitney told us we had to have *our* work done by Lincoln's Birthday, February 12. On the thirteenth, Court—General Whitney—gave our draft to the Japanese.

Q. How did they react?

A. In shock. In disbelief.

Q. What did Whitney say to make them change their minds?

A. He mentioned that the Emperor could be eliminated from the constitution, that he could even be tried as a war criminal. He said the constitution could be submitted to the coming general election over the government's head. He also alluded to their "atomic sunshine." And a B-29 flew overhead.

Q. How long did it take the government to agree to follow your draft as exactly as possible?

A. We gave them till February 22, Washington's Birthday, to accept the substance. Finally, we had a marathon all-night drafting session working out all the points of translation so it could be completed by March 5, as the General said it should. An imperial rescript the next day recommended its adoption.

Q. According to the Meiji constitution, who was supposed to adopt this new constitution as an amendment replacing the old one in toto?

A. Both branches of the Diet by a two-thirds majority. There was to be an election to the lower house of the Diet on April 10, 1946 so that could give the people a chance to express their feelings before action on our draft.

Q. Was it public knowledge that it was your draft?

A. No. But everybody inside the Japanese government knew it. The knowledge became public in Japan in 1952.

Q. Was the constitution an election issue?

A. Not at all as far as religion was concerned. I do not believe religious freedom had any special significance for most Japanese. It wasn't like France or Russia, for example. The only issues that got into the election were the status of the Emperor and Japan's renouncing of war. Only a small number of candidates talked about even these issues. Remember, too, that the press was under our censorship.

Q. When the constitution was adopted in the Diet was there much discussion of the religion clauses?

A. Not very much, but a few problems were signaled. I think, though, I first ought to set out what the religion clauses were and go back and tell you a little bit about where they came from.

Q. Go ahead.

A. We had our own constitution, of course. We had the 1935 constitution of the Philippines. It was really the only Asian country that had established religious freedom the way Americans knew it, and, of course, the General was familiar with it since he served in the Philippines in the '30s. The Philippine constitution had complied with certain mandatory requirements set out by our Congress in the Jones Act of August 29, 1916. The Jones Act went beyond our constitution in requiring that the Philippines not appropriate any money for the use of any church or any "sectarian institution." The constitution of the Philippines followed the Jones Act in that prohibition. We found it useful in putting a similar prohibition into the constitution of Japan. We did it under the heading of "Finance."

Let me give you what is a literal translation of the Japanese version of our draft. It's a little bit different from the official English because the Japanese language doesn't really have our mandatory "shall." Japanese has a softer form. Instead of saying, for example, "You shall go to the store for the rice," like a command, the Japanese would say, "You have to go to the store to get the rice," leaving it to you to decide whether you're being commanded or simply being told that if you want to get the rice you will "have to" go to where the rice is. So, literally, Article 89 reads: "As for public money or other property, one has to not expend or appropriate this for the use, benefit or maintenance of any religious institution or association, or for any charitable, educational, or benevolent enterprises not under the control of public authority."

That article caused questions from the Religious League of Japan, representing Shintô, Buddhist, and Christian leaders. Would it, for example, take away the tax exemption of the shrines, temples, and churches? The question was not directly answered by the government, but it was inferable that the government had no appetite to tax the shrines.

There was also a question or two about Article 20, which reads: "As for freedom of religion, one guarantees this to all. . . . No person will be compelled to take part in any religious act, celebration, rite, or practice." And then a peer—that's a member of the House of Peers, the upper branch

of the Diet—noted, there wasn't any definition of religion and worried,
"one can believe in anything and call it a religion." As there was no restriction on proselytizing, "there could be cases disruptive to the social order
and harmful to the citizens and the environment." The government
spokesman replied that religious faith was to be placed outside the jurisdiction of the state, but if a religious group engaged in something endan-
gering the public welfare, the government would have to interfere. I should
give you the rest of Article 20 as literally translated back from the Japanese.

Q. Go ahead.

A. "Religious organizations have to not receive any privileges from the
State or exercise any political authority. . . . The State and its organs have
to refrain from religious education or any other religious activity." Of
course that meant that the constitution outlawed Shintô as the religion
of the state and the religion of the schools.

Q. Did that cause much discomfort?

A. It caused some serious discussion in the House of Peers. The government noted that whether Shintô was a religion "had long been controversial among practitioners." It was observed that the position had been
taken by the old government that "shrines were not religious institutions,
but were institutions for praising the nation's ancestors." A peer observed:
"If we say shrines are religious institutions, forcing to worship at them
would violate the freedom of religion guaranteed by the present [Meiji]
constitution. That is the reason that one had labeled shrines as nonreligious institutions. Is that correct?" The government spokesman
replied, "You are absolutely correct." Of course the Shintô Directive did
not accept this semantic nonsense. And the government acknowledged
that the new constitution wasn't going to accept it either. The shrines
were to be regarded as religious, and under the new constitution no compulsion could be exercised to produce worship at them.

Another difficulty was the elimination of teaching religion in the
schools. That made members of the Diet wonder about how morality
would be taught in the schools. A member of their House of Representatives voiced his view that "religion is the foundation of democracy" and that the United States in particular had been "built on a strongly
religious foundation." With the divine Emperor no longer divine, what
was the basis of morality to be in Japan? The government said the schools
could teach about religions although they could not teach any particular religion. The government said: "The issue of morality is determined

on the basis of respect for human beings. In a sense, there is a possibility that a fairly great change will occur in the way the nation's morality is treated."

Q. So the new constitution opened up the possibility of changing the morality of the nation because the constitution was changing the religion of the nation. How long did the Diet debate it?

A. The House from June 25, 1946 to August 24; the Peers from August 26 to October 6. Time enough to explore the ins and outs. In the end, the MacArthur draft was swallowed whole.

Q. In the end, why wasn't there more resistance to the articles on religion?

A. Religion just wasn't that big a deal for the Japanese. They don't have a Westerner's concept of God. They don't have a sense of exclusively belonging to one religion. The religions they knew were not likely to criticize the government, so the government did not have an intense interest in their control.

Q. Do you think MacArthur was arrogant in imposing the new constitution on Japan?

A. "Arrogant" is too strong. Proud, yes. Winston Churchill said of Clement Atlee that he was a modest man with much to be modest about. Douglas MacArthur was a proud man with much to be proud about. It is hard to think of a greater gift than the gift of a working democratic constitution that among its wonderful features enshrines the American idea of religious freedom.

Q. As you are no doubt aware, between 1957 and 1964 Japan had an official commission on the constitution. That commission said about Article 89 on the use of money for any religious or any charitable enterprise not under public control, "This provision is unreasonable and not in accord with present circumstances in our country and should either be abolished or revised." That was the majority position on the commission. What do you say about that view of your reform?

A. Have they changed Article 89? No.

Q. Isn't there something terribly anomalous in transplanting a whole body of constitutional doctrine? How can you expect it to take root when it was not grown organically in the soil?

A. According to modern studies the wholesale transplant of legal systems is not unusual and can be highly successful. The principle of religious freedom in today's world has a universal appeal. As Article 97 of the constitution says, it is one of "the fruits of the age-old struggle of men to be free." It could be considered a natural law. It will flourish wherever it is planted.

THE PURIFICATION CEREMONY OF TSU

On January 14, 1965, the city of Tsu in Mie prefecture invited four Shintô priests from a nearby shrine to conduct a grounds purification ceremony (*jichinsai*) prior to construction of a new city gymnasium. The city council appropriated a total of 7,633 yen (about $39) for the ceremony—4,000 yen for an honorarium for the priests, and 3,663 yen for ceremonial offerings. A Communist city councilor, who had been invited to attend the ceremony, filed an "inhabitant's suit" under Article 242.2 of the Local Autonomy Act. He claimed that by expending public funds for the ceremony, the city had violated articles 20 and 89 of the constitution, and demanded that the city be reimbursed for the outlay to the priests, and that he personally be paid 50,000 yen ($259) for the mental suffering he experienced as a result of being forced to observe the ceremony. The district court held for the defendant; the court of appeals reversed. The case went to the Supreme Court of Japan.

On July 13, 1977, twelve years after the event, the Supreme Court ruled by a vote of 10 to 5. As a general matter, the court said, the principle of separation of state and religion means "the state's nonreligiousness, or religious neutrality." But the principle of separation of state and religion is not an absolute. Some involvement by the state in religion is virtually inevitable. An absolute separation of state and religion would produce a variety of untoward effects. If the state were prohibited from subsidizing religiously affiliated private schools as it subsidized other private schools, or from helping religious organizations to maintain their buildings and works of art, the result would be disadvantageous treatment of them. Discrimination against them would occur on the basis of religion. If ministries in prisons were forbidden so long as they showed evidence of religious character, the religious freedom of the prisoners would be restricted.

With these examples set out, the court concluded that the constitution's prohibition of "religious activity" by the state cannot refer to all state activity that bears a relation to religion. Rather, constitutionally pro-

scribed activity must be activity "whose purpose carries a religious meaning, and whose effect is to support, encourage, or promote religion, or
to oppress or interfere with it." In order to determine whether state activity is "religious," more has to be considered than merely the external
appearance of the activity: "There must be an objective determination,
made in accordance with prevailing social views, of all the circumstances:
where the activity took place, the ordinary person's assessment of the religious character of the activity, whether and to what extent the actor
had a religious intent, purpose or awareness in so acting, and what effect or influence the activity would have on the ordinary person."

With these cautious and comprehensive words, the Supreme Court of
Japan went on to make a distinction between paragraphs two and three
of Article 20. Under paragraph two a person cannot be compelled to take
part "in any religious acts, celebration, rite, or practice." Paragraph three
prohibits the state from "religious education or any other religious activity." The meaning of "any other religious activity" in paragraph three
is not necessarily identical with "religious acts, celebration, rite, or practice." The state may engage in what an individual could not be forced
to do.

The court turned to the grounds purification ceremony at issue and
candidly set out its religious characteristics. Ceremonies whose purpose
was to ask for the safety and well-being of a building project were indeed activities "carrying an involvement with religion." Those who carried out the ceremony were professional men of religion. They wore religious garb. They set up a specific site for the ceremony and used specific
implements. They were motivated by religious faith. But all of this did
not make the ceremony "religious activity" by the state. A steady process
of secularization had made it impossible to designate the ceremony as
"religious activity." "There can be no doubt that as times have changed,
the religious meaning of such activity has progressively weakened." Although the ceremony undoubtedly bore a connection to religion, "in the
view of the ordinary person, or of those persons involved in the ceremony, subordinate to the city of Tsu and the mayor who sponsored it,
the ceremony would be deemed secular activity and would not be recognized as having a religious meaning." The purpose of the ceremony
was to ask for a sound building site and safety in construction; the
ceremony was "primarily seen as something secular, the carrying out of
an observance in accordance with common social convention." Because
the ceremony had the effect neither of supporting, encouraging, or promoting religion, nor of oppressing or interfering with religion, it was not

"religious activity" proscribed by Article 20, paragraph three of the constitution.

Five justices, led by Chief Justice Ezikō Fujibayashi, dissented. The dissenters broadly endorsed the reasoning of the court of appeals, insisting on "a thoroughgoing separation of state and religion," and attacking as vague and unclear the majority's notion of state involvement with religion as forbidden only when the involvement "exceeds a level deemed to be appropriate." According to the dissenters, the majority opinion threatened to nullify the principle of separation of state and religion. For them the ceremony was clearly religious activity, and city sponsorship of the event had the effect of preferring Shintôism and aiding that religion.

Both the majority and dissenting opinions included brief historical excursuses on freedom of religion in Japan. Both opinions acknowledged that this freedom was incomplete under the Meiji constitution. Both opinions pointed to the Shintô Directive of 1945 as marking a fundamental shift in the role of Shintô in Japan. American precedent went unmentioned by the majority. The intermediate appellate court had stated that Japan's "strict separation of state and religion" was much like the one developed in the United States. In response, the appellant before the Supreme Court had sought to show that the separation of church and state in the United States fell short of being absolute. Judge Masuzo Fujibayashi, dissenting separately, noted that the First Amendment of the American constitution had exerted an influence greater than any other on Japan's conception of freedom of religion and its conception of the separation of state and religion; but he added that Japan's restrictions were even more "thoroughgoing" than the American. The majority implicitly rejected this contention. Taking twelve years to mature, the Case of the Purification Ceremony of Tsu gave a distinctive Japanese imprint to the constitution of 1946. But a religious ceremony that was not religious activity was not very different from the United States Supreme Court's view of legislative prayer and "ceremonial deism."

"GIVE ME BACK MY HUSBAND, O SELF-DEFENSE FORCE"

Before the Tsu case had been decided by the Supreme Court, and while the intermediate court decision was still in effect, a new case arose testing the extent to which an individual's religious freedom could impact the religious activity of the state. In 1968 Takafumi Nakaya, a member of Japan's army, the Self-Defense Force, was killed in a traffic accident while on active duty. His body was taken to his father's house and was incinerated, the ashes being set before a Buddhist shrine. His widow, Yasuko, took a few of his bones to be deposited at a memorial vault in her Christian church.

Three years later an application was made for Takafumi Nakaya's enshrinement in the local Defense-of-the-Nation shrine. The applicant was the local Veterans' Association, whose solitary employee was also a member of the Self-Defense Force and worked out of its offices. The Self-Defense Force saw no future for the Defense-of-the-Nation shrines unless they were used for the apotheosis of Self-Defense soldiers. The old army was dying out. Without the practice of enshrinement the morale of the Self-Defense Force would suffer.

The enshrinement accordingly took place. Takafumi Nakaya joined some fifty thousand other kami at the shrine. According to the usual ritual, in the evening the spirits to be deified were summoned by the priest of the shrine, were then transferred onto the branches of the sacred *sakaki* tree, were borne on a palanquin to the main structure of the shrine, and were placed within. There they were to be worshiped and would, in reciprocation, "watch over the supplications for household safety and health of all citizens along with the sound development of their descendants as they are born." The names of the deified were enrolled at the shrine, to be preserved in perpetuity.

Yasuko, the widow, pondered this event. She had a son still in grade school, whose life would foreseeably be made difficult if she raised her voice in protest. She had left her in-laws, who liked the idea of their son's apotheosis. She worked as a cook at the Garden of Felicitous Longevity, a nursing home. In 1969 a study group at her church had motivated an eighty-year-old widow, Takano Watanabe, to collect 30,000 signatures to oppose a bill in the Diet calling for government support of the national Yasukuni Shrine. Yasuko knew of her example. She had a minister, the Reverend Hayashi, a stubborn man who had struggled eighteen years to secure the acquittal of a man convicted of mass murder. With Hayashi's encouragement Yasuko decided to bring suit for vindication of her religious freedom.

Competent counsel was sought and obtained. Who would be the defendant? The shrine itself was thought of, but that would be to pit Yasuko's Christian religion against Shintô. It was decided to sue the Self-Defense Force and the Veterans' Association. Yasuko claimed that the participation of the Self-Defense Force in the apotheosis was a participation by the state in religious activity contrary to paragraph three of Article 20 and that this unlawful conduct had violated her own freedom of religion. She asked for damages and an annulment of the apotheosis.

The district court found that the Self-Defense Force had assisted the Veterans' Association in seeking the enshrinement; the Self-Defense Force was therefore a proper defendant. Yasuko's right of religious freedom included "engaging in religious feeling and thought in an atmosphere of tranquillity free from the interference of other persons"; that right had been violated by the apotheosis. The court analyzed the violation in terms of "compulsion": after the apotheosis Takafumi Nakaya became the object of popular veneration, causing mental anguish to his widow, compelled to suffer this unwanted attention to her husband. The apotheosis had a religious meaning and furthered the Shintô religion in violation of Article 20, paragraph three of the constitution. The object and effect of the apotheosis was religious in nature. The request to annul the apotheosis was dismissed as, in effect, moot: apotheosis had occurred. The damages of one million yen were granted. On appeal, the intermediate appellate court ruled that the Veterans' Association, a private organization, lacked the capacity to be a subject of Nakaya's suit. In all other respects the district court's ruling was upheld.

Independently of the litigation, there was public controversy over visits by the prime minister to the Yasukuni Shrine. Five bills to furnish government financial aid to the shrine failed of passage between 1969 and 1974. The public position of the Liberal Democratic Party, the ruling party, was that formal participation by members of the government at the shrine was unconstitutional. But the Association of War-Bereaved Families, joined by conservatives in the ruling party, continued to push for government recognition. In 1983 Yasuhiro Nakasone, the prime minister, paid tribute at the shrine at its spring festival. He declined to say whether he acted as the prime minister or in a private capacity. The Supreme Court's decision in the Tsu case encouraged the conservatives to go further. On August 15, 1985, the day that commemorated the dead of World War II, Nakasone led the cabinet to the shrine in his official role as prime minister. Instead of following the shrine rite of offering a sprig of *sakaki*, bowing twice, clapping twice, and bowing again, he offered only flowers and bowed once, apparently demonstrating that his public tribute to the kami was not a Shintô rite. Foreign reaction, notably in the countries that had been subject to Japan, was outrage. The Chinese press, in particular, denounced the Japanese government for worshiping at a shrine containing the weapons of war and apotheosizing "the glorious war dead," among them soldiers killed in invading China and military leaders who were Class A war criminals.

Against this background of increased political involvement in the shrines for the deified dead, Yasuko Nakaya's case was considered by the Supreme Court of Japan. On June 1, 1988, by a vote of 14 to 1, the Supreme Court reversed the decision in her favor. Usually an appellate court in Japan, as in the United States, accepts the trial court's findings of fact; but there are exceptions. Here the Supreme Court began by rejecting the district court's finding as to the role of the Self-Defense Force. The Veterans' Association had been dominant. As a result, the Self-Defense Force was not properly a codefendant. The state was effectively eliminated from the case.

The court could have stopped at that point, dismissing the suit; but the court had more to say. Apotheosis had taken place by the action of the shrine itself; a request from outside parties was not a prerequisite. To recognize Yasuko Nakaya's right to object to the apotheosis was to impinge on the shrine's own freedom of religion. Everyone, including shrines, was free under the constitution "to make someone the object of one's faith or to memorialize someone or seek the tranquillity of that person's soul through the religion that expresses one's faith."

Criticism of the opinion came from the sole dissenter, Judge Masami Ito (a former law professor), who wrote that the Self-Defense Force was an equal participant in seeking the enshrinement. He perceptively observed: "As is often pointed out, in the West basic human rights are said to have arisen from the guarantee of freedom of religion; that guarantee is held to be the core of all human rights. In Japan, by contrast, although a variety of religious views coexist, the general popular level of interest in religion is not very high, and people lack a sharp sense of the freedom of religion. This does not mean that it is acceptable to weaken the separation of state and religion—on the contrary, it requires us to be all the more faithful to the principle of this separation."

The majority opinion was greeted with glee by conservative Japanese. Yasuko Nakaya was deluged by hate mail as she had been at the beginning of the case. The intensity of the emotion expressed could be seen as evidence against Judge Ito's statement that "the general popular level of interest is not very high"; but the majority of his court might have interpreted the letters as expressing not religion but identification with the country. "If you don't like the verdict, get out! Go to a 'Christian country,' a foreign country" could be read like the comparable American putdown, "If you don't like it here, go back to Russia," as a political expression. That very possibility of a political interpretation pointed to the continuing difficulty: the unity of Shintô customs with the nation. The "religion of Japan," a half-American, half-Japanese woman writes, "is Japaneseness, which is best cultivated in daily life. Cultivated to the point of invisibility of daily practice, this religion is resistant to challenge even in its more concentrated, obtrusive forms as manifested at Yasukuni or the Defense-of-the-Nation shrines."

The extraordinary foreign intrusion of an ideal had half-succeeded. The culture had absorbed the ideal and molded it. The formal separation of the state from religion could not eliminate all the ties between them. Judicial review, it turned out, was as likely to bow to old cultural convictions as to implement constitutional imperatives. Still, a process had begun. In 1997 the Supreme Court of Japan ruled that donations of public money to Yasukuni were contrary to the constitution. The American commander was gone. The American contribution remained and was reckoned with.

CHAPTER 12

AMERICAN ADVISERS, AMERICAN MISSIONARIES

REBUILDING OF THE CATHEDRAL OF CHRIST
THE MOST HOLY SAVIOR, MOSCOW

*The photo, taken December 22, 1995 by William C. Brumfield,
is of the church's south facade, on the frozen Moscow River—
an icebreaker in the foreground, modern cranes and scaffolding
surrounding the body of the church (destroyed by Stalin).
Has the ice finally broken, or is the thaw deceptive?*

In 1914, on the eve of World War I, the Russian Orthodox Church—according to the report of the Chief Procurator of the Most Holy Governing Synod—had 64 dioceses in Russia and 4 missionary dioceses (the Aleutian Islands, Japan, Peking, and Urumiyeh [the modern Iranian Rezaiyeh]); 57,144 churches; 5,400,000 acres of land; 550 monasteries housing 11,845 monks and 475 monasteries housing 17,829 nuns; 3 metropolitans, situated in St. Petersburg, Moscow, and Kiev, and 166 bishops; 3,246 archpriests and 47,854 priests; 18,966 converts lessened by 10,610 fallen-aways; and 98,534,800 believers. Christianity had come to the land with the evangelization of the Eastern Slavs by Saints Cyril and Methodius and the reduction of the Russian tongue to the Cyrillic alphabet. The establishment of the Church dated back to Prince Vladimir of Kiev and the appointment by Constantinople of the first metropolitan, Saint Michael, in 991. In the nearly thousand years of its history the Church had known vicissitudes, dangers, defeats—the incursion of the heathen Mongols in 1237; the loss of the mother church with the fall of Constantinople in 1453; the rise of the Uniate Church formally affiliated with Rome in 1595; the schism in 1681 of the Old Believers who rejected an updating of the liturgy and were persecuted as dissidents; the assumption of the administration of the Church by Peter the Great, who in 1721 created the Most Holy Governing Synod and its chief procurator, a government official, to replace the patriarch and appoint the bishops; and the introduction of limited freedom for various other religions, most recently by law in 1905. The Russian Orthodox Church coexisted uneasily with other Christian bodies such as the Molokans (milk-eaters), who preferred milk to vodka; the Dukhbors (spirit-wrestlers), sectarians resembling the early Quakers, who had to be moved to eastern Russia or allowed to emigrate to Canada; the Stundists, who were practically Baptists in their prayer and Bible study; the ancient autocephalous Armenian Orthodox Church and the Georgian Orthodox Church; the Lutherans in the Baltic regions and Finland; a group of largely German

Mennonites; and 1,600,000 Catholics in Lithuania, Poland, and the Ukraine. The Russian Orthodox Church had had to accept the presence of millions unlikely to be assimilated by the Church—5,600,000 Jews, kept out of Russia before the czar's absorption of part of Poland, then supposedly confined to the Pale of Settlement running from Riga to Odessa and from Polish Silesia to Kiev, and 16,000,000 Muslims in Central Asia; the presence of disenchanted intellectuals, who formed urban circles of Tolstoyans, Theosophists, rationalists, atheists; and the existence of far-out sects such as the Flagellants and the Castrates, who took Matthew 5:29 literally. All but the last two enjoyed the freedom of worship accorded by the reform of 1905 in a law entitled On the Establishment of the Principle of Religious Toleration. It was no longer a crime to apostasize from Orthodoxy or to induce one to do so. The keen animosity felt toward schismatics had diminished, and it was even bad taste to deprecate the Old Believers as *Raskols*. But there was no doubt that the religion of Russia was Russian Orthodoxy.

The Church had not merely survived; it had secured its status. It had domesticated the Mongols. It had become autocephalous with its own patriarch after Christianity had lost Constantinople. It had resisted Catholic incursions, the Polish peril, the wiles of the Jesuits. "The Tale of the White Cowl," the story of how the Emperor Constantine's gift to Pope Sylvester eventually came to the Orthodox archbishop of Novgorod, was "the cornerstone of Russian national ideology." The Church had inspired the resistance to Napoleon, its role recognized by the great basilica of Christ the Most Holy Savior built by the czars in Moscow. It had made Russia the center and patron of Orthodoxy throughout the Balkans and the Middle East. It had become part of the apparatus of government and sustained the czar as God's vicar.

Other churches were "foreign religions," carefully regulated by law when permitted at all. Proselytizing by these foreigners was at first criminal and now frowned upon. A true Russian was Orthodox. As the religion of the state, Orthodoxy was naturally supported by the state. The budget of 1914 provided 54,000,000 rubles for parish operations alone. Political conformity was not considered a price that was exacted. The czar was Caesar, the power that existed, God's representative on earth. Christians were supposed to render unto Caesar what was his and to obey the powers in existence. State support was not seen as sapping the Church's energy and initiative. The Church grew as the empire grew, advancing in geographic range and in numbers.

The regime that it served, with which it was administratively and financially integrated, would not bear inspection. The empire's bureaucratic callousness, its secret police, its Siberian exile system, its pogroms (first tolerated, then encouraged) against the Jews, its fears made it odious; and the Gospel proclaimed by the Church did not dispel the empire's chauvinism, xenophobia, and anti-Semitism. Neither institution wanted to learn from American democracy.

The voice of America was small and distant, heard first in 1880–1881. John W. Foster, the American minister to Russia, protested the application to two American citizens, Henry Pinkos and Marx Wilczynski, of Russian law restricting Jewish residence in Russia. With Secretary of State James G. Blaine's blessing, Foster even discreetly encouraged the Russian foreign minister, De Giers, "in the direction of a liberal tolerance analogous to that which forms the fundamental principle of our national existence." But the laws were not changed. Ten years later, in 1891, De Giers took the initiative with Charles Emory Smith, the American minister, saying that he had had conversation with the czar on "recent publications in American newspapers respecting Russia and the Jewish question"; De Giers wanted to assure Smith that no new measures would be undertaken against the Jews, but that old laws might be enforced. The imperial conversation was a delayed effect of a resolution adopted in America on August 20, 1886 by the House of Representatives that asked the president for information about "proscriptive edicts against the Jews in Russia." Blaine, back as secretary of state, had then responded: "Such a step, if in reality contemplated, would not only wound the universal and innate sentiment of humanity, but would suggest the difficult problem of affording immediate asylum to a million or more of exiles without seriously deranging the conditions of labor and of social organization in other communities." Instructing Smith, Blaine continued to express this double concern for religious persecution as offensive to humanity and as a stimulus to an emigration the United States did not seek to encourage. Smith was told to read this instruction to De Giers. President Benjamin Harrison reported to Congress: "This Government has found occasion to express, in a friendly spirit, but with much earnestness, to the Government of the Czar, its serious concern because of the harsh measures now being enforced against the Hebrews in Russia." No official answer from the czar was reported.

The Church was weighted by the evils spawned by the system, but it was not intellectually dead. It had seminaries and theological journals. It had theologians, most notably Vladimir Solov'ev, and poets, most notably the Symbolists, and novelists, most notably Fyodor Dostoyevsky, and an avant-garde, the *Vekhi* authors. In sharp contrast to the heavy-handed bureaucrats, these writers focused on human personality and stressed compassion as well as humility. The Church had its contemporary saints, represented in fiction by Father Zosima in *The Brothers Karamazov* and in life by Saint Silvester of Kanev. The Church embodied beauty—beauty in the onion domes of the Kremlin and other churches, beauty in the iconostases that presented sacred persons to the worshipers, beauty in a liturgy that was long and elaborate and elevated the believer into a supratemporal world that became present. The beauty of the liturgy had moved the Slavs of the steppes to conversion in the tenth century. "The world will be saved by beauty," is attributed to Prince Myshkin in *The Idiot*. This famous line was later to be understood by Aleksandr Solzhenitsyn to be "a prophecy" by Dostoyevsky and, in the end, to be vindicated by the experience of Russia. In 1914, as war approached and intellectuals doubted and the disaffected plotted, the Church was where beauty still lived. But first, as in *The Idiot*, beauty was to be destroyed.

In the fall of 1917, in the midst of revolution, a council of the Church composed of bishops, priests, and a lay majority ended the governance of the Holy Synod and restored the patriarchate, electing Tikhon. The Church was formally free. Almost simultaneously the Bolshevik coup occurred. The atheists—a number of them ex-seminarians, abstract and absolutist in their thinking—controlled the state. The new Soviet man was meant to be an atheist, Soviet society was to be the achievement of man without the hindrance of belief in God, the believers—in Russian usage sometimes simply the Russian Orthodox but in modern parlance all those acknowledging the existence of God—were to be treated as a superstitious remnant of an old order that had passed with the czar.

BELIEVERS OF TWO KINDS?

That Communism itself was a religion has often been forcefully argued. It may be made to fit within the terms of at least one anthropological definition of religion as "a system of symbols which acts to establish powerful, pervasive and long-lasting moods and motivations in men by formulating conceptions of a general order of existence and clothing their conceptions with such an aura of factuality that the moods and motivations seem uniquely realistic." Communism did provide a system of symbols, conceptions of the world, an aura of factuality, which sustained powerful and relatively long-lasting moods and motivations. It had a scripture, provided by Marx and Engels. It had imagery, borrowed by them from the Bible. "Materialism," wrote Marx, "is the only-begotten son of Great Britain." The Trinity, the Creation, Original Sin, the Incarnation of the Son of God, the Redemption, the Apocalypse were all transposed to a materialist key. Man was presented as the master of his destiny, naturally good and naturally able without supernatural aid to overcome the social forces exploiting him. An otherworldly, afterdeath salvation gave way to salvation on earth. Class warfare, the destruction of the capitalist class, the rule of the proletariat were predestined; so ultimate salvation was predestined.

The Communist Party functioned as the church, communicating this vision and bringing it to fruition. As the Soviet constitution was to put it, "The leading and guiding force of Soviet Society is the Communist Party of the Soviet Union." The Party consequently had its hierarchy, its missionaries, its inquisitors. The whole enterprise—its evangelical élan, its zeal for converts, its doctrinal rigidity and severe discipline, its sense of purpose and its rationale for action—depended on faith. As long as belief in the vision held, the moods and motivations persisted. Disillusioned ex-Party members would write of "the god that failed." That Communism had a political mission and political embodiment did not lessen its religious status: Islam is a religion, although it is a militant faith and has political embodiments. Jacques Maritain has persuasively contended that Communism is a Christian heresy, a derivation that would account both for its messianic zeal and for the intensity of its hatred for the kind of Christianity it repudiated.

From a Durkheimian perspective, the Soviet state proved once more that the collectivity must create a religion, and the religion that the collectivity creates is the worship of itself. From a Durkheimian perspective, the separation of church and state proclaimed by the Soviet constitution was hollow hypocrisy: the church ruled the state. But as I have argued earlier, a functional analysis is an incomplete approach to religion if it eliminates the intentionality of the believers and ignores the reality of what they believe in. The Communists made no claim to having a religion; indeed the claim would have been incomprehensible to them. Religion was part of the superstructure that would change as the means of production were socialized. Once the expropriating classes were eliminated, their tool the church would disappear. The inevitable needed to be encouraged only by systematic scientific atheistic education. To foist upon these uncompromising unbelievers a set of beliefs labeled as religious is to deny them their own self-understanding, to force them into a category they despised. With no intention of loving, obeying, or worshiping God, they were what they proclaimed themselves to be, irreligious.

The Declaration of the Rights of the Peoples of Russia, issued on November 2, 1917, as the Bolsheviks took over the government, abolished all "national-religious privileges and restrictions"—a blow to the Orthodox and a bid for support from discriminated-against minorities such as the Jews and the Armenian Christians. Within two months, the lands of the churches were expropriated, church schools transferred to the People's Commissariat of Education, and the validity of all marriages made dependent on civil registration. On January 23, 1918, the Council of People's Commissars, headed by Lenin, set out the foundations of the new religious order, beginning with the single sentence, "The Church is separate from the State." With equal force the decree declared: "The school shall be separate from the Church." In lapidary legal language these provisions enacted Jefferson's wall of separation, reinforcing it with the promise that religious rites should not accompany "actions of the Government or other organizations of public law." Nothing like prayers in the legislature or the courts was to be acceptable. Separation was to be absolute. Recognition of "freedom of conscience" accompanied this righteous rule, fortified by the statement, "Each citizen may profess any religion or no religion at all."

Removed from their context, these major provisions read like Hugo Black's exposition in *Everson* of American constitutional doctrine. These texts did not, however, stand alone. The provision on the schools was amplified by a prohibition of any religious education in any school, public or private. The separation of church from state was modified by the provision assigning "all property" of all churches and religious associations to the state. As property holders the churches passed out of existence. To underline the point, the decree added that no religious association should "enjoy the rights of a legal entity."

The constitution, adopted by the Fifth Congress of Soviets on July 16, 1918, succinctly summarized the decree of January, adding an explanation and a new freedom: "To secure for the workingman true freedom of conscience, the church is separated from the state and the school from the church, and freedom of religious and antireligious propaganda is recognized as the right of every citizen." The felt need to use "true freedom of conscience" as the touchstone was remarkable. Reference to this ideal did not disappear even in the Stalin constitution of 1936. But conscience had class restrictions. The constitution of 1918 classified clergymen with "capitalists, merchants, former members of the police, criminals, and imbeciles": all were denied public office and the vote and as a collateral consequence suffered discrimination in food rations and housing. The constitutional freedom of religious propaganda was not honored. No Bibles, for example, were permitted to be printed in the first twenty-five years of Soviet rule. In sharp contrast, antireligious propaganda became the activity of a government department that trained what the Party called "antireligious agitators and propagandists" and sponsored posters, leaflets, books such as *The birth, life, and deaths of the gods and goddesses*, and a weekly newspaper, *The godless*.

The chief later legal addition to the decree and constitution of 1918 was the law On Religious Associations, issued under Stalin in 1929. In sixty-four separate articles this masterpiece of bureaucratic control minutely regulated the believers who would be entitled to lease for worship "the prayer buildings," that is, the physical churches. If amounting to at least twenty persons and registered with the local soviet, the believers could constitute "a religious society," which, although denied the rights of a legal entity, was the form through which religious activity was to be organized. That activity was to take place in the prayer building and was not to include any charitable or cooperative assistance, any organization for the teaching of religion, or any special meetings for "children, young people, or women." The activity of the clergy was restricted to "the area where the prayer buildings or premises are situated." The registered believers were liable for the maintenance and repair of the edifice and responsible for all the state property (chalices, crucifixes, vestments, etc.) entrusted to them by the government for purposes of worship. Surveillance over the activities of the religious societies was to be "exercised by registration agencies and in rural areas by village soviets." In this fashion the exercise of religion was confined to the physical churches, and the forms of religious life were determined and supervised by the state. The Communists could not with a stroke of the pen destroy belief. They put in place a system designed to deny belief any status, structure, stability, or support; to reduce to a minimum its manifestation by any group; to make it a kind of private aberration. No place at all was left for monasteries; in an atheist state for persons to dedicate their lives to prayer would have been a scandal. In 1929, the year of the enactment of the law On Religious Associations, Sunday was abolished as a day of rest.

Apart from the dispositions made by law, the Communists inflicted harm of every sort upon believers, at first in the midst of civil war when they identified their enemies, the Whites, with the cause of religion and then, more thoughtfully, in 1922 with the return of peace when they could give priority to the repression of religion. In 1922 the government provoked physical resistance as it expropriated sacred objects in the churches to sell them for famine relief. Over one thousand incidents of bloodshed occurred. Patriarch Tikhon was arrested. The patriarchate was suppressed. The Living Church, backed by the government, took over the administration of the Orthodox. Benjamin, the metropolitan of Petersburg, was shot. By the end of the year sixty-six Orthodox bishops were in prison or in exile and over twenty-five hundred priests, nearly two thousand monks, over three thousand nuns had been killed. In 1923 the few Catholic bishops in the country were imprisoned or exiled. In the same year Archbishop Nasarie of the Georgian Orthodox Church was executed and the members of his council imprisoned. Against Judaism, Bolsheviks who were ethnically identified as Jewish were used because "the participation of non-Jews would have smacked of the earlier czarist oppression of the Jewish religion." Jewish schools were a special threat. The use of Hebrew was made difficult. Orthodox Judaism, as much as Orthodox Christianity, was an affront to the atheistic state.

Persecution of religion, accompanied by intense atheistic propaganda, thereafter came in waves. The first ran from 1929 through 1932, coinciding with the collectivization of agriculture and the liquidation of the kulaks; it was frequently carried out with the closing of the village church and the deportation of the parish priest as a kulak. The second ran from 1937 to 1939, when Stalin staged the great purges and, as Khrushchev later put it, "no one was safe from arbitrary arrest or from the repression." The Orthodox Church was especially vulnerable. Its priests were forced into secular jobs, turned into beggars, subjected to forced labor, deported to eastern Russia, executed. In Leningrad, for example, the number of priests dropped from one thousand in 1930 to fifteen by the end of 1937. The hierarchy was nearly eliminated. From Vladimir Bogoyavlensky, metropolitan of Kiev, to Methodius, archbishop of the Far East, at least one hundred and thirty bishops became martyrs for the faith. The monasteries, the monks, the nuns were gone: to be a monk or nun was impossible. To be an active layman was to suffer discrimination and risk imprisonment as a counterrevolutionary. Tiny religious groups as well as the Orthodox were targets. In 1934, for example, in eastern Siberia the Red Army destroyed the Buryat way of life, uprooting in the process a Lamaist Buddhist monastery and killing the monks.

Equally vigorous efforts were made to wipe out the Church physically. Vandalism was, so to speak, the order of the day. Of the 57,000 Orthodox churches in existence in 1914, less than one percent remained as functioning centers for congregations by the end of 1937. Many had been blown up or attacked with wreckers and reduced to rubble, sometimes with a statue of Stalin replacing the ruin. Among the destroyed were the famous cathedral of Christ the Most Holy Savior in Moscow, the cathedral of Our Lady of Kazan, and the eleventh-century Monastery of St. Michael in Kiev. A handful were preserved as historic monuments. Most of those not physically removed were turned to secular uses such as housing.

Organized religion had almost been suppressed. But Russia was not like Japan in the seventeenth century where a fairly recent Christian community could be extirpated by sustained and ferocious pressure. The church had been in Russia for a very long time. Those harboring a faith in God still existed. They were believers, as Russians used the term. The census of 1937 asked bluntly a question that the government was confident would be answered correctly: "Are you a believer?" The government never published the results. The reasonable inference is drawn that there were too many Yeses.

Near the height of the wave of persecution in 1932 the United States, which had refused to recognize the Bolshevik regime, came in contact with the Soviet Union. The new president, Franklin D. Roosevelt, wanted to establish diplomatic relations. Very quietly, an agreement was worked out in an exchange of letters between Roosevelt and Maxim Litvinov, People's Commissar for Foreign Affairs. As a condition, the president asked for assurance that Americans in the Soviet Union would "enjoy in all respects the same freedom of conscience and religious liberty which they enjoy at home." Nothing was said of other people's religious liberty. The United States was not then a champion of human rights throughout the world. Both the left wing of the Democratic Party and American big business wanted the deal to go through without fuss. On the same day as the president's note, Litvinov, who was in Washington, replied that it was "the fixed policy" of the Soviet Union to accord to American nationals freedom of conscience and worship and religious education, all of which were "supported" by the public law of the Soviet Union; he went on to quote Lenin's decree of January 23, 1918. In this way the lip service paid to religious freedom by Soviet law was useful. Neither party to the exchange cared to point out how this decree in practice was applied. The president assumed, correctly, that Americans would not be harassed. It was as far as he sought to extend the lustre of the First Amendment.

Deliverance by the West came with terrible irony in a different way, by the revival of the role of the Orthodox Church as the partner of the state. On June 21, 1941 Germany invaded the Soviet Union and on the same day Sergius, Metropolitan of Moscow, issued a pastoral: "Our Orthodox Church has always shared the destiny of her people. . . . She gives her heavenly blessing to this sacrifice now to be made by the whole nation. . . . May God grant us victory." It took two years for the government to reciprocate and recognize the Church's patriotic part. Then everything was arranged by the government. Stalin met Sergius. Four days later a group of nineteen bishops was allowed to meet in Moscow. The patriarchate was restored. With little heed to the canons of the Church, Sergius became the patriarch. It was clear that a deal of some kind had been made between the Party and the patriarch. Bishops and priests who had survived the concentration camps returned. Church closings stopped. Some churches were repaired. Eight seminaries and two theological academies were opened. Twenty-five thousand Bibles were printed. Antireligious propaganda was discouraged. In the eyes of some Orthodox, the Church had undergone a resurrection. And the quid pro quo, beyond the patriotic support already supplied? A wonderful docility of the patriarch to his Communist patrons; the infiltration of the patriarchate by agents of the state; the use of the patriarch as an ally of the state in Eastern Europe, in the Middle East, in America, and in ecumenical assemblies; a sense on the part of some Orthodox that now there was "no unity between the policy of the Moscow Patriarchate and the Church."

Annexation of Estonia, Latvia, and Lithuania and of eastern Poland in 1939 had brought under Soviet control whole countries where religion had flourished up to the Soviet takeover and where churches and even monasteries still existed after the takeover. The German occupation of western Soviet territory had permitted the restoration of religious rites in these regions. Resumption of Soviet control meant new measures of repression. The Uniates, or Catholics of the Byzantine rite as they preferred to be called, were forcibly annexed to the Orthodox Church, and their bishops, headed by Joseph Slipyi, were sentenced to forced labor. But the Soviet pressures failed to destroy religion in the Ukraine. Elsewhere, Evangelical Christian Baptists grew in strength and, less institutionalized in structure, were less open to Soviet control than the Catholics or the Orthodox. Other Western groups—Adventists, Pentecostals, Jehovah's Witnesses—appeared. The total sum of religious activity within the borders of the Soviet Union became disquieting to the Communists.

The Party had always distinguished tactics from long-term goals. Religion had been accommodated, even rewarded, when necessary. Its continued existence after a half century of socialist rule was a contradiction of Communist premises. The contradiction could only be explained as a "survival of capitalism in the consciousness of the people." Communist doctrine called for ultimate suppression. The "moods and motivations" of Communist belief had to be reinvigorated. Nikita Khrushchev, known to the West for his denunciation of Stalin, balanced his bold castigation of the cult of personality with a compensatory Communist orthodoxy. To show adherence to the basic beliefs of the system, to warn potential troublemakers that destalinization was not decommunization, to quicken the pulse of the aging party, there was nothing better than to fall upon the old and fundamental and vulnerable foe.

In 1959, the campaign began. In every grade in every school a required subject was to be scientific atheism. An atheist perspective was prescribed for every subject taught. A "long-cherished dream" of the Party was realized by the creation of a center where atheism would be addressed in the highest intellectual style, the state-supported Institute of Scientific Atheism. The state published and made available quantities of atheistic literature. Atheistic agitators—so described in *Sputnik atheista*, or *Atheist's Companion*—were encouraged to carry their message to individual homes to drive out belief in God.

Positive propaganda was coordinated with negative sanctions. Believers did not face death in this last great persecution in the Soviet Union; they could be penalized by fines, exile, forced labor, or prison if they violated the laws as they were now applied. The persecutors relied on the letter of the law, narrowly read and harshly enforced, as the way of choking religion. The technique employed to the full the Soviet bureaucrat's fondness for stubbornly applying regulations, however absurd, the bureaucrat's morbid devotion to compliance with the rules, however cruel the result. The Council for the Affairs of the Russian Orthodox Church, a central government agency, was given supervision over observance of Soviet law by the Church and issued new restrictions on church activities. Local soviets used their formal power to register priests as a substantial power to control the clergy by making it impossible to ordain, assign, or transfer priests without first obtaining the oral consent of the leaders of the local soviet. Every citizen who wanted to baptize his children or be married in church or to receive anointing of the sick had to present his identification documents to the church council; the record of his reception of a sacrament was then scrutinized by local government authorities with a view to him being "worked over" at office or school and subjected to "administrative pressures." The law requiring a minimum of twenty believers to form a religious society was now interpreted as setting a maximum of twenty, depriving numbers of believing citizens of participation and, if one of the twenty dropped out, requiring reregistration and a closing of the church if reregistration was not immediately achieved. Inspection committees certified churches to be in need of repair; when the believers could not immediately provide restoration, the church was closed. A church too near a school endangered education; it was closed. (Many churches were in this category; state schools often occupied old parochial schools.) A church that attracted large crowds was a traffic hazard; it was closed. A remarkably beautiful church was classified as a national monument; it was removed from the control of believers. A church stood where a town plaza should be extended; it was destroyed. In these and comparable ways, usually but not always relying on the law and competing among themselves to close the most churches, local authorities by 1964 had locked down or eliminated entirely half the Orthodox churches that had come into operation during the fifteen years of thaw.

In the monasteries that had reappeared or had come within Soviet control, the monks themselves became the targets, subjected to physical examinations that found fit monks sick or mentally ill or classified them as illegal vagabonds. At Pochaev it was forbidden to supply the monastery with fuel; the monks could freeze. By an accumulation of petty tyrannies and, if these failed, by physical assaults, the monks were to be made to change their minds and ways.

Unprecedented efforts were undertaken to prevent the religious education of children. The law of 1929 on religious associations was interpreted to forbid any religious education of children by priests. The right of parents to educate their children religiously was challenged; children could even be removed from parents who had given them religious education; on removal, the children were to be sent to state boarding schools. A secret circular, issued in 1962, forbade children over three and under eighteen to attend church.

The patriarchate, coopted by the government, was silent before the new persecution. The Church was not totally still. Archbishop Ermogen of Kaluga protested to Patriarch Aleksii and was removed from office; but two Moscow priests in contact with him, Nicolai Eshliman and Gleb Yakunin, made an even bolder move. On December 15, 1965, using their own names and addresses, they sent an open letter to the heads of the Soviet government and the chief prosecutor accusing the authorities of illegality. Specifically, they cited acts of persecution that violated "the free exercise of religious worship." They pointed to the banning of children from religious services and other measures that ignored the separation of Church and State by administrative interference with the churches. The two priests asked that the illegalities be stopped. The patriarch suspended them.

Eshliman and Yakunin had given witness to the Christian faith and to what a constitutional guarantee of free exercise could mean. They had led the way in openly challenging the Soviet authorities. Later the intellectuals were to imitate their protest while seeking secular freedoms. Meanwhile, Yakunin formed a committee for the defense of believers' rights, elicited accounts of persecution, and smuggled to the West thirteen volumes of believers' testimony as to what they had experienced. For these deeds he was sentenced to five years of prison and seven years of exile to Yakutia, possibly the coldest spot on earth. It would be another generation before an appeal to basic civil rights would find a response.

In 1980, in the sober terms of prophetic judgment, Aleksandr Solzhenitsyn wrote that Communism has been "most ruthless of all in its treatment of Christians and advocates of national rebirth. In the early years this meant wholesale executions; later the victims were left to rot in the camps. But to this very day the persecution continues inexorably. . . . The authorities make no attempt to hide the fact that they are crushing the Christian faith with the full force of their machinery of terror."

In the words of a leading American authority on Soviet law, Harold Berman, the seventy-year Soviet campaign to root out all belief systems other than Marxist-Leninist Communism was "surely the most massive and the most powerful assault on traditional faith that was ever launched in the history of mankind." The sporadic persecutions of Christians in the Roman Empire, the generation of persecution of Catholics in seventeenth century Japan, the less than a decade of active persecution of Christians in revolutionary France, were more intense at their ferocious peaks but not comparable in duration; and they were campaigns against a specific faith not against all belief in God. Yet in the 1970s it was guessed that still some 40 percent of the people of the Soviet Union were believers.

THE CHURCHES AND THE NEW CONSTITUTION

On December 7, 1988, Mikhail Gorbachev told the General Assembly of the United Nations: "Our country is going through a period of truly revolutionary uplifting." The process of perestroika, or restructuring, was under way—restructuring of "politics, the economy, intellectual life, and ideology"; and restructuring of the Communist Party. The ideological commitment to root out religion went unmentioned, but now freedom of conscience was to be part of "the normative base" of Soviet society. Now, in 1988, no one was imprisoned on the grounds of religious belief. "Additional guarantees" were being drafted that "rule out any form of persecution on these grounds." The new laws would meet "the highest standards from the viewpoint of ensuring the rights of the individual."

Had the ice finally broken? Had not a February thaw, but full spring, come? The leader of the Soviet Union and the Communist Party spoke against persecution on religious grounds. Publicly and internationally he had committed himself to new guarantees of freedom. He had pledged the country to the highest standards judged in terms of the rights of the individual person.

The highest standards were not those set by the as yet unreformed Soviet Union but those established by international bodies since World War II. In 1948 the United Nations had issued the Universal Declaration of Human Rights, affirming freedom of religion as such a right, and the declaration had been elaborated in the covenant, which the Soviet Union under Brezhnev had ratified in 1973. The covenant specified that freedom of religion included freedom to manifest one's "belief, observance, practice, and teaching." That was not the Soviet standard. In 1981 the United Nations had issued its Declaration of the Elimination of All Forms of Intolerance and Discrimination Based on Religion or Belief, which detailed the rights of religion in a way going far beyond the Soviet understanding of them. The Soviet Union had subscribed, because subscribing cost the Soviet Union nothing: the declaration itself contained the caveat that a state could enforce general regulations designed to protect public safety, order, health, morals, or the fundamental rights of others; and if this clause would not justify any Communist qualification of freedom, the regular rule of Soviet law was that the laws of the sovereign state were not subject to international agreements. When Gorbachev announced that the Soviet Union would meet the highest standards, it could be hoped that he meant something new. That hope was sustained when in 1989 the Soviet Union agreed to the Vienna Concluding Document, a product of the Helsinki Conference on Security and Cooperation in Europe. Like the covenant, this new international declaration set out protections of religious freedom far exceeding Soviet practice and principle. The Soviet Union was not judicially bound by its assent; politically, it was propelled in a direction difficult to reverse.

In this way, through the filter of international standards, the American example of religious freedom reached Russia. The American influence was to become more direct and more personal. In 1989 the drafting of a new Soviet law, On Freedom of Conscience and On Religious Organizations, was begun. Twenty-six articles set out particular assurances of religious freedom in detail comprehensible only against the background of the harassment the Communist bureaucrats had inflicted on believers. The draft was sent for comment to a trio of American academics: Harold Berman, at once the sympathetic interpreter of Soviet law and a Christian critical of its militant atheism; Erwin N. Griswold, former dean of Harvard Law School, former solicitor general of the United States, a man of moral earnestness and moral weight; and Frank C. Newman, former dean of Boalt Hall, former justice of the Supreme Court of California, a zealous worker for human rights in international contexts. Their critique was reflected not in the final Soviet law, adopted October 1, 1990, but in the law On Freedom of Religion, adopted on October 25, 1990, by the Russian Federation.

Three desiderata of the American experts found their way into the Russian law. The binding force not only of treaties but of international "agreements" was recognized, thereby incorporating the Vienna Concluding Document as a source of law. Freedom of conscience was not only acknowledged, but "the right of citizens to exercise their freedom" was explicitly declared. Free exercise was extended to foreigners, including stateless persons. The rights of a foreign church, however, were qualified by a requirement that a foreign church register with the Ministry of Justice. Nonetheless, refusal of registration was carefully circumscribed and made reviewable in the courts; in contrast, the 1990 Soviet law had left registration in the hands of local executive committees and, while providing for judicial review, did not specify the criteria a reviewing court should use. The breadth of principle and the specificity of protections reflected the industry of the drafting committee and the insights of their American counselors.

The final act of the Soviet Union touching on these matters was the Declaration of Human Rights and Freedom, adopted on September 5, 1991, by the Congress of People's Deputies. This declaration's generous enumeration of rights was criticized by members of the Communist Party as "too American." But by November 1991 Yeltsin had replaced Gorbachev and had liquidated the liquidators: the Communist Party was no longer legal in Russia. In January 1992 the Union of Soviet Socialist Republics dissolved, and its constitution, treaties, laws, and declarations ceased to have effect.

A deeper foundation was wanted for the advanced legislation adopted by the Russian federation in 1990. The foundation was supplied by a new Russian constitution prepared by a parliamentary commission and revised by a presidential commission appointed by Yeltsin. The constitution was submitted to the electorate, which, on December 12, 1993, ratified it. The fundamentals nominally enumerated in 1918 were preserved—the freedom of conscience, the equality of religions before the law, the separation of religious associations (now the preferred term for churches) from the state. There was also the qualification present in the international declarations permitting restrictions "for the security of the state." But the orientation had changed. According to the constitution, "Man, his rights and freedoms shall be the supreme value. It shall be a duty of the state to recognize, respect, and protect the rights and liberties of man and citizen." Concretely, the commitment was spelled out by articles recognizing particular rights—"to freedom and personal inviolability"; to "freedom of thought and speech"; "to association"—and by denial of state power to restrict any rights "on religious grounds." Most importantly, Article 28 declared: "Everyone shall be guaranteed the right to freedom of conscience, to freedom of religious worship, including the right to profess individually or jointly with others, any religion, or to profess no religion, to freely choose, possess and disseminate religious beliefs, and to act in conformity with them." The right extended to everyone, including children, including foreigners. The old czarist, the old Communist restrictions were repudiated. Above all, in spectacular fashion, the constitution proclaimed the right to act in conformity with one's beliefs. Free exercise could scarcely be taken further.

Specific questions, to be sure, were unanswered. Did the constitution grant immunity from service to conscientious objectors to war? It depended on how the right to act on one's beliefs was reconciled with the state's ability to restrict a right injurious to state security. In Communist days there was no doubt how the question would have been answered. Under the new constitution the question was left to the courts, for the constitution recognized a judiciary independent of the executive and legislature and explicitly provided, "Everyone shall be guaranteed protection of his or her rights and liberties in a court of law." Decisions, actions, and nonactions by organs of the state or local governments or public associations or officials were made subject to appeal in the courts. The constitution set the trajectory for the courts. Rights and freedom were "the supreme value."

An additional guarantee was added: the standards and the procedures of international law. The preamble set the note. The Russian people adopted the constitution "being aware of ourselves as part of the world community." Article 46 then provided: "In conformity with the international treaties of the Russian Federation everyone shall have the right to turn to international organs concerned with the protection of human rights and liberties when all the means of legal protection within the state have been exhausted." As specifically as a constitution could, Article 46 created a linkage with the highest international standards protecting freedom.

Laws were needed to implement the constitution. In 1993, even as the draft constitution was being prepared, new legislation was considered at a conference of the drafters with representatives of nine religious bodies, officials of various government ministries, and nine outside experts, seven of them law professors from American law schools. The conference unanimously endorsed the adoption of the international standards, to be achieved with the recognition of Russia's "own history, its own culture, and its own challenges."

Russian history, culture, and challenges of the past became relevant as events developed in 1993. American religions had entered into vigorous competition for converts in Russia. They spread their message by pamphlet and book and television. They advertised religious revivals and conducted crusades for Christ. Newer religious groups such as the Unification Church, the Hare Krishnas, and The Family concentrated on enlisting the young. The Russian Orthodox Church saw its traditional place in Russia threatened by American-financed religions that had economic resources they did not possess. In the words of Patriarch Aleksii II, foreigners were using "the difficult living conditions of our people and rough pressure on personality" to get converts. Bribery, coercion, fraud were, in the view of the Orthodox, being practiced under the cover of religion. Among some Islamic communities religious terrorist groups were said to mobilize. The 1990 law on freedom of conscience had, it seemed to the critics, led to disruption of Russian society. Solzhenitsyn in 1980 had scourged American commentators on the Communist regime for "their almost total disregard for the spiritual history of a country which has been in existence for a thousand years, as though (as the Marxists argue) this had no bearing upon the course of its material history." For the believer who was both Russian and Russian Orthodox the spiritual history of the country was wrapped up with the Russian Orthodox Church. Unrestricted religious competition touched a raw cultural nerve, especially when the competitors came from outside Russia.

The position of all the churches was still precarious. Almost 50 percent of the population thought of themselves as believers, that is, in the Russian sense of believing in God; only about 3 percent were regular churchgoers. Meanwhile the patriarchate—in its present form so indebted to the old Soviet state—did its best to exclude its closest competitor, the Russian Orthodox Church Abroad, the Church that had separated in the 1920s from the suppressed Church at home. Russian parishes that wanted to affiliate with the Russian Church Abroad were informed that the patriarchate would not surrender control of the churches—an assertion of ownership by the patriarchate contrary to the pre-Soviet ownership of churches by the parishes. Past Soviet sponsorship had given the patriarch power he had not enjoyed under the czar.

Gleb Yakunin, the protester of 1965, returned to Moscow from exile and became a member of a parliamentary committee that examined the files of the KGB. The committee reported finding under a code name Aleksii II himself—the police infiltration of the patriarchate had reached to the top. The patriarch was now anxious to appear as the defender of the Russian patrimony. In 1993, he urged changes in the law on religious freedom: "On behalf of the Russian Orthodox Church, to which the majority of Russian believers belong, I testify that the proposed amendments and additions correspond to desires and needs of Orthodox clergy and church people."

The amendments the patriarch supported bore heavily on American-based or financed groups. Freedom to disseminate religious beliefs was to be the right of citizens alone. The right of foreigners to engage in any "missionary activity" within the Russian Federation was expressly denied. The state was empowered to exclude foreigners completely if their activities in other countries were found to "contradict the standards of public morality in the Russian Federation." Even the freedom of conscience of individuals was limited by the blunt qualification, "provided that the individual observes the laws of the State." In a move reminiscent of Patrick Henry in Virginia in 1785, the Orthodox proponents of the bill sought to enlist on their side all "the traditional confessions." An amendment made these bodies eligible for state support. It did not specify what the traditional confessions were. Pretty clearly such American newcomers as Hare Krishna, The Unification Church, and The Family were not.

On July 14, 1993, the Supreme Soviet passed the amendments. They could not become law without the assent of President Yeltsin. Aleksii II personally appealed to the president to sign. President Clinton, Senator Richard Lugar, and many others urged him not to do so. Yeltsin in effect exercised a pocket veto, returning the law, unsigned, with a sharp critique of its violations of the constitution and treaties of Russia. The Supreme Soviet promptly reenacted the bill. Yeltsin still did not sign, so the bill did not take effect.

In 1994 the new legislature, now called the state Duma, again took up legislation making it difficult or impossible for foreign religious organizations to operate. Skirmishes over alternative bills continued into 1997. Then the parliament passed a law which Yeltsin vetoed a month later, stating that it "contradicts" the Russian constitution and the norms of international law such as the Universal Declaration of Human Rights. The proponents of the legislation—a coalition of the Moscow patriarchate, nationalists, ex-Communists, and present Communists— continued to press for it, offering minor concessions and trying to split the Catholics from the Protestants. On September 27, 1997 the legislation was enacted and signed into law by Yeltsin. Entitled On Freedom of Conscience and on Religious Associations, it marked a new turn in the Russian treatment of religion. It was as though James Madison had been corrected by David Hume.

The new law repealed that of 1990, thereby diminishing the American contribution. It created two classes of religious associations: organizations and groups. Organizations were authorized to hold property, found religious buildings, receive tax exemptions, receive government aid and use state property, conduct religious services not only in their own buildings but in prisons, hospitals, and care centers, carry on charitable activities, create organs of mass media, establish seminaries, produce or import religious literature, carry on business undertakings, and teach religion in the schools. Groups were not recognized as having any of these rights. Only individual members of a group, not the group itself, could own property. Only the existing followers could receive religious education from the group; proselytizing was out. A gulf was opened between the two classes.

What had distinguished a religious organization from a religious group? The line was drawn in terms of previous existence in Russia. An organization had to have "existed on the given territory for no less than fifteen years," i.e. since 1982, and confirmation of this existence must come from the local government, implying that the existence must have been in accordance with the law since 1982. All the religious bodies that had surfaced since the thaw of 1988 fell into the category of "group." Not only obvious new arrivals like The Family but denominations like the Baptists might be relegated to this status if they could not get governmental confirmation that they had been in existence in the dark days. Recognition as a religious organization was made dependent on what the atheistic rulers of 1982 had recognized.

The mechanism of control was the required registration of organizations. The law gave the opportunity to a group of achieving the status of an organization by registering annually for fifteen years. As a second check on the new religions, registration could be refused if "the activity" of the group in any year involved violation of current law. What this provision meant was spelled out with greater force in an article of the new law providing for the liquidation of an organization or the banning of a group on a variety of grounds apparently described with specific American religious bodies in mind. The grounds included, for example, encouraging the refusal of medical help; hindering compulsory schooling; inciting citizens to refuse to perform their civic obligations—provisions respectively impacting the Christian Scientists, some Evangelicals, and the Quakers and Mennonites. Other grounds of liquidation appeared to have in mind Islamic bodies—e.g., "the formation of armed units," "the igniting of social, racial, national or religious dissention," and "hindering a citizen from leaving a religious association" by serious threats. The dangers the Moscow patriarchate had seen in unrestricted freedom of religion were transformed into reasons for depriving a religious group or organization of all legal status.

Religious organizations, privileged though they were, were put on a leash and required to file their charters, to describe their methods and annually to report their activities. The judicial organ of the state registering an organization was given authority to "monitor" the organization's observance of its charter. The Procurator of the Russian Federation was given authority to "monitor" the implementation of all aspects of the new law.

A final provision of the new law, intended to ward off foreign competition, was that an organization created outside Russia did not have the status of a religious organization in Russia although it might be granted the legal right to have "a representative" in Russia, a representative that could then be "attached" to a religious organization recognized by Russia. Only an organization that had existed in Russia for fifty years, i.e., since 1947, could use the word "Russia" in its name. Under this provision the Russian Orthodox Church Abroad was denied the use in Russia of one of its chief characteristics. The law showed how far the Moscow patriarchate would go. It wanted no rivals, especially no rival with a better claim to be the continuation of the prerevolutionary Church.

The same law stated that nothing in the law was to "be interpreted in such a way as to diminish or limit the right of man to freedom of conscience and freedom of creed as established by the Constitution of the Russian Federation or stemming from international treaties of the Russian Federation." The law added that foreign citizens legally present in Russia had the right to the freedoms of conscience and creed "on an equal footing" with citizens and that "the establishment of privileges or restrictions, just as any other form of discrimination on the basis of one's attitude toward religion, is not permitted." In short, a law giving extensive privileges to the Moscow patriarchate and possibly to a few other churches meeting the fifteen-year requirement, was to be interpreted as if it gave no privileges and treated all creeds alike. What Yeltsin had criticized in his veto message had not been substantially changed. Now what would happen depended on the administration of the law and on the courts.

The role of religion in Russian politics was symbolized in the rebuilding of the cathedral of Christ the Most Holy Savior, built by the czars and demolished by Stalin. The project began in 1994, sponsored by Yury Luzhkov, the mayor of Moscow. In January 1995 Aleksii II laid the cornerstone with Prime Minister Viktor Chernomydrin and Mayor Luzhkov in attendance. Supposedly the funds for construction were to come from donations; but the degree of official involvement and the estimated cost (as high as $300 million) made it unlikely that private charity alone would realize the result. At the cornerstone ceremony Mayor Luzhkov declared: "Let the reconstruction of the main cathedral stand as symbolic proof of hundreds of destroyed churches and millions of lost lives. Let this stand as proof that this great government deals not only in words but in prayers and in deeds—prayers to God, words to the people, and deeds of building for all of Russia." What the state had taken away the state returned. On the surface religion was restored. The achievement was assailed by independent Orthodox priests like Gleb Yakunin who saw the state as uniting with the Moscow patriarchate in an embrace inimical to religious freedom.

The decay of Communism was seen by some outside observers as an economic collapse due to a moral collapse due to a religious collapse. This view found support in the push to identify the revival of religion with the rebirth of Russia. In January 1996 the following article appeared in *Rossiiskaya Gazeta* under the headline "We Must Believe in Russia and Then We Will Live!"

> On January 7th, President Boris Yeltsin sent an address to His holiness Patriarch of Moscow and All Russia, Aleksei II, in which he congratulated the Head of the Russian Orthodox Church on Christmas and the New Year.

On that same day Boris Yeltsin participated in the Christmas celebration which took place at the restored Cathedral of Christ the Savior in Moscow. At this first patronal holiday of the Cathedral, which is dedicated to the Birth of Christ, the Patriarch of Moscow and All Russia, Aleksei II, led a brief service. Then the President of Russia and the Head of the Russian Orthodox Church performed the symbolic placement of the last stone in the Cathedral's outside wall.

Boris Yeltsin, meeting with journalists, observed that "the stabilization and elevation of Russia lie ahead" and "the Cathedral of Christ the Savior symbolizes this process." And the fact that they built it in one year shows that this is possible. "It means—Russia is alive, the Russian spirit is alive, the Orthodox Church—which has made a large spiritual contribution—is alive."

Boris Yeltsin expressed certainty that the rebuilding of the cathedral "will now revive belief in the people." "I am certain: this belief will bring about that Russia will now be revived more quickly than before. In this I see the chief significance of the Cathedral—besides its primary function, to be a Cathedral—it's a memorial to the war dead of the Patriotic War of 1812."

Had religious freedom come to Russia or had the state found it expedient, as had Stalin in 1942, to put the Moscow patriarchate in a privileged position as the state's good servant?

Free exercise in Russia remained an experiment. The bare phrase was not dispositive of any outcome. The history of the country, the politics of the moment, the example of the United States, and the advice of American advisors and the reaction to American religions all were factors affecting how the experiment would prosper. The voice of outside counsel was raised to suggest that the divided churches should enter into *sobornost*—dialogue, negotiation, spiritual harmony freely reached. To achieve that end there was necessary "the power of prayer." Free exercise was as much a religious as a legal issue; perhaps more so.

CHAPTER 13

THE LIGHT OF REVELATION
AND THE LUSTRE OF AMERICA

FOURTH SESSION OF THE SECOND VATICAN COUNCIL
Rome, 1965

*"This Vatican Council declares that the human person has
a right to religious freedom . . . founded in the very dignity
of the human person as it is known by the revealed
word of God and by reason itself."*

I turn from the impact of the American experience on the constitutional law of particular nations to a distinctively different encounter: the American mark upon the teaching of that church to which I adhere. It has always seemed to me presumptuous for America to put itself forward as especially favored by Providence, to be a model for the nations, to be almost as it were a second Israel. The Messianism that has characterized some Russians writing about Russia has always appeared to me to be a delusion, not to be mimicked by Americans writing about America. But as the evidence just reviewed in relation to France, Japan, and Russia has shown, the United States has had a light to contribute on the special subject of religious liberty. Is it unimaginable then that America had a contribution to make to an overtly spiritual institution possessing among its accumulated doctrinal accoutrements a militant thesis on the proper relation of the state to the Church? A condition of American religious variety, it has been suggested, is space; in the apparent openness of the continent there has been room for old religions and new. The Catholic Church, in arguable contrast, has cherished its continuity in time. Could this institution that had its own primordial charter and developed character, that had maintained its identity over so many centuries, that had coexisted with and survived so many forms of secular government, incorporate the insight which James Madison had so precociously articulated and asked his country to experiment with?

FATHER MURRAY FINDS HE'S THROUGH

The debate over religious freedom begun by John Courtney Murray I have already chronicled as part of my experience at the Catholic University of America, and it is time now to trace the debate's course after the 1940s. The American Jesuit Murray, it will be recalled, had challenged the reigning doctrine that the ideal Catholic state would suppress heresy; he had been vehemently opposed by a few traditional American theologians, led by Joseph Fenton; and Fenton had turned to Rome for help. It was, no doubt, a coming of age that such a debate occurred. American Catholic theologians had in the past docilely followed where European theologians had led. The Catholic Theological Society of America, the first professional association of these teachers (mostly men, mostly priests, mostly seminary faculty) was only three years old when Murray delivered his challenge; his was the first American voice to draw much attention from European Catholic theologians. The display of American independence was not welcome to Cardinal Alfredo Ottaviani, who as head of the Holy Office presided over the department of the Roman curia charged with policing heresy among theologians; his own *Institutiones juris publici ecclesiastici* took the conventional position assailed by Murray; his work had been published in Rome in 1948 the same year Murray had spoken in Chicago.

The debate continued from 1948 to 1953, when Ottaviani spoke in Rome, definitively restating his position, and Pius XII, a few months later, addressed the elements of the problem in a speech to Italian jurists and pointedly refrained from endorsing Ottaviani. Thereupon Murray was advised by Robert Leiber, the pope's Jesuit secretary, that Pius XII's words were meant as indication that Ottaviani's position was not necessarily the pope's. Murray then publicly interpreted the pope as deliberately rejecting what Ottaviani held. In response, Fenton argued that Pius XII had maintained the traditional thesis; no "careful, honest, and competent examination" could conclude otherwise. Ottaviani himself, his tenure at the Holy Office unaffected, pointedly noted Murray's "offensive" lecture in a letter to Cardinal Francis Spellman, archbishop of New York: a battle was under way, in Rome and in America.

Murray apologized to Ottaviani for any personal criticism the cardinal could have found in Murray's remarks; but the doctrinal issue was beyond personal feelings, and Murray's apology was not accepted. Jesuit headquarters in Rome, which had already shown some uneasiness over Murray's boldness, was now closely scrutinizing his writings. In conformity with the usual rules governing a member of a religious order, what he wrote was subjected to censors in advance of publication. In July 1954 a Jesuit censor in Rome declared that his article, "Leo XIII and Pius XII: Government and the Order of Religion," could not be published. The American assistant to the general of the Jesuits added, as he communicated this verdict: "It seems to me a mistake to wish to carry on with that controverted question under present circumstances." Murray replied, thanking him for his "delicate way of saying, 'You're through.'" The American assistant promptly answered, "You are far from through, I hope." Murray came back: "It was kind of you to say, 'You are far from through, I hope.' I do not share that hope." He had returned all the books on church and state to the library. Ottaviani with his American ally Fenton had won hands down. The six-year-old fight was over. The most knowledgeable man in America on the Catholic doctrine on religious freedom as it related to the American experience was effectively eliminated from the argument. Twice again he tried—in 1958 and in 1959—and twice again his articles were rejected by the Roman censors. He remained silent or, rather, silenced on the subject for a total of nine years.

JAMES MARITAIN LOVES JAMES MADISON

A foreshadowing of change had taken place in the archdiocese of Boston in the 1940s. Leonard Feeney, a Jesuit attached to the chaplaincy for Catholic students at Harvard, had seized upon an ancient patristic phrase, *extra ecclesiam nulla salus est*—"outside the Church there is no salvation." In the course of doctrinal development the sense of this expression had undergone metamorphosis, as theologians attributed to all sincere seekers of truth a kind of membership in the Church. Leonard Feeney, however, insisted that the phrase be taken narrowly so that on every side he saw persons damned by their unbelief. He was rebuked by Richard J. Cushing, archbishop of Boston, and by his own Jesuit superiors. He would not relax his tenacious grip on the literal meaning. His most fervent follower, a laywoman named Katherine Clark, wrote a small book whose climax was the imagined vindication of Feeney by the pope with the newsboys in Harvard Square shouting, "Extra! Extra! Extra! *Extra ecclesiam nulla salus est!*"

This apocalyptic fantasy was not realized. Feeney was dismissed from the Jesuit order and excommunicated—and so, for insisting that there was no salvation outside the Church, he found himself put out of it. For those writers of whom William Lecky is typical, who have insisted that the doctrine of the Church as the exclusive way of salvation was at the root of the persecuting mentality, the Feeney affair signaled the end of any belief justifying persecution. But as chapter two demonstrated, the duty to repress heresy was not formally dependent on a claim that salvation could be found only in the visible Church. Whatever the subterranean connection, the formal logic requiring persecution rested on the proposition that broken faith should be punished. The Feeney affair did show that the literal reading of a hallowed formula could be mistaken, that theological terms are capable of expansion, that the development of Christian doctrine requires spiritual discernment.

On January 25, 1959, the new pope, John XXIII, convoked a council of the bishops of the Catholic Church, and in due course suggestions were solicited as to what the council should consider. Archbishop Cushing wrote to Rome that "controversies have arisen about the relation of the Church to the modern State"; there was need for an exposition of fundamental principles, theological and juridical, in order to "supply a new conception of this relation, as the old concepts in force are rooted in political matters no longer in force." Murray's position, exactly. Nor had the Jesuits forgotten him. Their general, Jean Janssens, wrote of the desirability of a declaration by the council on the Church's relation to the state in today's circumstances. He added—whose work could he have meant but that of theologians like Ottaviani?—that the doctrine was sometimes "less aptly expounded" with "not small inconvenience." So America and Rome again interacted to keep the argument alive.

The task of addressing the issue was turned over to a new body, the Secretariat for the Promotion of Christian Unity, one of several committees set up to draft texts for the coming council. This choice was appropriate: what could be less encouraging to Christian ecumenism than any trace of the old teaching that heresy should be suppressed and the heretics themselves forced to conform? The first drafting session for a new declaration of the Church's position was held at the end of December 1960 in Fribourg, Switzerland. A Swiss bishop and a Swiss theologian, a Belgian bishop and a Belgian theologian were the draftsmen. The Belgian bishop, Emile Joseph De Smedt of Bruges, was to be the reporter of the document through its next five years of drafts and redrafts. The Fribourg draft stressed tolerance as a virtue and, beyond tolerance, Christian charity (shades of George Mason!), and it discarded the ideal of a Catholic state as the enforcer of orthodoxy. It was a good beginning, made exclusively by moderate Europeans.

To understand the point to which European thought had evolved—assisted only by a diffuse glow from America—a brief recall of the recent European past is necessary. Italy had experienced Fascism, Germany and occupied Europe had experienced Nazism, Eastern Europe was still suffering Communism. In reaction to these forms of modern totalitarianism Pius XI and Pius XII had increasingly insisted on the rights of the human person. *Mit brennender Sorge*, addressed by Pius XI to the bishops of Germany in 1937, spoke of "this fundamental fact that man as person possesses rights given by God, which must remain safe against every attempt by the community to deny them, to abolish them, or to prevent their exercise." In *Divini Redemptoris*, issued five days later, Pius XI declared that Communism "denigrates and denies the rights of the human person, his dignity, his freedom." So, during World War II, Pius XII stated that the human person must be acknowledged to have "the dignity with which God at the beginning endowed the human person." As this pope observed, the peoples who had experienced totalitarianism had become "questioning, critical, distrustful" of the state and wanted government "more compatible with the dignity and freedom of citizens." It was this new consciousness that was reflected postwar in the United Nations' adoption of the Declaration of the Rights of Man. The new nations that came into existence after the war chose constitutions setting out human rights, including the right of religious freedom.

The popes not only reacted, like the nations, against the totalitarian experience. They also followed and strengthened a line of Christian personalism, elements of which could be found in Christian tradition. The French philosopher Jacques Maritain had developed these elements into a compelling synthesis. Maritain came from a Protestant family of lawyers; he breathed the spirit of religious freedom and fidelity to law that Louis Méjan embodied; and he was a convert to Catholicism. On the one hand, as Maritain saw it, the bourgeois liberalism of the nineteenth century stressed the individual at the expense of the common good; it was this unrestrained individualism, each man for himself and each conscience free to make itself as it pleased, that the nineteenth-century Church condemned. At the other extreme, as a kind of built-in revenge, was the absorption of the individual by the collectivity that totalitarian doctrine presented in the twentieth century. The trick—if that is not too frivolous a term for a philosopher's analysis—was to say how both the common good and the uniqueness of each human being could be preserved.

Maritain's solution was to distinguish two aspects of every human being: the material, individuating each being in space and time, and the spiritual or personal, transcending space and time. The common good, for which the State has responsibility, relates to both the material needs of persons and their spiritual needs. The State in its care for the material welfare of the community is superior to any individual; but the State in its service to the spiritual welfare has limits set by the transcendence of the person. The common spiritual good consists in justice, beauty, truth, which the State properly cultivates. But in and through these goods the human person transcends this life. The human person is, indeed, ordained directly and ultimately to God as an absolute end, and this ordination "transcends every created good." The freedom of the human person is founded on this ordination beyond any material need. It is a freedom that the State does wrong by violating. Conserving the spiritual common good, the State may not intervene to coerce a person in the person's search for the truth; for it is the nature of a person to seek the truth freely. Who says "person" says freedom. The "right freely to believe the truth" is "the most basic of human rights."

If Maritain had written that the body belongs to the State, the soul to God, he would have had a wider if less discriminating audience. If he had said, without ontological preamble, that conscience cannot be coerced but man is part of a society that makes laws for him, his conclusion would not have differed from Madison's. But Maritain was a Thomist and rejected a Cartesian split between soul and body; he was a careful philosopher who knew of bourgeois excesses and socialist excesses; and he sought to find formulas that expressed the division and the unity of each human being, the enduring drive of each human being to a union with a Being beyond physical death, and the existence of spiritual values that the State should serve. So he wrote with a philosophical vocabulary focused on personhood, he made subtle and sometimes elusive distinctions, he taught at Princeton but did not declare himself a Madisonian. Old Bergsonian, neo-Thomist, epistemologist, and metaphysician moved by the horrors of European politics to plunge into the practical realm of political theory, he was the leading Catholic philosopher of his age. Refugee in America, later French ambassador to the Holy See, he could praise the constitutional arrangements of the United States, as being of "exceptional historic significance" and carry conviction at the Vatican.

Having translated into the language of person the traditional claims of conscience, Jacques Maritain spoke to and for those who cherished the idea of a Christian democracy in France, Italy, Germany, Belgium, and the Netherlands or chafed under its absence in Poland, Portugal, and Spain. His thought was equally attractive to those in Latin America who wanted no more military dictatorships. Maritain responded to the modern popes, and they to him. His deep piety, his gentleness, his gaiety of spirit assured him of friends. The future cardinal Charles Journet was his collaborator and the future pope Giovanni Battista Montini his admirer. And in his book *Man and the State* in the 1950s Maritain more than once quoted John Courtney Murray's writing on the subject. More broadly, like Tocqueville he saw and approved the American experience

of religious freedom, and he transmitted his enthusiasm to Catholic intellectuals at a time when human rights, including the right to religious
liberty, were becoming the accepted standards for measuring governments
in a large part of the world. If the Church's leading philosopher, if recent European experience, if common political discourse all pointed in
the same direction, was it not obvious that the Second Vatican Council
should bring the Church itself up to date? It was not obvious to a small
and strategically placed opposition.

THE GOOD GUYS COME TO TOWN

Two texts on religion and the state had been proposed for consideration
by the Council, one elaborated by the Fribourg group for the Secretariat
for Christian Unity, the other prepared by the Theological Commission,
a separate preparatory committee chaired by Cardinal Ottaviani. The
latter took the hard line of the past and put it forward as theologically
true. Which text would go to the floor of the Council? The committee
charged with sorting out jurisdictional disputes of this kind heard debate
as to which committee had right of way. The Theological Commission
insisted that the Secretariat had gone beyond its competence when it meddled with theology. Cardinal Augustin Bea warmly defended his
Secretariat. Cardinal Ottaviani, who had brought Father Fenton to Rome
as his adviser, pressed the claims of the conservatives.

The initial reaction of the Council's central commission was to abandon the whole enterprise of a declaration on religious liberty as "too controversial." John XXIII suggested that the two texts be brought together
in a compromise. It proved impossible. No draft on religious liberty was
presented to the first session of the Council as it opened in the fall of
1962. Only on October 22, 1962, did John XXIII determine that the Secretariat for Christian Unity had the right to present its drafts directly to
the Council, and only that decision kept open a channel for a declaration on religious liberty. The topic was still off the agenda.

The papal decision of October 22, 1962, however, showed how the
tide was turning against the curial conservatives, of whom Cardinal Ottaviani was the most prominent. These were the men who had staffed
the central administration of the Church, had policed doctrine and picked
bishops, and seen the Church survive the Fascists and the Nazis and the
Communists. They thought of the Church as well run and of its doctrines as well established. With all their hearts they did not want change.
With all their hearts they feared what change in one doctrine implied for

the stability and certainty of all doctrines. They had not wanted the Council. They had taken two years and eight months to prepare for it. Their proposals for action by it were restatements of old formulas. To the extent they could, they controlled the mechanisms of the Council. They were in a position to fight, they had the interior lines of communication so important to success, and, as they were certain that they were defending the truth, they felt assured of victory.

Those of us who had never seen a council—and none of us had—were familiar with the theology that treated as the last word in faith and morals the determinations of a council promulgated with the concurrence of the pope. Pictorial images of councils presented vast and still assemblages of learned males; in some paintings a light shone, or a dove representing the Holy Spirit hovered, above the solemn faces. The images were visual embodiments of the pouring out of grace upon the deliberations, which resembled the reception of revelation rather than a parliament of planners.

What we found in fact was a legislature in action. A legislature with a right, center, and left. A legislature with a variety of committees composing legislation, compromising disputes, considering amendments. A legislature of bishops guided by staffs of experts. A legislature interacting with the executive power possessed by the pope. A legislature surrounded by lobbyists on every issue.

The conciliar sessions themselves took place in the great basilica of St. Peter, a space suited to the size of the assembly—over two thousand bishops. The side altars of the basilica were turned into coffee bars where over an espresso one could engage in argument with other participants. At the end of each day's session there were press conferences, lunches, cocktail parties, dinners. The work of the Council went on not only in the nave of St. Peter, not only in its coffee bars, but around the town— in religious houses, in hotels, in embassies, in Roman congregations, and in the old palace of the Vatican. The experience of the Council was the experience of a demythologized church. Those experienced in biblical studies knew that in the documents gathered in Scripture God spoke through human tongues in human voices. Now the same phenomenon was observed in the flesh, as it were. The Council was the work of human beings. Faith would accept its conclusions as the will of God. But the conclusions did not come in a disembodied voice from heaven or carved on stone tablets.

When the bishops arrived from abroad, took stock of the process, and heard the experts, the great majority found themselves on the side of moderate change on a variety of matters and conscious that they could make improvements. In the context of the Council they were liberals. The two popes who presided over the Council—John XXIII, succeeded in 1963 by Paul VI—were liberals, too. In Catholic belief certain statements made by a pope are infallible expositions of faith and morals; but the conditions set for such statements are of a nature to be very rarely met; and there are no infallible means of detecting an infallible statement. Nonetheless, ever since the doctrine of papal infallibility had been proclaimed at the First Vatican Council, a kind of creeping pseudo-infallibilism had taken place in which many papal utterances were treated as if they were absolutely dispositive of the issue addressed. A type of fundamentalism thrived in which particular papal utterances were invoked the way a scriptural verse might be cited by a biblical fundamentalist. Hedged about by this quasi-infallibility, the pope had a place and enjoyed greater prerogatives than any secular president in relation to a legislature. The popes, however, were respectful of the machinery the conservatives had set in place and ordinarily ready to let the proceedings be governed by it. A liberal majority and a liberal pope could be frustrated, or at least the conservatives had the chance of frustrating them. The papal prerogatives were always trumps; but it is usually an illusion to think that the man at the top can do wonders alone without much support from below to sustain him and without prodding from below to push him forward. Support and prodding were at work in the aftermath of the first session.

In this period John XXIII commissioned an encyclical, *Pacem in terris*, which he issued in April 1963. Addressing questions of world peace and justice, the pope insisted on "the universal, inviolable, inalienable rights and duties" of the human person; among these rights he prominently put the right "to honor God according to the dictate of an upright conscience." The conservatives were left squirming room; did an "upright conscience" mean "a Catholic conscience" or an erroneous but uprightly formed conscience? John XXIII did not decide this question, but the championing of inalienable rights pointed in the direction of Maritain, Murray, and Madison. The principal draftsman of the encyclical was Pietro Pavan, a theologian from Treviso who had been a collaborator of Giovanni Battista Montini. Pavan was a priest capable of reading and taking in the American sources, of citing the Virginia Statute on Religious Freedom as the first of its kind, and of distinguishing the American concepts from those developed by the French Revolution. Over thirty times the encyclical used the phrase "the dignity of the human person"—the phrase that was in the end to introduce the document on religious liberty. Without *Pacem in terris*—so Pavan later observed—"it would have been difficult to come to that conclusion [on religious liberty] to which the Council came." In Pavan John XXIII had found the liberal expert he needed to advance ideas that the pope must have personally cherished.

Murray himself reappeared on the scene, not too dissimilarly from Joseph confronting the brothers who, according to Genesis, had thought him permanently disposed of. How had this rehabilitation come about? As usual, through the convergence of several factors. First, and possibly most importantly, a Catholic had run for president of the United States. What Murray had called "the neuralgic point" in ecumenical relations had become a sore spot in politics. Could a Catholic be trusted in the highest office? It seemed an insulting or silly question to many, but there was still a strain of Protestant thought that nourished itself on anti-Roman feeling, and in this constituency, largely Southern, the question seemed a good one, especially when fortified by reference to official Catholic documents. In the course of his campaign John F. Kennedy had to address the question and did so on September 12, 1960 before the Greater Houston Ministerial Association. The speech was read first to Murray: the Kennedy camp wanted to be able to say that Murray had not found it outrageous or untrue, even when the candidate avowed he believed in a separation of church and state that was "absolute." It was evident to everyone that the old line on an ideal government's duty to suppress heresy would have harmed the campaign. Kennedy's subsequent election made even more desirable a public doctrine of the Church that an American Catholic president could live with.

Murray, his importance acknowledged in the arena of affairs, had also been writing—not on Church and State but more comprehensively on "the American proposition." The book, as Murray described it, was "a primer of pluralism" and, without explicitly addressing the theological problems, celebrated American democracy and its freedoms and rooted them in European Christian tradition. *We Hold These Truths* appeared before the 1960 election. After the election, Henry Luce, a Republican but an admirer of Murray, put Murray on the cover of *Time*, whose lead story was "U.S. Catholics and the State." Celebrated in the media, consulted in a presidential campaign, the author of an acclaimed book, Murray could not be ignored in America even if Cardinal Ottaviani had made it clear that he was not welcome at the Council.

Almost simultaneously with the issue of *Pacem in terris* came an official notice from Rome: Murray was designated an expert of the Council and invited to participate in its proceedings. Murray ascribed the invitation to Cardinal Spellman, who, as he put it, "pried me in." No doubt the pragmatic Spellman responded to the American admirers of Murray; but the American intervention would not have succeeded if the conservative curial position had not already been weakened by John XXIII.

In November 1963, as the second session of the Council was under way, Murray appeared before the Theological Commission. The issue was whether the text prepared by the Secretariat for Christian Unity should be reviewed by another committee: John XXIII had died, and the conservatives had revived the jurisdictional objection. The chairman of the Theological Commission was Cardinal Ottaviani. Murray rose to speak, introduced by John Wright, bishop of Pittsburgh. "Who is that man?" asked Ottaviani, nearly blind and not hearing the introduction. "An expert, eminence," he was informed. The debate went on for two and one-half hours. At its conclusion Ottaviani's own commission voted 18 to 5 in favor of the Secretariat's text proceeding without further review. Murray reported the whole occasion to the Jesuit rector of Woodstock in the familiar parlance of an American Western. It was, he wrote, "a glorious victory for the Good Guys."

The Secretariat's text, however, was still not on the Council's agenda. Murray prepared a memorandum for the American bishops saying why the topic should be taken up. Meeting as a body in Rome, the Americans endorsed the memo. Cardinal Spellman presented the request to the presidency of the Council, a committee composed of the presiding officers of the assembly. The curial conservatives had taken care to assure that its membership would be predominantly in their camp; it was the focal point of their power; and it was not certain how the presidency would respond to the Americans' petition.

The new pope, elected in June, was Giovanni Battista Montini, Paul VI. His election had been a notable setback for the conservatives. In his first address to the Council, he observed that all the Council Fathers had "our reverence, our esteem, our confidence, our love." Difficult as these feelings may have been to cultivate, Paul VI maintained them in regard to old opponents such as Ottaviani, whom he did not remove from his place at the head of the Holy Office. By this modest spirit the pope made it possible for most of the conservatives to accept what they would have rebelled against if he had pushed his own agenda ruthlessly.

In the same opening of the second session of the Council, Paul VI expressed his regret that in certain countries "religious freedom, like other outstanding rights of man," were impeded. Superficial readers could see a standard reference to the Communists; close readers would see that

Paul VI was implying that if religious freedom was an outstanding right, it must be a fundamental one. With this pope succeeding John XXIII the conservatives remained caught between the supreme executive and the legislative assembly. With Paul VI's collaboration, the American request met with approval from the beleaguered council presidency. The draft on religious liberty prepared by the Secretariat was presented to the Council.

Presentation of the text was made by Bishop De Smedt, using a speech Murray wrote for him, which he "reworked in his own style." The *New York Times* promptly identified the true author. The report crisply set out four reasons for action by the Council:

1. The reason of Truth. Only by forming and following conscience could a human person obtain the end of human life, union with God.

2. The reason of defense. In a large part of the world atheistic materialists sought to deprive human persons of this liberty. The believers needed to assert it for all.

3. The reason of peaceful coexistence. In today's world there were no societies so closed that their actions of religious discrimination did not have repercussions elsewhere; human beings everywhere were called to live in peace with their neighbors throughout the world.

4. The reason of ecumenism. Many non-Catholics suspected Catholics of Machiavellianism in defending religious liberty when the Catholics were a minority while wanting to deny it to others if they became a majority. This distrust must be destroyed by frank commitment to freedom for everyone.

Religious liberty, the report continued, does not entail "indifferentism," as though it makes no difference what one believes, nor freedom from the human obligation to God, nor the relativism of truth, nor *pessimissimus dilettantismus*, that one has a quasi-right to be content with one's uncertainty as to religious truth and no need to search and struggle to discover it. The Fathers of the Council were asked not to take religious liberty in any of these senses. What did the term mean? Two things: positively, "the right of the human person to the free exercise of religion according to the dictate of the person's conscience"; negatively, immunity from all external coercion in such matters. Affirming the existence of religious truth and the duty to seek it, the report asked the Council to assert the inviolability of the person in relationship to God.

Could such a declaration be controversial? To the curial conservatives it was not only controversial but unthinkable. As they looked at their prospects for defeating the Secretariat's text in the Council, they concluded that there was not even time for discussion of the issue. De Smedt's presentation had been made on November 19; the second session was scheduled to close on December 4. Without taking a vote, the presidency of the Council postponed debate to the following year.

Earlier in 1963 Joseph Fenton had vigorously defended Ottaviani against those "who dislike the unchanging continuity of Christ's teaching within His Church." Ottaviani, he wrote, had "insisted on the need for stating Catholic doctrine, even when that doctrine is opposed to the tenets of the Reformers and the Modernists." It could not have been especially pleasing to the leaders of the American hierarchy to be implicitly identified with the Reformation and with the Modernist heresy of Alfred Loisy. After the close of the second session the ecclesiastical machinery moved. In January 1964 the following note appeared in *The American Ecclesiastical Review*: "In December 1963 Msgr. Joseph Clifford Fenton, after twenty-five years of outstanding service as Editor-in-Chief of *The American Ecclesiastical Review*, resigned because of poor health. Made Prothonotary Apostolic by Pope Paul VI, Msgr. Fenton is now Pastor of St. Patrick's Church, Chicopee Falls, Massachusetts." Recalled from his tenured position as professor of theology at Catholic University to his home diocese of Springfield, "Butch" Fenton had been removed from the combat: the American liberals, like the curial conservatives, knew how to press the levers of power. The defenders of religious liberty were not entirely committed to liberty of speech in the Church.

Murray, meanwhile, was instructing the American hierarchy further by a magisterial essay entitled "Right of the Human Person to Liberty on Matters of Religion." Acknowledging that there were "serious differences" in the Church on religious liberty, Murray neatly summarized "the First View" as presenting "intolerance wherever possible, tolerance wherever necessary." The First View was guilty of "Fixism," the doctrine that the Church's understanding could not develop; "Archaism," a rejection of the present age and a return to the past; and "Misplaced Abstractness," insistence on an ideal where there were only concrete conditions. In contrast, the "Second View" saw the nature of man as "a historical nature, whose rational exigencies manifest themselves progressively." The notion of religious freedom as a human right was "explicitly the product of a twentieth-century insight into the exigencies of the personal and political consciousness." The answer to the question of religious freedom was new because the question, in terms of this consciousness, was new. The tradition of the Church had to respond to the new insight. The tradition had a "growing end." The theologian's task—Murray's accomplishment in fact—was to discern the growing end.

Into a theological system that stressed continuity a dynamism was introduced. The key concept reflected the language of Bernard Lonergan, a Canadian Jesuit whose teaching at the Gregorian University in Rome had radiated an influence confirmed by his book *Insight*, a masterful modern treatment of theological method in general. Far more concrete than the fundamental work of Lonergan, and focused on a specific theological-political-juridical problem, Murray's paper was published in *Theological Studies* as the conciliar debate continued, his first sustained exposition of the issues since his silencing in 1954. Prior to publication the paper was circulated to the American bishops. Before the debate was over it had been translated into Dutch, French, German, Portuguese, and Spanish, finding everywhere readers who resonated to its theme.

Bishop De Smedt presented a modestly revised text of the Declaration on Religious Liberty to the third session of the Council. Debate opened September 23, 1964, with both sides well represented by speakers and by written submissions. Cardinal Ernesto Ruffini, archbishop of Palermo, said that there was a single true religion; other religions deserved only "patient and benign tolerance." The Catholic Church had never coerced anyone; but the Church did have concordats made in 1929 with Italy, in 1940 with Portugal, in 1953 with Spain, in 1954 with the Dominican Republic; according to the concordats the Church held a privileged position, Catholic feast days were civilly observed, the Catholic clergy was exempt from military service, and public education conformed to the dogmatic and moral principles of the Church. Would these concordats remain valid if the free exercise of religion was acknowledged? The negative answer that was implied was enough for Ruffini to reject the document.

Cardinal Ferdinando Quiroga y Palacios, archbishop of Santiago de Compostella, characterized the document as effecting "not an evolution, but a revolution." *Liberalismus*, many times formally condemned by the Church, was being offered for approval. Archbishop Marcel Lefebvre, head of the Fathers of the Holy Spirit, noted that the freedom recognized included freedom to follow the moral precepts of one's religion: so polygamy would have to be allowed to Muslims, a reductio ad absurdum in Lefebvre's book. Cardinal Ottaviani affirmed that Catholics had a natural and supernatural right to full religious freedom; but no one else did. Was the Church to say good-bye to the concordat with Italy, which safeguarded indissoluble Christian marriage and the Christian education of children? How could heretics be permitted "freedom of propaganda?"

Against this band so stubbornly and so loyally defending concepts of past centuries and the legal arrangements made by the Church in this century, were Cardinal Franz Koenig, archbishop of Vienna, representing the view dominant on the European continent; Archbishop Silva-Henriquez of Santiago, Chile, speaking for fifty-eight Latin American bishops; Cardinal Emile Léger, speaking for the majority of Canadian bishops; and Cardinal Cushing of Boston speaking "for almost all the bishops of the United States." Using Murray's language, Cushing described freedom as "the highest political end." He quoted deliberately from the American Declaration of Independence, telling the Fathers of the Council that the Church must show "a decent respect to the opinion of mankind."

The text was remanded by the Council to the Secretariat for Christian Unity to consider amendments offered by the Fathers. Murray was designated "the first scribe," his work immensely aided by the presence of Pietro Pavan among the drafters. The conservatives attempted to deflect treatment of the topic to a new "mixed commission," three of whose four members had declared themselves opposed to the Secretariat's draft. An appeal to the pope, followed by his rejection of the conservatives' maneuver, ended this barefaced attempt to smother the declaration. The text, as revised by the Murray-Pavan team, was printed and distributed to the Fathers on November 17.

On November 19, the presidency announced that no vote would be taken until the following year. That day, as Murray recalled, was "the day of Wrath" on the council floor: *dies irae, dies illa*, as the thirteenth-century hymn had it. Cardinal Albert Meyer, archbishop of Chicago, led the protest. Over eight hundred Fathers signed a petition to the pope asking him to overrule the presidency, which had come to its decision without consulting the assembly as a whole and without even consulting all of the members of the presidency. Paul VI declined to step in, assuring the American bishops that the Council would consider the matter next year. The bishops went home, more conscious than before of their own agreement and the tenacity of their opponents, and not a little nettled at being outmaneuvered.

Paul VI's Christmas broadcast showed again where his heart was; in language dear to Pavan, he spoke of "the human gasp for God" (*l'anelito verso Deo*) and said that public authority "exceeded its competence" when it entered this area of sacred breathing. On December 29, 1964, Cardinal Joseph Ritter, archbishop of St. Louis, wrote all the American bishops asking them to stand behind the declaration as distributed at the third session. Murray himself had his second heart attack of 1964. Recuperating, he wrote an article for *America*, in which he reported on "the day of Wrath"; he also noted some divergences between the American and French supporters of the text and observed that his tenacious opponents were not so much opposed to religious freedom as opposed to "the affirmation of progress in doctrine that an affirmation of religious freedom necessarily entails." With great candor he declared that "development of doctrine is *the* issue underlying all the issues at the Council" (emphasis Murray's).

In Italy the Secretariat drafted and redrafted, not attempting to meet the objections of the irreconcilables, but trying to accommodate nuances suggested in hundreds of amendments sent in by the Council Fathers. During the summer of 1965 Murray was well enough to negotiate with the French bishops a text that reflected their view that theology as well as juridical principles should have a prominent place in the document. Scripture, the French successfully insisted, grounded religious freedom; the seeds of liberty were planted by the Gospel.

The fourth session of the Council opened on September 14, 1965. The revised document was, as Paul VI had promised, the first order of business. With the Council not scheduled to end before December 8 there was plenty of time for discussion and voting. Cardinal Spellman opened the debate as the champion of the proposed declaration.

The old opponents were still vocal and unconvinced. As Archbishop Lefebvre put their position most succinctly in writing: "If what is being taught is true, then what the Church has taught is false." From every quarter of the world, bishops spoke to the contrary. Especially notable was the oration of Cardinal Wojtyla, the future John Paul II, speaking for the bishops of Poland: "In the very fact of Revelation is included the true and deep doctrine of religious liberty." Other bishops from the Communist countries, such as Joseph Slipyi, once a prisoner, now a cardinal, spoke of the essential need of a basis for the religious liberty of all persons regardless of their belief; only on a firm and universal foundation could the freedom of Christians from persecution be presented. The bishops from Eastern Europe were joined in this contention by bishops from the Islamic Middle East and Islamic Africa; they, too, had a sensitivity to present day persecution. Particularly eloquent, striking a note generally neglected, were the observations of Cardinal Joseph Beran, archbishop of Prague, who testified to what he had seen under the Communists in Czechoslovakia. When religious freedom was radically restricted, he said, there was "a serious danger" to faith and "very serious temptations" to hypocrisy and lying. But hypocrisy in professing faith hurt the Church more than the hypocrisy of those who hid their faith under pressure. And the Church had once fostered the former hypocrisy. The Catholic Church in Czechoslovakia "now seems to do sad expiation for faults and sins committed in its name in times past against liberty of conscience, such as the burning of Jan Hus, priest, in the fifteenth century, and in the seventeenth century the external compulsion of a great part of the people of Bohemia to again adopt the Catholic faith." The Church's reliance on the secular arm had "left a certain wound hiding in the hearts of the people" that was still an impediment to their progress in the spiritual life. Religious liberty, therefore, should be declared by the Council "in clear words and without reservations" and "in a spirit of penance for sins committed in this matter in past centuries." The concreteness of Beran's speech—Hus's execution candidly described as a *crematio*—was as startling as his acknowledgment of the sins committed in the name of the Church. The sins were a subject on which few articulate prelates wanted to dwell.

As of September 20, 1965, there had been sixty-two speeches and over a hundred written comments on the draft. The presidency of the Council saw its chance in this clamor of tongues. It decided that the text was not ready to be put to a vote. Once again there was a strong reaction by the Council Fathers. This time Paul VI acted. He required that the text be put to a preliminary vote. The clamor had been deceptive. The text passed 1,997 to 224. Under the rules the text was now "in possession" and could not be essentially changed; but amendments might be entertained by the drafting committee. Murray himself became *hors de combat* with a collapsed lung.

Also before this session of the Council, planned to be its last, was what was, in a sense, a companion document entitled *Gaudium et spes* (Joy and hope), whose subject was "The Church in the Modern World." Among the topics addressed was marriage. Among the positions taken was the right of every couple to determine in accordance with the consciences of husband and wife the number of children they should bring into the world. The curial conservatives were highly concerned with the relation of this document to contraception, whose treatment by a curial compromise had been withdrawn from the Council and turned over to a special papal commission.

As *Gaudium et spes* entered the final drafting stage, after being approved by an overwhelming conciliar majority, the conservatives staged a coup, producing before the drafting committee a note from the pope that apparently required the Council's reaffirmation of the rule on contraception; the special commission would be preempted. Heated discussion broke out in the committee. "Christ himself has spoken," declared Cardinal Michael Browne, a curial conservative. The liberals went to Paul VI. He qualified the directive delivered in his name. The text suffered, but not fatally. The tenacity of the conservatives in continuing to fight after so many defeats was cautionary.

Israel Shenker, the correspondent of the *New York Times* covering the Council, had formerly covered the Kremlin. He saw analogues in the subterranean ways he had observed there and what he now saw at the Vatican. As he observed the factional maneuvers that were producing the solemn doctrine of the Church, he asked me, "Why do you believe?" I answered, "Because the Church has the Gospel and the sacraments." I could have added, "Because God acts through human beings." How different Rome was from contemporary Moscow! Here without violence, in open debate and in written exchanges, and in personal confrontations and frank advocacy, the teaching of the Church was being purified. That in a context which was political, political moves should be made could surprise only those who expected an incarnational process to be purely spiritual. As to the final outcome one could only work, wait, and trust.

A slightly revised text on religious liberty was passed by the Council on October 26, 1965. More amendments were proposed. A further vote was taken on separate sections of the document on November 19; the opponents never numbered more than 249. The day before this vote, Murray with other selected experts celebrated mass with Paul VI in St. Peter's. The Good Guys were on the brink of victory. On December 7, a final vote was taken—70 no; 2,308 yes. On December 8, the feast of the Immaculate Conception, exactly 101 years after *Quanta cura* had denounced liberty of conscience as a madness, Paul VI promulgated the declaration as the teaching of the Church. Among those subscribing their names to the final text was Alfredo Ottaviani.

OF THE DIGNITY OF THE HUMAN PERSON

Known by its opening Latin words, *Dignitatis humanae personae*, the text as it finally emerged from debate and amendment bore the title Declaration on Religious Freedom and the subtitle On the Right of the

Person and of Communities to Social and Civil Freedom in Religious Matters. Cardinal Wojtyla had proposed that the solemn ecclesiastical term "doctrine" be used in place of "declaration." A slight concession to the minority could be seen in the retention of "declaration." But it had also been argued that "declaration" was appropriate for the Church making its mind known not only to the faithful but to the whole world; and the chosen word echoed the famous eighteenth-century declarations of America and France and the modern declaration of the United Nations. A clearer concession to the minority was the subtitle, making explicit that the declaration was not a recognition of total freedom from all obligation to God, but only of civic liberty.

The opening words of the Declaration declared that our day saw an increasing consciousness "of the dignity of the human person." The number of those had increased who wanted all to act "in free responsibility, not moved by coercion but by the consciousness of duty." Especially was this felt in what "concerns the free exercise of religion in society." The Council, attentive to these aspirations, had scrutinized the sacred tradition of the Church "from which it draws the new always in congruence with the old." In these succinct phrases the Council explained why it was taking up the topic at this point in history and acknowledged novelty while asserting continuity. In this area of political morality an evolving human consciousness was made a collaborator of the Church.

After this extraordinary exordium, there followed the fundamental teaching: "This Vatican Council declares that the human person has a right to religious freedom." The freedom was defined. The freedom consisted in immunity from coercion by individuals or by social groups or by "any human power," so that "no one in a religious matter may be compelled to act against his conscience or prevented from acting privately or publicly, alone or associated with others, according to his conscience, within due limits."

What followed was crucial: the basis for recognizing this right. The Council declared that the right was "founded in the very dignity of the human person as it is known by the revealed word of God and by reason itself." The repetition of the phrase "human person" (surely unnecessary when neither angelic nor divine persons were at issue) was an effort to emphasize the objective character of the right. It was in terms of the person—in terms of a "dignity" that pleonastically emphasized the person's special status and unique worth—that the Council marshaled revelation and reason on the side of liberty. The right belonged to each person because no one could satisfy, in a manner conformable to human nature, the moral duty to seek and adhere to the truth, except by "psychological freedom and immunity from external coercion." Using the approach of Maritain, the Council declared that human beings, directed as they are to God, "transcend by their nature the terrestrial and temporal order of things." The civil power "exceeded its limits" when it presumed to direct or impede this relationship to God. The right to freedom belonged to groups as well as individuals, because both human nature and religion have a social dimension.

A special section of the text was devoted to religious freedom "under the light of revelation." The teaching of Jesus Christ was manifest in his conduct. Christ compelled no one to believe. "Mild and humble of heart" in the words of the Gospel of Matthew, he had patiently attracted and invited his disciples; and he had testified to the truth not by the use of force but by submitting to death. The Apostles had followed the same path. The Fathers of the Church had unanimously taught that the act of faith must be voluntary, and so had the Church, "although sometimes in the life of the people of God in its pilgrimage across the vicissitudes of human history a way of action existed less conformed to the spirit of the Gospel and indeed contrary to it." The Gospel seed had nonetheless contributed in the course of time to the growing conviction that in religious matters all should be immune from compulsion.

As a review of history, *Dignitatis humanae personae* failed badly. It referred to slips in conduct but not in teaching. It mentioned only the freedom traditionally accorded the nonbaptized. It never acknowledged the long record of coercing the baptized when they were considered to be in heresy. Details like the *crematio* of Jan Hus were missing along with the penitential spirit recommended by Cardinal Beran. Even the lapses in coercing the act of faith were noted in oddly impersonal terms as if "the vicissitudes of human history" were explanation and apology enough for acts of persecution urged and undertaken by responsible Christians in the name of the Church.

As a juridical document, the Declaration had the vagueness that has attended every effort, from the Virginia Declaration of Rights to the present, to say that religious freedom is not without bounds. Thrice the Council returned to the topic. It was "to do injury to the human person and the very order established by God" to deny "the free exercise of religion in society, provided a just public order is preserved." No attempt was made to specify what constituted a just public order. In the next section "the just demands of public order" qualified the asserted freedom of religious associations (in itself a markedly liberal expansion of Madisonian doctrine; Madison had thought in terms of individual consciences, not churches). A little greater specificity was achieved in recognizing that these religious groups had a right to disseminate their beliefs but that "indecent or even less upright persuasion of the uneducated" was an abuse of the right. In section 7, again taking up this troublesome subject, the Council taught that civil society had the right to protect itself against abuses that could arise under the pretext of religious liberty. The Council acknowledged that the civil power had duties imposed "by the due care of public morality" (was Lefebvre's fear about polygamy being met and disarmed?). The Council concluded that the norm should be "that freedom is maximally recognized for human beings and not restrained except when necessary to the extent necessary." A doubly elastic formula.

The Declaration was wide open to interpretation in another area, that of establishment of a church by law. "Given the particular circumstances of a people," a religious association might be assigned "a special civil status in the juridical order." Responsibility for such arrangements was not attributed to anyone; as in the passage on "the vicissitudes of human history" a set of historical facts was referred to with no admission that the Church had brought these situations about; concordats went unmentioned. Such arrangements were neither condemned nor praised, but the Council insisted that the religious freedom of all should be respected and that the civil power "must provide that the juridical equality of citizens never be openly or hiddenly injured on account of religious reasons, nor any discrimination made among them." Was it really possible to have an established church and no religious discrimination? (Cardinal John Heenan, archbishop of Westminster, had testified in debate that such was the happy situation in England.) The Council went in two different directions.

Three large inadequacies, then—the failure to deal with history, the failure to deal with the implications of an establishment, the vague and tangled treatment of the civil power's right to limit actions based on religious convictions. In its failures, the Declaration reflected its character as a document composed by a committee issuing from a legislature-like assembly. It carried some wounds inflicted by the minority. It illustrated the practical impossibility of a worldwide church finding a single formula suitable for every country in the world. It demonstrated the difficulty of abandoning past precedents without appearing arbitrary and the difficulty of departing from one's ancestors without denouncing them. Although Murray had remarked that the development of doctrine was the underlying issue of the Council, the Declaration did not even sketch a theory of development, other than a postulated growth in human respect for freedom. Even on this point it was open to criticism. As Murray himself remarked, the change in consciousness had come in the eighteenth century. The Church came late "to a war that has already been won." Not only the development but the lag in development needed to be accounted for. A tiny minority remained unconvinced that the development could properly take place. For them, the Church had married the French Revolution!

If an unkind critic should remark that the Declaration was as inevitable —and of as little significance—as a declaration that modern plumbing is preferable to a world without bathrooms, he or she would have to be answered that what now seems inevitable came close to not happening, and that far from merely registering the obvious, the Declaration was dynamic in its implications for the future of a large spiritual society. If the unkind critic should observe that the implications have scarcely been faced let alone developed, he or she would have to be answered that time must pass for the implications of a profound change to be drawn. Finally, if this hypothetical critic should cynically observe that what has been changed could be changed again and that at some later time it might be advantageous to the Church to assert its old position, no disavowal of such a possibility might disarm him or her, but a believer would see a development of the kind that is organic and that can as easily be reversed as an oak can be restored to the acorn from which it came.

Despite the disappointing deficiencies, *Dignitatis humanae personae* was a substantial accomplishment. However characterized, this act of a world assembly of the bishops of the Catholic Church had set a new course for that body as the champion of religious freedom everywhere for everyone. The demand of human nature for such freedom had been affirmed. Psychological freedom from pressure to believe had been posited as essential. The quibbles and the qualifications of the text paled in the light of the central contention that linked freedom to the search for truth. "The truth shall make you free," John's Gospel taught. In freedom only shall you reach the truth, the Council added.

Implicitly the Council had a theory of development. First, asserting the need for psychological freedom in reaching the truth, the Council indicated the basic condition of development, free and open debate, such as had ultimately occurred in the Council itself but had been suppressed by ecclesiastical authority in the years preceding the Council and hampered for two years in the Council itself by its presidency. Second, pointing to the pedagogy of Christ as the model, the Council showed that development of Christian doctrine meant a deeper, more faithful response to Christ. Development was not to be unguided without binding criteria. Third, the Council proclaimed that the Church learned from human experience. In Murray's words, the Church here adopted "a principle accepted by the common consciousness of men and civilized nations."

The learning had been largely from the United States: from its Constitution of such extraordinary importance praised by Maritain and from the Virginian Declaration pointed to by Pavan; from its bishops who kept the issue alive as "*the* American issue" in the Council; from its theologian John Courtney Murray, who poured his energy and insight into the shaping of the new teaching. Impossible without the recent European experience and the support of bishops from around the world and the receptivity of Italian popes, the Declaration on Religious Freedom would not have come into existence without the American contribution and the experiment that began with Madison.

EPILOGUE

CHAPTER 14

TEN COMMANDMENTS

First. You shall conclude that the genealogy, the domestic environment, the educational exposure, the intellectual adventures, the friendships, and the professional life of anyone treating this topic influence the treatment; and you shall suspect that the spiritual life of the writer is relevant as well; and you shall know that no person, man or woman, historian or law professor or constitutional commentator or judge, is neutral in this matter.

Second. You shall acknowledge that the foundation of freedom in religion is the concept of the individual conscience; and you shall not worship an empty idol, attributing to "the Enlightenment" an insight that is of deeper and more ancient root.

Third. You shall respect the content and the context of the sixteen words creating religious freedom in the Constitution, and you shall not artfully divide the words from one another, nor omit any of them, nor impose two meanings on a single word.

Fourth. You shall read Tocqueville for his celebration of the holy union of freedom and religion, discount his excesses and omissions as an advocate, and meditate on his conviction that religion is the foremost of our political institutions.

Fifth. You shall observe that the free exercise of religion generated the moral energy and the bitter passions that produced the Civil War and led to the liberation of the millions held in bondage.

Sixth. You shall mark that government when it seeks to adjudicate the truth of a religion falls afoul of the First Amendment and when it attempts to adjudicate the sincerity of a believer enters on an enterprise beset by hazards.

Seventh. You shall realize that the words safeguarding religious freedom in the Constitution must be applied in order to achieve that end; that their application invites interpretation; that interpretation breeds disputes;

that disputes result in distinctions; and that only over time do the dominant distinctions become palpable, only then does a development of doctrine occur.

Eighth. You shall substitute neither State nor society for God nor suppose that religion may be analytically reduced to the self-worship of society.

Ninth. You shall recognize that the free exercise of religion can be divisive and dangerous to established institutions and customary ways as well as beneficent for believers and empowering for the forgotten, and that the price of our constitutional liberty is acceptance of this precarious condition.

Tenth. You shall acknowledge that religion itself requires religious freedom. Heart speaks to heart, spirit answers Spirit, freely.

NOTES

INTRODUCTION

Cradle of Liberty: Boston's double claim to this title on the basis of its revolutionary and its abolitionist activity is noted by William E. Gienapp, "Abolitionism and the Nature of Antebellum Reform," in *Courage and Conscience: Black and White Abolitionists in Boston*, ed. Donald M. Jacobs (Bloomington: Indiana University Press, 1993), 44; "the hanging of the Quakers": *infra*, chapter 2.

as Newman says: the phrase *cor ad cor loquitur* (heart speaks to heart) was adopted by him as the legend of his cardinal's coat of arms. It was an adaptation of a phrase he had earlier used from St. Francis de Sales. See Ian Ker, *John Henry Newman: A Biography* (Oxford: Clarendon Press, 1988), 719 and John Henry Newman, *The Idea of a University*, ed. Ian Ker (Oxford: Clarendon Press, 1976), 332 and 655.

CHAPTER 1

O'Connell's career: James M. O'Toole, *Militant and Triumphant: William Henry O'Connell and the Catholic Church in Boston, 1859–1944* (Notre Dame: University of Notre Dame Press, 1992), 72, 79, 94 (advancement in office); 113–120 (resistance in diocese); 194–195 (losses in Rome); 181, 195–196 (nephew's secret marriage); "The Puritan has passed": 121; "The march to our duty": 129; disapproval of Curley: 124–126; the lawsuit: *Boston v. Santosuosso*, 298 Mass. 175, 10 N.E.2d 271 (1937); "the walls": O'Toole, *Militant*, 125.

odd pockets such as Quincy . . . Republicans: so I was informed by Paul Reardon, secretary to Republican governor Christian Herter and later a justice of the Supreme Judicial Court.

David Ignatius Walsh: O'Toole, *Militant*, 122; Carroll: see 220 Massachusetts Reports.

O'Connell's politics and political friends: O'Toole, *Militant*, 129; defeat of the lottery bill: 138–139.

referendum on birth control: for the negative result see Mass. Gen. Laws 272, 20–21 (1956).

"this unholy, unpatriotic": O'Toole, *Militant*, 136; O'Connell and Sacco and Vanzetti: 164; "Almost hysterical": 137–138; "even before we have a chance":

131–132. On the Sacco and Vanzetti case, see *Commonwealth v. Sacco*, 261 Mass. 12 (1927); and Francis Russell, *Sacco & Vanzetti: The Case Resolved* (New York: Harper and Row, 1986).

Hawthorne's "The Gentle Boy": written before 1829, first published in 1832, revised and published in 1837 in his *Twice-Told Tales;* see Neal Funk, *Hawthorne's Early Tales: A Critical Study* (Durham, N.C.: Duke University Press, 1992), 158–161; John Greenleaf Whittier, "Cassandra Southwick," in *The Complete Poetical Works* (Boston: Houghton Mifflin, 1884), 18.

"our own perfect liberty": Brooks Adams, *The Emancipation of Massachusetts* (Boston: Houghton Mifflin, 1887), 342–343.

"the neuralgic point": John Courtney Murray, "Governmental Repression of Heresy," *Proceedings of the Catholic Theological Society of America* 3 (1948): 26.

"the doctrine of liberty of conscience": John A. Ryan, "Condemnation of *L'Avenir*," *Catholic Historical Review* (April 1937): 23–36.

"If there is only one true religion": John A. Ryan and Francis J. Boland, *Catholic Principles of Politics* (New York: Macmillan, 1948), 319.

"indifferentism": Gregory XVI, *Mirari vos*, August 15, 1832, *Acta Gregorii Papae XVI* (1901), ed. A. M. Bernasconi (1971), 1:171–172. The quotation is from Augustine, Letter 166. When Lamennais in a pseudonymous work, *Paroles d'un croyant*, criticized the encyclical, Gregory XVI responded in an encyclical aimed specifically at this book. He lamented "the madnesses of human reason seeking novelty and contrary to the warning of the Apostle seeking to know more than it is necessary to know and to find truth outside the Catholic Church." Gregory XVI, *Singulari nos*, June 25, 1834, *Acta Gregorii*, 1:434. *Deliramentum*, meaning "madness," is the term used by both Gregory XVI and Pius IX. It is sometimes softened by being translated "aberration"; but "madness" is what Gregory XVI chose to call liberty of conscience; and Pius IX repeated the term in *Quanta cura*, December 8, 1864, *Pii IX Pontificis Maximi Acta* (Rome, 1857), pt. 1, 3:690–691. Simultaneously with this encyclical the pope released a document denominated "A Syllabus Containing the Principal Errors of Our Time as Noted in Consistorial Allocutions, in Encyclicals, and in Other Apostolic Letters." Popularly known as "The Syllabus of Errors," it listed eighty propositions, rejecting all of them; the context of each original rejection shows the degree of condemnation. Among the condemned propositions was no. 55: "The Church should be separated from the State, and the State from the Church," rejected September 27, 1852, in Pius IX's allocution *Acerbissimum*. Among the errors specifically ascribed to "Today's Liberalism" was no. 79: "It is false that civil freedom for every religion and full power granted everyone of openly and publicly manifesting their opinions and thoughts leads to the easier corruption of morals and of souls and to propagating the disease of indifferentism," rejected December 15, 1856, in the allocution *Numquam fore*. Leo XIII invoked *Mirari vos* in *Immortale Dei*, November 1, 1885, *Acta sanctae sedis* (Rome: Vatican Polyglot Press, 1885), 18:173.

"I, for one": Francis Connell, intervention, *Proceedings of the Catholic Theological Society* 3 (1948): 100.

The hypothesis: notably defended in France by Félix Dupanloup, bishop of Orléans. See F. Lagrange, *Vie de Mgr Dupanloup* (Paris, 1883), 1:326, 348–349; compare the attack on Dupanloup for watering down *Quanta cura* and "recognizing the hypothesis as the law and the permanent state of affairs." V. Magnard, *Monseigneur Dupanloup et M. Lagrange son historien* (Paris, 1884), 137.

"Political experience has taught us": Murray, "Governmental Repression," 87–88.

the ideas of Félicité de Lamennais: see *L'Avenir*, November 1, 1830 and August 30, 1831, in *L'Avenir*, ed. Guido Veruccio (Rome, 1967), 119, 644–645. Gregory XVI, *Mirari vos*, August 15, 1832: *Acta Gregorii*, 1:172.

the attraction of Loisy's position: Alfred Loisy, *L'Evangile et l'Eglise* (Bellevue: Chez l'auteur, 1903); "synthesis of all the heresies": Pius X, *Pascendi dominici gregis*, September 8, 1907, *Acta sanctae sedis* (1907), 40:632.

the Church's prohibition of profit: John T. Noonan, Jr., *The Scholastic Analysis of Usury* (Cambridge, Mass.: Harvard University Press, 1957), 407–408.

"unrealistic": "The Supreme Court, 1952 Term," *Harvard Law Review* 67 (1953): 91, 111 (the authorship of the entire commentary was multiple; I recall my contribution). For further discussion of *Kedroff v. St. Nicholas Cathedral*, 344 U.S. 94 (1952), see chapter 7.

"wall of separation": Jefferson quoted in *Reynolds v. United States*, 98 U.S. 145, 164 (1879). For further discussion of the *Mormon Cases*, see chapter 9.

"makes no provision": *Permoli v. Municipality of New Orleans*, 44 U.S. 588, 609 (1845) (the First Amendment no barrier to a city penalizing a priest for officiating at a funeral outside an "obituary chapel").

freedom of speech and freedom of the press . . . Fourteenth Amendment: *Gitlow v. New York*, 268 U.S. 652, 666 (1925). Freedoms of speech, association, and assembly assumed: *Whitney v. California*, 274 U.S. 357, 371–72 (1927). Freedom of speech applied: *Fiske v. Kansas*, 274 U.S. 380, 387 (1927), *Stromberg v. California*, 283 U.S. 359, 368 (1931). Freedom of the press applied: *Near v. Minnesota*, 283 U.S. 697, 707 (1931).

successfully invoked freedom of the press: *Lovell v. City of Griffin*, 303 U.S. 444 (1938); the earlier free exercise appeal dismissed for "the want of a substantial federal question": *Coleman v. City of Griffin*, 302 U.S. 636 (1937).

"in the delusion of racial or religious conceit": *Cantwell v. Connecticut*, 310 U.S. 296, 310 (1940).

Holmes's 1905 dissent: *Lochner v. New York*, 198 U.S. 45, 74 (1905).

"discrete and insular minority": *United States v. Carolene Products Co.*, 304 U.S. 144, 153, n.4 (1938).

cases invalidating parts of the New Deal: e.g., *Carter v. Carter Coal Co.*, 298 U.S. 238 (1936); empire about to disappear: *National Labor Relations Board v. Jones & Laughlin Steel Corp.*, 301 U.S. 1 (1937); *Wickard v. Filburn*, 317 U.S. 111 (1942).

the "fundamental concept of liberty": *Cantwell*, 310 U.S. at 303; "unduly": id.

at 304; "in the exercise of a determination by state authority": id. at 307; "all others who respect": id. at 309.

CHAPTER 2

"**We must obey God**": Acts 5:29.

Nathan denouncing David: 2 Sam. 12:1–23.

"**Your very rulers are rebels**": Isaiah 1:22–23.

"**You know all the evil**": 1 Kings 2:44; see David Daube, *Ancient Jewish Law* (Leiden: E. J. Brill, 1981), 123–129.

"**Bad thoughts**": Cicero, *Pro Sex. Roscio Amerino*, in *Orationes*, ed. Albert C. Clark (Oxford: Clarendon Press, 1900), 67.

"**your mind's conscience**": Cicero, *Pro Cluentio*, in *Orationes*, ed. Albert C. Clark (Oxford: Clarendon Press, 1900), 159.

"**Is it a lighter matter**": Augustine to Boniface, governor of Africa, Letter 185, "The Correction of the Donatists," chap. 20, in *Patrologiae cursus completus, Series latina*, ed. J. P. Migne (Paris: Garnier, 1891), 33:802; that persecution worked: chap. 21.

The Apollinarians, the Arians . . . : *Theodosiani libri XVI cum constitutionibus Sirmonidianis*, ed. T. Mommsen and P. Meyer (Berlin: Weidmannos, 1962), 16: chap. 5, secs. 12, 25, 34, 38, and 39.

corollary of the absolute conviction: see William K. Jordan, *The Development of Religious Toleration in England: From the Beginning of the English Reformation to the Death of Queen Elizabeth* (Cambridge, Mass.: Harvard University Press, 1932), 396: "The man who is dominated by an absolute conviction of the truth of his belief is so certain of his faith and of the inspiration of God that he inevitably attempts to persecute, in one fashion or another, the error which is quite as clear to him as the truth of his own conviction."

"**Religion cannot be compelled**": Lactantius, *Divinarum institutionum libri*, 5:20, *Patrologiae* 6:614; "not by killing": 612. "None of us": 614; "against the law (*ius*) of humankind and against all established rightness (*fas*)": 613.

"**Those who differ**": Gregory I to Peter, bishop of Terracina, March 591, in Shlomo Simonsohn, *The Apostolic See and the Jews* (Toronto: Pontifical Institute of Medieval Studies, 1988), 1:3; that the Jews were to be won over by persuasion not force and that their religious rites were not to be suppressed was the pope's ideal program, generally observed by his successors. See also Gregory I to Paschasius, bishop of Naples, November 602, 1:23–24.

the Manichaean religion: *Theodosiani libri*, bk. 15, 8, 2; bk. 16, 5, 3 and 7, 9, 11, 18, 40, 62, 64.

Bernard of Clairvaux in a letter: to all Christians, Epistle 457, *S. Bernardi Opera*, ed. J. LeClercq (Rome: Editiones Cistercienses, 1957–1977), 7:432; for the debated interpretation of this letter, see Jürgen Mietke, *Bernard de Clairvaux: Histoire, mentalités, spiritualité* (Paris: Editions du Cerf, 1992), 492–495.

"**worthy of servitude**": Innocent III to Pierre de Courtenay, January 17, 1208, in

Simonsohn, *Apostolic See*, 1:93 (English translation in Edward A. Synan, *The Popes and the Jews in the Middle Ages* [New York: Macmillan, 1965], 226); "perpetual servitude": Innocent III to Pierre de Corbeil, archbishop of Sens, July 15, 1205, in ibid., 1:86 (English translation in Solomon Grayzel, *The Church and the Jews in the XIIIth Century* [Philadelphia: Dropsie College for Hebrew and Cognate Learning, 1933]). "Servitude" is not to be understood as physical slavery, legally enforced, but as a status inferior to that of free citizens. Salo Wittmayer Baron, *Ancient and Medieval Jewish History*, ed. Leon A. Feldman (New Brunswick: Rutgers University Press, 1972), 301, 320–322. Innocent III took a high hand as to the property rights of Jews, regularly remitting the obligations to pay them what he termed "usury" in blanket dispensations to crusaders as a reward for taking the cross. Innocent III to the archbishop of Narbonne, August 15, 1198, in Simonsohn, *Apostolic See*, 1:71; Innocent III to the archbishop of Magdeburg, December 31, 1199, in ibid., 1:78; Innocent III to the Christian faithful of Cologne, April 22, 1213, in ibid., 1:97.

"the rites of other infidels": Thomas Aquinas, *Summa theologiae*, 2–2, Q. 10, art. 10, ed. Pietro Carmello (Turin: Marietti, 1952).

To death if they were warned: ibid., Q. 11, art. 3.

"knows who are truly returning": ibid., ad. 1.

the famous conflict between Henry II and Archbishop Thomas Becket: see David Knowles, *Thomas Becket* (Stanford: Stanford University Press, 1970); John T. Noonan, Jr., *The Believer and The Powers That Are* (New York: Macmillan, 1987), 22–27.

the condemnation of Joan of Arc: see P. Doncoeur, S. J. and Y. Lanhers, *La Réhabilitation de Jeanne La Pucelle ordonnée par Charles VII en 1450 et le codicille de Guillaume Bouille* (Paris: Librairie d'Argences, 1956); Noonan, *The Believer*, 45–51.

"is in a certain way the dictate of reason": *Summa*, 1–2, Q. 19, art. 5.

"it is the same thing to flout": ibid., ad. 2; crass ignorance: ibid.

The Reformation . . . heretics . . . churches: Jean Leclerc, *Toleration and the Reformation*, trans. T. L. Weslow (London: Longmans, 1960), 1:162, 200, 328; Maximilian: 268.

Warsaw Confederation: A. Brückner, "The Polish Reformation in the Sixteenth Century," in *Polish Civilization*, ed. M. Giergielwic (New York: New York University Press, 1979), 81.

"desire above all the liberty": Cardinal William Allen, *A True, Sincere and Modest Defense of English Catholics that suffer for their faith both at home and abroad* (St. Louis: Herder, 1914), 2:148; "the free exercise of their religion": Marc' Antonio Morisini, Venetian ambassador in France, to the Doge and Senate, September 13, 1624. *Calendar of State Papers and Manuscripts Relating to English Affairs Existing in the Archives and Collections of Venice and in Other Libraries of Northern Italy*, ed. Allen B. Hinds (London: His Majesty's Stationery Office, 1912), 18:438. The princess and her suite: the marriage articles, enclosed in a letter from Zuane Pesaro, Venetian ambas-

sador in England, to the Doge and Senate, December 27, 1624 (524). By a
secret article added apart from the marriage contract, King James granted
Catholics "security of life and property without their being interrogated about
the Catholic faith, if they render the obedience they owe him" (525).

Sebastian Franck (1499–1542): Leclerc, *Toleration*, 1:166–175; Caspar Schweck-
enfeld (1489–1561): in ibid., 1:176–185. Menno Simons (1493–1561): Harold S. Bender, "A Brief Biography of Menno Simons," *The Complete Writings of Menno Simons*, ed. John Christian Wenger (Scottdale, Pa.: Herald Press,
1966), 1:4–28. On Sébastien Castillon's *Traité des Hérétiques* of 1554 see Jordan, *Development of Religious Toleration*, 310–313. Other writers who had
an impact on England include Jacopo Aconico, a Socinian from near Trent
who emigrated to England and in 1565 defended religious toleration in that
country, and Faustus Socinius, whose *Catechism of Rakau* (1609) rejected the
use of force in religious matters (Jordan, *Development of Religious Toleration*, 303–307); Jordan also reads the 1580 work of the English Jesuit martyr, Robert Parsons, *A brief discourse contagning certayne Reasons why
Catholics Refuse to goe to Church*, as arguing for universal civil toleration
(394). Jordan in his 1936 volume on toleration from 1603 to 1641 finds two
Baptist writers championing a freedom of religion that goes beyond mere toleration: Thomas Helways, *A Short Declaration of the Ministry of Iniquity*
(1612); and Leonard Busher, *Religious Peace; or a plea for liberty of conscience*
(1614). See William K. Jordan, *The Development of Religious Toleration in
England: From the Accession of James I to the Creation of the Long Parliament (1603–1640)* (London: G. Allen and Unwin, 1936), 275–286.

New Plymouth: John E. Pomfret, *Founding The American Colonies* (New York:
Harper and Row, 1970), 126–127; Massachusetts Bay Colony: Sydney E.
Ahlstrom, *A Religious History of the American People* (New Haven: Yale Uni-
versity Press, 1972), 139–150.

"a *Plantation religious*": John Norton, *The Heart of New England Rent at the
Blasphemies of the Present Generation* (1659), 58; "we through grace": 53.

In 1656 the General Court: *Records of the Governor and Company of Massachusetts Bay*, ed. Nathaniel B. Shurtleff (Boston: W. White, 1853–1854), vol.
4, pt. 1, 277–278; "alien" or "vagabond": vol. 4, pt. 2, 3; "directly or indirectly": vol. 4, pt. 1, 308; "approve of any known Quaker": 346; importation of Quaker literature: 278; penalty for proposing Quaker doctrine: 321;
"stranger" Quakers: vol. 4, pt. 2, 3; penalties for return: vol. 4, pt. 1, 329;
"severely" whipped: 308–309; death penalty: 346; death penalty for returning priests: 2:193; 3:112; death penalties applied in 1659: 3:383–384; death
penalty for Dyer: 3:407.

Provided Southwick and her brother: ibid., vol. 4, pt. 1, 366.

and Mary Dyer: Ruth Plimpton, *Mary Dyer: Biography of a Rebel Quaker*
(Boston: Branden, 1994), 181–189; "mercy and clemency": 181; "My life not
availeth me": 47.

"Would you not have thought it hard": Anne Coddington to Governor Endecott
and the General Court, July 7, 1660, reprinted in ibid., 192.

"the constable of the towne": *Records*, vol. 3, pt. 2, 348.

the new legislation enforced: Richard P. Hallowell, *The Quaker Invasion Of Massachusetts* (Boston: Houghton Mifflin, 1883), 183–187; George A. Sellek, *Quakers in Boston 1656–1854* (Cambridge, Mass.: Friends Meeting at Cambridge, 1976), 14–17.

"despising government": *Records*, vol. 4, pt. 1, 277.

"opinion of theirs of being perfectly pure": ibid., 386.

"the Quakers died": Endecott to Charles II, December 19, 1660, ibid., 451.

"a hideous Döppelganger": see Larzar Ziff, *Puritanism in America: New Culture in a New World* (New York: Viking Press, 1973), 139.

"For liberty of conscience": instructions of the General Court to its agents, Joseph Dudley and John Nichols, March 17, 1681: *Records*, 5:347; explanation to crown: 5:451.

as late as 1675 constables were instructed: November 3, 1675, ibid., 60; repeal of death penalty: 322; suspension of other laws against Quakers: 347.

"for or in respect of his or her religion": "An Act Concerning Religion," *Archives of Maryland: Proceedings and Acts of the General Assembly of Maryland, January 1637–September 1664*, ed. William Hand Browne (Baltimore: Maryland Historical Society, 1883), 246. George Calvert, principal secretary of state under James I from 1619 to 1625, was active in the negotiations for a Spanish marriage for Charles, negotiations that preceded, and set a precedent for, the negotiations that ended in the agreement with the French. Calvert announced his conversion to Catholicism in 1625, the year after Charles's marriage to Henrietta Maria was concluded. James made him baron of Baltimore and retained him in the Privy Council. William Hand Browne, *George Calvert and Cecilius Calvert: Barons Baltimore of Baltimore* (New York: Dodd, Mead, 1890), 6–13; Calvert had already obtained a patent from the king to Newfoundland, which he named Avalon, in honor of the legend that Christianity had first come to England at Avalon (16); when the area proved unpropitious for a colony, he sought a patent for land between the James and Passamagnus (Chowan) Rivers—and after Calvert's death in 1632, the patent was granted to his son Cecilius (30–31). The land was named Maryland in honor of Henrietta Maria (34) and, given its intended purpose as a colony for Catholics, in honor of the Virgin Mary. The instructions of Lord Baltimore of November 13, 1633, to those sailing on the *Ark* and the *Dove* to establish the colony insisted that the governor preserve "unity and peace amongst all the passengers on Shipp-board" (46). So from the outset religious peace was sought between Catholics and Protestants.

"such an infinite liberty": Roger Williams to the town of Providence, January 1654–1655, *The Complete Writings of Roger Williams*, ed. Perry Miller (New York: Russell and Russell, 1963), 6:278–279.

"*One* Almighty God": *Pennsylvania Charter of Privileges* in *The Federal and State Constitutions*, ed. Francis Newton Thorpe (Washington, D.C.: Government Printing Office, 1909), 5:3077.

"that the blood of so many hundred thousand souls": Roger Williams, preface to *The Bloudy Tenent, of Persecution; For Cause of Conscience, Discussed, In A Conference Between Truth and Peace*, in Williams, *Writings*, 3:3–4.

"no one can transfer": Baruch Spinoza, *Tractatus theologico–politicus*, in *The Political Works*, ed. A. G. Wernham (Oxford: Clarendon Press, 1958), ch. 20.

"I esteem that toleration": John Locke, *A Letter Concerning Toleration*, trans. William Popple, ed. Raymond Klibansky (Oxford: Clarendon Press, 1968), 59. As Locke himself wrote in Latin, Popple had to decide whether *verae ecclesiae* meant "the true church" or "a true church." Given Locke's ecclesiology, Popple made the correct choice.

"not armed with the sword": ibid., 65; "neither can nor ought": 67; "No way": 99; "can have no hold": 135; "those who refuse to teach": 133–135.

impact . . . on Isaac Backus: *Isaac Backus on Church, State, and Calvinism: Pamphlets, 1754–1789*, ed. William G. McLoughlin (Cambridge, Mass.: Harvard University Press, Belknap Press, 1968), 17.

"give some ease": Act of Toleration (1688), 1 William and Mary 74, chap. 18; confirmed by Act of Toleration (1711), 10 Anne 555, chap. 6.

"natural rights . . . God and nature have established": William Blackstone, *Commentaries on the Laws of England* (Oxford: Clarendon Press, 1765), 1:54. For medieval anticipation of natural rights theory, see Brian Tierney, "Natural Rights in the Thirteenth Century: A *Quaestio* of Henry of Ghent," *Speculum* 67 (1992): 58; and Brian Tierney, *The Idea of Natural Rights* (Atlanta: Scholars Press, 1997), 86–89.

"the principal aim of society": Blackstone, *Commentaries*, 1:124; "deformed by the daemon": 4:46; "the religious liberties of the nation": 4:432; "our minds from the tyranny": 4:49; "the persecution and oppression": 4:51; "the destruction of every principle": 4:57; "flourish in the highest vigor": 1:124; canons nor its book of common prayer: 4:40; publicly pledge: 4:54.

Catholics are subject: ibid., 56–57. Although "seldom enforced" the penal statutes against Catholics occupied "no less than seventy pages" in Burns's *Ecclesiastical Law* (see Mitford, speech in debate in the Commons on the Catholic Dissenters' Relief Bill, 1791, *The Parliamentary History of England, from the Earliest Period to the Year 1803*, ed. T. C. Hansard [London: T. C. Hansard, 1806–1820], 28:1262); and they had sufficient teeth so "that several lived under great terror, and some under actual contribution," in consequence of the statutes. George Saville, speech, May 14, 1778, debate on Sir George Saville's bill for the relief of the Roman Catholics, 19:1139–1140. For the covert character of Catholic worship in late eighteenth-century London, see the memories recorded half a century later, Wilfred Ward, *The Life and Times of Cardinal Wiseman* (London: Longmans, Green, 1899), 1:200. Even the 1791 bill repealing some disabilities of Catholics extended relief only to those willing to swear, "I acknowledge no Infallibility in the Pope" (31 Geo. III, c.22 [1791]).

no one can hold office: Blackstone, *Commentaries*, 4:59; can be naturalized: 4:59; "falsely pretend an extraordinary commission": 4:62; "for christianity": 4:59.

"When I mention Religion": Henry Fielding, *The History of Tom Jones*, ed. Fred-

son Bowers (New York: Book League of America, 1974), 1:127. For the unrest in the colonies produced by the Anglican establishment, see Bernard Bai-
lyn, *The Ideological Origins of the American Revolution* (Cambridge: The
Belknap Press of Harvard University Press, 1967), 246–71.

CHAPTER 3

"The Truth shall make you free": John 8:32.

JM's Notes: *The Papers of James Madison*, ed. Robert A. Rutland and William
M. E. Rachal (Chicago: University of Chicago Press, 1973), 8:197–199 (hereafter JM, *Papers*, with editors varying by volume).

He was baptized: editorial note JM, *Papers*, ed. William T. Hutchinson and William
M. E. Rachal (Chicago, 1962), 1:105, 1:3. JM's father: Irving Brant, *James
Madison* (Indianapolis: Bobbs-Merril, 1941), 1:51; Robertson's library and
Thomas à Kempis: 54; priest as tutor: 65. "Be always gratefully remembered":
JM to Thomas Martin, August 10, 1769, JM, *Papers* 1:42. "A man of both
learning and piety" and Latin he learned: William C. Rives, *History of the Life
and Times of James Madison* (Boston: Little, Brown, 1859–1868), 1:16.

"might be instrumental": John Witherspoon, *Works* (London: E. and C. Dilly,
1800–1801), 4:10; quoted as a key to Witherspoon in Varnum Lansing Collins,
President Witherspoon: A Biography (Princeton: Princeton University Press,
1925), 2:197.

"very early and strong impressions": JM, *Papers* 1:107; see also Douglas Adair,
"James Madison," in *Fame and the Founding Fathers*, ed. Trevor Colbourn
(New York: W. W. Norton, 1974), 128. See also Dennis F. Thompson, "The
Education of a Founding Father: The Reading List for John Witherspoon's
Course in Political Theory, as Taken by James Madison," *Political Theory* 4
(1976): 523–524.

"the magistrate ought to defend": John Witherspoon, "Lectures on Moral Philosophy," in *Works* 3:350; "we ought to guard": J. Edward Colhoun, Notes
on "Lectures on Moral Philosophy by John Witherspoon" (1774), Archives
of Princeton University. Witherspoon taught that some natural rights were
"inalienable" (e.g., the right to one's own knowledge, 84–85), and some rights
ought not to be alienated (e.g., the right of a man "to judge for himself in
matters of religion," 175). He cautiously said, "many are of the opinion" that
the magistrate should make provision for the worship of God agreeably to
majority sentiment (179), and more decisively taught that the magistrate
"ought to encourage piety by his own example" (176).

"to whom it gave more satisfaction": Rives, *History*, 2:518.

pages of commentary on the Gospels: JM, *Papers* 1:51–58.

He had become sick: Brant, *Madison*, 1:72–103.

"the only valuable friend": JM to Bradford, November 9, 1773, JM, *Papers* 1:101;
"callings in Life": Bradford to JM, August 12, 1773, 91.

"I cannot however suppress": JM to Bradford, September 25, 1773, ibid., 96.

"every vacant hour": Bradford to JM, November 5, 1773, ibid., 98.

"loose in their principals": JM to Bradford, November 9, 1773, ibid., 101; "The History and the Science of Morals." ibid.

"If the Church of England had been the established and general Religion": JM to Bradford, January 24, 1774, ibid., 105.

imprisonment of six Baptist preachers: editorial note, ibid., 107. Between 1765 and 1778, over forty-five Baptist ministers were jailed in Virginia. Sandra Rennie, "Virginia's Baptist Persecution, 1765–1778," *Journal of Religious History* 12 (1992): 48–61.

in Caroline County, a preaching Baptist: Rhys Isaac, "The Rage of Malice of the Old Serpent Devil: The Dissenters and the Making and Remaking of the Virginia Statute for Religious Freedom" in *The Virginia Statute for Religious Freedom*, ed. Merrill Peterson and Robert Vaughan (New York: Cambridge University Press, 1988), 139, 141–142.

"Political Contests are necessary": JM to Bradford, January 24, 1774, JM, *Papers* 1:105.

Mathematicians, it is believed: it has been observed that JM believed "in the undeniability of quasi-mathematical moral principles." Morton White, *Philosophy, The Federalist, and the Constitution* (New York: Oxford University Press, 1987), 221; JM had a Lockean epistemology that led him to believe that his belief was "a self-evident proposition or one that could be derived from a self-evident proposition" (28). See also Dahl's comment on no. 10 of *The Federalist* as "an almost mathematical piece of theory." Robert Dahl, *Preface to Democratic Theory* (Chicago: University of Chicago Press, 1963), 5.

"That Religion, or the Duty": JM, *Papers* 1:172–173.

"extreme modesty": Thomas Jefferson, *Writings: Autobiography*, ed. Albert E. Bergh (Washington, D.C.: Thomas Jefferson Memorial Association of the United States, 1907), 1:61.

"young and in the midst": JM, "Autobiographical Notes," Library of Congress: William C. Rives Papers.

He redrafted the text: JM, *Papers* 1:174.

Equality carried, at least to some minds: see Philip A. Hamburger, "Equality and Diversity: The Eighteenth-Century Debate about Equal Protection and Equal Civil Rights," *Supreme Court Review* (1992): 333, 349 n.135. The equality of men in a state of nature was foundational. If men were equal in this state they preserved that equality in society if they did not surrender it. It was both assumed and argued that the rights of conscience being unalienable were never surrendered to society. Therefore, the original equality remained, excluding not only restraints but privileges (302, 330, 342).

"no man or class of men": JM, *Papers* 1:174.

"a *natural* and absolute right": JM, "Autobiographical Notes."

"the unlawful assembly": Act of October, 1785, chap. 77: *The Statutes [of Virginia] at Large*, ed. William Walter Hening (1823), 12:182. On Jefferson's part in the drafting, see Jefferson, "Bill No. 51," in *The Papers of Thomas Jefferson*, ed. Julian P. Boyd (Princeton: Princeton University Press, 1950), 2:470–473. On Madison's management of the bill, 472.

"Steal away to Jesus": Albert J. Raboteau, *Slave Religion: The 'Invisible Institution' in the Antebellum South* (New York: Oxford University Press, 1978), 213. Despite the formal law that left all meetings of slaves at the discretion of their master, many slaves followed their own religious inclinations; in particular, during the last third of the eighteenth century in Virginia, the Baptists and the Methodists made thousands of converts (130–131). But, until slavery was abolished, the masters could prohibit or break up religious meetings of slaves and punish harshly those who disobeyed by attending them (214).

slaves were part of "the family": JM to James Madison, Sr., March 29, 1777, JM, *Papers* 1:190. JM and emancipation: JM, "Memorandum on an African Colony for Freed Slaves," ca. October 20, 1789, JM, *Papers*, ed. Charles F. Hobson and Robert A. Rutland (Charlottesville: University of Virginia Press, 1979), 12:437–438. In this memorandum JM anticipated the American Colonization Society, of which he ultimately became president.

By law, they were restricted: Hening, *Statutes*, 3:193 and 517. Husband and wife were "one person in law": William Blackstone, *Commentaries on the Laws of England* (Oxford: Clarendon Press, 1765), 1:430. But the two parties making up the single person had different rights. The wife was, in law-French, "a *feme covert*," covered by her *baron*, her husband, a condition that made all contracts "void or voidable" (1:430–432).

the new general assembly of Virginia repealed: Hening, *Statutes*, 5:358–62. See also Thomas Jefferson, "Query XVII," *The Papers of Thomas Jefferson: Notes on Virginia* (Washington, D.C.: Taylor and Maury, 1853), 2:217–220. Jefferson, for rhetorical purposes, emphasized the common-law sanctions against heresy that Blackstone treated as repealed by the statute of Charles II. Blackstone, *Commentaries*, 4:432.

"establishing religious freedom": Jefferson, "Bill no. 82," in *Papers of Thomas Jefferson*, 2:545–547. On the history of the bill, see editorial note, 547–550.

"religious slavery": Jefferson, *Notes on Virginia*, 220–221.

"Whereas the general diffusion": "A Bill Establishing a Provision for Teachers of the Christian Religion," conveniently reprinted as Supplemental Appendix to *Everson v. Board of Education*, 330 U.S. 1 at 72–74 (1947).

"The *Episcopalians*": Jefferson to JM, December 8, 1784, JM, *Papers* 8:178, "the exquisite cunning": JM to Jefferson, April 25, 1784, 8:30; for the history of Henry's bill, see editorial note, 295–297.

Memorial and Remonstrance: ibid., 298–304.

"met with the approbation of the Baptists": JM, "Monopolies Perpetuities Corporations Ecclesiastical Establishments," in "Madison's 'Detached Memoranda,'" ed. Elizabeth Fleet, *William and Mary Quarterly* 3 (1946): 555–556 (hereafter "Monopolies").

petition . . . signatories: editorial note, JM, *Papers* 8:297–298; voters in Virginia: Charles S. Sydnor, *Gentlemen Freeholders: Political Practice in Washington's Virginia* (Chapel Hill: University of North Carolina Press, 1952), 31; for voters in Orange County: see also 142; "crushed": JM, "Monopolies," 556.

"Almighty God hath created": an Act Establishing Religious Freedom: Hening,

Statutes, 12:84–86; "espoused by some members": JM, "Monopolies," 556;
"have in this Country": JM to Jefferson, January 22, 1786, JM, *Papers* 8:474;
"*natural* and absolute": JM, "Autobiographical Notes."

these radical conclusions: the same position that "religion is altogether personal"
and can never be subjected to the state is taken in the memorial of the Presbyterians of Virginia to the General Assembly, August 13, 1785, *American
State Papers*, ed. William A. Blakely (Washington, D.C.: Religious Liberty Association, 1911), 13. George Washington refused to sign Madison's Remonstrance: Washington to Mason, 1785, H. J. Eckenrode, *Separation of Church
and State in Virginia* (Chicago: Library Resources, 1970), 105.

"sure that the rights of Conscience": JM to Jefferson, October 17, 1788, and
"Repeated violations," JM, *Papers*, ed. Robert A. Rutland and Charles F. Hobson (Charlottesville: University of Virginia Press, 1978), 11:297.

"Is a bill of rights": JM, speech, June 12, 1788, JM, *Papers* 77:130.

"zeal for different opinions": JM, "The Size and Variety of the Union as a Check
on Faction," *The Federalist*, ed. Benjamin Fletcher Wright (Cambridge,
Mass.: Harvard University Press, Belknap Press, 1972), 131; "the security for
civil rights": JM, "Checks and Balances," 358.

"The political truths": JM to Jefferson, October 17, 1788, JM, *Papers* 11:297.

"The attempt was defeated": JM to Philip Mazzei, December 10, 1788, ibid.,
389.

had baptized 300 persons: Isaac Backus, *The Diary of Isaac Backus*, ed. William
McLoughlin (Providence, R.I.: Brown University Press, 1979), 3:1289–1290;
voters in election: editorial note, JM, *Papers* 11:309.

"the most satisfactory provisions": JM to George Eve, January 2, 1789, JM, *Papers* 11:405; "exert himself": George Nichols to JM, January 2, 1789, 408;
"many important Services": Benjamin Johnson to JM, January 19, 1789, 423;
"specific provision": "Extract of a letter from the Hon. James Madison, jun.
to his friends in this county," 429.

Madison was elected: editorial note, ibid., 438–439.

Leland wrote at once: John Leland to JM, ca. February 15, 1789, ibid., 443.

"first man": Fisher Ames to George Minot, May 31, 1789. *Works of Fisher Ames*,
ed. Seth Ames (Boston: Little, Brown, 1854), 1:35.

capacity of ghostwriter: editorial note, JM, *Papers* 12:120; "possess so much
power and influence" 121.

quiet reminder: George Washington to Fellow Citizens of the Senate and of the
House of Representatives [April 30, 1789], ibid., 123.

"The question arising": the address of the House of Representatives to George
Washington, president of the United States [May 5, 1789], ibid., 133.

Over two hundred amendments: ibid., 58; "No State shall violate": ibid.

Contents of Bill: JM, "Notes for Speech in Congress," ibid., 194–195; "The civil
rights of none" and "The people shall not be deprived": JM, speech June 8,
1789, 201.

"No religion shall be established": *Annals of Congress* (Washington, D.C.: Gales
and Seaton, 1789), 1:729 (August 15, 1789); "a support of ministers": 730

(August 15, 1789). The inadequacy of the informal reporting of the debates in the House (not to mention the absence of any report of the debate in the Senate) has been noted and made an objection to pontifications about "the original intent" of the framers. See Leonard Levy, *The Establishment Clause* (New York: Macmillan, 1986), 187–189. Nonetheless, the reporting of the House is no worse than that of the deliberations of most legislative bodies of the past, of legal arguments in the United States Supreme Court in the nineteenth century, or of English judicial opinions prior to modern times. The remarks attributed to JM square with his writings.

"Congress shall make no law": *Annals*, 1:796 (August 20, 1789).

"the most valuable": JM, speech in the House, ibid., 755 (August 17, 1789).

"Congress shall make no law establishing": *Journal of the First Session of the Senate*, 70 (September 4, 1789).

"Congress shall make no law respecting": U.S. Constitution, First Amendment. That "prohibit" in the First Amendment should be read to mean "inhibit," "hinder," is supported by Samuel Johnson's *Dictionary of the English Language* (London: W. Strahow, 1755), 5 at "prohibit" and also by JM, *Report on the Virginia Resolutions*, January 18, 1800. See Michael W. McConnell, "The Origins and Historical Understanding of Free Exercise of Religion," *Harvard Law Review* 103 (1990): 1486–1488.

In two prepositional phrases: as Justice Wiley Rutledge wrote: "'Religion' appears only once in the Amendment. But the word governs two prohibitions and governs them alike." *Everson v. Board of Education*, 330 U.S. 1 at 32 (dissent).

"Pleonasms, tautologies": JM to Joseph C. Cabell, Sept. 18, 1828, JM, *Writings of James Madison*, ed. Gaillard Hunt (New York: G. P. Putnam's Sons, 1910), 9:322–324.

The great ambiguity of the First Amendment: see Michael S. Ariens and Robert A. Destro, *Religious Liberty in a Pluralistic Society* (Durham: Carolina Academic Press, 1996), 88–91.

First Amendment . . . jurisdictional: see the sustained argument of Steven D. Smith, *Foreordained Failure: The Quest for a Constitutional Principle of Religious Freedom* (New York: Oxford University Press, 1995), 18–34.

"on the relation of Xnty to Civil Govt": JM to the Reverend Adams, [1832], JM, *Writings* 9: 484.

"every new & successful example": JM to Edward Livingston, July 10, 1823, ibid., 101–102.

"the danger of silent accumulations": JM, "Monopolies," 554; "4 great religious Sects": JM to Anon., March 1836, JM *Writings*, 9:610; "exorbitant advances": JM, "Monopolies," 557; "the most enlightened States": 554; "religious liberty is placed on its true foundation": ibid.; "any aberration from the sacred principle": 553

to incorporate the Episcopal church . . . to reserve land . . . for a Baptist church: editorial note to text in ibid., 558. JM himself mentions his vetoes without details.

"a palpable violation": ibid., 558; "already degenerating": 559; "religious proclamations": 563; "seem to imply": 560 (italics JM's); "a form & language": 562.

"oddly": Merrill D. Peterson, ed., *James Madison: A Biography in His Own Words* (New York: Newsweek, 1974), 26; "given up to a political religion": 405.

"Enlightenment" . . . a catchword: see Henry May, *The Enlightenment in America* (New York: Oxford University Press, 1976), xiii: "No definition of the Enlightenment fits all the men usually assumed to belong to it, or even those Europeans most directly influential in the United States, for instance Locke, Samuel Clarke, Montesquieu, Paine, and Thomas Reid—or, if one adds those who have been important as dangerous opponents and targets of polemic, Voltaire, Rousseau, and Hume." May goes on to identify four Enlightenments: the Moderate, preaching balance, order, and religious compromise; the Skeptical (Voltaire, Hume); the Revolutionary (Paine and Godwin); and the Didactic (Scottish; opposed to skepticism and revolution [xvi]). These categories, which seem to be tailored to particular authors, could no doubt be further refined; they demonstrate the ambiguity of "Enlightenment" unqualified by adjective. May goes even further as to John Witherspoon, Madison's teacher: he has "one foot in the camp of the Enlightenment" (xv; no adjective added, however). As for JM himself, May puts him with men "very difficult to allot to one camp or the other."

May reduces "the Enlightenment" in its religious meaning to two propositions: first, that the present age is more enlightened than the past and second, that man and nature are "best understood" through the use of natural faculties. The definition excludes John Wesley, William Blake, and Jonathan Edwards and "probably most people who lived in America in the eighteenth and nineteenth centuries" (ibid., xiv). Where Witherspoon and Madison fit is, May acknowledges, difficult to determine (xv). In America, what May calls the Moderate Enlightenment was "often inextricably mixed with Christian ideas" (xviii). The easy clichés about the Enlightenment dissolve under this analysis. While the Dark Ages have ceased to exist in the historian's vocabulary, their opposite, "the Age of the Enlightenment" continues to have a hardy existence, even among historians. It is not hard to tell why: the term has a polemical value, dear to modern secularists. Has not the time come to say of "the Enlightenment" what Richard Southern has said of "the Renaissance": the term "achieves the sort of sublime meaninglessness which is required in words of high but uncertain import." Richard W. Southern, "The Place of England in the Twelfth-Century Renaissance," *History* 45 (1960): 201. See also my "The Secular Search for the Sacred," *New York University Law Review* 70 (1995): 650–651.

"a principle which disclaims all control": David Hume, "Of the Coalition of Parties," in *Essays, Moral, Political and Literary* (London: Oxford University Press, 1963), 484–485; civil control of the church: "The Idea of a Perfect Commonwealth," in ibid., 506–511. I am indebted to Marc M. Arkin's article for bringing these essays to my attention in her "The Intractable Principle: David Hume, James Madison, Religion and The Tenth Federalist," *American Journal of Legal History* 39 (1995): 148.

"in the Annals of Heaven": JM to William Bradford, November 9, 1773, JM, *Papers* 1:101; his first biographer, William C. Rives, who knew JM in JM's old age and had taken personal measure of the man, comments on this letter: "The reader will not have failed to remark the elevated strain of religious sentiment which pervaded the preceding letter." Rives adds that JM's advice to pursue secular studies "with a due attention to the oracles of Divine truth was faithfully observed by himself." Rives, *History*, 1:22. For comparison with Voltaire's campaign to "wipe out" (*écraser*) Christianity, see chapter 10.

"a Theological Catalogue": JM to Thomas Jefferson, September 4, 1824, JM, *Writings* 9:203–207; "pretty full information": 203.

"beyond my depth": JM to the Reverend Frederick Beasley, November 20, 1825, ibid., 231; "probably America's most theologically knowledgeable President": William Lee Miller, *The First Liberty: Religion and the American Republic* (New York: Knopf, 1986), 90, quoting an unnamed editor of JM's *Papers*, while Miller himself doubts Madison's "religious interest in his maturity." See James H. Smylie, "Madison and Witherspoon. Theological Roots of American Political Thought," *Princeton University Library Chronicle* (spring 1966): 125: "In some sense Madison may be considered a lay theologian." Although describing him as "a rather passive believer," another biographer acknowledges that his overview of the human condition and society came from his Christian education. Ralph Ketcham, *James Madison* (New York: Macmillan, 1971), 47–48.

"the celebrated work": JM to Beasley, Nov. 20, 1825, JM, *Writings* 9:230.; Witherspoon's recommendation of Clark: notes of J. Edward Culhoun on Witherspoon's Lectures on Moral Philosophy (1774), Archives of Princeton University.

The Necessary Duty of Family Prayer: Ralph L. Ketcham, "James Madison and Religion—A New Hypothesis," *Journal of the Presbyterian Historical Society* 38 (June 1960): 73.

"the Ministry obliquely in View": see Miller, *The First Liberty*, "One can sense in his letters the forming, out of the earnest Princeton materials, of the high seriousness of purpose of the ministerial vocation that many of his classmates followed, transferred now to the realm of statecraft."

"the Christian Religion itself": Memorial and Remonstrance, JM, *Writings* 8:187.

"the true light": John 1:9.

"the total separation of the Church from the State": JM to Robert Walsh, March 2, 1819, JM ibid., 8:432.

"by giving to Caesar": JM, "Monopolies," 555; "a just and a . . . truly Xn": 554. See May, *The Enlightenment in America*, 96: JM came to "a consistent, lifelong defense of Christianity."

"There appears to be": JM to the Reverend Adams [1832], JM, *Writings* 9:485;
  "the Xn religion itself": ibid.
"spared no exertion": JM, "Autobiographical Notes," William Rives Papers, Library of Congress; "a mere duty": ibid.
"balancing": Mary Ann Glendon and Raul F. Yanes, "Structural Free Exercise,"
  Michigan Law Review 90 (1991): 477, 523.
theology underwrites the political theory: see White, *Philosophy, The Federalist,
  and the Constitution*, 33: "Madison's view of the logical connection between
  man's rationally discernible duties to God and man's unalienable right to religious freedom was generalized by other American colonists so as to apply
  to other unalienable rights." The generalizing begins with JM. As Michael
  McConnell observes in his magisterial article on the history of the free exercise amendment: "Far from being based on the 'respect for the person as an
  independent source of value,' the free exercise of religion is set apart from
  mere exercise of human judgment by the fact that the 'source of value' is prior
  and superior to both the individual and the civil society. The freedom of religion is inalienable because it is a duty to God and not a privilege of the individual." In light of that observation McConnell concludes: "The free exercise claim may well be the most philosophically interesting and distinctive
  feature of the American Constitution." McConnell, "Origins and Historical
  Understanding," 1497, 1512.
the faith . . . is fundamental: "The best reasons for protecting religious freedom
  rest on the assumption that religion is a good thing." John H. Garvey, *What
  Are Freedoms For?* (Cambridge, Mass.: Harvard University Press, 1996), 49.
  Garvey's approach in 1996 chimes with JM's insight.
"leaders and lawgivers": Ralph Waldo Emerson, *Representative Men: Seven Lectures* (Boston: Phillips, Sampson, 1850), 25–26.
"precipitates": Learned Hand, "The Contribution of an Independent Judiciary
  to Civilization," in *The Spirit of Liberty: Papers and Addresses of Learned
  Hand*, ed. Irving Dilliard (New York: Knopf, 1952), 180.
state like Massachusetts: see chapter 4.
"finally to a decisive test": JM to Frederick Adams [1832], JM, *Writings* 9:485;
  "admitted Umpire": ibid.
"a new Creation": JM to William C. Rives, March 12, 1833, JM, ibid., 511.

CHAPTER 4

Excerpts from the unpublished account: a cento that parallels and draws on Tocqueville's observations made during his 1831 expedition.
"There are two facts": see Alexis de Tocqueville, *Oeuvres: Voyage en Amérique*,
  ed. André Jardin (Paris: Gallimard, 1991), 74, quoting former president John
  Quincy Adams.
the most famous preacher: ibid., 77, quoting William Ellery Channing.
"moral and religious": ibid., 60–61, quoting Louis Dwight.

"conformable to nature": ibid., 44, quoting John C. Spencer, former congress-man, later secretary of war and then secretary of the treasury.

Declaration of the Rights of the Inhabitants: Massachusetts, Constitution, pt. 1 (1780).

"might as well expect a change in the solar system": Isaac Backus, *A History of New England with Particular Reference to the Denomination of Christians Called Baptists* (Newton, Mass.: Backus Historical Society, 1871), 2:201–202.

"to put the people's name in place of that of the king": Tocqueville, *Voyage*, 65, quoting Josiah Quincy, former mayor of Boston, then president of Harvard.

"piety, religion, and morality": Massachusetts, Constitution, pt. 1; "public, protestant teachers": ibid.

"principally attributed the peaceful empire": Alexis de Tocqueville, *De la démocratie en Amérique* (1835, 1840), 2:342 (my translation—and, for parallel cites in its English-language version, see *Democracy in America*, trans. Henry Reeve, rev. Francis Bowen and Phillips Bradley [1989], 1:308; "I am not afraid": ibid.).

"the Lord's Day": Act of October 22, 1782, Massachusetts, *Perpetual Laws*, 198–199.

sabbatarian legislation . . . characteristic of New York: see *The People against Ruggles*, 8 Johns 225 (N.Y. 1811); Virginia law: Virginia, *Revised Laws* (1819), c.141.

obligation, now reduced: Act of March 8, 1792, *Massachusetts Laws* 2:538; attendance was abrogated: Massachusetts, Constitution, amendment 11 (1833).

a man worked on the Lord's day: *McGrath v. Merwin*, 112 Mass. 467 (1873).

all public disputes . . . become judicial disputes: Tocqueville, *De la démocratie*, 2:310 (*Democracy*, 1:280).

"found to rest on the basis of immortal truth": *Barnes v. First Parish in Falmouth*, 5 Mass. 400 (1810).

a test oath required for eligibility: Massachusetts, Constitution, pt. 2 (1780); repeal: Massachusetts Constitutional Convention, 1820, *Journal of Debates and Proceedings*, 630, 634, 637.

"of the Protestant religion": New Hampshire, Constitution, pt. 2 (1784), Senate, House of Representatives, Executive Power—President. James Fairbanks Colby, compiler, *Manual of the Constitution of the State of New Hampshire* (Manchester: J. B. Clarke, 1912), 110, 112, 113. Amendments striking the religious qualifications were defeated by vote of the people, 15,297 to 5,799 in 1851 (209); they were eliminated by amendments only in 1877 (218–220), and Article VI of the Bill of Rights, forming part 1 of this constitution, authorized the towns to support "public Protestant teachers of piety, religion and morality." Amendments eliminating "Protestant" were put to the people in 1851, 1852, 1877, 1889, and 1902 and each time were rejected (238–239).

In Rhode Island, for example: Jacob R. Marcus, *The Colonial American Jew* (Detroit: Wayne State University Press, 1970), 1:438.

Baptists believe that the state: William G. McLoughlin, *New England Dissent*

1630–1833 (Cambridge, Mass.: Harvard University Press, 1971), 2:1088 and 1097.

Capture of the town meeting: *Baker v. Fales*, 16 Mass. 488 (1820); Jacob C. Meyer, *Church and State in Massachusetts from 1740 to 1833* (Cleveland: Western Reserve University Press, 1930), 177.

Even that amendment: Massachusetts, Constitution, amendment 11, see also McLoughlin 2:1230–39 on the vote; the golden handshake to the churches: Meyer, 181.

Story himself became indignant: André Jardin, *Alexis de Tocqueville*, trans. Lydia Davis and Robert Hemenway (New York: Farrar, Straus and Giroux, 1988), 203.

"cut off forever": Joseph Story, *Commentaries on the Constitution of the United States* (Boston: Hilliard, Grax, 1833), § 1847; "beyond the just reach": § 1876.

"should be hurt, molested, or restrained": Massachusetts, Constitution, pt. 1 (1780).

"few persons in this": Story, *Commentaries*, § 1874; "only for Protestantism": ibid.

"Church and State": Massachusetts, Constitution, pt. 2, chap. 5 (1780).

"to some extent and for certain purposes, a state institution": *President and Fellows of Harvard College v. Society for Promoting Theological Education & others*, 3 Gray (Mass.) 280 at 281, 293 (1855).

"reproaching Jesus Christ or the Holy Ghost": *Commonwealth v. Kneeland*, 37 Mass. 206 (1838); "frequently enforced": id. at 217.

blasphemy law of New York: *The People v. Ruggles*, 8 Johns 225 (N.Y. 1811); similar verdict . . . Massachusetts parallel, no federal appeal: Leonard W. Levy, *Blasphemy in Massachusetts* (New York: DaCapo Press, 1973), 493–505.

"exercises an immense power": Tocqueville, *Voyage*, 952; "anti-Christian books": ibid.

how closely Massachusetts had regulated: see John D. Cushing, "Notes on Disestablishment in Massachusetts, 1780–1833," *William and Mary Quarterly* 26 (1969): 174. Sanctions . . . unblessed unions: Act of February 17, 1785, Mass. *Perpetual Laws*, 203. Virginia bigamy law: Virginia, *Acts in Force*, chap. 104, 270–274 (1814); sanction modified, *Warren v. Commonwealth*, 4 Va. 95 (1817); on Jefferson's role, see John T. Noonan, Jr., *Persons and Masks of the Law* (New York: Farrar, Straus and Giroux, 1976), 48–52. Sodomy laws: An Act Against Sodomy, March 3, 1785, Mass. *Perpetual Laws*, 182; penalty reduced: Mass. *Revised Statutes*, code 130, sec. 14 (1835).

Christian religion . . . purity of morals: Tocqueveille, *De la démocratie* 2:337 (*Democracy*, 1:304).

chaplains for the House and for the Senate: see data collected in *Marsh v. Chambers*, 463 U.S. 783 (1983); for the modern development, see *Katcoff v. Marsh*, 755 F.2d 223 (2d Cir. 1985).

"religion, morality, and knowledge": Act of August 7, 1789, *United States Statutes*, 1:50, adopting the Northwest Ordinance.

"when among the members present": James Madison to Joseph C. Cabell, September 18, 1828, *Writings*, ed. Gaillard Hunt (New York: G. P. Putnam's Sons, 1910), 9:332.

Congress regulated the Northwest Territory: Gerard V. Bradley, *Church-State Relationships in America* (New York: Greenwood Press, 1987), 101.

Grant to Ohio Company: Act of April 21, 1792, *United States Statutes*, 1:257.

Reverend Mr. Cutler, in a sermon: William Parker Cutler and Julia Perkins Cutler, *Life, Journals, and Correspondence of Rev. Manasseh Cutler, LL.D.* (Cincinnati: R. Clarke, 1888), 1:342–346.

"Religion ought never to be made a political machine": Manasseh Cutler, sermon preached at Campus Martius, Marietta, Ohio, August 24, 1788, in *Life*, 2:447; "No one kind of religion": 444; "being burdensome to individuals": 448.

endowing the Moravian Brethren: Bradley, *Church-State*, 158.

"translating the sacred Scriptures": *Worcester v. Georgia*, 31 U.S. 515, 529 (1832); "the chief magistrate": 562.

all the leading colleges of the United States: Lawrence Cremin, *American Education: The Colonial Experience, 1607–1783* (New York: Harper and Row, 1970); on Harvard: 210–212, 222; on William and Mary: 321, 335; on Yale: 321, 558–559; on College of New Jersey: 299, 558–559; on Dartmouth: 328; on Queen's College: 328–329; on King's College: 345.

"no preferences or distinctions": James Madison, notes, *Records of the Federal Convention of 1787*, ed. Max Farrand (New Haven: Yale University Press, 1911), 2:616.

land grants to Columbian (later George Washington University): Act of July 14, 1832, *United States Statutes*, 4:603 (1832); grant to Georgetown: Act of March 2, 1833, *United States Statutes*, 6:538 (1833).

"As long as a religion": Tocqueville, *De la démocratie*, 2:344 (*Democracy*, 1:310); "upon the desire of immortality": 343 (*Democracy*, 310).

"The principal aim": Tocqueville, *De la démocratie*, 2:330 (*Democracy*, 1:299).

Félicité de Lamennais: see chapters 1 and 10; Jean-Baptiste-Henri Lacordaire: see mention in chapter 10.

men have diverged from women: see Ralph Gibson, *A Social History of French Catholicism, 1789–1914* (London: Routledge, 1989), 180–186.

fire on the earth: Luke 12:49.

Our family had suffered: see Jardin, *Tocqueville*, 7–9.

"You seem to me to have well understood": Alexis de Tocqueville to Eugène Stoeffels, July 24, 1836, Alexis de Tocqueville, *Oeuvres et correspondance inédites* (Paris: M. Lèvy Frères, 1861), 1:432 (emphasis in original).

The enactment in Virginia: Thomas Jefferson, *Writings: Autobiography*, ed. Albert E. Bergh (Washington, D.C.: Thomas Jefferson Memorial Association of the United States, 1907), 1:58.

in Massachusetts the disestablishment: McLoughlin, *New England Dissent*, 2:1189–1274, on the Establishment and Trinitarian Congregationalists, Universalists, and Baptists.

"What causes the religious tolerance": Tocqueville, *Voyage*, 43–44.

"strong security": James Madison, speech at the Virginia convention on the Constitution, June 12, 1788. Madison, *Papers* 8:130.

"In the depths of their souls": Tocqueville, *Voyage*, 86, quoting James Brown.

"Religion—which with the Americans never mixes": Tocqueville, *De la démocratie*, 2:338 (*Democracy*, 1:305–306).

the same syllogism: Washington's Farewell Address, September 17, 1796, in *Messages and Papers of the Presidents, 1789–1897*, ed. James D. Richardson (Washington, D.C.: Government Printing Office, 1896), 1:220.

CHAPTER 5

An extract from the correspondence: George Frothingham's letter, like Angélique de Tocqueville's commentary, is a cento. Contrast his views with the praise of Parker expressed by Octavius Brooks Frothingham in *Theodore Parker, a Biography* (Boston, 1874).

"our Savonarola": Ralph Waldo Emerson, "Historic Notes of Life and Letters in New England," in *The Complete Works of Ralph Waldo Emerson* (Boston: Houghton Mifflin, 1904), 10:341.

"Men and brothers": Theodore Parker, "The Mexican War," in *Collected Writings: The Slave Power* (1907–1911), 7:266.

"to talk the matter over," "Hangman Foote": Parker, "Discourse on Webster," in *Collected Writings*, 11:229.

he wrote the President an impudent letter: Parker's letter to President Fillmore, November 21, 1850, in John Weiss, *The Life and Correspondence of Theodore Parker* (1864), 2:100–101.

two runaways . . . marriage ceremony: William and Ellen Crafts, and their marriage in Henry Steele Commager, *Theodore Parker* (1947), 214–217.

"The noblest deed": ibid., 219; Parker and piracy: 221; "in an immortal pillory": 222; "The senator with a conscience": 256. On Brooks's caning of Sumner in the United States Senate: Moorfield Story, *Charles Sumner* (1900), 145–149.

"I have heard hurrahs": Parker, quoted in James Ford Rhodes, *History of the United States 1850–1877* (1910), 1:502.

"Why didn't he hit him?" . . . suspended: Commager, *Parker*, 236–237; ordered the return, see *Ela v. Smith*, 71 Mass. 121 (1855); law student, Albert Brown, Jr.: *The Boston Slave Riot and Trial of Anthony Burns* (Boston: Fetridge, 1854), 12.

indicted . . . let Parker off: Parker, *The Trial of Theodore Parker for the 'Misdemeanor' of a Speech in Faneuil Hall against Kidnapping* (1855); and Commager, *Parker*, 244–247.

a weak brother: the letterwriter's uncomplimentary reference to Justice Benjamin Curtis alludes to his dissent in *Dred Scott v. Sanford*, 60 U.S. (19 How.) 393, 564–633 (1857).

seminarian from Lane: his name was Amos Dresser. See "The Narrative of Amos

Dresser," in *Slavery Attacked: The Abolitionist Crusade*, ed. John L. Thomas (1965), 43–44.

"I do not find": Parker, *Trial*, 205; "I charge you with the death of that man": ibid., 204.

hanged for murder: the case of Dr. John W. Webster, professor in the Medical School, executed for the murder of his colleague, Dr. George Parkman. See *Commonwealth v. Webster*, 5 Mass. 386 (1850), and Simon Schama, *Dead Certainties* (1991), 73.

backed the invasion of Kansas: Commager, *Parker*, 249.

to patronize John Brown: Franklin B. Sanborn, "Parker in the John Brown Campaign," in *Saint Bernard and Other Papers*, by Theodore Parker, ed. Charles W. Wendte (1911), 394–419; "The fire of Vengeance": Parker to Francis Jackson, November 24, 1859, in ibid., 435 (emphasis in original).

"a general disgust": Franklin B. Sanborn, preface to *The Rights of Man in America*, by Theodore Parker, ed. F. B. Sanborn (1911).

"There writhe the wounded": Parker, "War," in *Collected Writings*, 9:313. "treads nations as grapes": 289, citing Isaiah 63:1–6; "aggressive war is a sin": 307.

"You know that I do not like fighting": Parker, "The Duty of Ministers under the Fugitive Slave Law" (a debate at the ministerial conference of the American Unitarian Association, 1851), in *The Rights of Man in America*, by Theodore Parker, ed. F. B. Sanborn (1911); and in Parker, *Collected Writings*, 12:151.

"This was certainly a direct appeal": Weiss, *Life and Correspondence*, 2:131.

"took him at once to Mr. Parker's": Sanborn, "Parker in the John Brown Campaign," 394; "the necessary supplies": 395; "some 500 or 1,000": John Brown to Parker, September 11, 1857 in ibid., 396; "establish a colony of freedmen": 401; Brown's constitution: 401; General McClellan's recent book: 406.

"To penetrate Virginia": Thomas Wentworth Higginson, *Cheerful Yesterdays* (Boston, 1900), 221; "in the direction of pure thought": 98.

"*A man held against his will*": Parker to Jackson, November 24, 1859, in Sanborn, "Parker in the John Brown Campaign," 422 (emphasis in original).

"had succeeded": ibid., 424–425; "Only I would paint": 425.

on the Fourth of July 1829: John L. Thomas, *The Liberator: William Lloyd Garrison* (1963), 92–93. A memorial plaque commemorating Garrison's oration is still on Boylston Street, Boston, outside the Park Street Church.

"a great and crying national sin": Amos A. Phelps, *Lectures on Slavery and Its Remedy* (1834; 1970), iii–iv.

Fifteen hundred merchants: Commager, *Parker*, 197; the newspapers: ibid.; the college presidents: 208; the churches: 198.

"Hunkers": Parker to Jackson, November 24, 1859, in Sanborn, "Parker in the John Brown Campaign," 427. "I cannot be otherwise": Parker, address, November 14, 1852, quoted in Perry Miller, "Theodore Parker: Apostasy within Liberalism," *Harvard Theological Review* 54 (1961): 271. Parker barred by Harvard Divinity School: Parker to the Members of the Twenty-Eighth Congregational Society of Boston, April 19, 1859 (hereafter Autobiographical Letter), in appendix to Weiss, *Life and Correspondence*, 2:501.

Lyman Beecher . . . baiting: Stuart C. Henry, *Unvanquished Puritan: A Portrait of Lyman Beecher* (1973), 156–157.

"I think I may call": James Russell Lowell, *A Fable for Critics* (New York: Putnam, 1848), 51.

"A Father and Mother Person": William Fairfield Warren, "Theodore Parker: The Good and Evil in His Opinions and Influence" (discourse delivered at the Bromfield Street Methodist Episcopal Church, Boston, Sunday, June 3, 1860; pamphlet available at the Harvard Divinity School), 18. Frothingham also borrows Warren's phrases "hybrid hermaphrodite" and "a being of hebetude": in ibid., 14 and 18.

believed Christ . . . a Christian church: Parker, Autobiographical Letter, 459; prosecution of minister for blasphemy: 461.

"Religion of Humanity": Orestes Brownson, quoted in R. W. B. Lewis, *The American Adam* (1951), 182–183; Brownson, a friend of Parker, declared that Parker's doctrine as preached in 1841 "forced my mind to take the direction it did," i.e., to conversion to the Catholic Church.

"I submit, sir, whether it is fair": Stephen Douglas, speech, May 8, 1854, *Congressional Globe*, 33rd Congress, 1st session, 1854, 656.

"The earliest thing you taught me": Parker, Journal, August 24, 1852, quoted in Miller, "Theodore Parker: Apostasy," 278.

"I thought it a wide place": Parker, Autobiographical Letter, 451; "no more divine": 454; "They did not dare affirm": 483; "intuition of the divine": 455; "the great fetish of Protestant Christiandom": 463; "the lust after property": 488; "the chief magistrate of the city" 493; "showing its enormous cost": 493; "more than any concrete wrong": 493; "According to my experience and observation": 488; "A woman is man's equal": 490–491; "The educated is also the selfish class": 489; "that the criminal": 477.

"An anti-slavery party": Parker to Jackson, November 24, 1859, in Sanborn, "Parker in the John Brown Campaign," 433. The passage within the quotation is from the Constitution of the United States, Article IV, sec. 4.

"strife between the Southern habit": Parker, Autobiographical Letter, 493.

"like a martyr and also like a saint": Parker to Jackson in Sanborn, "Parker in the John Brown Campaign," 436.

In memoriam: the memorial service at Faneuil Hall, another cento.

"projected a crusade": Parker, "Saint Bernard," in *Saint Bernard and Other Papers*, 1; "shed his luster": 2, "But if": 4. Parker's own crusade against slavery: anonymous review of *The Life and Correspondence of Theodore Parker*, by John Weiss, *North American Review* 203 (April 1864): 321.

"If they mean to have a war": quoted in Commager, *Parker*, 4; Captain Parker the first to fight: David Hacker Fischer, *Paul Revere's Ride* (1994), 149; the Parker line of descent: Commager, *Parker*, 3–4. How he drank: review of Weiss's *Life and Correspondence*, 317.

"I know that men urge in argument": Parker, "Sermon on Slavery," quoted in Commager, 205; "Christianity a Belief": 47.

"the rigid subordination": Warren, "Theodore Parker," 12.

model of a mature Unitarian: Stephen Fritchman, "The Hammer and the Forge" [a centenary sermon on Theodore Parker, First Unitarian Church of Los Angeles, 1960], in *For the Sake of Charity* (1992), 400–407.

"landmark": Cornelia Meigs, *Invincible Louisa: The Story of the Author of Little Women* (1968), 89–90.

"The law of God has eminent domain": Parker, "Function of Conscience in Relation to the Laws of Men," in *Collected Writings*, 11:395–396.

"practical atheism": elaborated by Parker in 1853 in "Of Practical Atheism, Regarded as a Principle of Ethics" in *Theism, Atheism, and the Popular Theology*, ed. Charles W. Wendte (Boston: American Unitarian Association, 1907), 87–103, where two Boston merchants deploring but justifying the kidnapping of Thomas Sims are given as examples of practical atheists (112).

"We must obey God": Acts 5:27–29.

a higher duty than to enforce: Parker, "Of the Chief Sins of the People" (sermon, April 19, 1851), quoted in *Trial*, 191; ready to tell jurors: 219.

apostrophized the legislators: Parker, "Discourse on Webster," 11:226; "But Mr. Webster would not": 231.

"Religion has nothing to do": Parker, quoted in Commager, *Parker*, 209.

"We see dimly in the Present": Parker, "Discourse on Webster," 11:247, quoting James Russell Lowell, "The Present Crisis," in *Poems* (1890), 1:181. As this edition notes, the poem was written in December 1844. Parker found its attack on compromise wonderfully apropos.

"When a boy": Parker, *Trial*, 220.

Living close to the ground: review of Weiss's *Life and Correspondence*, 319.

Parker's secret disciple: Garry Wills, *Lincoln at Gettysburg* (1992) 77–78, 91, 106–118.

"my Ideal": Herndon to Parker, May 13, 1854, quoted in David Donald, *Lincoln's Herndon* (1948), 55.

"that if God gave us the victory": quoted in Gideon Wells, *Diary*, 143 (entry of September 22, 1862); "It might be thought strange": ibid.

"that on this day": Abraham Lincoln, "Announcement of News From Gettysburg," in *Collected Works*, ed. Roy P. Basler (New Brunswick, N.J.: Rutgers University Press, 1953), 6:314.

"It has pleased Almighty God": Lincoln, Proclamation of Thanksgiving, ibid., 6:322.

"Direct Self-Government": Parker, "The Effect of Slavery on the American People: A Sermon Preached at the Music Hall, Boston, on Sunday, July 4, 1858," quoted in Donald, *Lincoln's Herndon*, 128.

"We here highly resolve": the Gettysburg address, in Wills, *Lincoln at Gettysburg*, 263.

"It may seem strange": Lincoln, Second Inaugural Address, *Collected Works*,

8:332–333. Scriptural quotations: "the judgments of the Lord": Psalms 19:9; "woe unto the man through whom the offense cometh": Matthew 18:7.

Over and over again: Carl Sandburg, *Abraham Lincoln* (1939), 4:361.

friend and close companion: Julia Ward Howe, in Commager, *Parker*, 105.

"Mine eyes have seen": Julia Ward Howe, "Battle Hymn of the Republic," *The Atlantic Monthly*, February 1862.

The chapter must end with the hymn; but it is not amiss to consider two tributes to Parker in Florence. The first is a distillation of his accomplishments, not an actual transcript; the second is an actual transcript.

THE MEMORIAL AT THE GRAVESIDE

The Protestant Cemetery, at the Porta Pinto, Florence, Italy—May 8, 1870

Three hundred and fifty years ago our ancestors crossed the sea for conscience's sake and found a land of liberty. From that stalwart stock came Theodore Parker. At his birth the land was in bondage. Conscience, coerced and compromised, cowered before lawless law. Wrong was in power. Right mumbled or writhed in silence.

Theodore Parker raised the voice of Right. Conscience, he proclaimed, knew no compromise. Conscience, he demonstrated, could not be coerced. Liberty, the birthright of the land, must be the law. Right must be restored.

Theodore Parker spoke as a minister of the Gospel, from the pulpit provided by the Church. He projected that pulpit into the public business of the State, for he was angered by that practical atheism which shapes the State while God is confined to the cloisters of the Church. He spoke the age-old message: the commands of the constable must yield to the commandments of conscience. The statutes of man must be judged by the ordinance of God.

Words are our appropriate tribute today to Theodore Parker's memory. For Theodore Parker, words were not enough. Deeds must accompany them or follow them. He acted to secure the freedom of escaped bondsmen and bondswomen. He was ready to undergo the loss of his own liberty to preserve the liberty of another. He fought for the freedom of three million Americans. He exhausted his vital energies, he gave his life for this comprehensive cause.

We have now gone through a great war. That war has brought about the end that Parker sought. He did not work, he did not die in vain. It is for us, his heirs in the Spirit, to ensure that that emancipation accomplished at such enormous expense of treasure and of blood shall be as full, as final, as fertile as Theodore Parker envisaged that it would be. To that tremendous task we dedicate ourselves anew.

Today Parker's burial place, the English Cemetery, is isolated by busy city streets. The grave is marked by a monument designed by William Wentworth Story, Joseph Story's son. Inscribed upon it are these words:

His Name Is Engraved In Marble
His Virtues In The Hearts Of Those He
Helped To Free From Slavery
And Superstition

An inscription at the entrance to the cemetery reads:

English Cemetery
(Swiss Property)
Burial Place
Of The English Poets
E. Barrett Browning
Arthur Clough
Walter Savage Landor

Of Frances Trollope
Mother of Anthony
And The Great
American Preacher
Theodore Parker

CHAPTER 6

"In the mountains": T. S. Eliot, "The Wasteland," in *The Complete Poems of T. S. Eliot* (New York: Harcourt Brace, 1952), 61.

Guy and Edna Ballard: Bruce Campbell, *Ancient Wisdom Revived: A History of the Theosophical Movement* (Berkeley: University of California Press, 1980), 163.

Not before, not since: In *United States v. Moon*, 718 F.2d 1210 (2d Cir. 1983), *cert. denied* 466 U.S. 971 (1984), the Reverend Sun Myung Moon was convicted of tax evasion—not for propagation of his religious beliefs. Part of his defense was that he held more than $1.7 million in trust for the Unification Church. To pass on this claim the court had to take account of the organization of the Unification Church, but the Church's teachings were not being examined for fraud. In another celebrated case Jim Bakker, a Protestant televangelist, was convicted of mail fraud, wire fraud, and conspiracy, and sentenced to a fine of $500,000 and imprisonment for forty-five years. His crimes consisted in selling partnerships in a vacation park, Heritage Village, that was attached to a Christian retreat center for families. Bakker raised $158 million by selling 152,000 partnerships carrying the benefit of annual lodging in Heritage Village. He used relatively little of the money to build facilities for lodging and used much of it to support his own lifestyle and pay the operating expenses of his corporation PTL (an acronym for Praise The Lord, or People That Love). The partnerships sold far exceeded the accommodations constructed. *United States v. Bakker*, 925 F.2d 728 (4th Cir. 1991). No fraud was alleged as to Bakker's religious teaching, and his conviction was sustained on appeal. His sentence, however, was reversed and the case remanded for resentencing because the district judge in sentencing him declared: "He had no thought whatever about his victims and those of us who do have a religion are ridiculed as being saps from money-grabbing preachers or priests." The appellate court held that Bakker was denied due process of law by the trial judge "factoring his own sense of religiosity and victimization into the sentence" (id. at 740). No doubt the severity of the sentence influenced the result.

John Rogge: *New York Times*, March 23, 1981, sec. B, 14; "a lot of complaints": Roosevelt to Robert Jackson, December 3, 1941, Jackson Papers, Library of Congress, Manuscript Division.

crime to use the mails to defraud: 25 Stat. 873 (1889).

"the darling of the prosecutor's nursery": *Harrison v. United States*, 7 F.2d 259, 263 (2d Cir. 1925).

"as *real* and *true*": Godfre Ray King [Guy Ballard], *Unveiled Mysteries* (Schaumberg, Ill.: Saint Germain Press, 1934), xvii (emphasis in original).

"fraud order": United States Post Office, *Fraud Record*, No. 7168. The hearing on the recommendation was held June 6, 1941 and the order issued on February 11, 1942. The ban was reported by the *New York Times*: "Coast Cult Banned From Mails," *New York Times*, February 14, 1942, 22.

version of the 1940 indictment: see *Ballard v. United States*, 138 F.2d 540 (9th Cir. 1943). Transcript of record upon appeal from the District Court of the United States for the Southern District of California, Central Division (hereafter *Ballard* trial transcript), 4:1551.

Horace Donnelly: *Who Was Who in America, 1974–1976* (Chicago, Ill.: Marquis Who's Who, 1981), 7:115; part in writing mail fraud statute: *Ballard* trial transcript, 3:1184. Joining Donnelly for the defense were two former assistant United States attorneys, David Cannon and Ames Peterson, who, government counsel noted, had long ago "learned, as they say, the ropes in trying criminal cases" (3:1183). They were backed by Ralph Curren, a graduate of the University of Chicago; W. I. Gilbert, a Stanford man; Joseph Rush, a graduate of Santa Clara; and Roland Woolley, another Georgetown graduate. An eighth Ballard lawyer, James R. Armstrong, was a retired judge of the criminal appellate court of Oklahoma and himself an I Am follower.

Following Yankwich's precedent, he ruled: *Ballard* trial transcript, 3:1178; "a patriotic service": 3:1182; $11,000 in five months: 4:1320; Goldberg on phonograph records: 3:1229; "he used Feenamint": 2:535; Dr. Brigham: 2:701–702; Ricord: 2:641; Edna's corrections: 1:430; La Ferrera: 2:491–492; King: 2:588; "I can make them believe": 2:711; Schall: 1:395, 398; Stevens: 2:713–714; Rogers: 2:730–732; "queen bee": 3:1299; Zimmerman: 2:937; Haldy: 2:947; Chamberlain: 2:950; Zimmerman: 2:937; Hawley: 3:998; Kelly: 2:961–962; Magnuson: 3:986–987; "I have never intentionally": 3:1125; "true, actual experiences": 3:1130–1131; "Doubt kills": 3:1143; "I represent the call": 3:1145; "this Ballard Racket": 3:1188; "a mild self-effacing man": 3:1219; "just as I might name": 3:1215; "real true adventures": 3:1218; "a glib prevaricator": 3:1244; Guy's letters to Edna: 3:1352–1353; "What man": 4:1489, quoting Matthew 7:9–10; "God to these people": 4:1439; "a Christian activity": 4:1409; "those things were claimed": 4:1460; "This case": 4:1571–1576.

its biblical base in the Christianity: see, e.g., on the power of prayer, Mark 1:12–14; on the Ascension of Jesus, Acts 1:9; on the "spiritual body" of the resurrected Christ, see Gustave Martelet, S.J., *The Risen Christ and the Eucharistic World*, trans. René Hague (London: Collins, 1976), 94; original, *Résurrection, eucharistie et genèse de l'homme* (Paris: Desclée, 1972). For the view that the Resurrection is an existential event that an individual apprehends under "the theological condition peculiar to the believer" see the work of another modern Jesuit, Xavier Léon-Dufour, S.J., *Resurrection and the Message of Easter*, trans. R. N. Wilson (New York: Holt, Rinehart and Winston, 1974), 246; original, *Résurrection de Jésus et le message pascal* (Paris: Editions du Seuil, 1971).

"showed most startling intimacy": William James, quoted in R. W. B. Lewis, *The*

Jameses (New York: Farrar, Straus and Giroux, 1991), 491; "by the ordinary waking use of her ears," 494.

came Helena Blavatsky: Maria Carlson, *"No Religion Higher than Truth": A History of the Theosophical Movement in Russia, 1875–1922* (Princeton: Princeton University Press, 1993), 29–34; she gives Elena Petrovna's married name as Blavatsky (39); see also Campbell, *Ancient Wisdom*, 2–28. *Isis Unveiled* as a syncretic mixture: Carlson, *No Religion*, 51. "Drew from the Astral light": Campbell, *Ancient Wisdom*, 34; "Somebody who knows": 34. The judgment of the Society for Psychical Research: Carlson, *No Religion*, 41–42. The fraud was exposed in 1894 in a work entitled *Isis Very Much Unveiled*: 50. Interestingly, in recent times, the Society for Psychical Research is reported to have withdrawn its charges. See "Blavatsky, H.P.," *Encyclopedia of Religion*, ed. Mircea Eliade (New York: Macmillan, 1987), 1:240–241; "unique, fiery talent": Vsevolod Solov'ev, *Zhritsa*, quoted in Carlson, *No Religion*, 49; "an untraditional, creative woman": 43.

"this great man": H. P. Blavatsky, *Collected Writings* (Wheaton, Ill.: Theosophical Press, 1950–1991), 1:109; "this great man . . . ," 3:128; "the Prince of Imposters," 9:229.

"went hand in hand with the Women's Movement": Carlson, *No Religion*, 67; suppression of Theosophists and later revival: 176–180; Annie Besant: 143–144.

Munch . . . spiritualism . . . Theosophy: see Norma S. Steinberg, "Munch in Color," *Harvard University Art Museums Bulletin* 13–14 (spring 1995): 41. Belyi: Carlson, *No Religion*, 8–9. Mondrian, Kandinsky, Yeats, Russell, Joyce: Campbell, *Ancient Wisdom*, 166–171; on Joyce, see also Stuart Gilbert, *James Joyce's Ulysses* (New York: Vintage Books, 1955), vii–viii, 32–37; "directive theme": ibid. Mocking of Russell: Leon Edel, *James Joyce* (New York: Gotham Bookmart, 1947), 179–180. "Met him": James Joyce, *Ulysses*, ed. Hans Walter Gabler (New York: Random House, 1986), 52; "I go to encounter": James Joyce, *A Portrait of the Artist as a Young Man*, ed. Hans Walter Gabler (New York: Garland, 1993), 218.

"I shall not want Pipit": T. S. Eliot, "A Cooking Egg," *The Complete Poems of T. S. Eliot*, 44. "It's no go": Louis MacNeice, "Bagpipe Music," *The Collected Poems of Louis MacNeice*, ed. E. R. Dodds (New York: Oxford University Press, 1967), 96–97.

"The earth exists": Rudolf Steiner, *The Gospel According to St. John*, 56, quoted in Carlson, *No Religion*, 132; "spiritual science," astral or etheric body: 128.

"the greatest popularity": Campbell, *Ancient Wisdom*, 163.

"the many discrepancies": *Ballard* trial transcript, 1:463; Buck: 3:987–988; Ade: 2:967; Kelly 2:959.

too raw to swallow: Paul Freund cleverly dispatches the Ballards in a phrase: "the record contained such items as the defendant's selection of the name Ray-O-Light for their celestial messenger after reading an advertisement for Ray-O-Vac flashlights." Freund, "Individual and Commonwealth in the Thought of Mr. Justice Jackson," *Stanford Law Review* 8 (1955): 9, 15.

"an institution of County Jail type": *Ballard* trial transcript, 1:188–190.

William Denman: Denman was a graduate of Berkeley and Harvard Law School; Stephens was the product of the University of Southern California and Stanford; Mathews had gone to Peabody College in Tennessee and then studied law on his own. Adult experience is always germane: all three had practiced law—Denman had taught at Hastings College of the Law and had then been a reformer in the corrupt San Francisco of the early 1900s and a major ally of Hiram Johnson in the Progressives' effort to cleanse California politics; Stephens had been a superior court judge in Los Angeles; Mathews had been attorney general of Arizona. Stephens professed no denominational identity, Mathews listed himself as an Episcopalian. Biographies of Denman, Stephens, and Mathews: *Biographical Dictionary of the Federal Judiciary* (Detroit: Gale Research, 1976), 70, 179, and 261; "In Memoriam Honorable William Denman 1872–1959," 262 F.2d 7–12 (1959); Denman's bequest "Denman's Estate to Educate Indians," *San Francisco Chronicle*, March 17, 1959, 3.

"We may try to see things": Benjamin Cardozo, *The Nature of the Judicial Process* (1921), 13; he quotes William James, *Pragmatism* (Cambridge, Mass.: Harvard University Press, 1975), 9.

"that some, at least": *Ballard v. United States*, 138 F. 540, 545 (9th Cir. 1943); "The district court did not give": id. at 546 (dissent).

the trial had consumed two months: O'Connor to Fahy, July 7, 1943, now in William O. Douglas Papers, Library of Congress, Manuscript Division.

other precedents: *New v. United States*, 245 F.710, 712 (9th Cir. 1917), cert. denied, 246 U.S. 665 (1918). Judge O'Connor also relied on *Crane v. United States*, 259 F. 480 (9th Cir. 1919), and *Post v. United States*, 135 F.1022. (5th Cir. 1905).

"probably the greatest blow": O'Connor to Berge, October 19, 1943, now in William O. Douglas Papers, Library of Congress, Manuscript Division; "Dear Bill": O'Connor to Douglas, October 20, 1943, in ibid.

justices' understanding of religion: John T. Noonan, Jr., *The Believer and the Powers That Are* (New York: Macmillan, 1987), 238–239; and *Biographical Dictionary of the Federal Judiciary* (1976). Jackson was an active enough Episcopalian to present the candidacy of the bishop of Buffalo at the diocesan convention in 1932 and to be the principal speaker in 1950 at the dedication of the two clerestory windows at the National Cathedral in Washington; he had a lifelong habit of reading the Bible. Eugene C. Gerhart, *Supreme Court Justice Jackson: Lawyer's Judge* (Albany, N.Y.: Q Corporation, 1961), 115.

"If there is any fixed star": *West Virginia State Bd. of Educ. v. Barnette*, 319 U.S. 624 at 642 (1943).

requiring their recusal: 28 U.S. Code § 24 (1940 ed.); today, a negative answer: see, e.g., *United States v. Arnpriester*, 37 F.3d 466 (9th Cir. 1994). Indictment dismissed at Jackson's request: see letters of congratulation to Jackson, February 1940, from Archibald MacLeish, Norman Thomas, Max Lerner, and others. Robert Jackson Papers, Library of Congress, Manuscript Division.

"a war" with Black: Jackson, quoted in Alpheus T. Mason, *Harlan Fiske Stone:*

Pillar of the Law (New York: Viking Press, 1956), 645. Made an issue: *Jewell Ridge Coal Corp. v. Local No. 6167, U.M.W.*, 325 U.S. 897 (1945).

"belief in their representations": *United States v. Ballard*, 322 U.S. 78, 84 (1944); no waiver: id. at 85; "The law knows no heresy": id. at 86, quoting *Watson v. Jones*, 80 U.S. (13 Wall.), 679, 728 (1871); "justified on other distinct grounds," 88; Douglas's first draft: text of March 21, 1944. In Douglas Papers, Library of Congress, Manuscript Division.

the state of one's mind: *United States v. Ballard*, 322 U.S. at 90 (dissent).

Jackson . . . voted to grant certiorari: memorandum from P.N., Jackson Papers; Jackson's intention to join Douglas: ibid.; Jackson's participation in services for a Theosophist: *Jamestown Sun Magazine*, April 8, 1951: ibid.; Jackson's dissent: *United States v. Ballard*, 322 U.S. at 92–94; "Some who profess": ibid. at 94. Jackson quotes William James, *The Works of William James: The Varieties of Religious Experience* (1920), 15:428.

"The religious views espoused": *United States v. Ballard*, 322 U.S. at 87; "I should say that the defendants": id. at 92 (dissent).

"usually the slaves": John Maynard Keynes, *The General Theory of Employment, Interest and Money* (New York: Harcourt, Brace, 1936), 383.

"The mother sea and fountain-head": William James, quoted in Lewis, *The Jameses*, 502; "the feelings, acts and experiences": James, *Varieties of Religious Experience*, 34; "as an external art": 32; "serious": 39. The anti-communitarian bias has been critically noted: by Mary Ann Glendon and Raul F. Yanes, "Structural Free Exercise," *Michigan Law Review* 90 (1991): 485, 501, 546; and by Michael J. Sandel, "Freedom of Conscience or Freedom of Choice?" in *Articles of Faith, Articles of Peace: The Religious Liberty Clauses and the American Public Philosophy*, ed. James D. Hunter and Os Guinness (Washington, D.C.: Brookings Institution, 1990), 74, 87.

"the high seriousness which comes from absolute sincerity": Matthew Arnold, "The Study of Poetry" in *The Complete Prose Works of Matthew Arnold: English Literature and Irish Politics*, ed. R. H. Super (Ann Arbor: University of Michigan Press, 1974), 9:184; see also G. H. Lewes, "The Principle of Sincerity," in *The Principles of Success in Literature* (San Francisco: Bosqui Engraving and Printing, 1885).

"a listless, vigorless summation": *Ballard v. United States*, 152 F.2d 941, 943 (9th Cir. 1945); "no single unfair act" id. at 945 (dissent).

Leslie Van Ness Denman.: San Francisco *Chronicle*, February 10, 1959; life became unbearable: Associated Press dispatch, March 1959, in personnel files, William Denman, Federal Record Center, St. Louis, National Archives.

himself addressed "Dear Franklin": Denman to the president, May 23, 1933; Denman to Thomas Walsh, February 3, 1933; Denman to the attorney general, June 16, 1933; applying for the appointment and listing supporters: Denman to the president, July 28, 1933; Archbishop Edward Hanna to the president, December 15, 1934. "At this moment when I feel stripped": Leslie Van Ness Denman to President Roosevelt, September 5, 1933. These letters are in the Denman file in the National Archives. I am indebted to David Frederick for copies of them.

"Hymn to the Mother of the Gods": "Rites and Ceremonies of the Indians of the Southwest, issued as Christmas greetings from Will and Leslie Denman, 1947" [Denman file, Bancroft Library, University of California, Berkeley]. "The modeller of gods" is quoted from Eli Faure, *History of Art: The Spirit of the Forms* (Garden City, N.Y.: Doubleday, 1937); "faith in a new power": Leslie Van Ness Denman, introduction to her *The Peyote Ritual* (San Francisco: Grabhorn Press, 1957), 1; "the messenger gods": 7; "the peyote man": 13.

"Well could a sensitive woman": *Ballard v. United States*, 152 F.2d at 952 (dissent).

"a body truly representative": *Glasser v. United States*, 315 U.S. 60, 86 (1944).

"the one large and vital religious group": *Ballard v. United States*, 152 F.2d at 951 (dissent); "You here! I did not believe": id. at 955; "Perhaps an agnostic psychiatrist": id. at 955.

"social history of the imagination": Clifford Geertz, *Islam Observed: Religious Development in Morocco and Indonesia* (Yale University Press, 1968), 19; "a confusion, endemic in the west": Clifford Geertz, *Works and Lives* (Palo Alto: Stanford University Press, 1988), 140. For analogous tension between the literal sense and modern theological interpretation, see Raymond Brown, *The Birth of the Messiah* (Garden City, N.Y.: Doubleday, 1979), 190: Infancy Gospels give "verisimilitude, not . . . history." According to Brown, religious imagination conceived the familiar Christmas stories to convey the great theological message—God has come among us. For discussion, see my "How Sincere Do You Have to Be to Be Religious?," *University of Illinois Law Review* (1988): 713, 720–722.

"not fungible": *Ballard v. United States*, 329 U.S. 187, 194 (1946); "the democratic ideal": id. at 195.

Vinson's religion: *Biographical Dictionary of the Federal Judiciary* (1976), 285; Burton's religion: *Who Was Who in America, 1961–1968*.

federal courts in California: *Ballard v. United States*, 329 U.S. at 206, n.2 (dissent).

The point had been abandoned: id. at 198 (Frankfurter called his opinion neither a dissent nor a concurrence); the religious issue unresolved: id. at 200–203.

T. Lamar Caudle's conviction: *New York Times*, June 14, 1956, 1.

fraud order revoked: United States Post Office, *Fraud Records*, case 7168.

the unjust judge of the Gospel: Luke 18:2–5.

CHAPTER 7

hill of which Winthrop once spoke: John Winthrop, "A Modell of Christian Charity," in *Winthrop Papers* (Boston: Massachusetts Historical Society, 1931), 2:294–295. Hill to which John Kennedy alluded: John F. Kennedy, An Address to the Massachusetts Legislature (1961), reprinted in *Cong. Rec.*, 87th Cong., 1st sess., 1961, 107:169, appendix.

It's like reading the Bible: cf. Hugo Black: "That Constitution is my legal bible; its plan of government is my plan and its destiny my destiny. I cherish every word of it from the first to the last, and I personally deplore even the slightest deviations from its least important commands." Hugo Black, *A Constitutional Faith* (New York: Knopf, 1968), 65.

'lay the article of the Constitution': Owen J. Roberts, writing for the court in *United States v. Butler*, 297 U.S. 1, 62 (1936).

'Congress' meant 'state': see *Cantwell v. Connecticut*, 310 U.S. 296, 303 (1940).

over two hundred cases: see John T. Noonan, Jr., *The Believer and the Powers That Are* (New York: Macmillan, 1987), 489–492.

a bit confused about Jefferson's part: "This Court has previously recognized that the provisions of the First Amendment, in the drafting and adoption of which Madison and Jefferson played such leading roles, had the same objective and were intended to provide the same protection against governmental intrusion on religious liberty as the Virginia statute." *Everson v. Board of Education*, 330 U.S. 1, 13 (1947) (per Black, J.). The error was pointed out by Justice Rehnquist: "Thomas Jefferson was of course in France at the time the constitutional Amendments known as the Bill of Rights were passed by Congress and ratified by the States." *Wallace v. Jaffree*, 472 U.S. 38, 92 (1985) (dissenting).

"The 'establishment of religion' clause": *Everson*, at 15.

'respecting an establishment' meant: see, e.g., *School District of Abington Township v. Schempp*, 374 U.S. 203, 309 (Stewart, J., dissenting): the provision was "primarily an attempt to insure that Congress not only would be powerless to establish a national church, but would also be unable to interfere with existing state establishments." See also Mary Ann Glendon and Raul F. Yanes, "Structural Free Exercise," *Michigan Law Review* 90 (1991): 477, 481, 497.

When it said 'No law': *New York Times v. United States*, 403 U.S. 713, 717–718 (1971) (Black, J., concurring).

He wrote those words: Thomas Jefferson to Messrs. Nehemiah Dodge, Ephraim Roberts, and Stephen S. Nelson, a committee of the Danbury Baptist Association: January 1, 1802, *The Thomas Jefferson Papers*, ed. H. A. Washington (1856), 8.

cutting the schools off from police protection: *Everson*, 330 U.S. at 17.

school field trips: *Wolman v. Walter*, 433 U.S. 229, 254 (1977).

state could buy textbooks: *Cochran v. Louisiana State Board of Educ.*, 281 U.S. 370 (1930), followed in *Board of Educ. v. Allen*, 392 U.S. 236 (1968).

maps and globes and tape recorders: *Wolman*, 433 U.S. at 249–250.

remedial help, therapy, and counseling: id. at 246–248; diagnostic services constitutional on premises: id. at 241–244; 'the pressures of the environment': id. at 247.

strictly supplemental help: *Agostini v. Felton*, 117 S. Ct. 1997, 2019 (1997), vacating the judgment of the district court after remand in *Aguilar v. Felton*, 473 U.S. 402 (1985).

some sorts of gerrymandering intolerable: e.g., *Shaw v. Reno*, 509 U.S. 630 (1993); *Bush v. Vera*, 116 S. Ct. 1941 (1996).

if the costs include both state exams and school exams: *Levitt v. Committee for Public Educ. and Religious Liberty*, 413 U.S. 472, 480 (1973); but if it's just state exams: *Committee for Public Educ. and Religious Liberty v. Regan*, 444 U.S. 646, 654 (1980).

generous funding for their buildings: *Tilton v. Richardson*, 403 U.S. 672 (1971); *Hunt v. McNair*, 413 U.S. 734 (1973), *Roemer v. Board of Public Works of Maryland*, 426 U.S. 736 (1976).

think of a tax break as aid: cf. *Walz v. Tax Comm'n*, 397 U.S. 664, 709 (1970) (Douglas, J., dissenting); and Boris Bittker, "Churches, Taxes, and the Constitution," *Yale Law Journal* 78 (1969): 1285.

present a substantial federal question: *Lundberg v. Alameda County*, 46 Cal.2d 644, 298 P.2d 1 (1956), appeal dismissed *sub nom. Heisey v. Alameda County*, 352 U.S. 921 (1956).

deduction of $40 . . . unconstitutional: *Committee for Public Educ. and Religious Liberty v. Nyquist*, 413 U.S. 756, 774 (1973); 'vitally different': *Mueller v. Allen*, 463 U.S. 388, 398 (1983).

'ad hoc judgments incapable of being reconciled': Jesse H. Choper, "The Religious Clauses of the First Amendment: Reconciling the Conflict," *University of Pittsburgh Law Review* 41 (1980): 673, 680; 'the incantation of verbal formulae': John H. Mansfield, "The Religious Clauses of the First Amendment and the Philosophy of the Constitution," *California Law Review* 72 (1984): 847, 848.

Something does not love a wall: see Robert Frost, "*Mending Wall*," *The Complete Poems of Robert Frost* (New York: Holt, 1949), 35. Cf. *Plaut v. Spendthrift Farm*, 514 U.S. 211, 240, and 245 (1995).

'the line of separation, far from being "a wall"': *Lemon v. Kurtzman*, 403 U.S. 602, 614 (1971).

a clergyman can't pray: *Lee v. Weisman*, 112 S. Ct. 2649 (1992); a city can't adopt: *Church of the Lukumi Babalu Aye v. City of Hialeah*, 508 U.S. 520 (1993); a state can adopt: *Employment Div. v. Smith*, 494 U.S. 872 (1990).

A prisoner seeks to receive sacramental absolution: *Mockaitis v. Harcleroad*, 104 F.3d 1522 (9th Cir. 1997).

'landmarking has burdened': Douglas Laycock, "The Remnants Of Free Exercise," *Supreme Court Review* (1990): 1, 49 n.203, citing the experience of New York City; the Yonkers case: *Yonkers Racing Corp. v. City of Yonkers*, 858 F.2d 855, 871 (2d Cir. 1988), cert. denied 489 U.S. 1077 (1989). For other examples of laws of general application that would trump religious practices, see Michael W. McConnell, "Free Exercise Revisionism and the Smith Decision," *University of Chicago Law Review* 57 (1990): 1109, 1142–1143. The articles by Laycock and McConnell provided solid scholarly support for the congressional intervention noted below.

'Government shall not substantially burden': Religious Freedom Restoration Act, 42 U.S.C. § 2000bb. For an example of the act's application, see *United States v. Bauer*, 75 F.3d 1366 (9th Cir. 1996), amended 84 F.3d 1549 (9th Cir. 1996).

"Congress exercised its power to protect First Amendment rights": e.g., the Privacy Protection Act of 1980, 42 U.S. Code §§ 2000aa–2000aa-12 (restricting government investigators seeking documents from the media and limiting the effect of *Zurcher v. Stanford Daily*, 436 U.S. 547 (1978)); the Church Audit Procedure Act of 1984, 26 U.S. Code § 7611 (strictly regulating "church tax inquiry" and "church tax examination" by the Internal Revenue Service); and the Exemption Act of 1988, 26 U.S. Code § 3127 (providing a special Social Security tax exemption for employers and their employees who are members of "a recognized religious sect" whose "established tenets" oppose participation in the Social Security Act program).

courts might shrink the meaning of religion: see Jesse H. Choper, *Securing Religious Liberty: Principles for Judicial Interpretation of the Religion Clauses* (Chicago: University of Chicago Press, 1995), 63.

The Supreme Court declared the legislation unconstitutional: *City of Boerne v. Flores*, 117 S. Ct. 2157 (1997); lack of congruence and proportionality: id. at 2168, 2169.

'panic, fear, and trauma': *Board of Ed. of Kiryas Joel Village School Dist. v. Grumet*, 512 U.S. 687, 692 (1994); 'fusion of governmental and religious functions': id. at 696–697, quoting *Larkin v. Grendel's Den*, 459 U.S. 116, 126 (1982); 'the Constitution allows the state to accommodate': id. at 705.

One who knows most: William Bentley Ball, who has acquired his knowledge in, as it were, the flesh by litigating on the side of religious freedom for the past quarter century. See Ball, *Mere Creatures of the State? Education, Religion and the Courts: A View from the Courtroom* (Notre Dame, Ind.: Crisis Books, 1994), 3–4. The court makes up the rules ad hoc: Ball, "Commentary on *Bd of Educ of Kiryas Joel*," *First Things*, November 1994.

'Be not conformed to this world': Romans 12:2.

'the very apex': *Wisconsin v. Yoder*, 406 U.S. 205, 213 (1972); 'fundamental rights and interests': id. at 214.

'published or distributed by a religious faith': *Texas Monthly, Inc. v. Bullock*, 489 U.S. 1, 5 (1989) (quoting Tex. Tax Code Ann. § 151.312 [1982]); 'state sponsorship of religious belief': id. at 15; tax on preaching unconstitutional: *Murdock v. Pennsylvania*, 319 U.S. 105, 112 (1943); 'in tension': *Texas Monthly*, 489 U.S. at 21.

state tax exemption for 'houses of worship': amici curiae defending exemption in *Walz*, 397 U.S. at 665–666; 'beneficial and stabilizing influences': *Walz*, 397 U.S. at 673; 'a social welfare yardstick': id. at 674; 'excessive government entanglement': id. The pedigree of this phrase is as follows: Madison in paragraph 3 of the Memorial and Remonstrance of 1785 stated: "The freemen of America did not wait till usurped power had strengthened itself by exercise, and entangled the question in precedents." Justice Rutledge, in attaching the Memorial and Remonstrance to *Everson*, declared that the realm of religion "should be kept inviolately private, not 'entangled . . . in precedents.'" Against this Madisonian background Justice Frankfurter declared that "the public school must keep scrupulously free from entanglement in the strife of sects." *Illinois ex rel. McCollum v. Board of Education*, 333 U.S. 203, 216–217 (1948) (dissenting).

'When the state encourages religious instruction': Walz, 397 U.S. at 672 (quoting *Zorach v. Clauson*, 343 U.S. 306, 313–314 [1952]).

sales tax . . . food served by religious organizations . . . wine: *Texas Monthly*, 489 U.S. at 29–33 (Scalia, J., dissenting); 'a new strain of irrationality': id. at 45 (dissent).

"the hobgoblin of little minds": Ralph Waldo Emerson, "Self-Reliance," *Essays* (Boston: Houghton Mifflin, 1865), 52, referring to "a foolish consistency."

Saint Paul told slaves: Ephesians 6:5.

take the Walnut Street Presbyterian Church: *Watson v. Jones*, 80 U.S. (13 Wall.) 679 (1871).

That rule would have stopped: see Thomas A. Brady, Jr., *The Politics of the Reformation in Germany* (New York: Humanities Press International, 1997), 129.

Russian Orthodox Church: Dimitry Pospielovsky, *The Russian Church Under the Soviet Regime, 1917–1982* (Crestwood, New York: St. Vladimir's Seminary Press, 1984), 1:19–25; the pre-Soviet regime: 31–36; the election of the patriarch in 1917, the Renovationists: 56–58. John Kedrovsky: "The Takeover of St. Nicholas Cathedral," *New York Times*, November 8, 1923, 21; dismissal of Platon and the response of the Detroit sobor: see *Saint Nicholas Cathedral v. Kreshik*, 164 N.E.2d 687 (N.Y. 1959), rev'd, *Kreshik v. Saint Nicholas Cathedral*, 363 U.S. 190 (1960). courts of New York . . . gave Kedrovsky: *Kedrovsky v. Rojdesvensky*, 212 N.Y.S. 273 (N.Y. App. Div. 1925), aff'd, 152 N.E. 421 (N.Y. 1926). Transfer of Orthodox churches to trustees headed by Platon: Pospielovsky, *The Russian Church*, 2:283.

New York . . . Religious Corporation Law: § 107 (McKinney 1990)

Venyamin Fedchenkov's appointment. Pospielovsky, *The Russian Church*, 1:71–72; 2:289, 485; Aleksii: 2:209–211.

the church rule controlled: *Kedroff v. Saint Nicholas Cathedral of Russian Orthodox Church in North America*, 344 U.S. 94, 120–121 (1952).

'Freedom to select the clergy': *Kedroff*, 344 U.S. at 116. On the significance of this development as it appeared at the time, see Mark DeWolfe Howe, "Forward: Political Theory and the Nature of Liberty, The Supreme Court, 1952 Term," *Harvard Law Review* 67 (1953): 91–95; 'a foreign and unfriendly state': *Kedroff*, 344 U.S. at 131 (dissent).

'a perversion of the implied trust': *Kreshik*, 164 N.E.2d at 694; gave St. Nicholas: *Kreshik v. Saint Nicholas Cathedral*, 363 U.S. 190 (1960).

'there are neutral principles': *Presbyterian Church in the United States v. Mary Elizabeth Blue Hull Memorial Presbyterian Church*, 393 U.S. 440, 449 (1969).

'forfeited all ecclesiastical privileges of the PCUS': *Lucas v. Hope*, 515 F.2d 234, 235 (5th Cir. 1975), cert. denied, 424 U.S. 967 (1976).

not find an 'implied trust': *Jones v. Wolf*, 243 S.E.2d 859, 863–64 (Ga. 1978), vacated, *Jones v. Wolf*, 443 U.S. 595 (1979), decided, *Jones v. Wolf*, 260 S.E.2d

84 (Ga. 1979), cert. denied, 444 U.S. 1080 (1980); neutral principles: *Wolf*, 443 U.S. at 602–603; 'so long as the use of that method does not impair free-exercise rights': id. at 608; 'In undertaking such an examination': id. at 604; fix up the deeds: id. at 606; neutral principles already applied: *Jones*, 260 S.E.2d at 85.

is 'startling': John H. Mansfield, "The Religion Clauses of the First Amendment and the Philosophy of the Constitution," *California Law Review* 72 (1984): 846, 866.

'were no more restrictive': *Protestant Episcopal Church v. Barker*, 171 Cal. Rptr. 541, 554 (Cal. Ct. App. 1981), cert. denied, 454 U.S. 864 (1981); 'If a Kentucky Fried Chicken franchisee': id. at 553; 'a constructive dissolution': id. at 556.

principle of double effect: Thomas Aquinas, *Summa theologiae*, 2–2, 64, 7.

preach on Sunday in a public park: *Fowler v. Rhode Island*, 345 U.S. 67 (1953); observance of Sunday constitutional: *McGowan v. Maryland*, 366 U.S. 420 (1961).

'of solemnizing public occasions': *Lynch v. Donnelly*, 465 U.S. 668, 692 (1984) (concurrence).

'for purposes of religious worship': *Widmar v. Vincent*, 454 U.S. 263 (1981); 'Sunday Mass': id. at 285–86 (dissent).

use of public-school property . . . evangelical group: *Lamb's Chapel v. Center Moriches Union Free School District*, 508 U.S. 384 (1993).

Wide Awake: *Rosenberger v. Rector and Visitors of University of Virginia*, 515 U.S. 819 (1995).

development of doctrine is a slow, laborious: John Henry Newman, *An Essay on the Development of Christian Doctrine* (London: W. Blanchard and Sons, 1846), 68–69; 'The development then of an idea': 37.

reading of these provisions . . . theological base: see Steven D. Smith, *Foreordained Failure: The Quest for a Constitutional Principle of Religious Freedom* (New York: Oxford University Press, 1995), 74 and 97.

'an experiment': see the discussion of JM's original insight, in chapter 3.

CHAPTER 8

My fellow Americans: the entire text is as follows:

THE PRESIDENT'S D-DAY PRAYER ON THE INVASION OF NORMANDY. JUNE 6, 1944

My fellow Americans:
     Last night, when I spoke with you about the fall of Rome, I knew at that moment that troops of the United States and our allies were crossing the Channel in another and greater operation. It has come to pass with success thus far.
     And so, in this poignant hour, I ask you to join with me in prayer:
     Almighty God: Our sons, pride of our Nation, this day have set upon a mighty endeavor, a struggle to preserve our Republic, our religion, and our civilization, and to set free a suffering humanity.

Lead them straight and true; give strength to their arms, stoutness to their hearts, steadfastness in their faith.

They will need Thy blessings. Their road will be long and hard. For the enemy is strong. He may hurl back our forces. Success may not come with rushing speed, but we shall return again and again; and we know that by Thy grace, and by the right-eousness of our cause, our sons will be triumphant.

They will be sore tried, by night and by day, without rest—until the victory is won. The darkness will be rent by noise and flame. Men's souls will be shaken with the vi-olences of war.

For these men are lately drawn from the ways of peace. They fight not for the lust of conquest. They fight to end conquest. They fight to liberate. They fight to let justice arise, and tolerance and good-will among all Thy people. They yearn but for the end of battle, for their return to the haven of home.

Some will never return. Embrace these, Father, and receive them, Thy heroic ser-vants, into Thy kingdom.

And for us at home—fathers, mothers, children, wives, sisters, and brothers of brave men overseas,—whose thoughts and prayers are ever with them—help us, Almighty God, to rededicate ourselves in renewed faith in Thee in this hour of great sacrifice.

Many people have urged that I call the nation into a single day of special prayer. But because the road is long and the desire is great, I ask that our people devote them-selves in a continuance of prayer. As we rise to each new day, and again when each day is spent, let words of prayer be on our lips, invoking Thy help to our efforts.

Give us strength, too—strength in our daily tasks, to redouble the contributions we make in the physical and the material support of our armed forces.

And let our hearts be stout, to wait out the long travail, to bear sorrows that may come, to impart our courage unto our sons wheresoever they may be.

And, O Lord, give us faith. Give us faith in Thee; faith in our sons; faith in each other; faith in our united crusade. Let not the keenness of our spirit ever be dulled. Let not the impacts of temporary events, of temporal matters of but fleeting moment—let not these deter us in our unconquerable purpose.

With Thy blessing, we shall prevail over the unholy forces of our enemy. Help us to conquer the apostles of greed and racial arrogancies. Lead us to the saving of our country, and with our sister nations into a world unity that will spell a sure peace—a peace invulnerable to the schemings of unworthy men. And a peace that will let all men live in freedom, reaping the just rewards of their honest toil.

Thy will be done, Almighty God.

Amen.

The Public Papers and Addresses of Franklin D. Roosevelt, ed. Samuel I. Roseman (New York: Harper, 1950), 13:152–153.

a comparable interest in treating scientifically: Emile Durkheim, *Pragmatism and Sociology*, trans. J. C. Whitehouse (New York: Cambridge University Press, 1983), 97.

"is a unified system of beliefs": Emile Durkheim, *The Elementary Forms of the Religious Life*, trans. Joseph Ward Swain (New York: Free Press, 1963), 62; "an eminently collective thing": 63; society creates the sacred: 242; society a religious phenomenon: 139.

"a sort of religion of which the majority will be the prophets": Alexis de Toc-queville, *De la démocratie en Amérique* (1835, 1840), 2:11 (my translation); "immense pressure": 330 (for parallel cite in its English-language version, see *Democracy in America*, trans. Henry Reeve, rev. Francis Bowen and Phillips Bradley [1989], 1:299). On the passages as anticipation of Durkheim, see Jean-Claude Lamberti, *Tocqueville and the Two Democracies*, trans. Arthur Gold-hammer (Cambridge, Mass.: Harvard University Press, 1989), 162.

"Taxes are the life-blood of government": *Bull v. United States*, 295 U.S. 247, 259 (1935).

were "allowed to challenge": *United States v. Lee*, 455 U.S. 252, 260 (1982).

Glebe lands of the Protestant: *United States Statutes* 2, 194 (1802); District of Columbia exemptions: id. 16, 153 (1870); refunds: id. 6, 116 (1813), 6, 346 (1826), 6, 675 (1836).

exempted the income: id. 38, 172 (1913), now 26 U.S. Code § 501; income tax deduction: 26 U.S. Code § 170.

"to conduct an institution": *Bob Jones University v. United States*, 461 U.S. 574, 579–580 (1983); "Charitable exemptions are justified": id. at 591–592.

Military chaplaincies: *Katcoff v. Marsh*, 755 F.2d 223 (2d Cir. 1985); "an ecclesiastical endorsing agency": id. at 225; "would suffer immeasurable harm": id. at 228; "so inherently impractical": id. at 236; "to make religion available": id. at 234.

"considered professional judgment": *Goldman v. Weinberger*, 475 U.S. 503, 508 (1986).

"There goes many a ship to sea": Roger Williams to the town of Providence, January 1654–1655 in *The Complete Writings of Roger Williams*, ed. Perry Miller (New York: Russell and Russell, 1963), 6:278–279.

"no person religiously scrupulous": *Annals of Congress* (Washington, D.C.: Gales and Seaton, 1789), 1:778. "No man can claim this indulgence of right": in ibid., 780.

"duly ordained ministers": *Selective Draft Law Cases*, 245 U.S. 366, 376 (1918). "And we pass": id. at 389–390.

Members of newer sects such as the Jehovah's Witnesses: Herbert Hewitt Stroup, *The Jehovah's Witnesses* (New York: Columbia University Press, 1952), 165–166.

"preparing for the ministry": *United States Statutes*, 54, 885 (1940).

"usually a political objection": *United States v. Kauten*, 133 F.2d 703, 708 (2d Cir. 1943) (per Augustus Hand, J.).

over five thousand Jehovah's Witnesses: Mulford Q. Sibley and Philip E. Jacob, *Conscription of Conscience, The American State and the Conscientious Objector, 1940–1947* (Ithaca: Cornell University Press, 1952), 84; for Robert Lowell, see Paul Mariani, *Lost Puritan: A Life of Robert Lowell* (New York: W. W. Norton, 1994), 105–109.

judicial deference to administrative: *Cox v. United States*, 332 U.S. 442 (1947). Justices Douglas and Black dissented.

"to give the selective service personnel": *Eagles v. United States ex rel. Samuels*, 329 U.S. 304, 309 (1946).

"the most prominent": see *United States ex rel. Levy v. Cain*, 149 F.2d 338, 340 (2d Cir. 1945); "Jewry is divided": Irwin Levy quoted in id. at 340 n.2.

Jacob S. Samuels and Henry Horowitz: *United States ex rel. Samuels v. Pearson*, 151 F.2d 801 (3rd Cir. 1945), reversed, *Eagles v. United States ex rel. Samuels*, 329 U.S. 304 (1946) and *Eagles v. United States ex rel. Horowitz*, 329 U.S. 317 (1946). Douglas assumed what was far from clear: that Samuels and

Horowitz could have discovered the identities of the panel members if they had chosen to seek them, *Samuels* at 314; "the variety of relgious faiths": id. at 313, quoting *United States ex rel. Goodman v. Hearn*, 153 F.2d 186, 188 (5th Cir. 1946).

Felix Frankfurter: *West Virginia State Board of Education v. Barnette*, 319 U.S. 624, 646 (1943) (dissent).

Jehovah's Witnesses were total pacifists: *Sicurella v. United States*, 348 U.S. 385 (1955).

"religious training": *United States Statutes at Large*, 62, 612 (1948).

"belief in and devotion": *United States v. Seeger*, 380 U.S. 163, 166 (1965); "sum and essence": id. at 168; "man thinking his highest": id. at 169. "A sincere and meaningful belief": id. at 177.

"by reading in the fields": *Welsh v. United States*, 398 U.S. 333, 341 (1970); "with the strength of more traditional": id. at 343, quoting *Welsh v. United States*, 404 F.2d 1078, 1081 (9th Cir. 1968); "whose consciences": id. at 344.

"the care that Congress realized": *United States v. Seeger*, 380 U.S. at 175.

"And more broadly, of course": *Gillette v. United States; Negre v. Larsen*, 401 U.S. 437, 462 (1971).

"The power to interpret": *City of Boerne v. Flores*, 117 S. Ct. 2157 (1997) at 2166.

Theoretically, the Constitution may be amended: amendments correcting decisions of the Supreme Court are the Eleventh, correcting *Chisholm v. Georgia*, 2 Dall. 419 (1793); the Thirteenth and Fourteenth, correcting *Dred Scott v. Sanford*, 60 U.S. (19 How.) 393 (1857); the Sixteenth, correcting *Pollock v. Farmers Loan & Trust Co.*, 157 U.S. 429 (1895); and the Twenty-Sixth, correcting *Oregon v. Mitchell*, 400 U.S. 112 (1970).

must decide what is the true church: see chapter 7.

a court cannot help giving the impression: *Shelley v. Kraemer*, 334 U.S. 1 (1948); followed in *Kreshik v. St. Nicholas Cathedral*, 363 U.S. 190, 191 (1960).

an establishment of religion: e.g., *Lemon v. Kurtzman*, 403 U.S. 602 (1971).

"Secular Humanism": *Torcaso v. Watkins*, 367 U.S. 488, 495 n.11 (1961).

If Secular Humanism was a religion: *Edwards v. Aguillard*, 482 U.S. 578 (1978).

"ceremonial deism": *County of Allegheny v. American Civil Liberties Union*, 492 U.S. 573, 596, n.46 (1989); see also id. at 630–631 (concurrence).

United States v. Ballard: see chapter 6.

"devastating": *Lyng v. Northwest Indian Cemetery Protective Ass'n*, 485 U.S. 439, 451 (1988); "Even if we should": id. at 451–452.

as in the case of monogamy: see chapter 9's discussion of the *Mormon Cases*.

" a *national* religion": see chapter 3.

"The flag represents a living country": 36 U.S. Code § 176(j).

states began enacting laws against flag desecration: see Albert M. Rosenblatt, "Flag Desecration Statutes: History and Analysis," *Washington University Law Quarterly* (1972): 193, 197. See, e.g., Mass. General Laws Ann. Code 264 § 5 (1919), *quoted in Goguen v. Smith*, 343 F. Supp. 161, 162 (D. Mass. 1972), *affirmed, Smith v. Goguen*, 415 U.S. 566 (1974); "any word, figure, mark": Wash. Rev. Code § 9.86.020 (1963), *quoted in Spence v. Washington*, 418 U.S. 405, 407 (1974).

"If they let that happen to Meredith": *Street v. New York*, 394 U.S. 576, 579 (1969); "It passes my belief": id. at 610 (Black, J., dissenting).

"America, the red, white and blue": *Texas v. Johnson*, 491 U.S. 397, 399 (1989).

Desecration of Venerated Object: Tex. Penal Code Ann. § 42.09(a)(3) (1989), quoted in id. at 400, n.1; "as readily signifies this Nation": *Texas v. Johnson*, 491 U.S. at 405; "the Government may ensure": id. at 417; the chief justice's examples: id. at 422–427 (dissent).

"All day long that free flag tost": John Greenleaf Whittier, "Barbara Frietchie," in *The Complete Poetical Works of John Greenleaf Whittier*, ed. Horace E. Scudder (Boston: Houghton Mifflin, 1894), 343, lines 45–46.

design of the flag: 4 U.S. Code § 1 (1947); time and occasion of its display: 36 U.S. Code § 174 (1976); position and manner of its display: 36 U.S. Code § 175 (1976); "conduct during hoisting": 36 U.S. Code § 177 (1976); flags given to families of deceased servicemen: 10 U.S. Code § 1482(a)(11) (1975); lowering of the flag on the death of the president: 36 U.S. Code § 175 (1976).

"symbolizes the Nation": *Texas v. Johnson*, 491 U.S. at 426; "the visible symbol": id. at 429 (dissent).

"mutilates": Flag Protection Act § 2, 18 U.S. Code § 700 (1989).

"suppresses expression": *United States v. Eichman*, 496 U.S. 310, 317 (1990); "national consensus": id. at 318; "create national symbols": id. at 318. "the symbolic value": id. at 319; "the spirit of our national commitment": id. at 321 (dissent).

"The Congress and the States": H.J. Res. 79, *Cong. Rec.*, 141st Cong., H6415–24 (June 28, 1995); the vote: H6439; the call for an amendment by 49 states: H6404.

CHAPTER 9

salute to the flag: David R. Manwaring, *Render Unto Caesar: The Flag Salute Controversy* (Chicago: University of Chicago Press, 1962), 56; Rutherford compared the compulsory salute: 30–31; two hundred children expelled: 56.

"The pledge of allegiance to the flag": *Nicholls v. Mayor and Sch. Comm. of Lynn*, 297 Mass. 65, 71, 7 N.E.2d 577, 580 (1937).

"an interest inferior to none": *Minersville School District v. Gobitis*, 310 U.S. 586, 595 (1940); "the basis for national security": id. Violence against Witnesses: Manwaring, *Render Unto*, 163–172; "flag desecration": *McKee v. State*, 219 Ind. 247, 37 N.E.2d 940 (1941) (reversing conviction); "which reasonably tends to create": *Taylor v. State*, 194 Miss. 1, 11 So.2d 663 (1943), rev'd, *Taylor v. Mississippi*, 319 U.S. 583 (1943); "primary object is a haven of rest": *Taylor*, 194 Miss. at 34, 11 So.2d at 673. New expulsions: Manwaring, *Render Unto*, 187.

"dangerously close": "Frankfurter vs. Stone," *New Republic* 102 (1940), 843; "the will of the majority": Edgar Fuller, "Constitutional Liberties of Pupils and Teachers," *Harvard Educational Review* 11 (1941): 76, 81–82; "Courts that will not protect": "The Court Abdicates," *Christian Century* 57 (1940): 846; "one of the most precious rights": Paul L. Blakely, "Flag vs. Oregon Case," *America* 63 (1940): 259.

A new case, from a West Virginia town: Manwaring, *Render Unto*, 208; Daniel and Esther before the court: 217; *Dred Scott* of modern constitutional law: 224. The biblical examples presented to the court: Daniel defies Darius, flouting the law of the Medes and the Persians and instead, observing the law of God in Daniel 6:9–15; Esther intervenes with Ahasuerus to prevent the execution of a decree against the Jews in Esther 5:1–14.

affirmed the injunction: *Barnette v. West Virginia State Board of Education*, 47 F. Supp. 251 (S.D.W.Va. 1942). Circuit Judge John Parker, writing for the three-judge district court, anticipated that the Supreme Court would reverse itself and was affirmed, *West Virginia State Board of Education v. Barnette*, 319 U.S. 624 (1943); "the action of the local authorities": *West Virginia State Bd.*, 319 U.S. at 642; "the right to differ": id.; "If there is any fixed star": id.

a "civil religion": Robert N. Bellah, "Civil Religion in America," in *Religion in America*, ed. William G. McLoughlin and Robert N. Bellah (Boston: Houghton Mifflin, 1968), 15.

"the genteel tradition": see George Santayana, *Character and Opinion in the United States* (reprint; New York: Braziller, 1955), 81; George Santayana, *The Genteel Tradition at Bay* (London: The Adelphi, 1931), 20.

"a symbolic and a sacramental act": Robert Lowell, "On the Gettysburg Address" in *Lincoln and the Gettysburg Address*, ed. Allan Nevins (Urbana: University of Illinois Press, 1964), 89; "the Christian sacrificial act": ibid.

nor is it a substitute for Christianity: Bellah, "Civil Religion," 10; the requirements of the civil religion: 20.

"a *reductio ad absurdum*": Robert N. Bellah, "Afterword: Religion and the Legitimation of the American Republic," in *The Broken Covenant: American Civil Religion in Time of Trial*, 2d ed. (Chicago: University of Chicago Press, 1992), 175.

"bemusement": Martin Marty, *A Nation of Behavers* (1976), 182.

"by Thy grace": for the full text of the president's D-Day prayer on the invasion of Normandy, June 6, 1944, see the first of chapter 8's notes, above.

distinctive personal cadence: typically Roosevelt's addresses were the result of interaction by the president with his ghostwriters, the president setting the direction and making the decisive revisions. See Samuel I. Rosenman, *Working with Roosevelt* (New York: Harper, 1952), 11; Betty Houchin Winfield, *FDR and the News Media* (Urbana: University of Illinois Press, 1990), 106–107.

Christians committed to social justice: see, e.g., Michael J. Baxter, C.S.C. "'Overall, the First Amendment Has Been Very Good for Christianity'—Not!," *De Paul Law Review* 43 (1994): 125.

quotation from Frankfurters: *Congressional Record* (June 28, 1995), H6411, H6440; "what makes us all": H6406; "makes this America": H6917. Flag desecration is not speech: H6908, H6934, H6440. Prayer distinguished:

H6407; "bless our great county": H6407. Religious affiliation (by members' self-identification)—in the Senate: Catholic 20, Episcopalian 14, Methodist 11, Baptist 10, Presbyterian 10, Jewish 9, Lutheran 5, Congregationalist 4, Mormon 3, Protestant 2, Unitarian 2, United Church of Christ 2, Assembly of God 1, Eastern Orthodox Christian 1, Greek Orthodox 1, no religion listed 4. Religious affiliation—in the House: Catholic 123, Baptist 53, Methodist 50, Presbyterian 44, Episcopalian 36, Protestant 25, Jewish 24, Lutheran 16, Mormon 10, Christian 9, Christian Scientist 4, Assembly of God 2, Christian Reformed 2, Church of Christ 2, Congregationalist 2, Greek Orthodox 2, Seventh Day Adventists 2, Unitarian 2, United Church of Christ 2, United Methodist 2, African Methodist Episcopalian 1, Christian Church 1, Disciples of Christ 1, Evangelical 1, Methodist Episcopalian 1, Nazarene 1, Pan African Orthodox Christian 1, Southern Baptist 1, no religion listed 12: *Congressional Yellow Book*, ed. Brian J. Combs, 1996. The amendment was defeated in the Senate: Senate Joint Resolution 31. The Senate's version received 63 to 36 votes, falling three votes short of the two-thirds necessary for a constitutional amendment (*Cong. Rec.*, 141st Cong., S18395 [December 12, 1995]).

colonialist anthropology: see Lawrence E. Sullivan, *Icanchu's Drum: An Orientation to Meaning in South American Religion* (New York: Macmillan, 1988), 6–12.

"I wonder whether you, Tom": Czeslaw Milosz to Thomas Merton, December 31, 1964, *Striving Towards Being: The Letters of Thomas Merton and Czeslaw Milosz*, ed. Robert Faggen (New York: Farrar, Straus and Giroux, 1997), 165.

"O Lord, give us Faith": the president's D-Day prayer.

"our united crusade": ibid.; see Dwight D. Eisenhower, *Crusade in Europe* (Garden City, N.Y.: Doubleday, 1948).

women entering the campaign through religion: Lydia Maria Child, *Anti-Slavery Catechism* (Newburyport: Charles Whipple, 1831); "who labor for the freedom": Maria Weston Chapman, *Songs of the Free and Hymns of Christian Freedom* (Boston: Isaac Knapp, 1836), vii–viii.

William and Ellen Crafts: Robert L. Hall, "Massachusetts Abolitionists Document the Slave Experience," in *Courage and Conscience: Black & White Abolitionists in Boston*, ed. Donald M. Jacobs (Bloomington: Indiana University Press, 1994), 93; Grimes and Burns: 91. On the Twelfth Baptist Church in the underground railroad: Roy E. Finkelbine, "Boston's Black Churches," also in *Courage and Conscience*, 176. "To all the Christian Ministers of Christ in Boston": *The Boston Slave Riot and Trial of Anthony Burns* (Boston: Fetridge and Co., 1854), 27.

"the crusade": anonymous review of *The Life and Correspondence of Theodore Parker*, by John Weiss, *North American Review* 203 (April 1864): 321.

"the story seems to me": Holmes to Norton, April 17, 1864, printed in Mark De Wolfe Howe, *Touched with Fire: Civil War Letters and Diary of Oliver Wendell Holmes, Jr.* (New York: DaCapo Press, 1969), 122. On Norton as the embodiment of the genteel tradition, see Santayana, *Genteel Tradition at Bay*, 3–4, 69.

"the woe due to those": Abraham Lincoln, second inaugural address, 4 March 1865, *The Collected Works of Abraham Lincoln (1864–1865)*, ed. Roy P. Basler (New Brunswick, N.J.: Rutgers University Press, 1953), 8:333.

"into the great day of the hustings": Stephen Douglas, speech, *Congressional Globe*, 29th Congress, 1854, 656.

"the imperative duty of Congress": Republican Party platform, 1856, in Donald B. Johnson, comp., *National Party Platforms* (Urbana: University of Illinois Press, 1978), 27.

"the almost universal excitements": Robert Taylor to President Buchanan, April 27, 1857, quoted in Norman F. Furniss, *The Mormon Conflict, 1850–1859* (New Haven: Yale University Press, 1960), 74–75; "root out polygamy": 82.

"circumstances permitting": *Reynolds v. United States*, 98 U.S. 145, 161 (1878); "would be damnation in the life to come": id.

chiefly Methodists, Presbyterians: see John T. Noonan, Jr., *The Believer and the Powers That Are* (New York: Macmillan, 1987), 195–196.

"An Act to punish and prevent": 12 *Stat.* 501–502 (1862).

"a matter between himself and God alone": John Taylor to the *New York Tribune*, quoted in Leonard J. Arrington, *Brigham Young: American Moses* (New York: Knopf, 1985), 375.

"would be to make the professed doctrines of religious belief": *Reynolds v. United States*, 98 U.S. at 167.

"my sermon on the religion of polygamy": Chief Justice Waite to Rev. D. Walbridge, January 20, 1879, quoted in Bruce R. Trimble, *Chief Justice Waite, Defender of the Public Interest* (Princeton: Princeton University Press, 1938), 244 n.18.

To prove polygamy: *Cannon v. United States*, 116 U.S. 55 (1885).

"I am not a member": *Davis v. Beason*, 133 U.S. 333, 334 (1890); "by the general consent of the Christian world": id. at 343; "However free the exercise": id. at 342–343; "Crime is not the less": id. at 345.

"Ever since Christ": John R. Tucker, speech, January 12, 1887, *Cong. Rec.*, 31st Cong., 2d sess., 18:593; Jesus on marriage: Mark 10:8.

"taught no dogmas but one": Joseph Bradley, "Esoteric Thoughts on Religion and Religionism," in *Miscellaneous Writings*, ed. Charles Bradley (Newark, N.J.: L. J. Hardhan, 1902), 431; "The organization of a community": *The Late Corporation of the Church of Jesus Christ of Latter-Day Saints v. United States*, 136 U.S. 1, 49 (1890); agreed to abide by the laws . . . returned its property: Leonard J. Arrington and David Bilton, *The Mormon Experience: A History of the Latter Day Saints* (New York: Vintage Books, 1979), 183.

early reformers for temperance: Norman H. Clark, *Deliver Us from Evil: An Interpretation of American Prohibition* (New York: W. W. Norton, 1976), 69–70; religious groups involved: 89; relation of Republican Party: 74; "individual Protestant churches as his basic organizational unit": 94. "The Protestant church in action": Andrew Sinclair, *Prohibition: The Era of Excess* (New York: Harper and Row, 1962), 65. "The church voters' list": Ernest Cherrington, *History of the Anti-Saloon League* (Westerville, Ohio: American Issue Publishing, 1913), 59. Saloons as centers for prostitution: Sinclair, *Prohibition*, 51.

"intoxicating liquors": U.S. Constitution, Eighteenth Amendment; "for sacramental purposes": National Prohibition Act, 41 Stat. 311 (1919).

"the black church coming alive": Rev. Joseph Lowery, quoted in Aldon D. Morris, *The Origins of the Civil Rights Movement* (New York: Free Press, 1984), 84–85.

"with Christian love": Lerone Bennett, Jr., *What Manner of Man: A Biography of Martin Luther King, Jr.* (Chicago: Johnson Publishing, 1968), 65; "What we are doing": 70; "Father, forgive them": 76; "God Almighty has spoken": 77. The significance of the last quotation is elaborated on by Michael Eric Dyson, "'God Almighty Has Spoken from Washington, D.C.': American Society and Christian Faith," *De Paul Law Review* 42 (1992): 129. The Supreme Court decision was *Owen v. Browder*, 352 U.S. 903 (1956). And for King, conscience was a trumpet: see Martin Luther King, Jr., *The Trumpet of Conscience* (New York: Harper and Brothers, 1967).

"most magnificent accomplishment": Bayard Ruskin, *Strategies for Freedom* (New York: Columbia University Press, 1976), 40. Officers and members of SCLC: Morris, *Civil Rights Movement*, 91–92; "direct action": 83; form of meeting: 97; imagery: 98; fundraising methods: 118; "The Crusade for Citizenship": 101–109.

"translated the message": Keith D. Miller, *Voice of Deliverance: The Language of Martin Luther King, Jr. and Its Sources* (New York: Free Press, 1992), 5, 11.

Crusade: see Ida B. Wells, *The Crusade for Justice*, ed. Alfreda M. Duster (Chicago: University of Chicago Press, 1970); King's biography: L. D. Reddick, *Crusader Without Violence* (New York: Harper and Brothers, 1959).

"Preacher, instead of preaching the Gospel": quoted in Morris, *Civil Rights Movement*, 105; "a systematic wholehearted battle against segregation": 251; the Birmingham demonstration: 250.

"just as the apostle Paul left his village": Martin Luther King, *Letter from Birmingham Jail* (Andover, Mass.: n.p., 1968). Distribution of the letter: Morris, 266; "music, religious oratory": 251; 758 demonstrations, 14,733 persons arrested: 274.

David Hume: see chapter 3.

"I come to send fire": Luke 12:49–52.

Once there were sixteen denominations: Roger Finke and Rodney Stark, *The Churching of America, 1776–1990* (New Brunswick, N.J.: Rutgers University Press, 1992), 25. They were Congregational, Presbyterian, Baptist, Episcopal, Quaker, German Reformed, Lutheran, Dutch Reformed, Catholic, Moravian, Separatist and Independent, Dunker, Mennonite, Huguenot, Sandemanian, and Jewish. For today's denominations, see Frank S. Mead, *Hand-*

book of Denominations in the United States, rev. Samuel S. Hill (Nashville: Abingdon Press, 1990). Number of new religions: see J. Gordon Melton, *The Encyclopedia of American Religions* (Detroit: Gale Research, 1989), xv.

Between 1791 and 1991: see Roger Finke and Rodney Stark, *The Churching,* 15–16. The authors acknowledge that their estimate of 17 percent churched Americans for 1776 is far smaller than that made by Patricia V. Bononi and Peter R. Eisenstadt, "Church Adherence in the Eighteenth-century British American Colonies," *William and Mary Quarterly* 39 (April 1982): 245. Finke and Stark are, however, persuasive in their criticism of Bononi and Eisenstadt. If we concede the necessity of guessing, and double Finke and Stark's percentage to 34 percent, the growth in percentage terms is striking.

the active monitor: see United States Department of State, Bureau of Democracy, Human Rights and Labor Affairs, "United States Policies in Support of Religious Freedom: Focus on Christians," July 22, 1997. In her Foreword to this document, Secretary of State Madeleine K. Albright declares: "freedom of religion is central to American history and identity" and is "basic to the life of every human being."

CHAPTER 10

Le Comité chargé: Champion de Cicé to Jefferson, July 20, 1789, *The Papers of Thomas Jefferson,* ed. Julian P. Boyd (Princeton: Princeton University Press, 1958), 15:291. Spelling is different from twentieth-century French.

Je sens toute ma malheur: Jefferson to Champion de Cicé, July 22, 1989, ibid., 298.

a slight contretemps when the great orator Mirabeau: editorial note, "The Mirabeau Incident," ibid., 15:243–256.

"A Charter of Rights": Jefferson to Lafayette, June 3, 1789, ibid., 15:165–166; Jefferson to Rabaut Saint-Etienne, June 3, 1789, 166–167. On Lafayette as a Mason, see Simon Schama, *Citizens: A Chronicle of the French Revolution* (New York: Knopf, 1989), 29; on Rabaut Saint-Etienne's religion, 569.

"Nature has made man free and equal": Jefferson, "Lafayette's Draft of a Declaration of Rights," in *Papers,* 15:230–231; Jefferson's annotations: Lafayette to Jefferson, July 6, 1789; "Be pleased to Consider": Lafayette to Jefferson, July 8, 1789.

expressed "eternal truths": Lafayette to the National Assembly, July 11, 1789, *Archives parlementaires,* 8:221, quoted in ibid., 15:231.

Lafayette . . . worshiper of Washington: Schama, *Citizens,* 28–29; Lafayette's role and age: 449.

"to Coalize": Lafayette to Jefferson, August 25, 1789, Jefferson, *Papers,* 15:354; "a neutral and passive spectator": Jefferson, *Autobiography,* quoted in ibid., 355; "and wine set on the table": ibid.

"It is impossible to desire better": Jefferson to Madison, August 28, 1789, ibid., 15:366; "the king, the mass": ibid.

"No one ought to be": *Déclaration des droits de l'homme et du citoyen*, Antonin Debidour, *Histoire des rapports de l'église et de l'état en France de 1789 à 1870* (Paris, 1911), 37–38.

public execution . . . of Lefebvre [chevalier de la Barre]: see René Pomeau, *Voltaire en son temps: "Ecraser l'infâme"* (Oxford: Voltaire Foundation, 1994), 293–305.

proposed the nationalization: Schama, *Citizens*, 482.

"all ecclesiastical goods": decree of November 2, 1789, Debidour, *Histoire*, 652–653; suppression of orders: decree of February 13, 653; the Civil Constitution of the Clergy: 653–663.

"ecclesiastical police": Mirabeau quoted in Schama, *Citizens*, 539; "the beginning of a holy war": 491.

l'erreur capitale: Debidour, *Histoire*, 68; drafters of the Civil Constitution: 64; the Jansenists' revenge: 68.

the Fête de la Fédération: ibid., 75–76; Schama, *Citizens*, 509–511.

great majority of French bishops: Debidour, *Histoire*, 80; the oath: 81; condemnation by Pius VI: 88.

le plus mortel ennemi: ibid., 90; the symbolic sense and the cause and effect relation of Voltaire to the Revolution: René Pomeau, *Voltaire en son temps: On a voulu l'enterrer* (Oxford: Voltaire Foundation, 1994), 350–351.

"des fêtes nationales": title 1, Constitution of September 3, 1791, *Les Constitutions et les principales lois politiques de la France depuis 1789*, ed. Léon Duguit and Henri Monnier (Paris, 1980), 5; "the freedom of every man": 4; incorporation of the Declaration: 1.

"The Tennis Court Oath": Schama, *Citizens*, 570–572.

10 percent of the male minority: ibid., 581; religious composition of Assembly: Debidour, *Histoire*, 96; emigration of bishops: 97; opposition of curés: 101; *suspects de révolte*: 101; excommunication by Pius VI: 107; measures of the Assembly in April and May 1792: 105 and 107; revolts: 111.

nineteen priests: Schama, *Citizens*, 633–634.

the National Convention . . . majority of its members: Debidour, *Histoire*, 112–113. The Jansenists' role in defending the Civil Constitution: Dale Van Kley, *The Religious Origins of the French Revolution* (New Haven: Yale University Press, 1996), 352. The electorate: Schama, *Citizens*, 646. Motion to stop salaries: Debidour, *Histoire*, 113–114; marriage blessing: 119; the oath extended: 117; "the dry guillotine": 117, 175; the offense of *incivisme*: 119.

"the holiest and most just": quoted in Schama, *Citizens*, 705.

soit directment: Debidour, *Histoire*, 121.

discarded that most potent of Christian reminders: Schama, *Citizens*, 771–772. New festivals and heroes for the schools: Debidour, *Histoire*, 125.

In the provincial cities, the commissioners (*représentants en mission*): Debidour, *Histoire*, 126; Fouché's order, 126–127 n.1. "The blood of kings": Schama, *Citizens*, 779.

constitutional archbishop and thirteen: Debidour, 128; fête at Notre Dame:

Schama, *Citizens*, 778. Temple of Reason, churches *désaffectées*, more resignations, scenes in the provinces, *deisme irrité*: Debidour, *Histoire*, 129; estimate of marriages of priests: ibid., n.1.

Throughout the country altars: François Souchal, *Le Vandalisme de la Révolution* (1993), 31–148; reliquaries, etc.: 40; statues: 40–41, 59, 62; churches: 39 and 283; cathedrals: 59–73; Cluny: 81; Clairvaux: 88; "one of the great cataclysms": 284.

Eighteen centuries of error: Debidour, *Histoire*, 130; an "angry, aggressive deism": ibid.

How many priests were killed: Donald Greer, *The Incidence of the Terror During the French Revolution* (Cambridge, Mass.: Harvard University Press, 1937), 106; priests killed without trial or as result of prison conditions: see 37, where the number of total victims dead "as a consequence of the terror" is put at twice the number executed after trial. Priests forced to leave: Donald Greer, *The Incidence of the Emigrations during the French Revolution* (Cambridge, Mass.: Harvard University Press, 1951), 83 (26,560 banished; 5,440 emigrated). Nuns killed: Greer, *Incidence of the Terror*, 96.

"vertical deportation": Schama, *Citizens*, 789.

the Carmelites: Francis Poulenc's opera *Dialogues des carmélites* (1957).

The Vendée . . . hideous massacres: Schama, *Citizens*, 791–792; Souchal, *Vandalisme*, 281–284.

"The French are not a people who": Schama, *Citizens*, 443, quoting the comte de La Blache.

None of these real factors explains: see François Furet, "Terreur," *Dictionnaire critique de la Révolution française*, ed. F. Furet and M. Ozouf (1988), 167; creation of a new order: 168; see Greer, *Incidence of the Terror*, 126.

"launch a crusade": René Pomeau and Christiane Mervaud, *Voltaire en son temps: De la cour au jardin* (Oxford: Voltaire Foundation, 1991), 338; Voltaire and Calvinism: ibid. *Ecraser l'infâme*: a phrase "inseparable from the name of Voltaire," first documented in writing as used by Frederick II of Prussia writing Voltaire on May 2, 1769, and probably a term first broached in conversation between Voltaire and the Prussian monarch. See Pomeau, *Ecraser l'infâme*, 5–8; "a horde of Arabs": see 215.

Christianity and a republic are incompatible: "Mais je me trompe en disant une république chrétienne; chacun de ces deux mots exclut l'autre." Jean-Jacques Rousseau, "De la religion civile," in *Du contrat social*, ed. Georges Liébert (1978), 364.

Voltaire . . . the Incarnation: Pomeau, *On a voulu*, 173.

"The French people and its representatives": resolution of the National Convention, December 2, 1793, quoted in Debidour, *Histoire*, 133.

une religion purement civile: ibid., 139; executions: 160; *Théophilanthropes*: 179 n.3; capture of Pius: 175–176.

"France, educated": Napoleon, speech to the clergy of Milan, June 5, 1800, quoted in ibid., 192–193.

les partisans les plus sincères: Anne Louise-Germaine Necker, baronesse de Staël,

Considérations sur les principaux événements de la Révolution française (1818), quoted in Debidour, *Histoire*, 185 (a contemporary English version of this posthumous work edited by the writer's husband and the duc de Broglie is *Considerations on The Principal Events of the French Revolution* [1818], 1:30).

gendarmerie sacrée: Debidour, *Histoire*, 184; Pius VII and Napoleon: 190–197.

"Le gouvernment de la République française": Concordat, ibid., 681; "to the prejudice of the State": ibid.

instructed the bishops to celebrate each August 15: André Latreille, *Le Catéchisme impérial de 1806* (1935), 62.

"Organic Articles": Debidour, *Histoire*, 221–223; Art. 39: 686.

"What are the duties": *Catéchisme à l'usage de toutes les églises de l'empire français* (1806), text as to Napoleon quoted in Latreille, *Catéchisme*, 80–81. The catechism of Bossuet had noted that the Fourth Commandment required respect for "all superiors, pastors, kings, magistrates, and others," 80. There was no pointed personal celebration of the reigning monarch.

"To the dogmatic union": Jean-Michel Leniaud, *L'Administration des cultes pendant la période concordataire* (Paris, 1988), 17; "attached to the public service": 27; laws defining the *cultes*: 9.

"a madness like that of a government": Charles Dumay in conversation with Louis Méjan, in L. V. Méjan, *La Séparation des églises et de l'état* (Paris, 1959), 49. French foreign policy and the concordat: 3.

deliramentum: Gregory XVI, *Mirari vos*, August 15, 1832, *Acta Gregorii Papae XVI* (1901), ed. A. M. Bernasconi (1971), 1:172. On Lamennais, see also chapters 1 and 13.

"I want my principle to be believed": Alexandre Vinet, *Essai sur la manifestation des convictions religieuses et sur la séparation de l'église et de l'état, envisagée comme conséquence nécessaire et comme guarantie du principe* (1842), 482; quotation of Tocqueville: 479–482, 484; mention of Julius and of Reed and Matheson: 484–485.

AMERICA WILL BE GREAT, IF AMERICA IS GOOD: Andrew Reed and James Matheson, *A Narrative of the Visit to the American churches by the Deputation for the Congregational Union of England and Scotland* (1835), 2, 197 (capitalization in original); influence of Vinet: Méjan, *Séparation*, 201.

"the bishops, priests, nuns": Louis Méjan, quoted in Méjan, *Séparation*, 440.

"Our priests": "nos prêtres ne sont pas ce qu'un vain peuple pense, / notre crédulité fait toute leur science." Voltaire, *Oedipe*, 4.1.58–59 (1719), in *Oeuvres complètes*, vol. 2 (Paris: Garnier, 1877).

"Mock on, Mock on": William Blake, "Poems and Fragments," in *The Complete Poetry and Selected Prose of John Donne & The Complete Poetry of William Blake*, ed. Geoffrey Keynes (New York: Random House, 1941), 586.

clerical press . . . Dreyfus: Méjan, *Séparation*, 487. Jean Denis Bredin, *L'Affaire* (Paris: Julliard, 1983), 269–272; Jean-Marie Mayeur, "Les catholiques français," in *L'Affaire Dreyfus de A à Z*, ed. Michel Drouin (Paris: Flammarion, 1994), 333–338.

Combes . . . a Spiritualist: Jean-Marie Mayeur, *La Séparation des églises et de l'état* (Paris, 1991), 18; *la loi Combes*: 17–19.

The legislative report: Aristide Briand, *La Séparation des églises et de l'état: Rapport fait au nom de la commission de la chambre des Députés* (Paris, 1905).

"Child-stealers": Alfred Loisy, *Choses passées* (1913), 19.

"The time must come": Brisson, quoted in Méjan, *Séparation*, 15–16.

"The Republic assures freedom of conscience": Briand, *Séparation*, 353.

"The English by their traditions": Benoist, discourse to the Chamber of Deputies, April 11, 1905, quoted in Méjan, *Séparation*, 160; "a guardian": 531; split position of the bishops: 285–286; the "green cardinals": 274–275.

the system employed in the United States: Ferdinand Brunetière, "Quand la séparation sera votée," *Revue des Deux Mondes*, December 1, 1906, 695–696.

"synthesis of all the heresies": Pius X, *Pascendi domenici gregis*, September 8, 1907, *Acta sanctae sedis* (Rome: Vatican Polyglot Press, 1907), 40:632.

"a great and pernicious": Pius X, *Vehementer nos*, February 11, 1906, *Acta sanctae sedis*, 39:6. Sacrilege to separate: Pius X, *Gravissimi*, August 10, 1906, *Acta sanctae sedis*, 39:385–390; see also Méjan, *Séparation*, 316.

"odious slavery": Briand, quoted in Méjan, *Séparation*, 515; his naturally religious temperament: Louis Méjan in ibid., 516.

"an inadmissible neologism": Louis Méjan quoted in ibid., 281; the bishops' rejection: Mayeur, *Séparation*, 137–140.

nearly 400 million francs' worth of foundations: ibid., 455–456.

inventory . . . a few deaths followed: ibid., 91–119; "the Dreyfusard revolution": Gabriel Le Bras, preface to Méjan, *Séparation*, viii.

the clerical enemy smashed: Mayeur, *Séparation*, 153.

Led by Cardinal James Gibbons, the American bishops: Claude Fohlen, "American Catholics and the Separation of Church and State in France," *Catholic Historical Review* 80 (1994): 741–756.

canonized Jeanne d'Arc: Benedict XV, *Acta apostolicae sedis* (Rome: Vatican Polyglot Press, 1920), 12:514–528 (May 9, 1920); the concordat . . . govern the eastern provinces: Mayeur, *Séparation*, 161; the state's contributions to repairs: Méjan, *Séparation*, 513; partial restoration of funds: 512.

Louis Méjan, Briand's counselor . . . read: Méjan, *Séparation*, 2–24, 208; his ideas on reform: 519.

CHAPTER 11

"not merely in numbers": C. R. Boxer, *The Christian Century in Japan 1549–1650* (Berkeley: University of California Press, 1951), 321; for statistics see Jesuit mission reports of 1612 and 1614 (320–322); the number of churches is an extrapolation.

fire or water or earth: imprisonment in filth: ibid., 348; water torture, 351; pit suspension, 353; crucifixion in ocean, 494. Immurement in bags: George Elison, *Deus Destroyed* (Cambridge, Mass.: Council on East Asian Studies, Harvard University, 1988), 216–217; death at stake: 188. Five to six thousand martyrs: Boxer, *Christian*, 361. Apostasy by *fumie*-trampling: Elison, *Destroyed*, 204; enrollment of ex-Christians: 205. Enrollment of everyone with Buddhists: Boxer, *Christian*, 318–319.

"Japan is the Land of the kami": decree of Hideoyoshi quoted in Elison, *Destroyed*, 115; "the country of the kami": see Boxer, *Christian*, 138 (Boxer uses "Gods" rather than kami).

Deus Destroyed: by Fabian Fucon (1642), translated by Elison and reprinted in *Destroyed*, 257–292; office of the inquisitor: 195.

Interview with Colonel J. P. McCaughan: a cento based on the sources cited.

"Freedom of worship": State-War-Navy Coordinating Committee, "United States Initial Post-Surrender-Policy for Japan," September 6, 1985, as excerpted by William Bunce for the Chief of Civil Information and Education; reprinted in William P. Woodard, *The Allied Occupation of Japan 1945–1952 and Japanese Religions* (Leiden: Brill, 1972), 285; organization of SCAP: 22–23. Freedom of religion "shall be established": the Potsdam Declaration, July 26, 1945, reprinted on 286 (as excerpted by Bunce).

"for centuries": Douglas MacArthur, quoted by Courtney Whitney, *MacArthur: His Rendezvous with History* (New York: Alfred A. Knopf, 1956), 273; "it was the collapse of a faith" and "a practicing Christian": 274; distribution of Bibles: 275.

We knew almost nothing about it: see Woodard, *Allied Occupation*, 285–286.

"set the tone of crusade": Whitney, *His Rendezvous*, 243; "to expedite the establishment": 23.

headed by Bill Bunce: see Helen Hardacre, *Shintô and the State, 1868–1988* (Princeton: University of Princeton Press, 1989), 187 n.8.

"Japanese subjects are, within limits": "Constitution of the Empire of Japan [the Meiji constitution]," in *The Japanese Legal System*, ed. Hideo Tanaka (Tokyo: University of Tokyo Press, 1976), 19. Limited meaning of freedom of belief: Hardacre, *Shintô*, 119; suppressions of new religions: 126–127; "maddeningly vague": 5; the early cults of kami and Shintô: 5, 9–11. The Religious Organization Law of 1940 and subsequent persecutions: David M. O'Brien with Yasuo Ohkoshi, *To Dream of Dreams: Religious Freedom and Constitutional Politics in Postwar Japan* (Honolulu: University of Hawaii Press, 1996), 45–46.

"the way of the kami": see Robert N. Bellah, *Tokugawa Religion* (Glencoe, Ill.: Free Press, 1957), 227 (Bellah uses "gods" rather than kami).

Meiji restoration made a kind of integration: Hardacre, *Shintô*, 28–32; "the nation's rites and creed": 33.

"The Emperor is sacred and inviolate": "Constitution of the Empire," 18. "The Emperor is Heaven-descended": official commentary, quoted in Woodard, *Allied Occupation*, 250. "Loyalty and filial piety": Hardacre, *Shintô*, 121–122; treatment of the rescript: 108–109.

a board game ... enshrinement at Yasukuni: Hardacre, *Shintô*, 91; number of souls deified at Yasukuni: 25.

"Shintôism as a state religion": John Carter Vincent, chairman of the State-

War-Navy Coordinating Committee, broadcast from Washington D.C., October 1, 1945, in Woodard, *Allied Occupation*, 54–55.

the Shintô Directive: ibid., 26, 62–65; "sponsorship, support": (English text, 293–299); "to separate religion from the state": 297; compliance with the Shintô Directive: 69–71.

"the false conception": Imperial Rescript, January 1, 1946, translated in Kyoko Inoue, *MacArthur's Japanese Constitution: A Linguistic and Cultural Study of Its Making* (Chicago: University of Chicago Press, 1991), 125; a hint: see 124–125; the religious structure ended: 126. In 1977 the Emperor Hirohito publicly denied that he had renounced being a manifest deity and had proclaimed his human character. O'Brien, *To Dream of Dreams*, 64. In 1990 the state paid for the religious rites attending the enthronement of the Emperor Akihito. *Id.* 206.

The General had told the Japanese government: on October 9, 1945—see John M. Maki, trans. and ed., *Japan's Commission on the Constitution: The Final Report* (Seattle: University of Washington Press, 1980), 67.

draft—we learned about on February 1, 1946: Inoue, *MacArthur's*, 12; drafting by Americans: 16. Lincoln's Birthday deadline: Whitney, *His Rendezvous*, 250. Reason for speed: Maki, *Final Report*, 71–72, 78. Washington's Birthday deadline: Whitney, *His Rendezvous*, 253.

What did Whitney say: Maki, *Final Report*, 76 (discussing debated evidence as to Whitney's reference to the emperor). "Atomic sunshine": Whitney, *His Rendezvous*, 251; threat of general election and risk to emperor: Charles L. Kades, Milo E. Russell, Alfred R. Hussey [officers with General Whitney], "Record of Events on 13 February 1946 When Proposed New Constitution for Japan Was Submitted to the Foreign Minister Mr. Yoshida, in Behalf of the Supreme Commander," text in Tanaka, 676–680.

adopt this new constitution as an amendment: Tanaka, 664.

everybody inside the Japanese government: Maki, *Final Report*, 79; discussion of the draft by candidates: 79–80.

the 1935 constitution of the Philippines: Woodard, *Allied Occupation*, 78.

"sectarian institution": the Jones Act, *United States Statutes* 39:545 (August 29, 1916); the Philippine constitution on financial support of sectarian institution: Constitution of the Philippines, Article VI, sec. 12, Jose M. Aruego, *The Framing of the Philippine Constitution* (Manila: University Publishing, 1936–1937), 2:530.

language doesn't really have our mandatory "shall": Inoue, *MacArthur's*, 83–84; see 98–100 on "the topic-comment construction" that begins a sentence "As for——"; translation of Article 89: 144.

questions from the Religious League: ibid., 145–146.

question or two about Article 20: ibid., 104.

"one can believe in anything": Yasuji Yûku, quoted in ibid., 133; "had long been controversial": Tokiyirô Kanamori, quoted on 137.

"If we say shrines": Narimitsu Matsudaira, quoted in ibid., 139; "religion is the foundation of democracy": Gisen Satô, quoted on 149; "The issue of morality": Kanamori, quoted on 158; length of deliberations: 32–35; religion just wasn't that big a deal: 104.

"This provision is unreasonable": Maki, *Final Report*, 333.

transplant of legal systems: see Alan Watson, *The Evolution of Law* (Baltimore: Johns Hopkins University Press, 1985), 66–76.

"the fruits of the age-old struggle": Article 97, "Constitution of the Empire," *The Japanese Legal System*, 14.

Case of the Purification Ceremony of Tsu: *Kakinaga v. Sekiguchi*, 855 Hanrei Jihô 24 (Sup. Ct., G.B., July 13, 1977): the summary of this case and translations from the judgments of the Japanese courts were done by Peter Stern. A German summary and translation of the judgments is in Ernst Lokowandi, *Zum Verhältnis von Staat und Shintô im Heutigen Japan* (Wiesbaden: Harrassowits, 1981), 89–151. The case and its critics are described in detail in O'Brien, *To Dreama of Dreams*, 84–88, 91–92, 94–97. O'Brien's very helpful book also contains an account of several lower court cases on freedom or establishment that did not reach the Supreme Court of Japan.

"Give Me Back My Husband": English translation of a Japanese account of the case by Nobusama Tanaka (Tokyo, 1988), summarized in Norma Field, *In the Realm of a Dying Emperor* (New York: Pantheon Books, 1991), 109–146; Nakaya's death and funeral: 129–130, 190; Veterans' Association employee: 144; Self-Defense Force's interest in enshrinement: 145; number deified at shrine: 148; enshrinement ritual: 149–150; "watch over the supplications": shrine pamphlet quoted on 149. The case and its implications are described in depth in O'Brien, *To Dream of Dreams*, 142–203.

Yasuko, the widow, pondered: see biography, ibid., 132–137; the example of Mrs. Watanabe: 124–125; Hayashi biography: 130; decision not to sue the shrine: 138.

"engaging in religious feeling": *Nakaya v. Japan*, 921 Hanrei Jihô 44, 68 (Yamaguchi Dist. Ct. March 22, 1979).

Five bills to furnish government financial aid: Hardacre, *Shintô*, 146–147; controversy over tribute at the shrine: 148–150; rites performed by Nakasone: Field, *In the Realm*, 139–140; reaction to rites: Hardacre, *Shintô*, 151.

Here the Supreme Court began . . . dissenter, Judge Masami Ito: *Nakaya v. Japan*, 912 Juristo 131 (1988). The case also involved an elaboration of the theme of the Grounds Purification Case, that a religious ceremony need not be religious activity by the state. The action of asking for apotheosis should be considered as only "indirectly" religious. The motive of the Self-Defense Force in seeking it was to raise its social status and improve its members' morale. The request for enshrinement neither aroused sympathy with a specific religion, nor encouraged any religion, nor interfered with any religion.

Judge Ito added, "In determining whether activity is 'religious,' it is appropriate to consider all the relevant circumstances. But under the current standard, which emphasizes the ordinary person's assessment of the religious character of a given activity and the effect and influence of that activity on the ordinary person (leaving aside cases such as the Grounds Purification Case, in which the court rules on the religious character of a type of secular activity), the possibility exists that, when the violation of an individual's religious interests is at stake, the majority may oppress the minority."

Yasuko Nakaya was deluged with hate mail: Field, *In the Realm*, 134–136.

The "religion of Japan . . . is Japaneseness": ibid., 147. The expression was popular in the 1970s. O'Brien, *To Dream of Dreams*, 17.

More steps in the evolution of free exercise: for those who like their cases in trilogies, a third decision of the Supreme Court of Japan rounds out the series.

The Memorial to the War Dead Case (*Kamisaka v. Nakai*, 815 Hanrei Taimuzu 104 [sup. ct., 3d p.b., February 16, 1993]). Again, I am indebted to Peter Stern for summary and translations. The case and implications are fully set out in O'Brien, *To Dream of Dreams*, 1–6, 11–16, 104–109, 126–136.

In 1916 the local chapter of the Imperial War Veterans' Association erected a monument to its war dead. The site for the memorial was that of the village town hall, adjacent to an elementary school. The veterans had asked the city for this space and had been granted it at no charge and in perpetuity. The Veterans' Association maintained the site and held memorial services there.

Following World War II, under the influence of the Shintô Directive, the Japanese government adopted a policy of removing war memorials from public schools, public buildings, and public spaces. In 1947 members of the Veterans' Association dismantled the memorial and buried its stones at a nearby location. In 1951 the stones were dug up and the memorial rebuilt at its former location by an organization of war survivors called the Association of War-Bereaved Families. This association was devoted to the mutual support of its members and to the mourning of the war dead. The Association of War-Bereaved Families took care of the site, and from 1955 sponsored an annual memorial service, held in April, at which Shintô and Buddhist rites alternated from year to year.

As time passed, the elementary school next to the memorial developed a need for more space. It became clear that the school would have to take over the site occupied by the memorial, and the city entered into negotiations with the Association of War-Bereaved Families about what to do with the memorial. The association agreed to vacate the site—but only if the city found another location for the memorial. This the city did: in 1975 it purchased land from a city development corporation at a cost of 78,826,824 yen (about $788,200), paid an additional 7,042,120 yen (about $70,400) to have the memorial moved to the new location, and gave the association a free, perpetual lease on the site.

Residents of the city filed an "inhabitant's suit" (as in the Tsu case), alleging that city officials—the mayor and members of the board of education—had violated the separation of state and religion. Initially there were two suits. In the first suit, the plaintiffs alleged that the officials had acted unconstitutionally in (1) providing land for the new site, (2) moving the memorial at city expense, and (3) turning over the land *gratis* to the association. This suit asked for the city to be compensated for the monies spent on behalf of the memorial. In the second suit, the plaintiffs charged that the officials had unconstitutionally permitted city and school facilities and supplies to be used as part of the annual services, and had attended services while being paid by the state. The plaintiffs asked for damages.

In the first instance, both sets of plaintiffs won a partial victory; the parties appealed. The five-judge panel of the Supreme Court began by restating the doctrinal bases of the grounds purification and apotheosis cases. The constitutional provisions making up the separation of state and religion provide a "systemic," "indirect" guarantee of freedom of individual belief; the constitution does not prohibit all government involvement with religion, but only involvement that, seen in the context of Japanese society and culture, exceeds a level compatible with the systemic objective of freedom of belief. "Religious activity" for purposes of article 20, paragraph 3, is activity whose purpose has a religious meaning, and which has the effect of supporting, encouraging, or promoting religion, or of oppressing or interfering with religion. The court's determination must be an objective one, based on all the relevant circumstances.

Turning to the case at hand, the court considered three sets of facts in finding that the city had not violated article 20, paragraph 3. First, both the memorial structure—in its original form and as rebuilt—and the concomitant memorial services were meant to honor and commemorate local war dead. In the postwar period, at least, the memorial's connection to religion was slight. The structure was not a "village Yasukuni" or a Defense-of-the-Nation Shrine (815 Hanrei Taimuzu at 106–107).

Second, the Association of War-Bereaved Families that controlled and managed the memorial had been formed primarily to provide mutual support to its members and to honor the spirits of the war dead. The association's main objective was not religious (id. at 107).

Third, although the memorial had at one time been dismantled, it was rebuilt after the war on city land with the city's permission. The city moved the memorial solely to facilitate necessary expansion by the elementary school. In a sense, the city owed the association a duty; it "couldn't very well not move the memorial to another location." And the city did no more than restore the memorial to its original condition (id.).

On the whole, then, the city's actions were primarily of a secular nature. There had been no effect of supporting, encouraging, promoting, oppressing, or interfering with a particular religion, and thus no action incompatible with freedom of religion, and no constitutional violation.

The court then considered whether the Association of War-Bereaved Families was a "religious organization" under article 20, paragraph 1, or a "religious institution or association" under article 89. These phrases, according to the court, do not comprehend all organizations "engaged in activity connected to religion." Rather, the language of the constitution refers to organizations "whose essential purpose is to engage in the activity—the faith, worship, proselytizing, etc.—of a particular religion." The Association of War-Bereaved Families was not such a group. Although the association participated in a broad range of activities, including some "tinged with" religion, such as encouraging worship at Yasukuni Shrine, its main objectives were the mutual support of its members and the honoring of local war dead. It had committed no constitutional violation.

Finally, the court examined the participation of city officials in the services held at the memorial. The involvement of the officials consisted primarily of placing a sprig of *sakaki* on the memorial's altar. The court concluded that participation in the ceremony—the expressing of sympathy for the war dead and their families—was a "social convention" incumbent on high public officials (108). Once again, in view of the memorial's function as a place of mourning and commemoration, the purpose of the service was primarily secular. The officials' participation in the services did not violate the constitution.

donations of public money: *Ehime Shrine Offering Case,* 1601 *Hanrei Jihō* 52 (1997). For a news report, see *Los Angeles Times,* April 3, 1997, Part A, p. 8.

CHAPTER 12

64 dioceses in Russia and 4 missionary dioceses: statistics in S. V. Troitsky, "Russian Church," *Encyclopedia of Religion and Ethics,* ed. James Hastings (New York: Scribner's, 1918), 10:875. The official statistics are scarcely reliably precise. The number of Old Believers in 1904, for example, is estimated to be 2 million or 20 million, "who knows." Gerd Stricker, "Old Believers in the Territory of the Russian Empire," *Religion in Communist Lands* 18 (1990): 31. The Church's history: E. H. Minns, "Russian Church," *Encyclopedia of Religion and Ethics*, ed. James Hastings (New York: Scribner's, 1918), 10:867–875. Statistics on the Catholics: Paul Mailleux, "Catholics in the Soviet Union," in *Aspects of Religion in the Soviet Union 1917–1967*, ed. Richard M. Marshall, Jr. (Chicago: University of Chicago Press, 1971), 364; on the Mennonites, Frank E. Epp, "Mennonites in the Soviet Union," in ibid., 285. For a convenient overview, see Harold J. Berman, "Religious Freedom and the Rights of Foreign Missionaries Under Russian Law," *The Parker School Journal of East European Law* 2 (1951): 423.

introduction of limited freedom for various other religions: Frederick C. Conybeare, *Russian Dissenters* (Cambridge, Mass.: Harvard University Press, 1921), 235–238; Robert Sloan Latimer, *Under Three Tsars: Liberty of Conscience in Russia 1851–1909* (New York: F. H. Revell, 1909), 39–100; Berman, "Religious Freedom," 423; and the Jews: Richard Pipes, *The Russian Revolution* (New York: Knopf, 1990), 89. On the unique mission of Russia in Slavophile literature, often maintained at the expense of the Jews, see Rowan Williams, "The Need for a Christian Critique of National Messianism," *Religion, State, and Society* 20 (1992): 57–59.

"the cornerstone of Russian national ideology": Serge A. Zenkovsky, *Medieval Russia's Epics, Chronicles, and Tales* (New York: E. P. Dutton & Co., 1963), 265.

John W. Foster . . . protested the application: see Foster to Secretary of State William Maxwell Evarts, October 20, 1880, *Papers relating to the Foreign Relations of the United States transmitted to Congress with the annual message of the President, December 5, 1881* (Washington, D.C.: Government Printing Office, 1882), 990–991 and subsequent correspondence, 991–1037. The Russian police stamp on Wilczynski's passport was peremptory: "The bearer of this passport, a North American citizen, a merchant and a Jew, Marx Wilczynski, is forbidden to reside in St. Petersburg"(990). Foster's actions were approved by Evarts and by Acting Secretary of State John Hay (993) and continued in 1881 at the direction of the new secretary of state, James G. Blaine (1012–1037). On July 29, 1881, Blaine instructed Foster to convey to Russian Foreign Minister De Giers the opinion of President Chester Arthur that the treaty of 1832 secured "to American citizens in Russia the treatment which Russians receive in the United States" and, if it did not do so in the Russian view, then "these stipulations should be made sufficient in these regards" and "in the direction of" (1035–1036).

"recent publications": Charles Emory Smith to Secretary of State Blaine, February 10, 1891. *Papers relating to the Foreign Relations of the United States, transmitted to Congress with the annual message of the President, December 9, 1891* (Washington. D.C.: Government Printing Office, 1892), 734; "proscriptive edicts": Blaine to Smith, February 18, 1891, 735; "Such a step": 738;

instruction to be read: 739; "This Government has found occasion": President Harrison to Congress, December 9, 1891, xii.

the *Vekhi* authors: Caryl Emerson, "'And the Demons Entered into the Swine' and The Russian Intelligentsia and Post-Soviet Religious Thought," *Cross-Currents* (summer 1993): 187.

The beauty of the liturgy had moved the Slavs: James Billington, "Christianity in the USSR," *Theology Today* 37 (1980): 202. "The world will be saved by beauty": Fyodor Dostoyevesky, *The Idiot*, trans. David Magarshack (New York: Penguin Books, 1955), pt. 3, sec. 5; "a prophecy": Aleksandr I. Solzhenitsyn, *The Nobel Lecture on Literature*, trans. Thomas P. Whitney (New York: Harper and Row, 1972), 7.

In the fall of 1917, in the midst: Nicholas Struve, *Christians in Contemporary Russia*, trans. Lancelot Sheppard and A. Manson (New York: Scribner, 1967), 21–26.

Almost simultaneously the Bolshevik coup: Joshua Rothenberg, "The Legal Status of Religion in the Soviet Union," in *Aspects*, 60–63; the Soviet theory of religion: Bohdan R. Bociurkiw, "Religion and Atheism in Soviet Society," in *Aspects*, 45–46; Billington, "Christianity," 200.

the believers—in Russian usage: Berman, "Religious Freedom," 427 (any theist) and 442 (a Russian Orthodox).

"a system of symbols": Clifford Geertz, *The Interpretation of Cultures* (New York: Basic Books, 1973), 90.

"Materialism . . . is the only-begotten son": Marx quoted in Reinhard Buchbinder, *Bibelparodien, theologische Vergleiche und Analogien bei Marx und Engels* (Berlin: E. Schmidt, 1976), 118; other examples: in ibid., 28–45; see also Jean-Yves Calvez, *La Pensée de Karl Marx* (Paris: Editions du Seuil, 1950), 594. "The leading and guiding force": Constitution of the Union of Soviet Socialist Republics, art. 6, reprinted in *Constitutions of the Countries of the World*, ed. Albert Blaustein (Dobbs Ferry, N.Y: Oceana Publications, 1989).

"the god that failed": see *The God That Failed*, ed. R. H. Crossman (New York: Harper, 1950); Communism as Christian heresy: Jacques Maritain, *The Person and the Common Good* (New York: Scribner's, 1947), 88.

a Durkheimian perspective: see chapter 8; critique of it: see chapter 9.

"national-religious privileges": Declaration of the Rights of the Peoples of Russia, in Rothenberg, "Legal Status," 62.

"The Church is separate": "On the Separation of the Church from the State and of the School from the State," January 23, 1918, *Aspects*, 437–438; all property" and "enjoy the rights": ibid. I follow Berman's translation of the title of the decree: Berman, "Religious Freedom," 425.

"To secure for the workingman": Rothenberg, "Legal Status," *Aspects*, 65; the 1936 constitution: *Aspects*, 437; "capitalists, merchants": Rothenberg, "Legal Status," 65.

antireligious propaganda: Joan Delaney, "The Origins of Soviet Antireligious Organizations," *Aspects*, 105–111; "antireligious agitators": 113; Bibles: Struve, *Christians*, 292.

On Religious Associations: translation in *Aspects*, 438–445; abolition of Sunday: Rothenberg, "Legal Status," ibid., 81.

Apart from the dispositions made by law, the Communists: Struve, *Christians*, 34–43, Mailleux, "Catholics," *Aspects*, 361–363; Georgian Orthodox Church: Elie Melia, "The Georgian Orthodox Church," *Aspects*, 229–231.

"the participation of non-Jews": Ziv Gitelman, "The Communist Party and Soviet Jewry: The Early Years," *Aspects*, 328.

The first ran from 1929 through 1932: Struve, *Christians*, 47–53.

"no one was safe": Nikita Khrushchev to the Twenty-second Party Congress (1961), quoted in ibid., 56; the list of martyred bishops: 393–398; the fate of the priests: 48, and see also Dimitry Konstantinow, *The Crown of Thorns: The Russian Orthodox Church in the USSR 1917–1967* (London, Ont.: Zaria, 1978), 17; the destruction of the Buryat way of life: *National Geographic* 181, 28 (June 1992).

Of the 57,000 Orthodox churches in existence: Konstantinow, *Crown*, 14; examples of destruction: Struve, *Christians*, 52.

"Are you a believer?": Billington, "Christianity," 205. The Russian sense of "believer": Berman, "Religious Freedom," 427.

"enjoy in all respects": Roosevelt to Litvinov, November 16, 1933, *The Public Papers and Addresses of Franklin D. Roosevelt* (New York: Random House, 1938), 2:476; "the fixed policy": Litvinov to President Roosevelt, November 16, 1933, 477. On the orchestration, see Harold Ickes, *The Secret Diary of Harold Ickes: The First Thousand Days* (New York: Simon and Schuster, 1953), 111, 113; on the business interest, see William Leuchtenberg, *Franklin D. Roosevelt and the New Deal 1932–1940* (New York: Harper and Row, 1963), 200–207.

"Our Orthodox Church": Sergius, quoted in Struve, *Christians*, 59.

The patriarchate was restored: ibid., 66–67, 88–89; the patriarchate and the state: 90–94 (and see Konstantinow, *Crown*, 22–26); infiltration: Walter Kolarz, *Religion in the Soviet Union* (New York: St. Martin's Press, 1961), 91.

"no unity": Konstantinow, *Crown*, 22.

restoration of religious rites in these regions: Struve, *Christians*, 77; other religious groups: Bociurkiw, "Religion and Atheism," *Aspects*, 55; Byzantine-rite Catholics: Mailleux, "Catholics," ibid., 369–375.

"survival of capitalism": Khrushchev to the Twenty-second Congress of the Communist Party, quoted in Donald A. Lowrie and William C. Fletcher, "Khrushchev's Religious Policy 1959–1966," *Aspects*, 133.

In 1959, the campaign began: ibid., 133–144; "long-cherished dream": *Nauka i religlia* (Science and religion) September 1964, quoted at 153; "Atheistic agitators": *Sputnik atheista*, quoted at 141.

propaganda was coordinated with negative sanctions: Struve, *Christians*, 317; Konstantinow, *Crown*, 263–267; Berman, "Religious Freedom," 426; forms of bureaucratic persecution: N. E. Eshliman and G. P. Yakunin to the chairman of the Supreme Soviet, N. V. Podgorny, December 13, 1965, translated in Struve, *Christians*, 404–417. The effect of one of the twenty believers dropping out: Rothenberg, "Legal Status," *Aspects*, 80. Surveillance of sacraments: Konstantinow, *Crown*, 254–258; controls on children's religious upbringing: 262–263; see also Lowrie and Fletcher, "Khrushchev's Religious Policy," *Aspects*, 134, 144–145.

The patriarchate, coopted by the government: Konstantinow, 254; Archbishop Ermogen's protest: Alexander A. Bogolepov, "The Legal Position of the Russian Orthodox Church in the Soviet Union," *Aspects*, 219–220; Eshliman and Yakunin's letter: 219–221; and see also Struve, *Christians*, 404–417.

Meanwhile, Yakunin formed a committee: in October 1994 Gleb Yakunin spoke at Princeton, New Jersey, under the auspices of CREED, an organization devoted to the Christian renewal effort in emerging democracies. I was present, learned these biographical details orally, and saw and spoke to this man who had the moral fervor of a Theodore Parker and the spiritual composure of a saint.

"most ruthless of all": Aleksandr Solzhenitsyn, "Misconceptions about Russia Are a Threat to America," *Foreign Affairs* 58 (1980): 815.

"surely the most massive": Berman, "Religious Freedom," 424–425; 40 percent guessed to be believers: 427.

"Our country is going through": Gorbachev to the General Assembly of the United Nations on December 7, 1985, *New York Times*, December 8, 1988, A16.

That was not the Soviet standard: W. Cole Durham, Jr., Lauren B. Homer, Pieter van Dijk, and John Witte, Jr., "The Future of Religious Liberty in Russia," *Emory International Law Review* 8 (1994): 13; the Declaration of the Elimination: 17–18; the Concluding Document: 20–22. The old Soviet position on treaties: Ger P. Van Den Berg, "Human Rights in the Legislation and the Draft Constitution of the Russian Federation," *Review of Central and East European Law* 18 (1992): 212–213.

The draft was sent for comment: Harold J. Berman, Erwin N. Griswold, and Frank C. Newman, "Draft USSR Law on Freedom of Conscience, with Commentary," *Harvard Human Rights Journal* 3 (1990): 137–156; reflection of critique in the law of Russia: Durham, "The Future," 4 n.5; Berman, "Religious Freedom," 432.

Declaration of Human Rights: Van Den Berg, "Human Rights," 197–198; "too American": 198 n.5.

supplied by a new Russian constitution: Constitution of the Russian Federation in *Constitutions of the Countries Of The World: The Russian Federation Supplement*, ed. Albert P. Blaustein and Gisbert H. Flanz (Dobbs Ferry, N.Y.: Oceana Publications, 1993). Freedom of conscience: Article 28. Equality of religions and separation from state: Article 14. Qualification on rights: Article 55.3, see Articles 29.2 and 13.5. "Man, his rights and freedoms": Article 2; "to freedom and personal inviolability": Article 22.1; "to freedom of thought": Article 29.1; "to association": Article 30; no restrictions on religious grounds: Article 19; "Everyone shall be guaranteed the right": Article 28. "Everyone shall be guaranteed protection": Article 46.1; "being aware of

ourselves": Preamble, clause 9. "In conformity with the international treaties":
Article 46.3.

The constitution was submitted to the electorate: Durham, 26.

"own history": statement of the conference held March 21–23, 1993, James E.
Wood, Jr., "The Battle Over Religious Freedom in Russia," *Journal of Church
and State* 35 (1993): 495. The conferees from American law schools were
Harold J. Berman (Emory); Albert P. Blaustein (Rutgers); Jesse H. Choper
(Berkeley); Robert A. Destro (Catholic University); W. Cole Durham, Jr.
(Brigham Young); and Edward M. Gaffney (Valparaiso).

"the difficult living conditions": Aleksii II to members of the Supreme Soviet, July
14, 1993, translated and quoted in Durham, "The Future," 9 n.10; examples
of what was objected to: 8. As of September 1, 1993 a total of 9,489 religious
associations were registered under the RSFSR Law. Of that number, the following religious denominations were most numerous: Russian Orthodox
Church (5,019); Old Believers (121); Russian Orthodox Free Church (64); Muslim (2,639); Roman Catholic (90); Buddhist (59); Jewish (48); Lutheran (86);
Evangelical Christian Baptist (49); Evangelical Christians (49); Pentecostal
(165); Seventh-day Adventist (130); Charismatic (73); Hare Krishna (68); Christian nondenominational associations (137). In addition there were 21
Methodist associations, 41 Presbyterian, 47 Jehovah's Witnesses, 3 Mormon,
and 1 Unification Church (Moon). The types of associations registered include
religious centers, congregations, monasteries, convents, religious educational
centers, nursing centers, and missions. Berman, "Religious Freedom," 432.

"their almost total disregard": Solzhenitsyn, 801.

"On behalf of the Russian Orthodox Church": quoted in Durham, "The Future,"
9 n.10. On "missionary activity": Law of the Russian Federation on Freedom
of Conscience and Religious Belief, (1993 draft), Article 21 (quoted in ibid.,
59); "contradict the standards": ibid.; "provided that the individual": Article 3 (48); "the traditional confessions": Article 8 (48). The religions intended
to be excluded: Berman, "Religious Freedom," 436.

President Clinton, Senator Richard Lugar, and: see Senator Richard G. Lugar to
President Boris M. Yeltsin, July 15, 1993 [copy in the author's files]; Yeltsin's
pocket veto and letter and the bill's reenactment: Berman, "Religious Freedom," 434; skirmishes of 1995: 438–440.

"contradicts" the Russian constitution: Yeltsin to the president of the State Duma,
G. N. Selenez, and president of the Federation Council, E. S. Stoer, July 23,
1997. *Radonezh* (August 12, 1997).

James Madison corrected by David Hume: see *supra*, ch. 3.

the new law repealed: *Emory International Law Review* 12 (to be published in
1998): "Russian Federation Federal Law: 'On Freedom of Conscience and on
Religious Associations'" (Lawrence A. Uzzell trans. 1997) (visited November
21, 1997), <http://www.law.emory.edu/E1LR/special/97law.html> art. 27.6.

Organizations were authorized: ibid., art. 16.1 (found religious buildings); 21
(own buildings); 4.3 (receive tax exemptions and receive government aid); 22
(use state property); 16.3 (conduct religious services in hospitals, etc.); 18.1

(charitable activities); 18.2 (organs of mass media); 19.1 (seminaries); 17.1 (religious literature); 23 (business undertakings); 5.3 and 4 (teach religion).

"existed on the given territory": ibid., arts. 9.1 and 11.5; required registration: 11.1; registering annually: 27.3, R. F. Law No. 125–F3, *Ross. Gazeta,* 10/1/97.

"the activity" . . . involved violation of current law: ibid., art. 12.1; liquidation on a variety of grounds: art. 14.1.

required to file: ibid., 11.4; "monitor" the observance: 25.2; the Procurator: 25.1.

"a representative" in Russia: ibid., art. 13.2; "Russia in its name": 8.5.

"be interpreted in such a way": ibid., art. 2.3; "on an equal footing": 3.2; "the establishment of privileges": 3.3.

the administration of the law: even before the passage of the statute, the collaboration of the Moscow patriarchate with the Ministry of the Interior in training officers of the ministry was critically noted: V. Polosin and G. Yakunin, "Federal Authorities and Freedom of Conscience," *Emory International Law Review* 12 (to be published in 1998). However, the supreme court of one of the constituent republics of the Russian Federation had held that the law of that republic restricting missionary activity violated the constitution of Russia. Decision, March 5, 1997 of the Supreme Court of Udmurt (Keston Institute trans. 1997) (visited November 21, 1997) <http://www.law.emory.edu/E1LR/special/97law.html>.

the rebuilding of the cathedral of Christ: see *Current Digest of the Post-Soviet Press,* October 12, 1994; laying of the cornerstone: *Moscow Times,* January 10, 1995. "Let the reconstruction": address of Mayor Luzhkov, quoted in ibid.; estimates of cost $100 million: *London Sunday Times,* September 11, 1994; $300 million: *Moscow Times,* January 10, 1995; assailed by independents: Polosin and Yakunin, "Federal Authorities."

The decay of Communism was seen: see Harold J. Berman, "The Challenge of Christianity and Democracy in the Soviet Union," in *Christianity and Democracy in Global Context,* ed. John Witte, Jr. (Boulder, Colo.: Westview Press, 1993), 293–294.

"On January 7th": "We Must Believe in Russia and Then We Will Live!" *Rossiyskaya Gazeta,* January 10, 1996, 1, translated by Jeff Trexler.

"the power of prayer": Berman, "Religious Freedom," 446. A division of opinion among American consultants and commentators on religious liberty in Russia centered on whether the Russian Orthodox Church should have special recognition of its historical identification with the culture and spirituality of Russia. I observed this division at a conference on religious human rights, held at Emory University, Atlanta, October 6–9, 1994, attended by Russians involved in the legislative drafting and American legal experts.

CHAPTER 13

A condition of American religious variety . . . space: see Sidney Mead, *The Lively Experiment: The Shaping of Christianity in America* (New York: Harper and Row, 1963), 11.

The debate over religious freedom: Donald E. Pelotte, *John Courtney Murray: Theologian in Conflict* (New York: Paulist Press, 1976), 13–16, 34–46; Ottaviani's address of March 2, 1953, "Church and State: Some Present Problems in the Light of Teachings of Pope Pius XII," was published in shortened form in the *American Ecclesiastical Review* (hereafter *AER*) 128 (May 1953): 321–334; Pius XII's address to the Italian jurists, *Ci riesci*, December 6, 1953, *Acta apostolicae sedis* (Rome: Vatican Polyglot Press, 1953), 45:794–802. Robert Leiber's advice: Murray's notes, quoted by Pelotte, *Murray*, 47; Murray's challenge to Ottaviani: in ibid., 46–47. "Careful, honest, and competent": Joseph C. Fenton, "Toleration and the Church-State Controversy," *AER* 130 (May 1954): 341. Murray's "offensive" lecture, Francis Spellman to Alfredo Ottaviani, April 5, 1954, quoted in Pelotte, *Murray*, 47; Murray's apology: Murray to Vincent McCormick, August 18, 1954, quoted at 49; nervousness at Jesuit headquarters: McCormick to Murray, November 15, 1953, quoted at 39; Jesuit censor's refusal of approval and "It seems to me a mistake": McCormick to Murray, July 9, 1955, quoted at 52; "delicate way of saying": Murray to McCormick, July 15, 1955, and "You are far from through, I hope": McCormick to Murray, July 21, 1955, and "It was kind of you": Murray to McCormick, August 3, 1955, all quoted at 53.

Twice again he tried: see J. Leon Hooper, *The Ethics of Discourse: The Social Philosophy of John Courtney Murray* (Washington, D.C.: Georgetown University Press, 1986), 126.

"controversies have arisen": Richard J. Cushing to Amleto Cicognani, secretary of state, August 3, 1959, *Acta et Documenta Concilii Oecumenici Vaticani II Apparando*, series 1, *Antepraeparatum*, vol. 2, *Consilia et Vota Episcorporum et Praelatorum* (Vatican City: Vatican Polyglot Press, 1960), pt. 6, 379; "less aptly expounded": Jean Janssens to Cicognani, August 25, 1959, pt. 8, 125.

The first drafting session for a new declaration: Jérôme Hamer, "Histoire du texte de la déclaration," in *La Liberté religieuse, déclaration "Dignitatis humanae personae,"* ed. J. Hamer and Y. Congar (Paris: Editions du Cerf, 1967), 53; content of the first draft: 55–56.

a brief recall of the recent European past: Pietro Pavan, *Libertà religiosa e pubblici poteri* (Milan: Ancora, 1965), 13–151.

"this fundamental fact": Pius XI, *Mit brennender Sorge*, March 14, 1937, *Acta apostolicae sedis* (1937), 29:159; "denigrates and denies": Pius XI, *Divini Redemptoris*, March 19, 1937, in ibid., 72.

Jacques Maritain had developed these elements: Jacques Maritain, *The Person and the Common Good*, trans. John J. Fitzgerald (New York: Scribner's, 1947), 81–83; individuation by matter and transcendence by spirit: 25–28; the common good as serving the person: 66; the immaterial components of the common good: 53 and 73. "Transcends every created good": Jacques Maritain, *Man + the State*, ed. Richard O'Sullivan (London: Hollis and Carter, 1954), 136; as the preface to its English edition notes, this book was written in English by a Frenchman living in America. Maritain's *The Person and the Com-*

mon Good, as the acknowledgments explain, contains lectures given between 1939 and 1945, including one delivered at the Pontifical Academy of St. Thomas in Rome on November 22, 1945. At that time he was the ambassador of France to the Holy See and in contact with Giovanni Battista Montini.

The "right freely to believe": Maritain, *Man + the State*, 137; "exceptional historic significance": 169; quotation of Murray: 144, 146, 149, 150.

Which text would go to the floor: Pavan, *Libertà religiosa*, reprinted in *Scritti del cardinale Pietro Pavan* (Rome: Città nuova, 1989), 1:270–272; Pelotte, *Murray*, 81.

"too controversial": Murray to Leo Ward, June 20, 1963, quoted in Pelotte, *Murray*, 81; no text presented: Hamer, "Histoire du texte," 61; the crucial decision of John XXIII: ibid.

"it would have been difficult": Pietro Pavan, "Il momento storico di Giovanni XXIII e della *Pacem in terris*: Sua influenza negli atti conciliari e nella vita della chiesa e sua influenza nella societa contemporanea," in *Scritti*, 4:108; Pavan on the American sources: Pavan, *Libertà religiosa*, reprinted in *Scritti*, 1:142–143.

not too dissimilarly from Joseph: Genesis 45:1–8.

"the neuralgic point": John Courtney Murray, "Governmental Repression of Heresy," *Proceedings of the Catholic Theological Society of America* 3 (1948): 26. "absolute": John F. Kennedy, televised address to the Houston Ministerial Association, *New York Times*, September 13, 1960, 22. The speech was read to Murray over the telephone by Theodore Sorensen as Sorensen stood by the side of a plane about to leave for Houston. In the question period one minister asked Kennedy if he would ask Cardinal Cushing to present Kennedy's "sincere statement" to the Vatican, "in order that the Vatican may officially authorize such a belief for all Roman Catholics in the United States." Kennedy replied that he would not intervene with the Vatican. At the same time he said that as president he would stand "around the globe" for "the right of free religious practice." See Pelotte, *Murray*, 76.

"the American proposition": John Courtney Murray, *We Hold These Truths: Catholic Reflections on the American Proposition* (New York: Sheed and Ward, 1960). "a primer of pluralism": Murray's notes, quoted in Pelotte, *Murray*, 75. "U.S. Catholics and the State": *Time*, December 12, 1960. Not welcome at the Council: Murray to Richard J. Regan, February 23, 1967, quoted in Pelotte, *Murray*, 109.

an official notice from Rome: Amleto Cicognani to Murray, April 4, 1963, quoted in Pelotte, *Murray*, 81; "pried me in": Murray to Leo Ward, June 20, 1963, quoted at 82.

"a glorious victory": Murray to Michael F. Maher [rector of Woodstock], November 22, 1963, quoted in ibid, 82; Murray's memo and Spellman's presentation: ibid.

"our reverence": Paul VI, allocution, September 29, 1963, *Acta Synodalia Sacrosancti Concilii Oecumenici Vaticani Secundi* (hereafter *Acta Synodalia*) (Vatican City: Vatican Polyglot Press, 1973), 2:1, 184; "religious freedom, like other outstanding rights of man": 196. The significance of the pope's words: Pavan,

Scritti, 1:237. Paul VI characterized the rights as *praecipua* (= "principal" or "paramount" or "outstanding"), which Pavan translates as *fondamentali*.

Presentation of the text was made: De Smedt, November 19, 1963, *Relatio, Acta Synodalia*, 2:5, 485–491. "reworked in his own style": Murray to Maher, November 22, 1963, quoted in Pelotte, *Murray*, 84; postponement of debate: ibid.

"insisted on the need": Joseph Fenton, "Cardinal Ottaviani and the Council," *AER* 148 (January 1963): 53. "In December 1963, Msgr. Joseph Clifford Fenton": *AER* 150 (January 1964): 1.

"intolerance wherever possible": John Courtney Murray, "The Problem of Religious Freedom," *Theological Studies* 25 (December 1964): 509; Fixism, Archaism, and Misplaced Abstractness: 560–562; "a historical nature": 559; "explicitly the product": 568; a "growing end": 569. The original title and circulation to the American bishops: Pelotte, *Murray*, 88; its translations: 111. On the influence of Lonergan see Hooper, *Ethics of Discourse*, 124–125, 138, 140.

"patient and benign tolerance": Ruffini, *Oratio*, September 23, 1964, *Acta Synodalia*, 3:2, 355; concordats: 356; "not an evolution": Quiroga y Palacios, 358; danger of polygamy: Lefebvre, September 24, in ibid., 491; Catholics' supernatural rights and "freedom of propaganda": Ottaviani, September 23, in ibid., 375; Léger: 359; Silva-Henriquez, 369; Koenig, 470; Cushing, 361–362.

"the first scribe": Pelotte, *Murray*, 94; collaboration with Pavan: 94–95, quoting Murray to Richard J. Regan, January 31, 1967; the mixed commission gambit: 95; the squelching of a vote and "the day of Wrath": 96.

"the human gasp for God": Paul VI, Christmas broadcast, December 22, 1964, *Acta apostolicae sedis* (1965), 57:181. Paul VI's assurance to the American bishops: Pelotte, *Murray*, 97, quoting Joseph Ritter to the American bishops, December 29, 1964; Murray's two heart attacks: 99.

reported on "the day of Wrath": John Courtney Murray, "This Matter of Religious Freedom," *America* 112 (January 1965): 40; "the affirmation of progress": ibid.; "development of doctrine": 43. Negotiations of Murray with French bishops: Pelotte, *Murray*, 97. The French view: John Courtney Murray, "Religious Freedom," in *Freedom and Man*, ed. John Courtney Murray (New York: P. J. Kenedy, 1965), 139–140.

"If what is being taught": Lefebvre, September 20, 1965, comment, *Acta Synodalia*, 4:1, 792. "In the very fact of Revelation": Cardinal Wojtyla, *Oratio*, September 22, 1965, in ibid., 4:2, 11; "a serious danger": Beran, September 20, in ibid., 4:1, 393; "in clear words": 394.

The presidency of the Council . . . Paul VI acted: Pietro Pavan, "Testimonianza per papa Paolo VI," in *Scritti*, 4:391–392.

The text passed: Hamer, "Histoire du texte," 106–108. Murray's lung: Pelotte, *Murray*, 99.

a special papal commission: it was in connection with this commission that I was in Rome. To cite briefly my own experience, peripheral to the issue of religious freedom but illustrative of the freedom of argument that characterized the Council, I declared myself neutral on the question of contraception. "No historian worth his salt was ever neutral," exclaimed F. X. Murphy, the Redemptorist historian largely responsible for the pseudonymous Xaiver Rynne's account of Vatican II. With this prompting my position became clearer. With F. X.'s aid, I expounded the subject to Cardinal Heenan, archbishop of Westminster, and his sidekick George Dwyer, archbishop of Birmingham; I talked to Cardinal Léger, who anxiously wondered what "they" wanted to happen; led by Mark Calegari, S.J., through the corridors of the Vatican palace in the best tradition of *The Three Musketeers*, I spoke to Paul VI's close collaborator, Cardinal Journet. The time was open for argument and reargument.

"Christ himself has spoken": so I heard at the time from persons present at the meeting of the drafting committee. Text and footnotes of *Gaudium et spes*: September 20, 1965, *Acta Synodalia*, 4:7, 766–771.

Murray with other selected . . . mass with Paul VI: Pelotte, *Murray*, 100.

Among those subscribing their names: *Acta Synodalia*, 4:7, 807.

"doctrine" be used in place of "declaration": Cardinal Wojtyla, *Oratio*, September 22, 1965, ibid., 4:2, 11. On the title chosen and reasons for it: Yves M. J. Congar, "Que faut-il entendre par 'déclaration'?" in *La Liberté religieuse*, 50–52.

"of the dignity": Second Vatican Council, *Dignitatis humanae personae*, sec. 1, *Acta Synodalia*, 4:7; "This Vatican Council declares" and "founded in the" and "Mild and humble," citing Matthew 11:29: sec. 2; "although sometimes": sec. 12; "to do injury": sec. 3; "the just demands": sec. 4; "by the due care": sec. 7; "Given the particular circumstances" and "must provide": sec. 6. The example of England: John Heenan, *Oratio*, September 28, 1964, *Acta Synodalia*, 3:2, 572.

"to a war that has already been won": Murray, "This Matter of Religious Freedom": *America* 109 (November 1963), 704; "*the* American issue," John Courtney Murray, "On Religious Liberty," *America* 112, 40 (January 9, 1965) (cf. the German bishop Walter Kompe citing Murray for making "the American contribution to the Council": Pelotte, *Murray*, 101).

married the French Revolution: Lefebvre refused to subscribe to either *Gaudium et spes* or *Dignitatis humanae*; see Jean-Anne Chalet, *Monseigneur Lefebvre* (Paris: Pygmalion, 1976), 158–159. Subsequently he entered into schism, denounced the Council for "marrying the Church to the [French] Revolution," and declared that prior to the council, for a century and a half, the popes "condemned liberal Catholicism, refused this marriage with the ideas of the Revolution" (Lefebvre, "Homily at Lille," August 29, 1976, quoted in ibid., 209–210). Leonard Feeney had put himself outside the Church by insisting that there was no salvation outside of the Church. Marcel Lefebvre was at the point of leaving the Church, insisting that, in an ideal state, there should be no freedom for a Christian to deny the teachings of the Church.

INDEX

Compositor:	Integrated Composition Systems
Text:	10/13 Sabon
Display:	Bauer Text Initial; Copperplate Gothic Bold; Sabon
Printer and Binder:	Haddon Craftsmen